Advance Praise for

# UNDERSTANDING THOSE
# WHO CREATE

"Jane Piirto brings to her readers a unique perspective on the study of creativity from her dual life as a long-time educator and as a professional writer. Her chapters on the biographies of talented individuals are alive with special insights into the processes and struggles they experienced. The literature on talents in the various disciplines is presented in such a way as to highlight the connections and distinctions among the talent areas, providing an important contribution to the field."

Dr. Rena F. Subotnik, Hunter College

"A genuine magnum opus on creativity! Piirto has masterfully synthesized and translated the major research on creativity and giftedness into a comprehensive and readable book. Pulling from her many years of experience as an educator and creative writer, her book is rich with personal insights, anecdotes and case studies that bring the subject alive in a most refreshing and edifying way. Never losing sight of clarity, Piirto unravels the theory, research, and practice on creativity and then ties it all together for the reader. A final chapter of practical, creativity-enhancing suggestions for parents and teachers brings the book full circle. A very creative synthesis and a welcomed addition to the literature."

Dr. James Alvino, Past President, Council for Exceptional Children — The Association for Gifted

"When, within our souls and psyches we are made aware of a soft but insistent drumbeat, repeated like butterfly wings in motion, we sense the message . . . that our innerself has begun its search for freedom. For some of us, this comes late in life. For some it begins its insistence too early for recognition, and is often ignored and misunderstood. And for some, it is never experienced at all, and that is the saddest of human fates — never to experience the soul's haunting demands for freedom.

"Piirto explains in her book what these demands are, why they are so often ignored and lost. She exposes reasons why educators and parents must provide children with experiences that make them strong enough to shake off the shackles of boundaries, negative expectations, and blind adherence to someone else's standards when such obedience is essentially detrimental to the soul's searching for itself.

"Her coverage of the history of creativity is scholarly; her research has been a search in itself for answers that will change the denial of inner urges to be creative. Her book is fair, objective and positive. It is well done; it is good."

Dr. Mary Meeker, Co-founder, Structure of Intellect Institute

# UNDERSTANDING THOSE WHO CREATE

**Jane Piirto**

Ohio Psychology Press
1992

Published by Ohio Psychology Press
P.O. Box 90095, Dayton, Ohio 45490
Copyright © 1992

#24792819

Library of Congress Cataloging-in-Publication Data

Navarre, Jane.
    Understanding those who create / Jane Piirto.
        p.   cm.
    Includes bibliographical references and index.
    ISBN 0-910707-19-7
    1. Creative ability.
    2. Creative ability — Testing.
    3. Creative ability — Case studies.
    4. Creative ability in children.   I. Title.

BF408.P87     1992
153.3'5 — dc20                                    91-41971
                                                  CIP

For my creative mother,
who taught us to love the arts
and to use the public library.

*There have appeared, from time to time,
individuals who grew to maturity without losing
the full inventory of their innate, intuitive, and
spontaneously coordinate faculties. These unscathed
individuals inaugurated whole new eras of
physical environmental transformation so important
as, in due course, to affect the lives of all ensuing
humanity. . . . such unscathed, comprehensively
effective, and largely unidentified articulators
are the artist-scientists of history.*

— Buckminster Fuller

# CONTENTS

# Preface

One summer nineteen United States educators were awarded Fulbright-Hays grant to study in Argentina for six weeks. The Argentinean co-ordinators of the learning project assumed that the participants were fluent in Spanish and thus had scheduled the lectures in that language, with no translation. But six Americans — and I was one of them — didn't speak Spanish. It was only through the kindness of people in our group and other hastily provided translators that we were able to learn what we were supposed to learn from our esteemed professors.

As a teacher of teachers, I notice that my students are often baffled by the language of researchers in psychology and gifted education. A woman who taught Advanced Placement English at a very good high school said "Ugh!" when I passed around some research journals. "I hate reading that stuff! I quit after my Master's degree in English rather than read more deconstructionist criticism!" She passed it on with a shudder. I then explained that articles in such journals are written in the language used in the profession, and that she would get used to it.

A teacher of enrichment mathematics for the gifted at a fine elementary school said, " Who do those writers think they are talking to?" And then he answered his own question: "Each other."

This book is my attempt to help anyone who is baffled by the jargon of scholars. I am going to try to translate, as my friends translated for us in Argentina, so that some of the "good stuff" in journals and books can be read by the general public. I am also attempting to synthesize some of the pertinent research on creativity and creative people, so

i

what has been learned by the researchers can be known and perhaps put to wider use.

I can lend the practitioner's perspective to the great seesawing debates on the place of creativity in our lives. Perhaps I can lend the novelist's perspective as well. Above my desk is a shelf of books with creativity as part of their titles: *The Creative Process; Higher Creativity; Creative Dreaming; Creativity and Personal Freedom; Creative Visualization; Gifted, Talented, and Creative Young People; The Search for Satori and Creativity; The Creativity Question; The Creative Attitude; Creativity; The Nature of Creativity; The Courage to Create; The Creative Vision; Creativity and Intelligence; Creative Mythology.* And there are more. I must hire a carpenter to build more shelves.

My reading over the past twenty years has led me to believe that there is no such thing as an expert on creativity, though many people would assert they are such. Creativity is a swampy concept. Some people may be experts within their own academic, artistic, or scientific fields, but often those who purport to capture creativity as a theory find it wiggling out of their clasping hands — like a fish just caught, it jumps back free, joining silver fins with silver water.

The purpose of this book is to make sense of the research and theory concerning what is called "creativity." The field of gifted education usually recognizes the construct "creativity" as one of several separate types of giftedness, yet few can explain definitively how and why creativity is giftedness. Most of the literature on creativity is idiosyncratic, theoretical, and highly dependent on the particular author's predispositions. This book attempts to synthesize some of the approaches to creativity and creativity training.

Creativity is more than numbers, lines, diagrams, dots, and arrows that expert speakers and writers generate when they try to describe their research from the perspective of their field's bias. Creativity is manifested in creative people and so a major emphasis of the book is on psychological studies, biographies, autobiographies, and memoirs. I have also tried to let the creative people speak in their own words, in a belief that we learn through stories, as aptly demonstrated by Robert Coles in *The Call of Story* (1988). In style, I have tried to be readable and in so doing have related personal experiences. This may offend some readers' need for the comfortable "rhetorical ritual" of scholarly work, as commented on extensively by Marshall and Barritt in their 1990 article, "The Rhetoric of AERJ."

The book is organized into four main sections. The first explains what creativity is, how creativity and giftedness are interrelated, and what takes place during the creative process. Part II covers creativity testing, training, and checklists. Part III discusses types of creative people according to specialty, with visual artists, writers, scientists, mathematicians, inventors, musicians, actors, and dancers featured. There is also a chapter on young writing prodigies whose work I have analyzed from my perspective as a creative writer and former English teacher. Readers will notice that I have not included several types of creative people, such as entrepreneurs and psychologists. That is for lack of space, not lack of intention. Part IV gets practical: it tells what teachers and parents can do for a creative child. The Appendix briefly summarizes various theories of creativity according to domain.

In preparing this book, I have been fortunate to have help. Michael Piechowski read the completed draft promptly and sent it back to me, chapter by chapter, with scrawled comments that were sometimes so frank they made me wince. He also provided me with extensive suggestions and comments that sent me back to the sources. He was more than a reader at the end; we had long talks about the various points I was trying to make. I appreciated the opportunity to talk out loud with him. He was unfailingly patient and helpful. I took many of his suggestions; others I ignored. The faults of this book are to be blamed solely on me.

Carolyn Nault Cummings, one of my oldest and most valued friends, also read and commented on the full manuscript, and her incisive professorial eye and critical judgment have been most valuable. Thanks to Rena Subotnik, who, in the course of reviewing a late draft of the book, added valuable suggestions just under the deadline. Thanks to John Fraas, and to my students Carol Ebel, Cherry King, Pam Oberholtzer, and Mark Solars, for reading and commenting on selected chapters. Thanks to John Stratton and Michael Hudson. Thanks to Sue Ellen Ronk at the Ashland University library, for prompt and helpful acquisitions and quick searches. And thanks to my editor, Beth Frank.

Let me begin.

Jane Piirto
Ashland University
Ashland, Ohio
44805

# PART I

## WHAT IS CREATIVITY?

*It was a convention for teachers of the gifted. Katherine had just been hired to teach the pullout program for fourth, fifth, and sixth grade gifted students. She was glad of the opportunity, for during student teaching experiences she had always gravitated towards the bright students, the ones whom her cooperating teachers called "too big for his britches" or "too mouthy." Her new superintendent, who had received an announcement for this state convention, had told Katherine that he would pay her way to go, so she could learn what she was supposed to teach.*

*There was no written curriculum to guide her. While teaching, Katherine was also to develop a curriculum. As in most states, Katherine's state did not require her to have any special training in how to teach gifted children. Katherine, her superintendent said, was bright, young, and not jaded, and besides, the school district could afford to hire her because she had no teaching experience and would come in on the lowest rung of the salary scale.*

*In her education courses, Katherine had not been taught anything about gifted children, though she had a course in the education of other special children. She had gone to the state university library in a town nearby to do some reading for her interview, and she memorized the categories of giftedness. Among these were "creative" children. Katherine was curious about what creativity was, and felt quite unsure who "creative" children were. Were they the ones who colored outside the lines? Or looked a little weird?*

*She stepped into the large convention hotel ballroom, took a cup of coffee, and prepared to hear the first keynote speaker. The conference organizer introduced him as a national expert on creativity. "Oh good," Katherine thought, and settled in. He told a joke or two, and was a little mussed, his hair caught into a fashionable ponytail, his cowboy boots and jeans in contrast with his blazer and striped tie. Through the microphone snapped to that tie his voice boomed throughout the ballroom of the hotel. Katherine had not expected so many people — almost a thousand! Were all of them educators of the gifted?*

*Overhead transparency after overhead transparency bloomed behind him on a giant screen — diagrams and curves and arrows and dots and lists. He illustrated his points with cartoons from* Peanuts. *There was a list of tests, too, but Katherine found it hard to believe that you could actually give a test for creativity.*

*Well, he must know. She scanned the program as he spoke, underlining all the sessions that were on creativity. If he was a keynote speaker, and* his topic was creativity, obviously she must learn to teach creativity. This would be her main emphasis at this convention. She collected the handouts of the lists and diagrams and psychological words, and hurried down the hotel hallway to a small room.

There, behind a table, a smaller screen, and another overhead projector, were two middle-aged women. They were local coordinators in a faraway corner of the state, and were going to talk about how to enhance creativity in elementary school children. They, too, had many blooming overheads, and had the group play some simple games. It was fun, and everyone relaxed. But Katherine was getting anxious. The coordinators were quite good speakers, and were using words like "fluency" and "flexibility" and "elaboration," and they talked about creativity as if it were "problem-solving."

Well, they must know, Katherine thought, for they've been in this field a lot longer than I. But in the back of her mind, she thought that creativity was a bit more than fun and games and generating alternative solutions. Katherine attended seven more sessions that day and the next, where "creativity" was part of the title of the session. By Friday night she was exhausted, and she had a briefcase full of stapled handouts, with dots and arrows and curves and diagrams and key words highlighted with graphic bullets. She had played games and had practiced techniques. She had packets of concrete ideas for lessons. But she still didn't know what creativity was. Oh well, she'd think about it next week.

On Saturday, she and her fiance, Brad, a computer consultant who had been infamous as a hacker during his high school and college years, were going to a weekend retreat at a camp in the woods about fifty miles away. The retreat workshop was on transformational empowerment. Brad was really into nature and preserving the environment, as well as the New Age, and he wanted Katherine to appreciate the mystery and beauty of inner contemplation. This was the third monthly session they had been to.

Katherine had been raised in her family's traditional Protestant church, and her mother was not pleased that she was attending these workshops. "I don't want you to be influenced by a cult," her mother said.

"Mother!" Katherine said. "We just do meditation and visualization and relaxation. Brad wants us to take our place to save the earth and in order to do that, we first have to understand our inner selves. We want to be the best that we can be. Why don't you come sometime? I feel very creative when I visualize and meditate. You will, too. It's like when you went to that church retreat for a weekend and took that intensive journal workshop a few years ago. Remember?"

*Just then Katherine realized she'd used that word again: "creative." All the way to the camp, she sat silently, thinking about the teachers' conference, and thinking about how wonderful she always felt when she and Brad sat with the group and meditated. Then she remembered her high school track coach. He had the girls visualize running the track before competition. Was this "creativity" as much as the lists and lessons she'd collected for use with her children at her new job?*

*She had a lot to learn, she knew, but she felt good about it. Though she felt confused, she knew she would sort it all out sooner or later.*

# Chapter 1

## Creativity and Giftedness

*The secret at the heart of all creative activity has something to do with our desire to complete a work, to impose perfection upon it, so that, hammered out of profane materials, it becomes sacred: Which is to say, no longer merely personal.*

— Joyce Carol Oates

*Because it denotes rare and valued human accomplishment, creativity should be considered interchangeable with giftedness.*

— Abraham Tannenbaum

A colleague in the art department gave workshops on creativity for art teachers. I asked him whether I could attend his Saturday workshop, and as we talked our conversation got around to the extreme difficulty educators in various disciplines have in discussing creativity. We all seem to have different definitions in mind. His primary purpose for offering the workshop, he said, was not to focus on definitions, but to help teachers help their students generate ideas for their projects since even his undergraduate art majors often get stuck looking for ideas.

He stated that he wasn't going to use that "education and psychology baloney and gobbledygook that no one can even understand," but instead simply a book about lateral thinking by a man called de Bono. I reminded him that de Bono is an educator, and pointed out that this creativity interest clearly was crossing disciplinary boundaries. I inquired whether he would show his students how to brainstorm. He responded that, yes, brainstorming is a good way to generate new ideas.

I could tell that he, an artist, like I, a writer, was struggling to make sense of creativity. That the mechanistic practice of group brainstorming to enhance creativity should have moved from its beginnings in 1955 at the Buffalo, New York, Creative Problem-Solving Institute to the art studio illustrates the wide impact of the work on creativity enhancement in the last forty years. That this evolved term, "creativity," literally the making of something new, should come to mean so much to all sorts of people, is a wonder.

One thing I have found — we all have a proprietary interest in creativity. Every discipline, every field, every person, has a separate definition, and each believes in creativity as something that really exists. As I was beginning to write this book, I ran into an administrator friend who asked what I'd been doing lately. When I told him, he said he had just read in an airline's magazine a wonderful article on what's wrong with the schools, namely that schools don't allow children to be creative. We suppress their creativity.

I argued that what I had been reading indicates otherwise. In current teachers' manuals for any reading series you'll find activities that emphasize teaching children to think creatively. Brainstorming is a popular activity. That is "fluency" training in creativity parlance. "Flexibility" training is also common, where children are asked to come up with alternative solutions. Teachers now have numerous activities which can be photocopied or dittoed, activities that did not exist in reading series a few years ago. The teaching of creative thinking has come into the mainstream, where it once was the province of the pullout "gifted" class. This "spillover" is a common effect that the burgeoning of gifted education programs has had on mainstream education in the last twenty years.

Critics of education often point to the lack of emphasis on creative thinking. A popular 1960s song by Harry Chapin spoke of a child learning to make a flower just like everyone else's flower, meaning that as the child was socialized, he was forced to lose his innate creativity. The creativity researcher Theresa Amabile often begins her lectures with an anecdote about her first grade teacher having the students copy prints of great masters in "art" class. The romantic notion inherent in these examples is that children are intrinsically creative and the school takes it out of them.

Things have changed. The drudgery of the basal reader, the flood of purple dittos, the numbing call of drill and response have given way to such flexible challenges as Young Authors, where children write their own books; Odyssey of the Mind events, where children make new products; Invention Conventions, where children invent gadgets; and Future Problem Solving contests, where children solve the problems of the world. Creativity is in. Everyone uses the word these days. This was not always the case.

## The Term "Creativity"

The root of the words "create" and "creativity" comes from the Latin *creatus*. This means, "to make or produce," or literally, "to grow." The word also comes from the French base *kere*, and the Latin *crescere*, and *creber*. The Roman goddess of the earth, Ceres, is an example, as is the Italian corn goddess, Cereris. Creativity as a word has roots in the earth. Other similar derived words are *cereal, crescent, creature, concrete, crescendo, decrease, increase,* and *recruit*.

The term "creativity" is a nineteenth and twentieth century invention. A relatively new noun, "creativity" came into parlance much as have the words "to prioritize" and "to network," and the noun, "infrastructure." Melville used the word "creativeness" in 1851 in *Moby Dick,* in describing the mechanical creativeness of a lightning storm, thereby illustrating that a noun form of the verb "to create" was in use. But use of this relatively new word, "creativity," has blossomed in the past twenty years. By 1990, the term was used in over 6,500 references to titles of books and articles. A run through the ERIC Clearinghouse (Educational Resources Information Centers) computer files from 1982 to 1990 showed 1,750 references on creativity and education. The Psychlit database has similar numbers, as does the Modern Language Association (MLA) database. Probably most of those authors purported to be expert.

Until recently, the study of creativity was called the study of imagination, as exemplified by Rugg's 1963 book on that subject. In the nineteenth and early twentieth century, the study of creativity was called the study of genius. Even so, the *Oxford English Dictionary* indicated that by 1958 certain jobs in classified advertisements were categorized as "creative"; among these were jobs in advertising, designing, modeling, public relations, television production, and magazine work. Even earlier, in 1930, reference was made to a "creative sales policy." "Creative education" was discussed by a panel in 1936. The term has even been used to infer something misleading, as in the term "creative bookkeeping." All of these uses of the word apply today.

## American Usage of the Term "Creative"

A 1964 college edition of U.S. English usage, Webster's *New World Dictionary of the American Language* did not even list "creativity," and gave short shrift to "creative." To be creative was to be productive or inventive. The 1988 Webster's stated that creativity is "creative ability; artistic or intellectual inventiveness." By 1988 the *Random House Dictionary of the English Language,* Unabridged Edition, noted that the term "creativity" was first recorded in English between 1870 and 1875, and described creativity as an ability to "transcend traditional ideas, rules, patterns, relationships or the like, and to create meaningful new ideas, forms, methods, interpretations, etc." That creativity is an ability has been an assumption now made by educators for several years.

To be "creative" is to have the "quality of creating," to be "given to creating," or to be "originative." Originative is an interesting word, which implies making something new. *To be creative, then, is to make something new. To make something new is to make novel.* The word "novelty" appears and reappears in various definitions of creativity. Therefore, to be an expert on creativity is to be an expert on those who make something new, or on teaching people how to make something new, or even on making something new.

## Philosophical, Psychoanalytic, and Religious Overtones

Although psychologists have conducted the most studies of creativity, the philosophers, the psychoanalysts, and even the clergy also have vested interests. Freud, the father of psychoanalysis, stated that the "source of creativity" is the "sublimation of energy into acceptable and fruitful channels." (Note the agricultural word, "fruitful," and the word "channels," a word with mystical roots.) Several philosophers, such as Nikolai Lossky, Berdyaev and Wieman, have held that creativity is what is common to both man and God. Berdyaev, a Russian Orthodox mystic, further noted that all creativity is what is good in humans, and what brings humans into communion with God. Wieman, an American theologian, further specified that there operates in the world a "four-fold creative event," resulting in good. This event is God. The tying of creativity to divinity is truly an ancient notion which goes back even further than the Greeks who, themselves, called poetry "divine madness."

To relate "creativity" to "creation" expands the term. To Judeo-Christians, God created the world in seven days. He filled the void. As we shall see, this identification of creativity with spiritual oneness with God is quite common to many who consider the creative process. In *Creative Mythology,* the 1986 volume of his mega-tome, *The Masks of God,* Joseph Campbell traced the history of the searches for God, the Grail, purity, and the prevalence of individual (not group) sacred quests for discovering meaning and value. The focus of creative thought, Campbell explained, was always the search for the elemental, the true, the archetypal.

These original connections of creativity with divinity, agricultural growth, newness, and intuition, still resonate today. For example, the metaphor of the seed is often used by educators when they speak of enhancing creativity in children. Allow them to grow, we say. Nurture them. Don't stifle them. The natural child is popularly thought to be very creative. The school, the family, and the society "ruin" the natural child's creativity by civilizing the child. Thus, creativity dies. This common metaphor is part of our American educator folklore, and is what my administrator colleague was referring to when he said the article he read was about how children's creativity is ruined by schooling. With a glimpse into the roots (another agricultural metaphor) of the word, we can see some of our unconscious beliefs about creativity surfacing.

### The Term "Giftedness"

But what of the gifted child? Is the gifted child, that highly intelligent child, creative? Does that child have creativity? Well, yes and no, in our common popular and educational definitions of giftedness.

From Homer to Einstein, from the patriarch Moses to the matriarch Grandma Moses, human society has struggled to define and deal with those individuals who stand out by virtue of their abilities, and especially, at least to educators, their abilities at school. The recognition that people differ in their aptness for study was seen at the very roots of Western culture. In Greece, Plato, in his ideal society led by the philosopher-king, said that people should serve society with their strongest abilities; he recognized that different people had different abilities.

This recognition of the special qualities of certain people has continued throughout history and two foci have emerged: (1) the intellective quality of quickness, or rate, of learning; and (2) the presence of the nonintellective quality of persistence. We call the former a "gift," implying hereditary origins, and we imply the latter has environmental genesis. An intellective quality implies a close relationship with the brain or mind; a nonintellective quality has to do with personality. Though often not a very clear distinction, it is one increasingly made by educators of the gifted, especially Tannenbaum in his book, *Gifted Children* (1983). For example, the necessary nonintellective quality of persistence is presently called "task commitment," after Renzulli's 1978 definition, which is very popular in contemporary U.S. schools. On a Venn diagram of three intersecting circles, Renzulli places giftedness at the juncture of "creativity," "above-average intelligence," and "task commitment."

Giftedness historically has been viewed with distrust, not only because of the difficulty in defining it, but also because of the connotation that a "gift" is inherited, and therefore not deserved. Similar to the disregard with which the accomplishments of people with inherited wealth are held, the term "gifted" often has a connotation of elitism, anathema in our supposedly egalitarian society.

Not surprisingly, then, the term "gifted" has, in this century, been used indiscriminately, and with great frequency. A cursory look at the *New York Times Book Review* one week yielded ten uses of the word to describe people — from being gifted in describing nature, to being gifted in relationships with people. The term "gifted" is used in connotation almost as often as the term "creative," and with the same lack of specificity.

## Origins of the Term "Gifted"

The word "gift" emanated from Old Teutonic; originally it meant payment for a wife. Another root of the word is in Old French, where it meant "poison." In the mid-nineteenth century, the term was used in connection with "genius," as A. Gray, in 1839, referred to Christopher North as "a gifted genius." However, Plato obviously had made the connection, for by 1875 Jowett was translating Plato using the term with reference to an educated mind, when he had Socrates say, "The most gifted minds, when they are ill educated, become the worst." There is no record of when "gifted" came to mean having "high intelligence."

The field of psychology has taken seriously the study of intelligence; researchers from Galton to Gardner, from Binet to Sternberg, from Spearman to Guilford have studied what intelligence is. These psychological test-makers and theoreticians have had great impact on the field of education, more impact than the philosophical theorists or the aesthetic theorists about creativity. The field of education has taken its knowledge base after psychology, and has sought to measure and to quantify both creativity and intelligence.

However, the psychologists who have influenced the field of gifted education with their theories of creativity and giftedness have not, seemingly, permeated the field of the psychology of creativity. A perusal of the *The Handbook of Creativity,* a 1989 book edited by Glover, Ronning, and Reynolds, yielded no references to the thinkers who are usually featured at gifted education research conferences. For example, a 1991 Research Symposium at the University of Iowa featured such researchers as the information processing theorist Robert Sternberg, the developmental psychologist David Feldman, and the social psychologist Dean Keith Simonton, who spoke of their creativity research, none of whom were featured in this *Handbook.* This *Handbook* also had no references to the cognitive scientist Howard Gardner, who is also widely admired in the field of gifted education, and, though it was dedicated to E. Paul Torrance, it contained only brief references to other seminal thinkers in gifted education. This, to me, illustrates again that people in many branches of psychology and education do not talk to each other, but yet many people purport to be experts on creativity.

Despite the lack of communication, researchers into the education of gifted children have generally stated — implicitly and explicitly — that being gifted is being of high intelligence, as determined by having scored high on a group or individual IQ test. The Terman study, a longitudinal study begun in the 1920s, is often used to justify the use of intelligence tests to define giftedness. Terman revised the Stanford-Binet Intelligence Test early in the century. He chose 1,500 high IQ children in 1922, and followed them throughout their lives. Most of them had relatively successful lives. Their success was used to justify the use of the IQ test as a way to define giftedness. Recently, it has been pointed out that most of them were from nurturing environments as well, and some critics of the IQ test have alleged that the environment, and not the IQ is what contributed to their adult success.

## Guilford and His Children

In 1950, J.P. Guilford, then President of the American Psychological Association, gave a speech that is often hailed as the beginning of the modern interest in creativity as a measurable phenomenon. Guilford had developed a theory called the Structure of the Intellect, where he theorized that there are 120 kinds of measurable intelligence factored across five operations, four contents, and six products. In his 1967 landmark exposition of this theory, *The Nature of Human Intelligence,* Guilford proved that it was possible to measure *divergent production.* (In 1988 Guilford modified his model of the intellect, adding visual and auditory contents, and dividing memory into memory recording and memory retention).

In his 1950 speech, Guilford called for research on two questions: (1) how to find the promise of creativity in our children; and (2) how to enhance the development of the creative personality. In particular, he called for the analysis of several factors within divergent production. Following are Guilford's original definitions of relevant key terms, all of which have gained wide acceptance in the creativity enhancement world.

1. **Fluency.** ". . . the person who is capable of producing a large number of ideas per unit of time, other things being equal, has a greater chance of having significant ideas."

2. **Novelty.** "The creative person has novel ideas."

3. **Flexibility.** ". . . the ease with which he changes set."

4. **Synthesizing ability.** "The ability to put unlike ideas together."

5. **Analyzing ability.** "Much creative thinking requires the organizing of ideas into larger, more inclusive patterns . . . Symbolic structures must often be broken down before new ones can be built."

6. **Reorganization or redefinition of already existing ideas.** Many inventions have been in the nature of a transformation of an existing object into one of different design, function, or use."

7. **Degree of complexity.** "How many interrelated ideas can the person manipulate at the same time?"

8. **Evaluation.** " Creative work that is to be realistic or accepted must be done under some degree of evaluative restraint." (1987, pp. 42-47)

An interesting point, though not widely reported, is that in this address, Guilford specified that these factors are probably only characteristic of those who are creative scientists or technologists. These factors probably do not describe those who have creative planning abilities — the economists, the political leaders, the military leaders. Nor do they describe writers, graphic artists, or musical composers. Yet today it is not uncommon to have programs in creativity training that emphasize fluency, flexibility, and novelty (or originality) for all students, not just future scientists or technologists.

What ensued has been a scramble among many researchers to measure divergent production. The trouble is that divergent production has been equated with creativity. Divergent production can be measured easily, but is it creativity? Guilford himself demurred from going so far. He said

> Quite a number of studies have lent support to the claim that Divergent Production factors and tests have relevance in connection with the measurement of creative potential, but creative potential is very complex and at times and in divergent ways involves abilities outside the divergent-production and the transformation categories, which are most important in that connection. (1970, p. 170)

Others, especially psychologists such as Gardner and Sternberg, have denounced such attempts to measure creativity by giving people paper and pencil tests as too commonplace.

Guilford's most famous disciple was E. Paul Torrance, the developer of the Torrance Tests of Creative Thinking (TTCT). Despite these tests' name, Torrance himself has never claimed that these tests, which measure divergent production, measure creativity. But often the tests have been confused with creativity. These tests are discussed in detail in Chapters 3 and 4.

The definitions of giftedness most commonly used by the schools stem from the Marland Report of 1972. Sidney Marland, then the U.S. Commissioner of Education, listed six types of giftedness, including high intelligence and creativity as two of those types. Prior to the Marland Report several psychologists had made studies that ostensibly showed that there is a difference between intelligence and creativity, and that they are made up of separate factors.

Guilford, as noted above, had formulated his Structure of the Intellect, differentiating between "convergent" intellect as a mode of cognition, a way of thinking, that emphasized what is known, being able to learn what exists, and being able to save that information in one's brain. "Divergent" intellect was a mode of cognition, or thinking, that emphasized the revision of what was already known, of exploring what would be known, and of building new information. People who prefer the "convergent" mode of intellect supposedly tend to do what is expected of them, while those who prefer the "divergent" mode of intellect supposedly tend to take risks and to speculate.

## Getzels and Jackson's *Creativity and Intelligence*

The most cited study that has taken these two modes of intellect into account is *Creativity and Intelligence* (1962), by Getzels and Jackson, who studied sixth through twelfth graders in a private school in Illinois. Students who scored high on paper and pencil tests that supposedly measured the "divergent" mode of intellect were called "creative." Those who scored high on paper and pencil tests (i.e., the Stanford-Binet or the Henmon-Nelson intelligence tests) that supposedly measured the "convergent" mode of intellect, were called "intelligent."

The Getzels and Jackson study made the assumption that everybody has some creative ability, and some intelligence, and that all children have some "creative potential":

> Our research interest focuses on "creative potential" in the same way that a music instructor is interested in assessing the musical potential of a child. Just as the children who possess fine tone discrimination or a highly developed sense of rhythm do not achieve distinction in music, so all children who possess outstanding creative thinking abilities do not achieve creative distinction. Nevertheless, the existence of these abilities might lead to a prognosis or probable failure in creative accomplishment. (p. 17)

The implications of this statement have resonated throughout education for the past thirty years, as practitioners have tried to sort out those with "creative potential" from those with "intelligence." Supposedly the Getzels and Jackson study showed that those who had the highest creative potential as measured by the paper and pencil tests of word associations, of uses for things such as a brick, of discovering hidden shapes, and of supplying the last lines for fables, scored below the top on intelligence tests. These were called "high creatives." The "high intelligence" students scored below the top twenty percent of scores in the divergent paper and pencil tests mentioned above, but were in the top twenty percent of those who took the Stanford-Binet or the Henmon-Nelson tests. The researchers stated that those "who were high in both intelligence and creativity were of course also excluded." Why?

The Getzels and Jackson study has been widely interpreted to mean that those with high creative potential need a certain threshold of intelligence, but not necessarily the highest intelligence. Attempts to replicate the Getzels and Jackson findings by such researchers as E. P. Torrance, Wallach and Kogan and others, were mostly unsuccessful or inconclusive, and similar results when they occurred were only found in similar, private, upper-middle, and middle-class schools.

## Wallach and Kogan's *Modes of Thinking*

Wallach and Kogan in their 1969 study, *Modes of Thinking in Young Children,* made the most cited attempt. Replicating the Getzels and Jackson study with fifth-graders, they found that an untimed, open-ended, nonthreatening testing atmosphere produces better responses on the divergent mode of intellect paper and pencil tests. They likewise concluded that creativity and intelligence were separate constructs: "We can assert with high confidence, then, that the ability of a child to display creativity as we here conceive of it, has little to do with whether or not he exhibits the behavior that will earn him high scores on measures of general intelligence."

Wallach and Kogan, however, never asserted that creativity testing was the whole of what creativity is. Because enhanced performance on these tests took place in a gamelike atmosphere, they proposed that special teachers be hired to go from classroom to classroom to "play games" with the children in order to foster their associational ability and associational processes. They said such training would provide the high intelligence-low creativity children with experiences that would make them view the relationship between the metaphoric and the affective domain (they called it "physiognomic sensitivity") more positively. For the high creativity-low intelligence children, the training would help improve their self-concepts. The high intelligence-high creativity children would receive inductive teaching by the discovery method. For the low-creativity, low-intelligence children they had no suggestions, except that these children should not be relegated to the "academic waste pile."

## Torrance's *Tests*

E. P. Torrance specifically set out to create and validate tests that would identify creative potential as reflected by divergent thinking. His Torrance Tests of Creative Thinking (1966) began to be widely used in schools. These tests were similar to the Guilford tests of divergent production, and quantified fluency, flexibility, and the like. The higher the score, the more potentially creative the child was believed to be. In attempting to show that paper and pencil testing of aspects of the divergent mode of intellect can truly identify creative potential, Guilford, Getzels and Jackson, Torrance, Wallach and Kogan, and others, began a controversial practice that still continues today.

Mainstream educators of the gifted have continued to attempt to identify creative potential by calling "creativity" a separate type of giftedness, rather than a necessary aspect of all giftedness. Their reasons for doing so have to do with a need to be inclusive. That is, those children who have creative potential may not be found by other means, but they could become included in programs by the use of paper and pencil vehicles such as tests and checklists of creativity. This separation of creativity and intelligence has led to much confusion in the practitioners' sector.

## Contemporary Definition of Giftedness: The Influence of the Marland Report

Is giftedness general intelligence, or IQ, measured by an intelligence test such as the Wechsler or the Stanford-Binet? Educators of the gifted have said both "yes and no." Current U.S. and Canadian definitions are variations of the 1972 Marland Report which lists six forms of giftedness, and is the first bureaucratic mention of creativity in this context. These six forms are; superior cognitive ability, specific academic ability, creativity, leadership ability, visual and performing arts ability, and psychomotor ability.

## Giftedness: High IQ or High Academic Ability

Having a high IQ is called "superior cognitive ability," superior because it is a score that falls into the top two or three percent, or above the 97 percentile. On most IQ tests, this usually translates to an IQ of about 130 or so. A second form of giftedness is having a "specific academic ability." This is usually defined as scoring above the 95 percentile on the school's standardized achievement test (e.g., The Iowa Test of Basic Skills, The California Achievement Test, The Metropolitan Achievement Test), in one area, for example mathematics, or reading.

## Giftedness as Creativity

A third form of giftedness is "creativity." Schools often operationally define "creativity" as scoring above average on an IQ test, *and* having some measure of creative potential (for example ranking high on a creativity checklist or scoring high on a standardized creativity test). They separate creativity from high intelligence, following upon Getzels and Jackson, and Wallach and Kogan. As noted above, this is called the threshold theory, the theory that creative people have above average IQs, but not necessarily the highest IQs.

Renzulli, as mentioned before, devised a definition of giftedness, portrayed in a Venn diagram, wherein creativity, above-average intelligence, and task commitment intersect. Renzulli is the only current theorist whose work has been widely adopted by the public who insists that the gifted person must have "creativity" and not simply a high IQ. Other theorists such as Sternberg and Feldman, who have also said creativity is a necessary aspect of giftedness, have not yet seen their theories receive much practical application in schools.

Marland's inclusion of creativity as a *type* of giftedness, rather than as giftedness, has posed many problems for contemporary educators. They struggle to make the distinction between high IQ and creative potential, wrestle with thresholds of test scores and measures of ability, and try to meet demands for accountability which are narrowly defined as numerical outcomes.

## Leadership Potential Type Giftedness

Marland cited a fourth form of giftedness as possessing the quality of leadership. Leadership is best identified by a person's past leadership roles, though many attempts have been made within the field of gifted education to identify children with leadership *potential,* much as the attempts, described in this book, to identify children with creative *potential.* Interestingly, gifted education programs are often justified in school districts by saying that gifted students will be tomorrow's leaders.

## Giftedness in the Visual and Performing Arts

Marland's fifth form of giftedness was having talent in the visual and performing arts, painting, drawing, acting, music, dance, sculpture, etc. This talent is identified by experts and professionals evaluating a person's performance by means of a portfolio or an audition. That visual and performing arts giftedness is different from creative giftedness is difficult to understand. Aren't visual artists creative? Aren't actors creative? Aren't dancers creative? Aren't musicians creative? The difficulty that educators have in separating the two types of giftedness is evident in their identification procedures and programs. It seems educators think that visual and performing arts students have *talent,* which, as in the Getzels and Jackson definitions above, is not necessary for creative potential. At least such a distinction is implied by having two separate categories.

## Physical Giftedness

A sixth type that Marland posited was psychomotor giftedness. This was eliminated from the Federal definition in the late 1970s, not because it isn't a form of giftedness, but because schools already have plenty of support and funding for their athletes and teams. Psychomotor giftedness in many forms is highly valued throughout the world, as witness the millions of dollars paid to heavyweight boxers for one fight. Dancers, though, who are also psychomotor people, struggle through grueling physical challenges with very little financial reward. For Marland to include psychomotor ability as a separate category of giftedness has presented many difficulties to contemporary educators. How is psychomotor giftedness different from visual and performing arts giftedness? Isn't the soccer player as much a performer as the actor?

## Controversies Over the Marland Definition

Critics have attacked the Marland definition of giftedness as being too difficult to identify and measure. In a 1988 article, Hoge called for a renewed definition of what he calls the "construct of giftedness." He said that educators have misused the tests to identify giftedness, and that the tests have become definitions in themselves. Instead he called for an explicit definition of giftedness: what are the traits of the gifted person, what behaviors and aptitudes does this person exhibit, and in what situations does a gifted person show his or her giftedness?

Currently, the typical scenario for the identification of giftedness goes like this: the school board develops a definition that corresponds with the Marland definition; it's usually close to the one that has been developed by the state or county. This definition summarily states that the gifted have high levels of intellectual potential, or high aptitudes in something like mathematics or reading, high motivation levels, and are creative. All are vague, and globally defined. Thus, the school district resorts to using a high IQ or high achievement test score as its definition because these potentials can be stated numerically and defensibly, while motivation and creativity are less easily translated to numbers.

## Creativity Since the Marland Report

Since the Marland Report and its huge impact on practitioners in gifted education, many researchers have attempted to define creativity. This is not to say that the researchers were interested in gifted education, but rather that the educators of the gifted were interested in what the researchers were finding. A somewhat uneasy marriage has occurred between educators of the gifted and psychologists (especially cognitive scientists and psychometricians).

### Gruber's *Darwin on Man*

One approach to the study of creativity has been the case study, most notably done in Gruber's study of Charles Darwin, *Darwin on Man* (1974). Gruber evolved a systems theory, an attempt to connect the development of the creative person with the milieu in which the creative person functions. Subsequently, in 1982, Gruber called for a unified effort in studying what he called the "development of extraordinariness." If we simply study giftedness and do not study the creative process in adults, we are off the track. Saying that "human extraordinariness is too important to be left under the sole guardianship of preformationists and psychometricians," Gruber suggested that we start with known creators and apply our knowledge of human development to discover how these people have synthesized knowledge, emotion, and their creative purposes.

Gruber said that we know quite a lot about adolescence and later, "but we know very little about the childhood that leads to creative adulthood": he reiterated that test scores predict quite imperfectly which children will be creative adults, but by reasoning backwards, from adult to child, we could perhaps come up with up with some determinants of creativity and giftedness.

## Getzels and Csikszentmihalyi's *The Creative Vision*

In their 1976 ground-breaking study of problem-finding in visual artists, Getzels and Csikszentmihalyi thought that creativity was an attempt to reduce tension that may not be perceived consciously. The way artists did this was to seek problems that could be symbolically solved through human imagination. When the problem was identified and a temporary solution found, the tension was released, but this differed from the simple concept of equilibration which Piaget had described years earlier. Piaget had said that we learn when we are put into disequilibrium by new information. We must assimilate that information into our existing scheme of knowledge, and then must accommodate it by changing our scheme of knowledge, and, perhaps, by changing our behavior. When this happens we can feel a sense of equilibrium again. This process happens repeatedly as we learn.

Getzels and Csikszentmihalyi took this one step further when describing what happens when an artist works: "the key to creative achievement is the transformation of an intangible conflict into a tangible symbolic problem to which the creative solution will be the response." The conflict the artist feels is changed, within himself, into a problem. In other words, the artist "finds" a problem that will lead to a work of art. The work of art is the symbolic solution to that problem. This happens again and again as the artist works. This concept will be discussed in detail in Chapter 5.

## Albert's and Amabile's *Work with Intrinsic Motivation*

Robert Albert's (1983) social psychological approach to creativity has focused on genius, continuing in the wake of Galton, Lombroso, Hollingworth, Terman, and Oden. Albert asserted that creative people begin the creative production early in life, are productive throughout life, have certain personality traits and family environments. Theresa Amabile, author of *The Social Psychology of Creativity* (1983), made important contributions with her experiments utilizing practicing artists. In *Growing Up Creative* (1989), Amabile made a three-ringed Venn diagram similar to Renzulli's, where she described creativity as occurring when intrinsic motivation intersects with the skills required to master the domain and with the skills of creative production.

## Simonton's *Scientific Genius*

Following upon Albert, and the Goertzels, whose work will be discussed in Part III, the social psychologist Dean Keith Simonton demonstrated in *Scientific Genius* (1988) that creativity is the result of the work of a life and that this lifetime has to encompass certain aspects of environment, depending on the type of creative product the creator is making. In a 1991 address, Simonton emphasized that his work concerns only "first-rate geniuses" and the social factors that impinge on the genius from birth to grave.

Simonton built upon Campbell's (1960) formulations that creativity is the measure of a total number of variations an individual can produce. By combining a consideration of rates of information processing, age at career onset, developmental antecedents, and other phenomena such as lifetime productivity, the sheer quantity of output as compared to the quality of output, and what Simonton calls "the swan-song phenomenon" (which is an odd but notable increase in the quality and nature of a creator's output five years before his death) Simonton has employed a statistical technique called historiometry. His deductions from the statistics generated by studying these features of a genius's life are described in Chapter 8.

## Feldman's *Nature's Gambit*

In *Nature's Gambit* (1986), David Feldman, a developmental psychologist, provided another approach to the forming of a creative adult. By studying extraordinary talent in young people, the phenomenon called "prodigy," Feldman said that we might better understand rapid human development as well as Gruber's assertion that the development of creativity has evolutionary implications. Feldman also extended the definitions of creativity. He pointed to the need for insight and illumination that can lead to the transformations necessary for the creative process. One of the most useful conclusions is that creativity is an extension of giftedness. Feldman, in 1982, noted: (1) giftedness is achieving advanced mastery within a field, or domain, of activity; (2) creativity is extending that mastery to find new meaning within that field of activity; (3) genius is remaking that field so that everyone has to think in new ways.

In his essay, "Dreams, Insights, and Transformations" (1988), Feldman called creativity "a special form of development that yields a product that is new and valuable not only to an individual but also to a field." He used the word "transformations" to describe these products. In a 1990 speech, Feldman diagrammed his developmental theory of creativity, emphasizing that the truly creative contribution is only made when the field is transformed. The creative person works within a domain within a field, and stretches the knowledge of that domain within that field. For example, a poet works within the poetry domain within the literature field; a painter works within the visual arts field in a domain called painting.

Every field and domain of knowledge in which creativity can be demonstrated has novice levels, apprenticeship levels, expert levels, and special jargons. People at the expert levels use methodologies that are distinct to the practitioners in the field in which the creativity is demonstrated. Creative people reach the expert levels and then transform and extend the field and domain. Feldman said there are several "regions" of development in creativity. The creative production, or the transformation, is achieved through insight that occurs only when the creative producer is developmentally ready.

## Frames of Giftedness

Giftedness takes many forms. Howard Gardner, in *Frames of Mind* (1983), cited seven different intelligences. In his essay, "Creative Lives and Creative Works" (1988), he said that several of these, alone and in various combinations, would probably yield a conception of giftedness, with giftedness implying outstanding achievement or ability in each or a combination of the seven intelligences. The intelligences are: (1) Linguistic Intelligence; (2) Musical Intelligence; (3) Logical-Mathematical Intelligence; (4) Spatial Intelligence; (5) Bodily-Kinesthetic Intelligence; (6) Inter-Personal Intelligence; and (7) Intra-Personal Intelligence. Gardner is himself a recipient of one of the so-called "genius" awards, the MacArthur Fellowship grants given to people who are thought to be contemporary geniuses.

In Gardner's theory, creativity is an aspect of each of these intelligences as they are perfected and developed, and not a separate intelligence or ability. Gardner asserted that creativity cannot take place without the odd interaction, or "asynchrony" of place, time, talent, and morality. He said,

> Creative individuals often are marked by an anomalous pattern of intelligences, by a tension between intellectual and personality styles, and by a striking lack of fit between personality and domain, intelligence and field, and biological constitution and choice of career. Indeed, it sometimes appears as if the very lack of fit served as a primary motivation for the individual to strike out in a new direction and, ultimately, to fashion a creative product. (1988, p. 320)

## Of Triarchies and Hierarchies

In *The Triarchic Mind* (1985), cognitive scientist Robert Sternberg named three types of giftedness. One of these is creative giftedness, the ability to adapt to what is novel, or the ability to make something new. Sternberg, in "A Three-facet Model of Creativity" (1988), defined creative ability as essential to giftedness:

> Those individuals who make the greatest long-range contributions to society are probably those whose gifts involve coping with novelty — specifically, in the area of insight. Creative and insightful individuals are those who make discoveries and devise the inventions that ultimately change society. (p. 74)

He called his theory "triarchic," insisting that each intelligent act incorporates planning, research, and finally, doing the act. Like many contemporary psychologists and educators, Sternberg suggested that many people who have high IQs do not have successful lives, perhaps because they lack all three components of intelligence. Again we see the evolving idea that creativity is necessary for giftedness, and not separate from it. In a 1991 address called "Creative Giftedness," Sternberg focused on everyday creativity that is exhibited when one leads an intelligent life. He said that creativity is not a matter solely of cognition, but that it occurs within the context of a certain environment. The six facets of creativity are: (1) creative intelligence; (2) specific knowledge within the domain; (3) a certain style of mind; (4) certain aspects of personality; (5) motivation; and (6) a nurturing environment. None of these aspects of creative giftedness is earthshaking or new, and by 1991, consensus had been reached that these were necessary.

## Of Moseses and Others

The patriarch Moses was led into the wilderness and spoken to by a burning bush, whereby he received the power of divinity and his abilities led the chosen people out of Egypt. Grandma Moses lived as an ordinary homemaker and mother for many years, and her great artistic talent was not realized until she was at an age where most of her contemporaries, male and female, were enjoying retirement or were dead. Both these people would be defined as gifted, and yet both are different. That Plato was a great philosopher, that Gardner is a cognitive scientist, that Moses was a prophet, that Grandma Moses was an artist whose talent was not recognized until she was aged, illustrate that giftedness, or the manifestation of giftedness, takes many apparitions, or elusive forms, in adulthood.

No one would argue that Moses was creative in the various ways he devised to fool the Egyptians, though many would say he was divinely inspired. On the other hand, no one would dispute that Grandma Moses was creative. Howard Gardner is one of our contemporary geniuses and reportedly wrote a book on China in just a few weeks (Shekerjian, 1990), a very massive as well as a creative endeavor. Plato, in his metaphor of the Cave, creatively captured the imaginations of all ensuing western civilization.

*Creativity is the underpinning, the basement, the foundation, which permits giftedness to be realized.* The high score on the intelligence test merely suggests that the person who gets that score may have the potential to do well in school, not necessarily in life. Doing well in school often permits a person to get more education and, in doing that, to get a good job. Certainly, to be creative is necessary in order to realize a life of giftedness, but with all due respect to Mensa, having scored high on an intelligence test may not be necessary.

## Why Are We So Interested in Creativity, Anyway?

To provide an interdisciplinary flavor, and not give short shrift to other fields with proprietary interests in creativity, let us see what the philosophers say. In "The Rationality of Creativity" (1981) the philosopher I. C. Jarvie alleged that the current literature on creativity is both impoverished and irrational. Problems exist, he said, because (1) the problem to be solved by the study of creativity is not clearly stated; (2) researchers and thinkers treat creativity as an issue of psychological, but not logical, import; (3) when one explains creativity, one explains it away; and (4) creating an explanation that explains creativity, also, paradoxically, must explain itself.

### Reasons of Quantity

Jarvie pointed out that the aim of people who attempt to discover and promote creativity is, presumably, not to increase the flood of papers, inventions, and works of art that already inundate publishers, galleries, critics. Every day in the United States 5,000 books are published. Who wants more? The educated consumer of literature cannot even keep up with what is now being published.

Too many creative people are struggling for recognition, acceptance, and financial award, another argument goes. Let me use myself as an example. I am a published poet, novelist, and short story writer. In 1989 alone, I had my second novel rejected, several short stories rejected, a collection of already published poems called *The Company* rejected, a collection of already published short stories called *Blueberry Season* rejected, and a nonfiction book called *Principal,* about my sojourn as the principal of a school for gifted children in New York City, rejected. That year I totalled over forty rejections of these materials. The people who ask me to do public readings of my work, and even pay me for doing so, consider me a talented writer. But at the moment it is clear that my talent is not wanted or needed by the world of commercial publishing. Too many novels, poems, and nonfiction books are being written, and too few being read, is the implication here.

My experience is not unusual for creative writers. A 1990 contest at Cleveland State University Press chose three manuscripts from the 975 manuscripts of poetry submitted. The poet Neal Bowers has said even those contests as prestigious as the National Academy of American Poets' contests, and those of university presses, are a racket: "The winning poet is the only writer to benefit in any immediate way. . . . The other 999 poets receive only a printed rejection letter or a hastily scribbled note of regret." Many are writing poetry, but not enough are reading and buying it.

Art schools are turning out artists. Yet most of these artists' work will not see the track lights of a one-person show in a gallery. Music schools turn out musicians, composers, teachers. Yet most composers, from even the most elite schools, will never see their work performed, especially if their work is orchestral. Even that most brutal of performing arts, dance, has hopefuls studying, dancing, seven days a week, for a chance to get into the *corps de ballet*. New York City has the best-looking waiters and waitresses in the world, most of them struggling actors and actresses, auditioning like crazy, studying like crazy, waiting for their big break. The United States Patent Office receives thousands of applications annually for patents. Do we need more creative production? As Jarvie pointed out, more output can certainly not be the reason we promote the development of creativity.

### Quality as Creativity

A particularly complex reason alleged to underlie the interest in creativity is the drive to produce quality creative works. Given the plethora of production noted above, an underlying implication is that most of the creative output nowadays is substandard. What is art to some is trash to others, as witness the controversy over the 1990 Robert Mapplethorpe exhibit, which included several homoerotic photographs. The fallout from this brouhaha almost left the National Endowment for the Arts without funding, and prompted Federal guidelines verging on censorship for works of art. Of note, though, the jury of nonartists in Cincinnati ruled in favor of the Contemporary Arts Center in the 1990 obscenity trial. (That is, they considered it art).

The often heard comment about abstract art, that a child or a monkey could do it, also illustrates the argument about quality. The subject matter chosen by the artist, the use of materials, the genetically inherited body — for who can be a ballet dancer without long legs and the right turn of instep? — all point to the necessity for quality. But whose idea of quality? The creator's or the public's? When Andy Warhol painted a Campbell's soup can, the public screamed about lack of quality. When Elvis sang "Hound Dog" the public bemoaned the passing of an era, and a new age of rock and roll was born. When Stravinsky's *Rites of Spring* premiered in the early 1900s, the audience rioted. The suggestion that a bomb could be built from nuclear fusion prompted the world to shake its head with disbelief, and then with horror.

A most perplexing question in judging a creative product is the question of quality. Most often quality is recognized by peers who, with expert eyes, see the merits of creative work. This is not necessarily the judgment of the marketplace, or of popular taste, however, and people buy art to match their couches rather than because the artist has won peer recognition. Censorship often results when popular taste is pitted against qualified peer judgment. That is why we have two Vietnam memorials; one for the Congressmen and one for the public.

*Creativity and Nationalism*

Others have said we should develop our children's creativity for nationalistic reasons. In the late 1950s, and throughout the Cold War, a nationalistic spirit prevailed in the U.S., especially after the Russians put Sputnik into orbit. Creativity was deemed necessary to keep the U.S. ahead of Russia. As Guilford noted in 1970: "the most urgent reason [for studying creativity] is that we are in a mortal struggle for the survival of our way of life in the world." Mid-century psychologists saw creativity as necessary for combatting the Soviet threat. Jarvie quoted Razik (1970) thus:

> In the presence of the Russian threat, "creativity" could no longer be left to the chance occurrences of the genius; neither could it be left in the realm of the wholly mysterious and the untouchable. Men had to be able to do something about it; creativity had to be a property in many men; it had to be something identifiable; it had to be subject to the effects of efforts to gain more of it.

In other words, creativity could (at least in part) be controlled, manipulated, engineered, and predicted. In fact, it had to be. (Jarvie, 1981, p. 134)

In recent years, the popular culture has used the same nationalistic argument concerning competition with the Japanese and the Europeans. A common assertion among patriotic educators of the gifted is that the U.S. still leads the world in patent applications, and that American inventors design, while the Japanese and Germans can only improve on the basic designs. These people then repeat their call for an emphasis on creativity training in the schools.

## Creativity and Equity

A fourth reason for emphasizing creativity has racist and classist overtones, usually implicit rather than stated explicitly. It goes like this. People in the middle and upper socioeconomic classes score better on IQ tests and achievement tests than people in the lower socioeconomic classes, no matter the ethnicity. Poor people don't score particularly well on IQ tests. But we do know that poor African Americans have invented American popular music, rhythm and blues, and jazz, and they have also revolutionized all sports they have been exposed to. African Americans have been stereotyped as having musical creativity and superior physical giftedness. Latinos have also had great influence on popular dance and music — tango, cha-cha, lambada. Therefore, such creativity should be nurtured in the schools in order to identify for gifted programs those who might not score so well on IQ tests.

The implication seems to be, let us admit to our programs those students with "creative potential," and hope that these will be students from lower socioeconomic classes, students who would not be in the programs if we only used high IQ and high achievement as criteria. Thus, by implication, poor people are creatively gifted and not intellectually gifted. Alternative high schools such as the La Guardia High School for the Performing Arts in New York City attract more poor and minority students than do Stuyvesant High School or the Bronx High School of Science or Hunter High School, even though all the high schools are tuition-free alternative schools and admit students from all five boroughs of New York City by competitive standards. Stuyvesant, Hunter, and the Bronx High School advertise themselves as academic high schools for intellectually gifted students, and although great efforts are made to enroll Hispanic and African American students, the majority of the students are white and Asian.

Although creativity, as argued here, is the highest form of giftedness, the graduates of the academic high schools go on to elite colleges in greater numbers and thus have tickets to join the establishment when they enter professions. Since the students supposedly have different potentials for giftedness, some being intellectually gifted and some being creatively gifted, their segregation is permitted. Here, creativity is often meshed with the visual and performing arts. For example, the specialties of vocal music and theater at La Guardia attract more poor minority students than do the specialties of instrumental music and dance, for one does not need special lessons in vocal music and theater in order to be picked out as talented in the competitive auditions.

The grave disparity in numbers of certain ethnic minority and lower socioeconomic children in gifted education classes has led to a concerted effort by the U.S. Office of Education. In 1990 and 1991, millions of dollars in grant moneys, called Javits Grants, were awarded to foster ways to identify and serve gifted children who were disadvantaged, culturally different, or handicapped. In 1991, an advisory panel to the U.S. Office of Gifted Education proposed a revised definition of giftedness that was motivated by political concerns for the inequity in participation in programs for the intellectually gifted. The definition would propose that giftedness occurs in all groups across all cultures and giftedness is in the product and not in the test score. The definition does not mention creativity.

## Creativity and the Future

Perhaps another reason we want to identify creativity is to increase it in specific ways. The justification for educating gifted children has often been that these children have special talents that can be used creatively to save the world from itself. We want our gifted students to be creative leaders, a notion which also implies that giftedness and creativity are meshed and not separate.

A popular nationwide program called Future Problem Solving, where teams of children solve current problems such as overpopulation or acid rain, is an illustration. Students doing Future Problem Solving use a creative thinking program called the Creative Problem Solving (CPS) model, developed by Osborn and Parnes and promoted by the Creative Education Foundation at the State University of New York in Buffalo, and by E. Paul Torrance at the University of Georgia. One of its goals is to enhance the creativity of bright children by having them solve real problems according to the model. This model will be discussed in more detail in Chapters 2 and 4.

Most educators of the gifted take for granted that creativity can be enhanced, and believe there is a need for more, as well as higher quality, creative production. In all the educational literature on creativity, no one questions these premises. The corollary premise is that creative promise, or "creative potential," as it is often called, can be identified by the means available to school personnel. These premises are shaky ones, as we shall see.

## What Place Does Creativity Have in the Schools?

Few even question whether enhancement of creativity is the proper province of the schools. But to identify and nurture a child who is gifted in creativity may require the use of means that far exceed what schools are supposed to do — which is to teach children to fit into society by (1) civilizing them, and (2) teaching them to read, to write, and to figure, i.e., making them literate. The schools today have their hands full doing both tasks, although some argue that teaching children to be more creative enhances their self-esteem and thus helps them to learn the basics more easily.

### Creativity as Human Freedom

*Creativity is the ability to produce something new — if not new to the world, at least to the person producing.* The concept of creativity has been invested with a lot of serious interest and research in the last forty years. Whereas Guilford in 1950 said he researched creativity and had come up with only a few articles, now there are thousands of experts, thousands of speakers at conventions, thousands of people doing research. It is all very confusing. Many theories have been espoused by many theorists (overwhelmingly men, by the way, to put a gender factor into the discussion). These are often complicated, and if you are interested, I have outlined some of them in the Appendix.

Why all this theorizing about creativity and the creative process? Another look at the philosophical point of view of Jarvie provides an answer. There is strong interest in unmasking the mystery of creativity precisely because it is so unexplainable. We write so much and think so much about creativity because we simply want to explain the creative achievement, to find out the truth about what makes a creative product. However, once we think we discover the process, it eludes us.

One reason philosophers study creativity is that creativity implies a kind of human freedom. The existentialist philosophers especially were concerned with freedom, and thinkers such as Wittgenstein and Sartre said that human beings have the freedom to thus create themselves. Despite what Calvinists and astrologers may say, a life is not pre-determined and a person thus demonstrates creativity in how she makes her life productive. This philosophy is a very popular one today, as shall be seen in the subsequent description of New Age thinking and the creative process in Chapter 2.

On the other hand, the psychologists' reason for studying creativity is very practical. They have attempted to identify the creative, as opposed to the noncreative, personality. Psychologists set out to make up tests that would ferret out the people who would be able to produce creative products. The psychologists are also interested in what happens in the mind while a person is being creative. They also write about the creative process, which creative persons supposedly go through in order to produce creative products. This fascination with these three — personality, process, and product — continues.

Domain specialists, creative people such as artists, writers, mathematicians, and dancers, are not very interested in what happens in the mind while a person creates, or in what the personalities of various creators show. Practitioners of the various creative disciplines are more interested in the products that the creator makes. Is it new? Is it valuable? Does it extend the field?

### Can a Person Be Creative Without a Product?

A major concern of creativity theorists is whether one can be a creative person without a creative product. Logic suggests that without judging the creativeness of the product, we cannot conclude that a person is creative. But that is essentially what we are doing in education, when we talk about creativity, or creative potential, as a type of giftedness. We often identify children with what we call "creative potential," without reference to the products they have or will produce. If we say the creative product is a person's life, then we don't need to have a concrete thing, a composition, a poem, a pot, a theorem. The children of Guilford have highly influenced the schools by leaving the impression that a young child who scores well on a paper and pencil test will be an adult who will produce a creative product.

## Creativity of the Moment and for the Ages

A related concern is how to objectively judge whether or not a product is "creative," that is, a valuable novelty. For example, take the recent soaring prices of Van Gogh's work. Van Gogh himself made nothing from his paintings. His work was not valued by the art galleries, critics, and auction houses of his day, but only by a few of his artist peers. Yet auction houses and rich buyers of today have parlayed some of his paintings into a net worth of upwards of fifty million dollars. Was Van Gogh creative? Are his paintings examples of creativity? If we had given Van Gogh a Guilford test of divergent production or a Torrance Test of Creative Thinking, would he have scored high enough to get into our creative thinking program? Did Van Gogh have an IQ over the threshold?

If we had been Van Gogh's teachers, we probably wouldn't have rated his products creative in comparison to others, because of the violent emotion and blinding color that his paintings showed. Even his art teachers did not think he had much potential. Van Gogh was probably a very scary boy, as well as a difficult man. He mailed his ear to a woman who spurned him, then did a self-portrait. Yet less than a hundred years later, his creativity is the most valued — in monetary terms — in the art world. This could be called the creativity theory of posthumous value which accrues after death. It is often the creator of the moment or of the past whom we praise, and not the creator of the future. Creators of the moment are probably those who extend the knowledge of the field just a little bit, enough so that we can understand it, just as leaders of the moment are people with whom we can identify, just a little smarter than we are, but not so much smarter that we can't relate to them.

In the past, creators of the future have had their works destroyed because their contemporaries didn't value them. In particular, many women, poor people, and minorities were creative but their work wasn't valued during its time, and so was lost. Historical re-examination may help their works to surface for future generations, if they haven't been destroyed.

Many contemporary writers emphasize that creativity cannot be recognized as such without reference to the times in which the creative product was made. That is why creativity must be judged within the context of the historical milieu and the readiness of the population to accept the creativity.

## Creativity Can Take Place Without Mastery

Though Feldman might disagree, I believe a person can be creative while learning the discipline. In fact, many disciplines are never truly mastered, for example, music, dance, creative writing, and other arts. The pianist who has practiced and prepared himself for years to interpret the master work achieves a novel interpretation — he transforms what he has done before and even transforms, to an extent, the individual work. I believe this person is creative, even though he hasn't extended the discipline for any record books, but only in the temporal and ephemeral memories of his audience. For example, the work may not be recorded, and thus the people in the field do not know whether or not that person has extended the discipline, but the judges know whether or not he has been momentarily creative. This "momentary" creativity comes as the result of years of preparation.

The same holds true for dancers. Much dance, because it is physical movement, has not been notated. The dancer achieved certain moves that the choreographer just described. The collaborative nature of the medium recognizes the choreographer as the more creative one. But wasn't the dancer also? The dancer achieved mastery within the domain, and in performance, extends the field. But if the dance was not videotaped, the only record would be in the memories of the audience. The trained dancer or choreographer watching the performance could watch and replicate it, but nuances of stretch and gesture would still be peculiar to the interpreter.

The people who face the blank page and the canvas are also creative while doing their work. The master novelist may win the National Book Award, or the Nobel Prize, but then again, the judges for the prizes have been notoriously partial to mainstream novelists, and have not been kind to those who experiment, except for such novelists as Gabriel Garcia Marquez, certain other Latin Americans such as Borges, and the odd phenomenon of Egypt's Nobel prize-winning novelist Naguib Mahfouz arising from a culture that doesn't write novels. The winner of the National Book Award or the Nobel Prize may be the "artist of the moment" but not the artist of the ages. But experimental novelists are often working in areas at the edges where the discipline would be extended. Perhaps the experimental novelists are those who will be hailed as geniuses, long after their deaths.

For example, Sinclair Lewis, who is rarely read these days except when required in college courses, won a Nobel Prize; Tom Pynchon is being read more and more, even though he hasn't won any major prizes. The visual artist with the mute lump of clay or the empty white canvas is also creative, for she, like the writer, is finding a problem. Her problem is not defined. She defines it as she works with her medium. The artist defines the problem as she creates. She is choosing the problem to solve, finding it, and in doing so is being creative. Often the choice of the problem is motivated by personal reasons, personal need, personal pathology. The execution of the solution of the problem uses the media provided by the field's constraints. Thus, a creator can be momentarily creative. This most often happens once she has gained substantial background knowledge, reasonable skill, and some recognition by peers. This allows the person who is not quite a "master," whatever that is, to be creative.

## The Existence of Talent

In all of my readings, there has been a given, a taken-for-granted — the creatively productive person must have something called "talent." This raises the problem of heredity and environment. Is a person born with talent, or can a person acquire talent? Although giftedness and talent are often used synonymously, discussions of the creative product say that the producer had talent first, developed that talent, and then produced that product. Aspects of talent are physiological and psychological, genetic as well as environmental. A musician needs dexterity. A visual artist needs visual acuity. A scientist needs curiosity. A writer needs verbal facility. An actor and a dancer need physical suppleness.

Talent is called a natural proclivity. Developed talent is necessary for creativity. In studies of eminence, such as Galton's back in 1869, talent was thought to be inherited, or evolved, in certain families. The immigrant experience in the United States has shown that even children from extremely poor families, when given the proper nurturing and

environment, often have significant talent, and that the propensity and ability to create is more common than many classist evolutionary hereditists have thought. The third section of this book will specifically consider several kinds of talent.

## Summary

1. Many fields have a proprietary interest in creativity. Among these are psychology, psychoanalysis, philosophy, the arts, business, and the sciences.

2. The term "creativity" is a relatively new term.

3. Creativity has come to be considered either a form of giftedness, or to be synonymous with giftedness; to be synonymous with genius, or to be a form of genius.

4. Psychologists, both psychometricians and cognitive psychologists, have had a great impact on the field of education in its definitions of creativity and giftedness.

5. Some people believe that a person can be creative without a product; some people believe that such creativity is not creativity at all.

6. There are many reasons for our emphasis on creativity. Some are reasons of quantity, quality, equity, national competition and pride, and reasons of freedom.

7. Talent is probably genetic, but some questions exist.

# Chapter 2

## The Creative Process

*The artistic experience, at its highest, was actually a natural analogue of mystical experience. It produced a kind of intuitive perception.*
— Thomas Merton

*The way to rock oneself back into writing is this. First, gentle exercise in the air. Second the reading of good literature. It is a mistake to think that literature can be produced from the raw. One must get out of life . . . one must become externalised; very, very concentrated, all at one point, not having to draw upon the scattered parts of one's character, living in the brain.*
— Virginia Woolf

*I called the Muse;*
*she pleaded a headache.*
— Derek Walcott

*The daimon of creativity has ruthlessly had its way with me.*
— Carl Jung

There is much mystical, magical, phenomenological writing about what goes on before and while a person is creating. The creative process engages many thinkers because they feel that if the process can be duplicated, more people will be creative. Some of the most interesting writing about creativity is written by creative people, describing the process they go through. It is probably most interesting because they are interesting people: writers, artists, scientists, mathematicians, composers, inventors, psychologists. This chapter discusses some of the most cogent theories.

## Traditional Theories of the Creative Process

For centuries people have tried to explain what happens when a person creates. Our interest in "the creative process" has stemmed from our deepest, most unconscious being and our most ancient mythologies. From the visitation of the muse to Wallas's four steps in the process; from Ghiselin's anthology of how creators have worked to "aha's" and "Eureka!'s"; from magical dreams to mysterious coincidences; from ritualistic obsessions to hypnotic trances; the creative process is intriguing, fascinating, and frustrating.

### The Visitation of the Muse

A popularly held conception, originating centuries ago and common in many cultures, was that the creative person went into a sort of trance while creating. This trance was caused by the visitation of the Muse. In fact, in Greek mythology there were nine Muses — all daughters of Memory (Mnemosyne) and of Jupiter. Each had her own province in music, literature, art, and science, according to Bulfinch in his 1855 *Mythology*. The muse of epic poetry was Calliope; the muse of history was Clio; the muse of lyric poetry was Euterpe; the muse of tragedy was Melpomene; the muse of choral dance and song was Terpsichore. Erato was the muse of love poetry, and Polyhymnia was the muse of sacred poetry. Urania was the muse of astronomy, and Thalia, the muse of comedy.

The muses came to symbolize the feminine principle; the male principle was symbolized by the Seven Spheres. Thus, "The Music of the Spheres" symbolizes the union of the male and female principles, the male being the animus, and the female being the anima. The male creator unites with his anima, or female side, and the female creator unites with her animus, her male side, according to Jungian thought. Dante had his

Beatrice, Lancelot his Guinevere, Tristan his Isolde, Ilmarainen his Maid of North Farm. At the beginning of Homer's *Iliad*, the blind poet invokes the muses in order to help him tell his story. For our purposes here, though, suffice it to say that the muses were inspirations to creative men.

Do creative women have muses? "Yes," said Carolyn Kizer in her 1990 essay, called, appropriately, "A Muse." This Muse was her mother; but women's muses are not always their mothers. Creative women, as well as creative men, often have desired sexual partners as muses. Inspiration comes in response to a feeling for someone, quite possibly a sexual feeling, certainly an emotional identification. Everyone has written a secret love poem to a love, requited or unrequited. Getzels and Csikszentmihalyi, in *The Creative Vision* (1976), specifically suggested that one primary reason artists make art, poets write poems, musicians compose music, is the erotic reason. They called it the "libidinous" reason, the longing for sexual connection.

For example, the painter Magritte said that seeing a catalogue of Futurist paintings in 1919 changed the course of his art explorations, as he realized that "one pure and powerful emotion, eroticism, kept me from falling at that time into a more traditional search for formal perfection" (Gablik, 1976). The contemporary homoerotic works of Eric Fischl, David Hockney, Robert Mapplethorpe, and Judy Chicago come to mind, as do the heterosexual paintings of Andrew Wyeth, the longing lyrics of the Brownings, and the romantic ballets of Balanchine. The place of erotic desire and longing for sexual union — not unlike yearning for the muses — cannot be underestimated in considering the products of any artist. Poets write love poems. Choreographers make ballets. Visual artists paint nudes. Many of these works are efforts to express eroticism within the boundaries of the medium within which the artists are working. Several poet friends have experienced whole new surges of poetic energy when they fell in love later in life, after they thought sexual love was lost to them. They wrote what they considered the best poems of their careers, works that combined mature skill with innocent longing.

Muses are virginal, pure, and faithful. The artist longs for the muse, and in the process of longing, creates a song, a play, a poem, a theorem. Many creative people, especially poets, still speak about their work in muselike terms. Poems "come" to them. "I awoke with this poem," a friend of mine said. "I'm waiting for poems," remarked another.

When the creative person is being visited by the muse, he or she often feels possessed, and enters another world, a world of reverie, of be*mused* silence. This state can be likened to how a person feels when driving alone for a long time on a boring interstate highway, deep in thought. Many people get their best ideas while driving. Suddenly a car crosses the median and the driver slams on the brakes. The adrenalin flows. Alertness. A beating heart. She has awakened from the creative, meditational, half-awake yet alert state, and is thrust suddenly back to an awareness of daily life.

In relation to the mystique of the muse, some novelists describe their characters as having lives of their own. Others can't believe they wrote what they did, that they were capable of it. They feel as if they were go-betweens, mediums. The composer, Brahms, called it a state of "semitrance": "I have to be in a semitrance condition to get such results — a condition when the conscious mind is in temporary abeyance, and the subconscious mind is in control." (Abell, 1946)

## The Old Chestnuts

Several basic old chestnuts appear and reappear when one is reading about the creative process. For example, Graham Wallas's list of steps in the creative process, the story about Kekule's dream of snakes coiling, providing the clue to the benzene ring, Poincare's trust in the unconscious to solve his mathematical problems, Albert Einstein's vivid visualization, without words, of his thoughts, Coleridge's use of opium while writing "Kubla Khan," or A. E. Housman's meditative walks after lunch and a pint of beer. Though old, these stories can be instructive.

Here is Wallas's oft-quoted summary of the process, from his 1926 book, *The Art of Thought*. Wallas, a pioneer in critical thinking, worked out of the tradition of John Dewey and Horace Mann. He said that there are four stages in the creative process: (1) preparation; (2) incubation; (3) illumination; and (4) verification. In the first stage, the person does both formal and informal work — she readies herself for the act of creation by studying, thinking, searching for answers, asking people, etc. In the second state, the process rests, is in gestation, and the person is pregnant with the creative product. The unconscious is working on the problem. In the third stage, a solution arises, and light is thrown on the problem. The most famous example of this is in the creativity literature: the vision of Archimedes rising from his bathtub and running naked through the streets shouting "Eureka! I have it!" when he understood the theory of the displacement of water. Then the creative person has to prove the theory, to see whether it is, indeed, valid. This is the fourth stage.

## The Work of Brewster Ghiselin

Brewster Ghiselin, a fine poet, became better known for editing an anthology of essays called *The Creative Process* (1952), than for his poetry. His own essay, the introduction to the book, summarized and explained what many creative people have said about the process experienced when they create. Often they describe a feeling of oceanic consciousness, which precedes the almost automatic producing of the work. Emotion is often present, and is expressed as the creator exercises intense concentration in her field.

*Oceanic consciousness.* The creative process may begin in the creative person with what Ghiselin called "primitive, a condition of complete indecision." Describing it as "yielding to oceanic consciousness," he likened it in some people to an intense or vague religious experience, the surrender of the self to some internal necessity, some call that seems greater than the self, greater than the puny ego. It may be a yearning or a hunch, but it is usually preverbal, vague, an "intimation of approaching or potential resolution."

What is to be invented then appears partially and spontaneously:

> . . . sometimes in the form of a mere glimpse serving as a clue, or like a germ to be developed; sometimes a fragment of the whole, whether rudimentary and requiring to be worked into shape or already in its final form; sometimes essentially complete, though needing expansion, verification, or the like. (p. 15)

*Automaticity.* The work then is done with some automaticity. This automaticity, already highly developed in the creator, has arisen as he has acquired the necessary tools within the domain of creative activity. Ghiselin pointed out that the part of the creative process most often underplayed is the enormous preparation that creators must do within their fields. The viewer sees the finished work, and forgets the "sweat and litter of the workroom." He said, "The impression it gives of unlabored force is not to be trusted." Bloom, in *Developing Talent in Young People* (1985), and Bamberger, in a 1988 essay about the development of musical talent, likewise highlighted the need for the creative person to learn the field to the point where expression becomes almost automatic. Automaticity will be discussed in more detail in Chapters 5 through 9.

*Restlessness.* The process is characterized also by restlessness, and creative people often move on to other projects just when the rest of the world is beginning to catch on to what they have done. The word "movement" as in "Romantic Movement," "Neoclassical Movement," or "Abstract Expressionist Movement" illustrates this restlessness. It was said of Picasso that he was not in any movements; he started them. Ghiselin pointed out that the creator casts himself loose from the "ties of security," and this requires a certain courage and a willingness to work alone, counter to the popular taste, and with a certain amount of uncertainty. A person who is too formalistic and follows the current rules, will probably create nothing. This is perhaps why the inventors and entrepreneurs who are not employed by large companies are often the most innovative.

*A sense of aesthetics.* Whatever the creator's field, emotion is needed — a feeling for aesthetics, for the beauty unique to that field. Mathematicians admire the elegant proof. Scientists marvel at the beauty of cells and theories. Artists notice unique patterns in the visual world. Poets write about details in the ordinary world that no one else notices. The creator is drawn toward activity in a specific domain, and expresses this aesthetic appetite by a passion for working within a certain field.

*Organic unconsciousness.* However, Ghiselin pointed out that the unconscious work in any field of creativity is done organically, and is not "canny calculation governed by wish, will, and expediency." Even so, the creative mind during the creative process is not undisciplined. It needs to be managed in order to discover what needs to be done next, and to assure that movement toward the end product is economical and certain. Much of the work done is imitation, especially in young creators, but the creator must go on, "for only on the fringes of consciousness and in the deeper backgrounds into which they fade away is freedom attainable."

*Massive concentration.* Ghiselin also emphasized the physical manifestations of the creative process, the massive concentration that the creator exhibits. One could say that the person is in kind of a concentration or trance, almost like being hypnotized or sleepwalking. But this state differs from hypnotism or trance, for the person is collected, autonomous, and watchful. This trancelike state is common to all creative activity, but it is an indirect result and comes from the creator's passion for the particular domain, not as a direct intention: "In short, the creative discipline when successful may generate a trancelike state, but one does not throw oneself into a trance in order to create."

In an interview for the famous *Paris Review* "Writers At Work" series, John Hersey, the writer who changed the world with his portrait of Hiroshima's devastation, described his creative dreamlike state: "When writing is really working, I think there is something like dreaming going on. I don't know how to draw the line between the conscious management of what you're doing and this state." Hersey said that this dreamlike mood happens during the first stages, during the drafts of his work, in a process similar to daydreaming. "When I feel really engaged with a passage, I become so lost in it that I'm unaware of my real surroundings, totally involved in the pictures and sounds that passage evokes." He then speculated that this mysterious feeling may be one of the things that attract those of us who write. Csikszentmihalyi probably was referring to this feeling when he described the "flow" experience in his book, *Flow* (1990). The flow feeling occurs "when a person's body or mind is stretched to its limits in a voluntary effort to accomplish something difficult and worthwhile."

Similarly, in my own process of creating, I find that I often lose consciousness about hours of time while I am writing, especially poetry and fiction. In poetry I work, revise, see it, revise, see it, revise, walk around, think, pace. I look up and it's several hours later. An artist friend reported the same phenomenon. She begins in the morning only to look up to discover it's dark out. She said that's why she gave up painting. When her kids came home from school, she'd look up surprised to realize she had done no housework, run no errands, and had an angry husband. Her husband and her children did not understand her passion for her work. Many creative women have experienced much shame, guilt, and conflict about their work.

*The will and organic form.* In the creative process, a willingness to sit down and concentrate is not enough. Though the will to create is important, alone it is not sufficient, for "will belongs to the conscious life only," Ghiselin noted. Though will can keep a person at her desk, and can help in organizing a project, will can also stultify and inhibit the development of what is truly new. Virginia Woolf, in *A Writer's Diary* (1954), wrote how she had planned and organized the structure of her novel, *Mrs. Dalloway,* but had to abandon that organization when it didn't work. She then proceeded blindly, without a plan. Clearly the previous plan had not been what she needed in order to express her impulse in writing the book. Therefore, the plan must be organic.

Julian Green in his 1961 diary described teaching fiction writing at Goucher College. His students expected him to give them a recipe for writing a novel, but Green told them, "I know of no other rule for writing a novel than sitting down at a table and starting off with Chapter One." John Irving, on the other hand, in an interview in *Poets And Writers,* said that he preferred to "not only know the end of the novel before the end of the novel, but the end of the chapter before I begin the chapter, the end of the scene before I begin the scene." (Stanton, 1991)

*The need for hard work.* Organic needs must also dictate the subject of the creative project; choosing a subject the creator is not inclined to, and forcing his mind to elaborate on that subject, is not productive. As Ghiselin said, finally this inspiration must be realized by good hard work.

After the work is completed, the process is not finished, however, for the creator must determine whether his excitement over the work has created something new, fresh, and useful. Often he will find that the value of the work has been in its intrinsic benefit to his development. When he submits it to critical review, it may be found wanting. Then he may work on it some more, or reject it and begin again. Shelley, for example, left behind many parts of poems because he didn't like to revise.

Ghiselin's "Introduction" still remains among the best summaries of what happens during the creative process.

## The Importance of Rituals

The creative process also often has ritualistic aspects. For example, some creators like to work in the morning, some at night. Some can work anywhere, but most have a place to work, a studio, a workshop, an office. Some find that their minds get excited with certain stimuli, such as music heard in solitude, chemical agents, certain company, reading, or exercise. Like dogs who circle before lying down, or athletes who put their uniforms on in a certain order before the big game, creative people often instinctively follow certain rituals before and while working.

## Illuminations and Aha's

Much has been written on the illumination phase, for that is the most dramatic. A very entertaining book by Madigan and Elwood called *Brain-*

*storms & Thunderbolts: How Creative Genius Works* (1984), described the Aha!'s of many creative people. This book would be a good resource for enrichment; kids would love it. The illuminations, or inspirations, come from the following types of experiences:

1. **"Triggers and flashes"**: For example, a sunset and a poem by Goethe inspired Tesla's design for an alternating current motor.

2. **"Obvious connections"**: Buckminster Fuller discovered the stability of the triangle, which later became the basis for his geodesic dome, in kindergarten while building structures from toothpicks and dried peas.

3. **"Visions and voices"**: Harriet Beecher Stowe saw the image of Uncle Tom on the ice chunk, trying to escape, while she was in church; this inspired her writing of the serialized novel that was instrumental in the cause of Abolition.

4. **"Dreams and drugs"**: Mary Shelley dreamed the idea for her book about Frankenstein after several days at a retreat with other writers trying to make up the most scary ghost story; and Isaac Singer dreamed the solution to the sewing machine problem — that the needle had to have its eye in its point. In fact, much has been written on the place of dreaming in the creative process, and creative people often keep journals of their dreams, hoping their dreams will give them insight. Feldman, the psychologist, wrote an essay, "Dreams, Insights, and Transformations" (1988), on what insights two dreams had given him.

5. **"Reflections on death"**: The death of Selman Waksman's sister from diptheria greatly influenced his developing streptomycin, for which he later won the Nobel Prize. Alfred Lord Tennyson began an elegy for his dear friend, Hallam, that became the poem for which he is most famous, "In Memoriam."

6. **"Being in love"**: The Taj Mahal was built in Agra, India, as a tribute to the wife of Shah Jehan, Mumtaz Mahal. Although he did not design it, she inspired its creation. Also, certainly many poems and stories are inspired by the yearning for a loved one.

7. **"Following trains of thought"**: Rorschach, who invented the inkblot test, belonged to a poet's group who wrote poems about what inkblots suggested to them. He was an artist, and had gone to art school before he decided on medical school. The Rorschach test resulted from this chain of interests.

8. **"Suggestions"**: Janov's Primal Therapy was suggested by a comedy act one of his clients had seen.

9. **"Plain old creative thievery"**: Velcro, invented by the Swiss inventor George de Mestral, was suggested by burrs sticking to hunting clothes. The idea for the process to make it came from barber's thinning shears. Vaseline petroleum jelly, refined by the chemist George Cheesebrough in 1870, was an idea cribbed from oilmen who complained about the rod wax that clogged oil pumps.

10. **"Fakes, mistakes, and accidents"**: Ivory soap, the soap that floats, was supposedly discovered when a worker went to lunch and left his whipping vat on. Too much air was whipped into the batch; he was afraid he would be reprimanded, so he poured it into the frames, and Ivory soap was born.

These accounts of how creative products and ideas were attained are interesting and fun to read. All illustrate that the creative product comes about from strange and wonderful processes, intentional and accidental. The purpose of creativity training, say some experts, is to make the accidental seem intentional by creating the proper atmosphere in which creativity can flourish.

## Newer Theories of the Creative Process

Writing and interest in creativity has burgeoned in the last thirty years. Many of the writers have focused on the creative process. Brain research has been popularized, and simplistic theories of right and left brain thinking have evolved. The outgrowth of the 1960s Vietnam War and the civil rights movement led to what was called the "me" generation in the 1980s, where people worked to make themselves the manifestation of creativity. Research on the influence of substances on the creative process has been done. Psychologists and psychoanalysts have begun to consider that creativity is the work of a lifetime and not of the moment. Cognitive scientists have sought to isolate what happens during the moment when the creator is creating. All of this has led to some interesting postulation.

### Right/Left Brain and the Creative Process

One popular cultural myth has been that creativity is the province of the "right brain," while noncreativity is the province of the "left brain." A favorite pastime of the 1980s was for people to say they were "right-brained" or "left-brained." Speakers went from company to company, school district to school district, giving pop psychology tests that purportedly showed the test-taker's brain dominance. Teachers were overheard saying, "Well, I'm right-brained, and my husband is left-brained, so that's why we don't get along. He's so organized, and I'm so disorganized." Right-brained people were supposed to be creative, and left-brained people were supposed to be methodical, sequential. Many books and articles were written on the subject, many researchers joined in to prove or disprove, and many interesting workshops were held to help people tap into their right brains. In *Drawing on the Right Side of the Brain* (1979), Betty Edwards taught people how to draw from the right sides of their brains by using upside-down techniques and reversals to prevent verbal codes from interfering with abilities to see. Gabriele Rico also taught people how to write the "natural" way. Her book was subtitled, *Using Right Brain Techniques To Release Your Expressive Powers.*

I took workshops from both Edwards and Rico. Edwards had all of us draw our "best" drawing. We laboriously reproduced a drawing from our left-brain memories, that first grade house with a sun, that second grade snowman with a dog, that fourth grade horse which mother had kept framed on the wall for all these years. Edwards pointed out that we had all stopped drawing at such developmentally early stages because we couldn't draw well enough to suit our own standards, and so had fallen into codes and symbols in our drawing. Her point was that we were censoring our right brains with our left brains.

Rico had us write after webbing our ideas, going back in our associational memories to early childhood. The experience was so powerful that a man behind me let out a sob, and later commented that he hadn't thought of that experience for years. I have also used a similar technique in workshops — a reminding chain or memory probe. Holding up an object such as a Granny Smith apple, I remind the participants that this apple first came to the United States from New Zealand on the other side of the world, telling a story about its voyage, talking about how it is winter here but summer down there, turning their perceptions topsy-turvy. While playing soft music, baroque or New Age, in the background, I then ask them to write on the first line, "The Granny Smith apple reminds me of," and someone might write, "of a green spring day," or whatever. Then the person continues: "A green spring day reminds me of," and I go with them through the first few lines, then leave them to write, saying they must use concrete images from their associational memories and not abstractions like "love," "peace," "happy," or "sad." People have described how this simple associational memory exercise unleashed memories they thought they'd forgotten, sometimes even from preschool years.

Rico, after she got her book contract, was stuck. Finally she took her own advice, put butcher paper all over the kitchen floor and, using associational thinking, outlined the book that has gained such popularity (personal communication, Gabriele Rico, August 1984). Whether one side of the brain or another is dominant in such activities, the creative process was indeed enchanced by paying attention, in Edward's workshop, to edges and contours, and, in Rico's workshop, to associations brought on by other associations.

*Substances and the Creative Process*

Many people have used substances to enhance the creative process, to put themselves into that semitrance state of creative production. Jack Kerouac supposedly wrote *On The Road* on amphetamines and alcohol at his girlfriend's house, typing nonstop on a roll of butcher paper. Aldous Huxley experimented with mescaline in the late 1920s, and wrote *The Doors of Perception*. Carlos Castaneda also used mushrooms to enhance his journey to spiritual awareness. Heroin was used by many musicians and writers, including Charlie Parker, Stan Getz, and William S. Burroughs. Alcohol is the drug of choice for many performers, writers, and creative writers, and absinthe was popular at the turn of the century. A list of the clients at the Betty Ford Clinic, as reported by *People* magazine every week or so, includes many of the most respected talents in the arts. The tragic death of the actor John Belushi, of the singer Janis Joplin, of the rock star Jimi Hendrix — to mention just a few examples — all point to the attraction of drugs for creative people.

Alan Bold edited an anthology of prose about drinking, called *Drink To Me Only* (1982). His introduction noted that the association of creative people with alcohol is so longstanding that the word "drunken" has become "the essential epithet of the poet"; people have come to believe that there is a "close relationship between booze and the muse. The artistic temperament is indissolubly associated with drunkenness and we expect musicians to perform outrageously and painters to make exhibitions of themselves."

Linda Leonard in her 1989 *Witness to the Fire: Creativity and the Evil of Addiction* made the point that creative people often use substances such as cocaine or alcohol to artificially achieve states where they feel they can be creative, but then they risk becoming addicted to those substances. But, she noted, addiction and creativity are parallel processes, not "causal." She said "both descend into chaos, into the unknown underworld of the unconscious. Both are fascinated by what they find there. Both encounter death, pain, suffering." But there is a difference, for other addicts are pulled without choice; the person who is creative "chooses to go down into that unknown realm." But even though some creative people can continue to create, many lose their creativity early to addiction, and as Leonard explained, "they must eventually choose to find form and meaning from the chaos."

McAleer (1989) said that lowered metabolism and attention that's allowed to be unfocused also seem to encourage creative thinking. Runners and other solitary aerobic exercisers — crosscountry skiiers, walkers, climbers, bicyclists, swimmers — have often spoken of "the runner's high," a feeling of euphoria and timelessness that occurs after exercising for a certain amount of time, usually about half an hour. They speak of solving their life's problems while running, or of coming up with answers. Running becomes addictive for some people, as they run to pass that threshold into altered consciousness. The increase of endorphins (brain peptides containing amino acids resembling opiates) produces a feeling of euphoria, the feeling runners and athletes attain after exercising.

*The Need for Solitude*

But beyond the presence of rituals, of right and left brain, of Aha's, and Eureka's, of substances and the dangers of addiction, the core of the creative process is solitude. Perhaps group creativity trainers would disagree, or teams of comedy writers, or teams of problem solvers in industry. They would allege that cooperation and group process are essential, for example, in the brainstorming that precedes the solving of a problem. Yet, in the early 1960s, researchers found that group brainstorming was less effective than they thought. Robert Weisberg, in *Creativity: Genius and Other Myths* (1986), reviewed these studies and concluded, "working in groups is less effective than working alone." However, recent emphasis in industry and in schools on cooperation and group problem solving may disprove these notions. The Ford Motor Company said that the revolutionary design of the Taurus, for example, was accomplished through unprecedented group cooperation. The emphasis on "cooperative learning" in the schools of the U.S. is a recent trend.

Indeed, our society emphasizes group creativity and group belonging. In *Solitude* (1988), Anthony Storr noted that modern society believes that people are their best selves when they are in human relationship. People without human relationships, who are not married, in love, or in a family are viewed as somehow sick. The connection to other human beings within a relationship has been viewed, ever since Freud, as the highest form of communion.

Storr, however, marshalled evidence that such is not necessarily the case. People strive for what in the creative process is called the illumination, or the feeling of wholeness, an inner unity, and having a relationship is only one way of attaining this. In creative people's lives, their work is often the most important thing. Others achieve inner peace through their spirituality or religious contemplations, the contemplation of nature, art or music, or through exercise. All of these are usually done alone. Creative people may be solitary, but that doesn't make them neurotic or unhappy.

Storr described the journey of Admiral Byrd to Antarctica, and his solitude there, the meditative state he achieved while tending a weather base. Byrd wrote that on his daily walks, he "paused to listen to the silence" and while doing so, noticed at sunset, "great peace. Here were imponderable processes and forces of the cosmos, harmonious and soundless" and he realized, "Harmony, that was it! That was what came out of the silence — a gentle rhythm, the strain of a perfect chord, the music of the spheres, perhaps."

These experiences that take place when a person is alone need not occur with external stimuli, Storr wrote, but there is something transcendental about such experiences, where the person is suddenly able "to make sense out of what had previously appeared impenetrable, or with a new unity by linking together concepts which had formerly seemed to be quite separate." For many creative people, a main frustration is not being able to achieve solitude. Virginia Woolf wrote in her *Writer's Diary*:

> And every time I get into my current of thought I am
> jerked out of it. We have the Keynes; then Vita came;

then Angelica and Eve; then we went to Worthington, then my head begins throbbing — so here I am, not writing — that does not matter; but not thinking, feeling, or seeing — and seizing an afternoon alone as a treasure. (p. 142)

Jung was one psychoanalyst who encouraged solitude, encouraging his patients to set aside part of each day to enter a reverie of active imagination. Among the first to deal with middle-aged people in depression or crisis, he encouraged this reverie particularly to help them rediscover themselves. This active imagination is similar to what Maslow called "self-actualizing behavior," as well as to the creative process. Maslow said that when the creative person is being inspired, he suspends time, and seems unconscious of time passing, being so concentrated that the moment is all that is there. In an essay called "Creativity in Self-Actualizing People" (1968), Maslow elaborated that this ability to become "timeless, selfless, outside of space, of society, of history is the prerequisite for creativeness."

Storr likewise said that a "state of reverie" seems induced by solitude, and that many ideas are generated in this solitude. In the state between sleeping and waking, the subject is relaxed, allowing images and ideas to come so that attention can be paid. What is important is a state of passivity and receptivity. Some people achieve this while cooking, cleaning, or sewing alone, others while driving or doing a monotonous task.

One of my favorite books is May Sarton's *Journal of a Solitude* (1973). The author of many novels, books of poetry, and nonfiction works, Sarton chronicled one year of her life. Here, briefly, is what she had to say about solitude and the creative person. "The value of solitude — one of its values — is, of course, that there is nothing to cushion against attacks from within, just as there is nothing to help balance at times of particular stress or depression." During this year Sarton was not a hermit; she was doing public readings and speeches; she was seeing her friends. But her real work was what she encountered in her solitude. Virginia Woolf called solitude "real life" and went on to say, "I find it almost incredibly soothing — a fortnight alone." It is indeed odd that educators and theorists rarely mention the necessity for solitude in most of their advice on how to be creative.

## Visualization, Imagery, and New Age Creativity

The 1970s and 1980s saw the rise of the New Age Movement. An outgrowth of psychotherapy, the Vietnam War, and the hippies' counterculture, this movement utilized psychological and religious meditational techniques. Solitude was encouraged, as people took up Buddhism and Hinduism. However, the purpose of the solitude was not to produce creative work, but to produce creative selves, true selves. The word "creativity" was used with great frequency by the proponents of New Age thinking.

To enhance people's creativity, self-proclaimed experts used such methods as visualization, imagery, metaphorization, chanting, and the formulation of affirmations. People fondled scared objects such as quartz crystals and sat beneath pyramids. The creative process was viewed as the province of every human being, and not just of those who wanted to make creative products. In fact, creative products such as music, poems, paintings, or mathematical formulas were viewed as mere by-products by people who had attained full creative development. People's lives were to be their creative products.

An outgrowth of the humanistic psychology movement, particularly such humanistic psychologists as Carl Rogers and Abraham Maslow, and of such gestalt psychologists as Fritz Perls, generated what was called a new consciousness, and centers devoted to it sprang up. Like others, I attended workshops in the mid-1980s at The Open Center in New York City and at The Omega Institute at Rhinebeck, New York, where I learned to seek the truth of my inner self through an intensive journal workshop, dream workshops, singing workshops, empowerment workshops, improvisational theater workshops. All of these, no matter what the topic, had common threads. We were there to probe our inner psyches and to make our lives our works of art, to reach inner placidness as human beings. Many people reacted strongly and positively to these experiential exhortations. Talk shows abounded with psychological experts who said we must work on ourselves first; then happiness and fulfillment would follow. Nevertheless, as we shall see in Part III, many creative producers of works in the arts and sciences are not necessarily what is popularly considered psychologically healthy.

The vehicles for discovering one's self were breath control, meditational technique, visualization, imagery. Several workshops I attended were remarkably similar. The leaders took us through relaxation exercises where we progressively relaxed our toes, our feet, our legs, and the rest of our bodies, breathing deeply. We mentally placed ourselves in a setting, often a beach with the waves crashing, or a forest with the birds singing and the leaves rustling, or the ramparts of a castle looking over the purple plain. Soft synthesizer music or tinkly bells played in a tape recorder controlled by the group leader, and we visualized ourselves in these places.

These group relaxation techniques were supposed to help us contemplate our inner selves, discover our inner truths, quiet us to the point where we would pay attention to what was going on inside, calm us, and release us from the pressures of the hustle bustle. Of course, the popularization of these workshops and techniques focused on truths creative and spiritual people had known for ages. Creative people, mystics, ascetics of all religions had long known that calming inner solitude was essential for true knowledge of self.

The connection of the spiritual with therapy was implicit, and therapists were often viewed as priests, or gurus. Indeed, this investiture of psychology with religious import began with the advent of psychoanalysis. In *Returning* (1988), an account of his return to the church, the novelist Dan Wakefield said that for his generation of young, creative people in the 1950s, psychotherapy replaced God. He said, "I entered psychoanalysis with the high seriousness of purpose and commitment of any acolyte taking his vows to a religious order. Like many in my generation, I had already made the intellectual substitution of Freud for God."

By the 1970s and 1980s, connections between spirituality and creativity were made explicit. One of the most popular authors and speakers about this process, Shakti Gawain, in her best-selling book, *Creative Visualization* (1979), most openly exhorted that visualization aids in creating the self:

> Creative visualization is not just a technique, but ultimately it is a state of consciousness. It is a consciousness in which we deeply realize that we are the continuous creators of our universe and we take responsibility for that at all moments. There is no separation between us and God; we are divine expressions of the creative principle on this level of existence. (p. 120)

Gawain likened living to art: "I like to think of myself as an artist, and my life is my greatest work of art." She called her life (not her creative products) "a magnificent art form."

*Creative Imagery and Athletics*

Another expanded definition of the creative process has been in the use of meditation, visualization, and imaging in athletics. Athletes imagine their performances beforehand; they visualize the ski run, or the football play, or the course for the marathon, and imagine themselves on every part of that course. Adoption by athletes has given these methods respectability and cachet. Books such as *The Inner Game of Tennis* are an example, prompting athletes to meditate and put on their "game faces" before athletic events.

Some people are afraid of these methods now in common use by coaches and teachers, asserting that children are being hypnotized, or brought to Satanism. They say that this is a new religion, anti-Christian and pro-Hindu and Buddhist. Such a definition of this movement is too simplistic, though essentially the impulse behind the New Age movement has been a spiritual impulse intertwined with a creative impulse. Upon trying relaxation and visualization techniques as a means of enhancing children's creativity, or to prepare the children to take standardized tests, teachers often have been closely questioned by parents. When this happens, teachers often refer the parents to the coaches, because athletes use visualization so extensively nowadays.

But there is evidence, besides the uncritical yet enthusiastic chanting of mantras and the progressive relaxation of toes and knees, that altered consciousness did aid people in one measure of divergent thinking. In a 1982 study, Cowger and Torrance trained twenty-four undergraduates in meditation, and ten undergraduates in relaxation. The meditators gained significantly on the Torrance Test of Creative Thinking in heightened consciousness of problems, perceived change, invention, sensory experience, expression of emotion and feeling, synthesis, unusual visualization, internal visualization, humor, and fantasy. Those trained in relaxation lost in verbal fluency and originality, and figural fluency and originality, but had gains in synthesis and unusual visualization. This use of a standardized creativity test is one way of showing that meditation and relaxation do have some relationship to perceived processes of creativity, at least on paper and pencil measures. For more on divergent production testing, see Chapter 3.

Even one session of aerobic dancing can help students on creative thinking tests, according to a 1987 study by Gondola. After a twenty-minute aerobic dance class, posttest analysis found that the twenty-one subjects showed significantly more flexibility, different ideas and more original ideas than did the sixteen control subjects.

## Creativity as the Process of a Life

The influence of New Age thinking, where creativity is not the creation of works of art or thought but the power to create oneself, can be seen in any chain bookstore where shelves are filled with how-to books by authors fond of the term "creativity." The great popularity of these speaks to the resurgence of a spiritual yearning in people. The New Age books explore channeling, out of body experiences, reincarnation, and meditation. They sell much better than poetry or novels, and their sales rival book sales in the self-help sections. A poet friend marketed her book as a New Age book, because she thought people would be more likely to buy it. She was right.

### Transpersonal Psychology

In psychology, New Age thinking is related to what came to be called the Human Potential Movement, which has evolved to a field called Transpersonal Psychology. This field, as Brown (1988) said, seeks to understand how inspiration, insight, intuition, imagination, and creativity operate. Higher states of awareness are produced in people through this branch of psychology, and that is why it is called "trans" personal. Transpersonal psychologists often speak of "empowerment," meaning a sense within the human being of being able to move, to act, to be all that she can be. (The field of education has adopted the word recently also, in the sense of "empowering" teachers, parents, or students).

The experience of attaining a sense of unity with all the universe is also a part of transpersonal psychology, and devotees speak of using their creativity for enhancing a global consciousness. The result of visualization, imagery, solitary and group meditation was to produce the ultimate creative product: a peaceful world order, a universal consciousness. The earth is personified into a female creature called Gaia, and we are all charged with not harming our Mother Earth by burning forests in the Amazon nor by polluting blue coral in Japan. Harman and Rheingold spoke of "higher creativity" in their 1984 book of the same name. The product was not any painting, poem, or mathematical theorem, but many such — all made for the purposes of achieving a global unity. Such creative work could only begin with personal affirmations; " thus, we view higher creativity not as an abstract idea, but as an experience." Harman and Rheingold thought that the person who wants to contribute to global unity — the ultimate creative product — should, several times a day, for six months, imagine these statements to be true: "I am one with all. I can trust. I can know. I am responsible. I am single-minded."

The people who are creating their selves and their lives view their creativity and their creative processes as producing works of life art that are universal, that transcend the personal, and affirm the human spirit. One such work was the First Earth Run, in 1986; teams of runners circled the globe, beginning and ending at the United Nations, carrying a torch that symbolized earth. Hundreds of thousands of people participated.

Others besides New Age thinkers have also viewed the creative process as more than simply involving an altered consciousness, an immense concentration, or an attainment of solitude. That is, we can look at the entire process of a creative person's life. Gruber, for example, in his 1974 psychological biography, *Darwin on Man*, looked at Darwin's life from a psychological perspective, to see how lifelong creativity unfolded and developed. Simonton, in *Scientific Genius* (1988), has done similar work with a method called historiometry, using published biographies of creative persons, especially scientists.

## Seeing as if for the First Time

Ghiselin (1952) pointed out that ultimate achievement through the creative process demands not only concentration while doing a project, but "the concentration of a life." Certainly, concentrating one's life upon a field may not be sufficient if talent, milieu, and even chance aren't there. Concentrating one's life on a field often results in viewing the world in fresh, new ways, particularly if the creative person remains open to eccentricity and deviation, a facet that Ghiselin has emphasized. If a person is suspicious of deviation, the likelihood of being inventive is reduced because everything that is new "is liable to seem eccentric and perhaps dangerous." Creative people are obligated to pay attention to the odd, the strange, the eccentric:

> The alien, the dangerous, like the negligible near thing, may seem irrelevant to purpose and yet be the call to our own fruitful development. This does not mean that we should surrender to whatever novelty is brought to attention. It does mean that we must practice to some extent an imaginative surrender to every novelty that has even the most tenuous credentials. (1952, p. 31)

While Ghiselin called this aspect of the creative process, "imaginative surrender," Getzels and Csikszentmihalyi described creative visual artists as having a similar characteristic which they called "naivete," and Julian Green in his 1961 *Diary* similarly stated that such naivete is a component of "talent" and elaborated that:

> One of the secrets of real talent is to see everything for the first time, to look at a leaf as though one had never seen one before, for then only can it appear to us in all its newness. The power of marveling makes up the genius of childhood, so quickly blunted by habit and education, and no one will ever be able to fit words together in an acceptable order unless he knows a little how to see creation through Adam's eyes. In art, truth lies in surprising.
>
> When one looks at a stone as though it were a miniature mountain, one begins to see it as it really is. (p. 105)

Likewise, Ferrucci, in *Inevitable Grace* (1990), said that the "true" artistic person shows himself through his "attitude to what is ugly and banal."

> Neither repulsion nor judgment is present, nor, on the other hand, morbid pleasure; rather, we find an attitude of universality — the ability to love and appreciate even the most unlikely subject — as in the "old women's throats" to which Leonardo devoted hours of attention and observation for several of his drawings; or even in cigarette butts, in which the Russian painter Wassily Kandinsky claimed he could see the "secret soul" of things. (p. 57)

Ferrucci similarly quoted a letter in which Van Gogh said that he saw "drawings and pictures in the poorest huts, in the dirtiest corner. And my mind is drawn toward these things by an irresistible force."

## Concentration of a Life

This basic personality characteristic of creative people — the attitude of naivete, of acceptance and curiosity about the odd and strange — appears necessary, but not sufficient. Storr noted three key periods in the process of the creative life. The first is the imitative stage, the period where the young creative person learns what already has been done and spends much time imitating. During the second period, the creative person dispenses with what has been done, and enters an assured and masterful period of production in which the need to communicate with a wide public is clear. In the third period, the creative person withdraws from the need to communicate and may turn to unconventional forms without rhetoric or posing, while continuing to explore areas that are not intrapersonal but perhaps spiritual or universal.

Similarly, LeoNora Cohen, in an article in *Creativity Research Journal* (1989) adopted a life view when she proposed a developmental theory of creativity, specifying that creativity evolves on a continuum of "adaptive creative behaviors," from infancy to adulthood. She outlined seven levels of development:

1. Learning something new; universal novelty.
2. Making connections that are rare compared to peers.
3. Demonstrating talents.
4. Producing information.
6. Creating by extending the field.
7. Creating by revolutionizing the field.

Mary Catherine Bateson, in *Composing A Life* (1989), adopted a slightly different focus, at least in creative women's lives, where there is a sense of making it up as one goes along. Although creative development may follow general stages, the paths often show sudden changes. She studied five prominent women, and in each of their lives found there had to be the willingness to drop everything and change plans, often to subsume their creative work to the needs of their husbands and growing families. These women spoke of the implications and repercussions of small choices, and of a constant sense of conflict between their creative work and their family's needs.

Likewise, Nachmanovitch, a jazz musician, in *Free Play* (1990), spoke of the creative life as improvisation, "risky business," noting that "to follow your own course, not patterned on parents, peers, or institutions, involves a delicate balance of tradition and personal freedom, a delicate balance of sticking to your guns and remaining open to change."

Dabrowski and Piechowski (1977), in a particularly rich theory, also spoke to lifelong development, but of life as a process rather than a series of stages. Higher forms of development are achieved as a person moves beyond primitive drives, selfishness, and feelings of inferiority, to transcendence, self-determination, and "sustained creativity and lucidity of the mind in spite of infirmity of the body." In the Dabrowski theory of emotional development, with reference to the creative person, creativity is manifested in the person's overexcitability, or "enhanced and intensified mental activity distinguished by characteristic forms of expression which are above common and average." Creative people, artists at least, characteristically have strong emotional sensitivity and intensity, a great range of feeling, as well as having high imaginational overexcitability, which is "spontaneous activity of a mind that freely makes unexpected associations, reaches into invented realms, takes any form as a stimulus to perceive other forms, including nonverbal ones." (Piechowski, Silverman, and Falk, 1985, p. 545)

The Dabrowski theory describes several levels of development — levels I through V — which can support creative production. An example is the writer Antoine de St. Exupery, whom Piechowski in a 1978 monograph described as having reached Level IV, a level similar to Maslow's concept of self-actualization, almost the highest level of human development. Eleanor Roosevelt was described as having reached Level V, which is the highest level. Piechowski and Tyska (1982) noted that few people reach this level. Level V, as Piechowski described in an essay called "Emotional Giftedness" (1990), encompasses "incomprehensible freedom found in total selflessness, in love truly unconditional, expecting nothing in return, love that accurately perceives the divine spark even in the most darkened soul."

Certainly, creativity can be present in any of these levels, but the process of a life can also be viewed as creativity. The most widely conceived theories of the creative process encompass the beliefs that creativity is not merely momentary, but lifelong; that creativity has a universal purpose; and that creativity evolves developmentally.

# The Creative Process as Cognitive Science

Cognitive science uses scientific analysis to answer questions that have long troubled philosophers. It is an interdisciplinary field, combining philosophy, neuroscience, anthropology, psychology, and artificial intelligence. Howard Gardner, in his ground-breaking history of cognitive science, *The Mind's New Science* (1985), said that the questions cognitive scientists answer should "provide a cogent scientific account of how human beings achieve their most remarkable symbolic products: how we come to compose symphonies, write poems, invent machines (including computers), or construct theories (including cognitive-scientific ones)." The emphasis here is on the word "science." The previous explanations for the creative process could have been gathered under the rubric of "humanities."

The cognitive psychologist and philosopher David Perkins in 1981 tested many creative process postulations that have been described in this chapter. His book, *The Mind's Best Work,* is one of the most interesting cognitive psychological creativity books in the literature. Perkins made what he called "propositions" based on the prevailing thought about the creative process. He then examined what the evidence had shown, and refuted or modified the propositions, calling them "revised propositions." Results of psychological experimentation were primarily used to generate the revisions. How creative people form schemata, how creative people recognize patterns, how creative people solve problems, were a few. Among the techniques he used was the observation of working poets and artists, interrupting them while they were painting or writing and asking them what they were thinking. Here are some of his propositions and their revisions.

*The Expert Witness Proposition.* Many accounts have been written by creative persons about what was happening when they were creating. Some believe that people like Coleridge and Poe were trustworthy witnesses of their own creative processes. Perkins, however, said that people writing about their own creativity don't give valid accounts, because we can't tell whether or not they are telling the truth, or whether they remembered what happened correctly. Thus autobiographical accounts of the creative process are quite unreliable and shouldn't be taken seriously.

*The Notebooks Proposition.* Some believe that one can psychoanalyze what happens in the creative process by painstakingly reading the diaries, notebooks, scribbles, doodles, and other notes left by creative people. Perkins said such physical evidence seldom or never shows "the judgments, aims, and alternatives making up the process and the ways these emerge in the mind of the maker."

Much has been written about great mental leaps that creative people make when they receive the illumination. Here are three propositions commonly made about mental leaps, and Perkins's responses:

*Mental Leap Proposition 1.* — that mental leaps occur very rapidly and are characterized by no conscious thought. They solve problems that a person has been stuck on, and help achieve insight into problems or situations that seemed impossible. Perkins pointed out that a mental leap may seem a quick unitary event, but there are some discernible steps. These steps are progressive, and the mental leap seems to just skip a few logical steps, and produce the insight more quickly than if logical thought had been used.

*Mental Leap Proposition 2.* — that mental leaps are the result of long unconscious processing that suddenly comes to the consciousness of the person. Perkins said, "Extended unconscious thinking does not occur." Such strategies as "deferring a troublesome problem and returning to it later" work sometimes, but this has nothing to do with what is going on in the unconscious.

*Mental Leap Proposition 3.* — that mental leaps are faster, compressing much thought into a short time. Perkins showed that the process of "recognizing and realizing" account for mental leaps to a much greater degree than previously suspected. We may call it a mental leap when it helps us organize material that we were unable to organize before.

*The Discovery Proposition.* In past views of the creative process, the word "discovery" was often used, implying that the inventor had come upon the product by accident or chance. For example, who "discovered" penicillin? Who "discovered" America? Who "discovered" the light bulb? The word "discover" means that this person is the first to find out, to realize. Some people believe that the processes in discovery are special. Perkins showed that a person makes discoveries when she wants to discover.

Memory, paying attention or noticing, forming metaphors and analogies, and combining unlike things are helpful in making discoveries, but the *intention* to discover is most important. Many accounts of the creative process emphasize that the person who is doing the creating, especially in the arts, is in a state of heightened emotion, but that creation cannot take place without using the rational processes of mind. Perkins insisted that emotionality and rationality are parts of the same whole. Thus, although some people believe that affect (feeling) and cognition (knowing) "enter distinctively and essentially into creating," Perkins disagreed. Instead, he said, "Cognition and affect are not distinct aspects of creative experience." Emotions are affective ways of cognition, or knowing.

Ultimately, according to Perkins, the creative process is a process of selection, and as such there is not much that is mysterious about it. This selection involves ten ways that the creative person selects in order to come up with the creative product. The selection methods used are the backbone of his theory of creativity. During the creative process, the creative person

1. Notices opportunities.
2. Notices flaws.
3. Directs the memory to pertinent information.
4. Notices the critical reactions of others and of self while the work is in progress, and forms judgments based on those reactions.
5. Looks at the work in progress with certain criteria in mind.
6. Sets the work aside for awhile and comes back to it.
7. Makes long searches for options during the process, generating and rejecting solutions until a sound option is found.
8. Figuratively climbs a hill during the process, as each option is tried, with a step up the hill being a narrowing down and a step back down the hill an opening up for new options.
9. Is familiar with the schemata of the field.
10. Can find new and challenging creative problems to work on.

Perkins might say that there is no such thing in the creative process as genuine surprise, even though many people have had such surprises. Such a position implies that a genuine surprise only comes to the person who is prepared to recognize the implications of that surprise. You may think that Perkins has taken the mystery out of the creative process, has deflated its connection with the spiritual, and has lessened its connection with the search for truth. But demystification is the job of cognitive science, even though some have commented on the difficulty in applying science to the study of the creative process. Edward Wilson, in his foreword to Findlay and Lumsden's *The Creative Mind* (1988), called the creative process the "grandmother of problems in the human sciences." The creative process is intractable and is "the gale of destruction that destabilizes the study of human evolution, reduces much of the social sciences to hermeneutics, and threatens to maintain the chasm separating the sciences from the humanities." Thus the work of demystification, such as that of Perkins and the other cognitive scientists, is particularly important in understanding the human process called creativity, even though many of us would like to retain the mystery.

Schools also use the Creative Problem Solving Process — called CPS — that is prosaic and practical rather than poetic. It is a widely used system that purports to help ordinary people be creative. Talent is not necessary. This process seems to represent the logical extension of the wish to equate creativity with divergent problem solving. Based on the work of Osborn (1953) and Parnes (1981), and brought to gifted education by Donald Treffinger and his colleagues, the Creative Problem Solving Process has five steps: (1) Fact-finding; (2) Problem-finding; (3) Idea-finding; (4) Solution-finding; and (5) Acceptance-finding. Usually it is a group process.

Beginning with a "mess," the group of problem solvers asks IWWMI (In What Ways Might I — make a new dish for dinner? Solve the problem of the destruction of rain forests?). Nothing says that this process should be done in a group, and in fact the sourcebook of Isaksen and Treffinger (1985) said it can be done alone, but since brainstorming is one of the major devices used to generate ideas, the process is more fun in a group. Groups generate more ideas than do individuals, especially as people begin to "piggyback" or follow trains of thought. As the problem solvers go through the process, each step has a divergent phase, where fluency, flexibility, elaboration, and originality are encouraged, and a convergent phase, where analysis and synthesis are encouraged.

Some critics have said that CPS is too mechanical, too structured, but Perkins (1981) pointed out that no one says the problem solver must go through all the phases in linear fashion, and people doing the Creative Problem Solving process often find it "too roundabout." In doing rudimentary training and teaching of the process, I, too, have found that people will just skip phases if they arrive at a potentially good solution early on. In his essay, "The Possibility of Invention" (1988), Perkins also said that training in fluency and flexibility "appears misguided"; the value of such training is in "inducing related values" and by putting such techniques as brainstorming "into people's behavioral repertoires."

Unfortunately, the creative problem solving model is the only process offered by educators of the gifted in many schools. This was not the intention of its inventors, I am sure.

Perhaps the suggestions in this chapter on the creative process — that the process is rich, sometimes mysterious, and certainly complicated — will result in an expanded repertoire by educators seeking to enhance creativity. What we have learned and what we continue to learn about the creative process will, ultimately, help us understand the world, help us understand ourselves, reconcile the humanities and the sciences, help us be more creative, help us make better products, save the world, heal the world. It all depends upon your point of view.

## Summary

1. The creative process has engaged the best thinkers of the world from prehistoric times.

2. Common mythological perspectives have viewed the creative process as the visitation of the Muse.

3. Historically, the creative process has been tied with erotic desires, desires for spiritual unity, and with the need for personal expression.

4. The use of substances to enhance the creative process has been prominent in the lives of creative people.

5. Many creative products have resulted from insight, illumination, and unconscious processing.

6. Solitude seems to be a necessary condition during some aspects of the creative process.

7. The creative process must be viewed in the context of a person's life and the historical milieu.

8. Contemporary psychological and religious thought have emphasized that the creative process has universal implications.

9. What is popularly called "right-brain thinking," as well as visualization, metaphorization, and imagery seem to help people in the creative process.

10. The creative process is a concern of scientists as well as humanists. Scientific experimentation has demystified many popular creative process beliefs.

11. The repertoires of educators, who often use only the CPS process in enhancing creativity, should be expanded.

# PART II

## HOW CAN CREATIVITY BE MEASURED?

*Several months have passed since the state conference. Katherine Miller has been so busy she hasn't had time to think about what creativity is, or about what comprises the creative process. She has sixty fourth, fifth, and sixth graders during the week. She uses several levels of basic textbooks, supplemented heavily with materials from the media center. She has coached a team for the Odyssey of the Mind Competitions, and her students have joined the Math Olympiad team and the Academic Challenge team. These kids are truly something!*

*Although she spends every weekend preparing for the next week and hardly sees Brad at all, she feels on fire. She's working with kids who really want to learn. One morning she has a note in her mailbox from the regional coordinator, who also serves seventy-nine other schools. It's time to begin selecting kids for the fourth grade class of next year. Has she given the creativity test and checklist to the third grade teachers yet?*

*"What test? What checklist?" Katherine wonders aloud.*

*The principal overhears her on his way to the coffee pot. "You have to identify kids for next year. Just call the regional office and ask how to do it. It has something to do with special tests. But don't ask me what. Testing was never my strong point."*

*Katherine and the regional coordinator play phone tag for several days. Then there's another note. "What test are you planning to use? Half the districts are using the Renzulli and half are using the Torrance. Let me know, and I'll drop them off for you."*

*"Don't counselors give tests? Isn't that what they do?" Katherine asks the principal.*

*"Our elementary counselor serves seven buildings," he said, "and we need her for testing the other types of exceptional kids. Just read the directions and give the test — or the checklist if you prefer. What did you learn when you went to that workshop? Didn't you tell us at the teacher's meeting that you attended a lot of sessions on creativity? What did they say?"*

*Katherine goes back to her convention handouts and notes. She hasn't had time to do much with them. But there, among her notes from one of the sessions is, "How To Choose A Creativity Test — If You Really Must."*

*You may be tempted to skip this section, especially if you dislike testing or fear the numbers, but don't. What Katherine is about to learn is important, especially since testing is now a major part of every child's life. Important decisions about children are made as a result of their taking tests.*

# Chapter 3

## Creativity Testing and Training

*The most important thing was to keep your references fashionable and to avoid, for fear of being discredited, all mention of the authors used for this purpose in the preceding decade.*

— Julio Cortazar

*It is our impression that there are very few people who continue to believe that there is a scientific method that natural scientists use that can be applied to the human world.*

— Margaret Marshall and Loren Barritt

Mrs. Larson, the teacher, gets the test from the teacher of the gifted, Katherine Miller. It is a paper and pencil test, and the directions are simple. Mrs. Larson makes sure her third graders all have sharpened pencils, scratch paper, that they can hear her and that she can see them all. "All right, boys and girls," she says. "Today we are going to test your creativity. Listen carefully. I am going to read some directions, and you will do some tasks according to my directions. Are you all listening?"

Bobby, the class clown, who brings Calvin and Hobbes cartoons each day, is restless. He can't seem to sit still. Bobby, like Hobbes, also has an imaginary playmate, only his is a boy just his age. Bobby is an only child and is lonesome at home because his mother and father are divorced. He carries his key on a string around his neck and must spend two hours locked in his house after school, until his mother returns from her job at the telephone company.

"Boys and girls, listen now. Here are a group of squiggles. We are going to do some drawing." Mrs. Larson follows the instructions, and points to the squiggles on the page, making sure all the children have their eyes on her. "Bobby, are you watching? Bobby, I want your eyes on me," she says kindly, walking over to him and putting down the pencil that he has clutched in his hand, making doodles on the squiggles already. "Bobby, you must wait until I say 'Begin.'" She finishes the directions, about making the squiggles into whatever they want to make them into, anything is okay, and then says, "Begin."

Bobby has lost interest in making the squiggles into something different, and proceeds to make them into letters of the alphabet, some cursive and some printed. Then he begins to change them into a sketch of his imaginary playmate. But the time is up. Mrs. Larson goes on to the next part. "Now you are going to write a story about one of these. The story must begin with these words, but you can end it any way you want. 'Let's pretend' are the words. Begin your story with 'Let's pretend.'"

All the children dutifully begin their stories, clutching their pencils and laboriously forming the letters into shapes, proud of their writing. They have studied the Writing Process, and Mrs. Larson is pleased with their daily work. But this is a test. This is different. Bobby begins to write about a television show he saw last night while his mother was passed out from the marijuana she had smoked with her boyfriend. He begins it "Let's pretend I got high on marijuana," but has trouble spelling it, crosses it out, and puts "grass." Then he realizes this is not right, and crosses out the whole story except for the first two words, "Let's pretend." Bobby has a whole notebook of stories at home; he writes while he sits in front of the television watching the soap operas and the children's quiz shows. In one of his stories a third-grade boy chosen for the quiz show wows them all by throwing a tomato into the face of a bigger boy. This boy becomes known as Ketchup to millions of adoring fans, and begins a whole new way of dealing with bullies.

In another story Bobby and his imaginary playmate, Tony, sneak into a neighbor's basement to spy on him, because the neighbor looks like a spy from a foreign land. The neighbor carries a cane and wears a pointed beard and sunglasses; Bobby and Tony believe that he carries secret maps rolled up in the cane. Bobby wonders whether he can write any of those stories, but it's too late.

"Time," Mrs. Larson says. "Now, let's go do something different." She is reading from the manual that the coordinator of programs for the gifted has given her. "Let's turn to this page, boys and girls," and she shows a page with many numbers on it. "Let's see how creative you can be with numbers." The directions are a little confusing for the children. Perhaps they should add and perhaps they should subtract. "How many ways can you think of to get to 43?" the directions say. Just as Bobby is figuring out that 43 is made up of no prime numbers, Mrs. Larson says "Time." Bobby's father is an engineer and sometimes, when Bobby visits him and he's not yelling about what a horrible person Bobby's mother is, he does math with Bobby. Bobby's father taught him about prime numbers last week.

Bobby looks over at the girl next to him, and the boy across from him, and sees that they have both filled out all the blanks with numbers such as $42 + 1$, and $44 - 1$. All the blanks! In fact, all the squiggles are made into interesting drawings on the boy's paper, and all the lines for the story are filled with neat penmanship on the girl's paper. All Bobby has done is get confused, and just when he got an idea, Mrs. Larson called time.

This scenario illustrates some of the difficulties with creativity testing. The test will probably be scored according to set scoring rules as the test scorer has been trained. Among the first scores is that of fluency. Fluency means "how many," and Bobby will score all right on the first test, because he did use all the squiggles to make letters of the alphabet. On the second, Bobby's slow motor skills will hamper him as well; and even though the test is normed with other third grade boys who have similar motor developmental problems, perhaps Bobby's slowness has to do with a sense of quality as well as speed. On the third, Bobby's fluency score will be low because he took too much time thinking of the problem, and didn't write down the easy answers that his friends did. No matter that Bobby's thoughts were about prime numbers, there is no way the creativity test can judge that. So the ones with the greatest fluency scores will ultimately get the higher scores.

Another way these tests are scored is for flexibility, or the variety of different ideas the test taker had. In the first test Bobby had only two ideas, even though he used all the squiggles. Letter of the alphabet is one idea. On the second test, Bobby's hesitancy, in changing his mind about what to write was his downfall, and he will receive a fluency score of 0 or 2, depending on whether the manual allows the "Let's pretend" stem. He gets no points for crossing out, or censoring himself. And again, nothing for the numbers test.

While Bobby is probably too young to even be tested with a creativity test, such tests are in wide use in our schools, and for a very good reason. They are practical and they seem to be objective. That is, they don't discriminate against Bobby because he lives in a single parent home or because he has a mother who smokes marijuana. But Bobby didn't do very well on the test.

Katherine Miller wants to be sure that youngsters like Bobby aren't missed, and so she gives the teachers a checklist as well. She has chosen the one recommended by the State Department of Education — clearly, then, the best checklist available. She has even looked up the checklist in the latest *Mental Measurements Yearbook,* where the reviewer also called it the best creativity checklist available. The checklist format is called a Likert Scale, where the teacher has to consider the child as she knows him, and check "sometimes," "always," "never," and points in between. Does he exhibit such behaviors as curiosity? Does he have a sense of humor? Does he ask questions?

The checklist doesn't ask whether he can write, sing, dance, draw, do science experiments, or think of new mathematical ideas, because this is a checklist of whether Bobby has the characteristics that lead to being a creative adult. Why the checklist doesn't ask such obvious questions is strange, isn't it? These questions are not there because the experts have led educators to believe that creativity exists as a separate kind of behavior, separate from the ability to dance, sing, write, or draw. These experts have also led the school to believe that such a thing as "creative potential" exists and that it can be found if the teachers fill out a checklist. If Bobby is gifted in creative thinking, then he does not need to be able to dance, sing, write, act, or draw, do science experiments, or think of mathematical ideas.

At first, Mrs. Larson didn't even get a checklist for Bobby because his school ability index (falsely called an IQ by many educators), which was extrapolated from the Iowa Test of Basic Skills taken last year when her students were in second grade, came out to be 113. The rules for the gifted education program state that children who are identified by a creativity checklist must have IQs of 118 minus the standard error of measurement, and Bobby is one point below that. Everyone in the school knows that you must fill out one of those checklists giving the kids you think are particularly creative 4's on each item of the Likert Scale checklist, or else they won't get into the program. She asks for a checklist for Bobby. Bobby takes unusual books out of the school library. Last week he took out *Moby Dick*. The librarian was amazed, and told Mrs. Larson. "Why did you take out *Moby Dick*, Bobby?" Mrs. Larson said. She herself has never been able to get through it. "Isn't it just a little hard for a boy?" "Well, I like whales," Bobby said. "Let me know when you finish it," Mrs. Larson said. They had a laugh in the teacher's lounge on that one.

Mrs. Larson has a suspicion about Bobby, from the *Moby Dick* incident, and tells Katherine Miller, the new teacher of the gifted. Katherine calls the regional coordinator of the gifted. "My hands are tied," the coordinator tells her. "We've got parents calling and wanting their kids in the program for the gifted, and we've go no room. All the kids have IQs over 130, from last year's Iowa, and we just don't have any room. Besides, his IQ isn't high enough, and what's to say that a kid who wants to read *Moby Dick* is gifted in creative thinking? Have you heard from his mother?"

Bobby's mother was too busy to come to parent teacher conferences last Wednesday night. Bobby brought the announcement home, and the letter of invitation mailed by the principal arrived a few weeks ago, but she's had so much work these days, and when she gets home at 7:00 p.m. she wants to relax, and not go out again to the school. Besides, if something was wrong, the school would let her know, wouldn't they? She adores Bobby. He is her only child so he gets lonely, she's sure, but he never complains. You should see his notebook! Now he's doing sketches along with his stories, and they have to set a place for his imaginary friend Tony, right along with them, when they eat supper together. Of course, they rarely eat together because of their schedules. Bobby's mother just brings home some hamburgers, or stops for a pizza, or when she has to work so late, Bobby opens some Chef Boyardee and zaps it in the microwave.

Bobby's dad wrote and called the school, asking when the parents' night was, but he can't seem to get on the mailing list, though the school says that both parents of the child of divorce should be involved. He angrily calls the principal. How the heck can he get involved, if he doesn't get the announcement, he wants to know. And when he calls Bobby's mother, they just get into the old recriminations about custody. Bobby's father had wanted joint custody, but Bobby's mother pulled out that little indiscretion he'd had, the cause of their divorce. Now Bobby doesn't even want to come every other weekend anymore, since he started living with his new girlfriend. This time it's going to last, Bobby's father hopes, and Bobby will have a stepmother and everything can return to normal.

Bobby feels pulled between his parents and wants to please them both. He does like school, though. School is fun. Last week when he told a joke, the rest of the kids laughed. It was when Mrs. Larson had her back turned, writing the day's schedule on the board. Bobby rolled his eyes up and sat back, his heels hitting the floor, and said, "Oh, my God! She's got a tail!" and everyone laughed. He starts writing more jokes in his notebook.

In high school Bobby's mother used to sing with a rock 'n' roll band. She has a great collection of records, and sometimes Bobby plays them while waiting for her to get home from work. He asked her for music lessons. He wants to learn to play the guitar, or maybe the drums. She buys him a keyboard, and a book of chords, and surprisingly, he finds the notes are easy to learn, and learns the B-flat scale. In music class, the music teacher notices that he has a good ear, and sets him up for a small solo for the Halloween program. Bobby asks his mother to come, but she forgets.

Mrs. Larson has to spend a little more time thinking about Bobby, but she quickly fills out a form for Christine, the adorable girl who starred in *The Nutcracker* last Christmas. Christine's mother is active on the advisory committee for the academically talented program, and has helped in the classroom with birthdays. Mrs. Larson gives the girl all 4's, even though Christine is already in the program for the gifted, under the "academically talented in specific ability" guideline. The girl is a fantastic reader and even better in the Writing Process.

Does Mrs. Larson know enough about Bobby's secret life to fill out the checklist? Well, it's October, and she's only known him since September, and while he's certainly a sweet boy, she notices he comes to school with a strange smell on him, sort of like tobacco, a stale smell. Often . his hair isn't combed, his jeans are rumpled — and he only wears one pair of jeans each week. The flaps on his shoes are always loose, and he has an annoying habit of zipping the Velcro back and forth while she is reading aloud to the children. He gets so involved in the story, he doesn't know he's doing it. Finally, last week, she told him to take his shoes off during story time. Bobby's reading level is fine, but he's not in the top group because he has no patience for prefixes. He tries, but he's just a whole word reader, and not a phonics person. Mrs. Larson, while she's attended several workshops on the Whole Language Approach, is still a firm believer that phonics is the way to teach reading. New fads come and new fads go, but Mrs. Larson knows that phonics teaching is the best way and no one can change her.

Is Bobby a child gifted in creative thinking? In this case, the tests didn't work, and we'll see about the creativity checklist. His behavior at home could be a predictor, but who knows about that? His mother doesn't even know the full extent of his creative activities. His slowness in timed tests, and his lack of flexibility in the tests operated against him. Perhaps his tumultuous home life and his retreat into secret notebooks, sketchbooks, music, and isolated thought, operated for him. But even if Bobby had done well on the timed creativity test, could the test predict that he would be a creatively productive adult?

## Why Try to Measure Creativity?

Why assess, why measure creativity, if such a thing can even be done? In a 1987 article, Donald Treffinger gave seven reasons the schools should attempt to do so: (1) to recognize individual strengths so that students can do well; (2) to go beyond IQ and achievement testing; (3) to give schools, charged with practical concerns, some basic data so they can compare their students with norms; (4) to include creativity information in the basic profiles of students; (5) to help teachers discover their own creative talents; (6) to advance the research about nurturing and developing behavior that is creative; and (7) to take away the mystery from the consideration of creativity.

## Two Schools of Thought

Two schools of thought exist on the value of testing for creativity — or, more accurately, testing for the ability to do divergent production. The aspects of divergent production, defined by Guilford, were described in Chapter 1. They include fluency, flexibility, elaboration, and the like. On the one hand, Isaksen, in editing *Frontiers of Creativity Research* (1987), said that "there is mounting evidence that creativity can be assessed systematically and scientifically." He mentioned Treffinger's work, as well as that of Biondi and Parnes, Khatena, Guilford, and Torrance. Biondi and Parnes are associated with the Buffalo Center for Creative Thinking, which promotes the Creative Problem Solving Method discussed in Chapter 2, and Khatena and Torrance are longtime developers of creativity tests and checklists.

On the other hand, the Eastern establishment of cognitive psychologists insists that creativity testing has little value. Robert Sterberg of Yale, in *The Nature of Creativity* (1988) noted: "such tests [psychometric tests of creativity] capture at best only the most trivial aspects of creativity." Howard Gardner of Harvard, in *Art, Mind, and Brain* (1982) also commented on the studies of adolescent creativity, saying that "the measures on which they have relied in their studies have almost all been brief tasks — learning word lists, mastery of a maze — which can be surmounted in a matter of minutes (and which are even more rapidly forgotten)." James Borland of Columbia Teacher's College, a specialist in gifted education, in a 1986 article likewise raised questions saying "There are reasons to consider the basic issue as to the extent of the realm of divergent production," and noted that the Educational Testing Service (Princeton, NJ) has dropped tests for spontaneous flexibility and originality from their battery called Factor-Referenced Cognitive Tests.

The discussion lines are thus drawn between one group who has spent the last forty or so years trying to develop tests that have validity and reliability and another group who insists that creativity is a process that is explainable by noticing how creative people think. Among the latter is Perkins (discussed in Chapter 2) who, in an essay called "The Possibility of Invention" (1988) called for including motivation in the assessment of creativity. After all, what are people creating for? Why does the writer write, the painter paint, the inventor invent, the scientist experiment? Thus, he said, the creativity testing people may be off base: "Whereas testing for creativity typically emphasizes flexibility, fluency, and similar indices, values and patterns of deployment seem to offer the best predictors of creativity." That is, Bobby has motivation to do creative activities, on his own, at home. His mother values his creativity. He does many types of activities, none of which were represented when he was tested for flexibility and fluency.

Amidst all this controversy is the bewildered professional responsible for educating the gifted, whose state may require that children with creative thinking potential be identified using creativity tests or checklists. The busy educator often has neither the time nor the propensity to wade through the research evidence, and the research itself is confusing and often done by the people who can benefit most from showing that their own tests and checklists have validity and reliability.

## Validity

Validity is best described as the test's truthfulness. That is, does the test measure what it says it will measure? There are three kinds of validity: (1) content/construct validity; (2) criterion validity; and (3) concurrent validity.

### Content/Construct Validity

Content, or construct, validity is necessary in order to determine whether the test has covered what it says it measured. To determine whether a creativity test is valid, you must look at what it measures. Divergent production is not creativity, and creativity is not only divergent production. Creativity is called a "construct," which means that it is an unobservable phenomenon that helps to explain a person's behavior. The lack of a universal definition for creativity, and the complexity of creativity is the major problem in developing any test or measures. Some researchers use one aspect of creativity — for example, divergent production of figural units, or free drawing within circles, and squares — and then conclude that people who were pretested and posttested on that one test were improved in "creativity." That is certainly not so. This where consideration of content of what is measured comes in. Creativity is too complex to be measured by a simple five-minute test, or even an hour-long test.

But researchers are still developing tests, and, it is hoped, they are doing so with a larger view of creativity. Kalsounis and Honeywell, in an article published in 1980, said that there were, that year, seventy-seven creativity tests available for research, though they were not yet available commercially. Donald Treffinger (1987), noted continued test development in the areas of: (1) the quality of creative products; (2) the personalities of creative people; (3) imagery as a creative activity; (4) creative problem solving; (5) the scoring of tests for aspects of creativity; and (6) finding creativity in young children.

People using tests that are called "creativity" tests should look carefully at the content of the test. Is filling in blanks or drawing within boxes "creativity"? Even if the tests are called "divergent production" tests, do such tests by implication translate themselves to creativity? Certainly, many state guidelines require divergent production tests to assess creative potential, but is it valid to equate divergent production with creative potential?

Treffinger also said that construct validity should be concerned with creativity testing as a total field, and not simply with individual tests: "Construct validity refers`. . . to the total pattern of research evidence that supports an instrument." He cited Khatena's work on creative imagery and imagination, Rimm and Davis's work on GIFFI, their personality and product instrument, Guilford's work on divergent production in the Structure of Intellect, Torrance's Tests of Creative Thinking, Mednick's work on the Remote Associates Tests, Wallach and Kogan's work on their test, and concluded "although there are still many isolated, fragmented studies, then, there have also been some promising signs of progress in validating several specific creativity assessment procedures." Those who argue that no creativity assessment procedure can possibly measure the construct of creativity would disagree, saying that no battery, no matter how widely conceived, can measure the creativity construct.

The subject is a difficult one, and the practitioner must trust in the authorities, for wading through the contradictory evidence of the studies is a mammoth task. Most districts do not have a testing or measurement person, and even if they do, this person might be swayed by the charming personalities of those who go from conference to conference, propounding one system of creativity assessment over another. It is not my place to recommend, but simply to clarify the issues involved. Additionally, Carolyn Callahan, in a 1990 essay called "The Assessment of Creativity" offered a thorough review of creativity tests and checklists.

Another issue related to construct validity is whether or not creativity stands separately from intelligence. On the one hand, Zarnegar, Hocevar, and Michael examined the construct of original thinking in a 1988 study, and determined that original thinking was definitely distinct, conceptually, from measured intelligence as indicated by IQ scores on the Stanford-Binet. Respondents in this study were asked to give only one original response, so that originality would not be confused with fluency of ideas. Original thinking is only one of the ways the tests are scored. The difficulties in separating originality factors from divergent production factors presents an ongoing problem. The tests that were related to originality were those called "Unusual Uses" and "Improvements," which "tap the ability to focus on high quality answers," and a test called "Consequences," which is the ability "to create remote associations without qualitative reflection."

Earlier, Hocevar in a 1980 study called "Intelligence, Divergent Thinking, and Creativity," found that when ideational fluency (how many ideas) was taken out of these tests of divergent thinking, the flexibility and originality scores were shown to be "unreliable." Likewise, Borland, in his 1986 investigation of flexibility and originality, showed that these may not exist as valid cognitive factors. Like Hocevar, Borland also found that ideational fluency was a factor that "could even be a general factor analogous to Spearman's "g" (1927). ("g" is general intelligence, the unity underlying abilities in special fields such as math ability). Borland cautioned, "Despite the certainty with which many educators of the gifted speak about fluency, flexibility, and originality, this is a murky area." Thus content/construct validity presents many problems when considering whether a test can measure creativity — or even the aspect of creativity called divergent production.

## Criterion Validity

Criterion validity is how much the test scores can predict one's performance in other areas, especially one's performance later on in life. For example, does a high score on a creativity test given in elementary school predict that a person will be a true creative achiever when she is an adult, or even when she is in high school?

## Predictive Validity of Creativity Tests

Why test children with such instruments if the tests don't show something about how the person is going to be as an adult? Torrance has spent a lifetime testing children, following them up, trying to find out whether their scores on such tests as his Torrance Tests of Creative Thinking have predictive validity. Unfortunately, the answers are mixed.

Optimally, predictive validity studies would be independently done. Instead, often the test-maker must take the responsibility for proving the validity. The issue of bias towards the instrument being validated is a real one, for who wants to spend a lifetime working on a test, and studying its validity, only to report the results were not what were planned? The temptation to suppress such results must be enormous. While independent reviewers and researchers do some validation work, much is done by the test-makers, who may design studies that are likely to prove that their test works.

Here is an example of one of the Torrance studies. A predictive validity study by Torrance and Safter (1989) was done on the Just Suppose Test, that is part of the Torrance Tests of Creative Thinking. The data were from the 1981 follow-up of sixty-four children in Minnesota who had taken the experimental forms of the Torrance Tests of Creativity in 1960-61. The follow-up forms examined five indices of creative achievement: (1) number of high school creative achievements; (2) number of post-high school achievements; (3) number of creative life-style achievements; (4) quality of highest creative achievements; and (5) creativeness of future career image. Post-high school achievements were such things as articles in professional journals, having written novels or poems and having received literary awards, obtaining patents, receiving creative arts awards, demonstrating leadership, or starting or innovating a business. These measures were correlated with flexibility, originality, emotional expression, fantasy, elaboration, analogies, and an overall Creativity Index. Correlations were statistically significant in almost all of the thirty-five possible ways, but the Creativity Index was most significant. Torrance and Safter in this article, called "The Long Range Predictive Validity of the Just Suppose Test," said "fluency, originality and elaboration seem to be the best individual predictors of young adult creative achievement."

But in the 1980 study, Hocevar pointed out that divergent thinking tests do no better than intelligence tests in predicting real-life creativity. Even in those studies that support the predictive validity of divergent thinking tests, the correlations are low, less than .30. He believed that telling people to be original in the directions for these tests would improve predictions of real-life creativity. He cautioned that researchers have assumed that divergent thinking and creativity are synonymous, and thus have made the mistake of using the test as the definition of creativity rather than clearly stating that the test may be related to the total construct of creativity, and emphasized the importance of using measures of how people had actually achieved creatively in the real world.

## Concurrent Validity of Creativity Tests

Concurrent validity establishes whether the test correlates with what real people in the field supposedly being measured really do. Khatena in *The Creatively Gifted Child* (1978), reported a concurrent validity study of his inventory called Something About Myself, and a checklist called Onomatopoeia and Images. In 1973, the Something About Myself inventory had been combined with Torrance's What Kind of Person Are You inventory, and subsumed under the title Khatena-Torrance Creative Perception Inventory.

In subsequent years, Khatena, Torrance, and colleagues have attempted to establish the validity of these inventories. For example, Morse and Khatena published "The Relationship of Creativity and Life Accomplishments" (1989) showing how the Something About Myself inventory and the What Kind Of Person Are You inventory were related to an index of life accomplishments. The researchers asserted that this study demonstrated the concurrent validity of the inventory, meaning that what the inventory measures is what real live creative individuals manifest. Here is a brief description of the study. The creative adults completing this biographical inventory were twenty-four male and twenty-two female conference leaders attending the annual Creative Problem Solving Institute at the Creative Education Foundation at State University College at Buffalo, New York. The creative productivity of the adults was determined by a point system over eight categories: (1) job/vocation; (2) interests; (3) leadership; (4) membership in the Creative Education Foundation; (5) artistic endeavors and accomplishments in an artistic field; (6) musical accomplishment; (7) miscellaneous accomplishment, or accomplishment is any field of the performing arts other than visual arts or music; and (8) creative production, or products other than visual arts, music, or performing arts.

Only the last four of these categories, for one point each, had anything to do with creative production in mind. Yet, (1) job/vocation — the number of different positions the person had held; (2) the number of subgroups within the Creative Education Foundation the person belonged to; and (3) leadership — the managerial positions the person had held, all had a possibility of three points. For example, a writer who has published many well-reviewed novels would only get one point, in category (8). Likewise a ground-breaking scientist or mathematician would only receive one point. But someone who had joined many special interest groups, an activity creative people are not known for (as will be discussed in Part III), would receive three points.

The results were that the adult creative producers studied here had accomplishments higher than the norms in the technical manual (Khatena and Torrance, 1976), and that the Something About Myself Questionnaire items were related moderately to biographical information. The authors concluded, rather weakly, that "some evidence for the validity of self-report measures such as the Khatena Torrance Creative Performance Index can be mustered." They further concluded that "such measures can and do have validity as indicators of creative potential." This is an illustration of an attempt to establish concurrent validity.

## The Threshold Theory

Runco and Albert in a 1986 article stated that the so-called threshold theory — that one needs above-average intelligence in order to be creative — is incorrect. They pointed out that some studies done on creativity and its relationship to intelligence have used IQs derived from ability tests, such as the Stanford-Binet. Other studies, however, have used IQs derived from achievement tests, such as the California Achievement Test. But as they noted, tests such as the Stanford-Binet and the California Achievement Test are not equivalent measures — that is, they do not measure the same things. Even though the tests were not measuring the same things, many researchers assumed that they were, and thus conducted experiments based on false initial assumptions caused by differences in the tests. Thus, statements that one must have above-average intelligence in order to show a good score on a creativity test remain unproven. Runco and Albert said, "For now, it appears that the traditional view of the threshold of intelligence necessary for creativity is at least partly a psychometric artifact." By psychometric artifact they mean that the results were due to characteristics of the tests being used, rather than being due to real differences among people. Criticisms in the threshold area were also made by Davis, in the 1989 article called "Testing for Creative Potential." Davis commented on the Runco and Albert study, and pointed out that "The threshold idea probably cannot be evaluated fairly only with divergent thinking tests and fifth-grade children."

Confused? Don't be shy about admitting it. This experiment demonstrates the complexity of research into creativity testing. Many eminent researchers are spending their professional lives trying to help us make sense of things. Unfortunately, the schools make decisions based on contradictory research. School leaders choose the research and justify their decisions saying they are "research based." But what research, and how well was the research conducted? A long-standing cry exists in the education profession for the research to be translated to solid practice, and maybe someday it will be. But for now, two carriage horses called inertia and practicality are the main pullers of practice.

In general, the validity studies of tests of divergent production have been weak to mixed. Mark Runco, in the book *Divergent Production* (1990), has shed much light on these studies, and you may wish to consult his extensive and expert evaluations for more information on this subject.

## Reliability

Three interrelated types of reliability must be considered by the person using creativity testing. These are: (1) stability; (2) equivalence; and (3) internal consistency. Is the test stable? If a person takes the test one day, and then takes the test again, will the results be the same? The best way to assure this is to administer equivalent alternate forms of the test, a reason why most standardized tests have Form A and Form B. The ideal is that the person taking Form A will score the same on Form B, and thus assure that the score is stable, consistent and equivalent. However, in the field of creativity testing this is very difficult because of what is being measured. An analogue would be to compare the scoring of a multiple choice test with the scoring of a divergent production test. It is easy to mark a multiple choice test. But in an open-ended format with no right answers, it is very difficult to make items equivalent. Is asking a person to list unusual uses for a ball equivalent to asking a person to list unusual uses for a bat?

Another way to establish equivalence is to examine internal consistency; that is to see whether the scores from one half are about the same as the other half, using odds and evens or other ways of splitting the test. This split-half reliability, however, is also difficult to accomplish in testing for creativity.

Reliability of tests can be increased by administering the tests in a standardized way, by using objective scoring measures, by having item difficulties that are equal, by having the test measure only one aspect of creativity, and, in general, by increasing the number of items on the test. But administering the tests in a standardized way and scoring them objectively is particularly difficult for divergent production tests. Mrs. Larson followed the directions printed on her direction sheet, as she should have done for reliability, even though her "standardized" administration of the test left Bobby confused and behind.

## Administering Tests

Lissitz and Willhoft, in "A Methodological Study of The Torrance Tests of Creativity" (1985) found these tests to be highly sensitive to how the directions were given, or "experimenter manipulation." That is, "the degree to which test-takers feel restricted or encouraged may well have a critical effect on their performance." They gave different directions to four groups: one was administered the test in the standard way, a second was told to be "practical and reasonable," a third was told to list as many ideas as possible, and a fourth group was told to include "unusual, weird, or illogical" ideas. After finding that such differences in giving directions changed the results, they cautioned others that "studies using the Torrance Tests should be viewed with extreme caution." More to the point, schools should remember that they are using the tests for making decisions about children's lives, their educational futures.

Runco, in two studies in 1986 and 1987, similarly found that directing talented and nongifted children (meaning they did not have high IQs) to be original increased their fluency (i.e., the number of responses they gave), but that directing high IQ students to be original did not. Since fluency is always a large proportion of the total scores in such divergent production tests, increasing the fluency raises the child's test scores; but, if some test-givers tell the children to be original and some do not, the test scores will not be comparable.

## Scoring

Scoring is also a problem. Scoring is not merely marking which multiple choice questions the student answered correctly or incorrectly. The responses are as varied as the people taking the test; however, they have been codified into classes, so that the scorer, with training, can recognize certain patterns. For example, a response is called original if it only occurs once or twice in a group of thirty people. The scorer must remember who has done what and how many times it has occurred. I have received and given extensive training in one particular form of divergent production testing and have scored thousands of divergent production tests. Yet there is still inconsistency in my scoring, especially for humor or the macabre. My mood may be different from day to day, or my understanding of the children's recent assignments may not be clear.

Once I scored a group of stories for a divergent production test. Most of them ended with a moral. If a story ended with a moral, a child received a higher score, according to the directions. It turned out that the students had been writing fables for two weeks. If I had tested them one month later or one month earlier, the morals at the ends of the stories would have been less frequent, their scores would have been lower, and the decisions ultimately made on the basis of those scores may have been different. That is why it's better to have several people score the same tests independently — that is, to be interraters. If they come up with similar scores, their scoring is called reliable. The scoring is said to have high interrater reliability. Another way to score such difficult tests is wholistic scoring. Several people score the same test, and the scores are averaged, throwing out the highest score and the lowest score. Such Advanced Placement tests as the Composition tests are scored in this way.

Scoring the tests also presents difficulties of overrating and underrating the test information, or of giving the same student high scores, but for substantially different reasons (Halpin and Halpin, 1974; Rosenthal et al., 1983). This means that even if scorers are highly trained, there still will be differences that affect the final scores in the areas of originality, say, or in elaboration. Sending the tests in to be hand-scored by the publisher is perhaps the best idea. A school district trying to save money by having local people score the tests should factor in the dollar value of the local scorers' time and the cost of properly training local people. Often the district will find that sending the tests to be scored will save money.

Other researchers have examined the assumption that the figural Form A Torrance Tests of Creative Thinking measures fluency, originality, and elaboration. In a 1988 study of the Torrance Tests, Heausler and Thompson found that since the same set of responses is scored several different ways, with the scorers looking for different aspects of divergent production during each scoring, there is too much relatedness in the scoring. They concluded that people who use the Torrance Tests should be "cautious" in thinking that the subscales derived from the scoring "provide meaningfully different information." Although their cautions are well taken, it must be noted that the experiment was conducted with kindergartners and second graders, a young group for any standardized testing.

The next chapter continues this discussion of standardized creativity testing and research. When Katherine Miller was hired to teach gifted children, she had no idea she would be asked to give creativity tests, nor did she have a suitable background for deciding what tests to give, why she should give them, and how to interpret the scores once she obtained them. Chapter 4 discusses how creativity checklists are used, and how creativity training has mushroomed in the past few years. You are now halfway through the most difficult section of this book. Congratulations!

### Summary

1. Teachers are often not well trained in administering creativity tests and checklists.

2. School districts should understand the research base that went into the checklist or creativity test.

3. Sometimes the research is confusing, since validity and reliability can be presented in different ways.

4. Predictive validity of creativity tests, creativity training, and creativity checklists is most difficult to establish because the tasks on the tests have little relationship to real life creativity.

5. Scoring is also difficult on creativity tests because the scoring requires subjective judgment and scorers must be trained.

6. When reading the results of studies that say the treatment made the group "more creative," see whether or not that meant more fluent, flexible, etc. and judge the results accordingly.

# Chapter 4

## Significance, Creativity Training Questionnaires, and Checklists

*And besides, in quoting others, we cite ourselves.*
— Julio Cortazar

*The language that separates teachers from researchers invests researchers with authority and power and allows the practices of researchers on behalf of teachers to remain unchallenged except by other researchers.*
— Margaret Marshall and Loren Barritt

Chapter 3 dealt with creativity testing and its difficulties. This chapter continues along the same lines, but focuses on what having "significant" results means to people who use the creativity tests. I'll use an example of creative adolescents to illustrate. Creativity checklists and personality questionnaires will also be discussed.

## Studies of Significant Results

Beyond the concern of whether tests are valid and reliable comes the consideration of whether or not there are significant results. If the results were "significant," people in the schools decide to pay attention. But "significance" is the play territory of college professors of statistics. The level of significance is shown like this: (1) $p < 0.05$, which means that the results have a one in twenty likelihood of having occurred simply by chance; (2) $p < 0.01$. which means that the results would occur 1 percent of the time, or less, by chance; and (3) $p < .001$, which means that the results would have occurred by chance less than one time out of a thousand.

But statistical significance does not necessarily imply that the results are meaningful. For example, many studies of creativity testing are correlational. This means that one test is compared with another to see whether the tests are related. If the tests are related more than would be expected by chance, the results are "significant." But few researchers question whether the tests are in fact measuring creativity, and have construct validity. Other studies try to isolate the factors being measured by the tests. If the researchers find factors that are, indeed, separate and isolatable, the results are "significant." These theoretical studies are necessary — but they're not very helpful to the practitioner.

And even if the study is not correlational or factorial, but experimental, and the results are "significant," what does that really mean? For example, Torrance, in a 1987 essay called "Can We Teach Children To Think Creatively" reviewed 142 studies that taught children to think creatively. For 103 of those studies, significantly enhanced creativity was determined by using the Torrance Tests of Creative Thinking as a indicator. But what did these really mean? He said, "I am particularly aware that many researchers are likely to discredit most of the 142 studies . . . because 103 of them have used performance on the Torrance Tests of Creative Thinking as criteria." He also said that "while I strongly favor and have used more real-life criteria" he nonetheless defended the validity of his test.

Despite the limitations, his study found that the most improvement in creative thinking was when the Osborn-Parnes training program was used. Next, in descending order, were programs that involved both thinking and feeling when the students practiced creative thinking. Other packaged programs such as the Purdue Creative Thinking Program also scored high. Using the creative arts as a vehicle, especially out of school, brought success. Again, remember that the success was measured by posttesting on a paper and pencil test.

## A Flawed Study of Creative Adolescents

I did a study of creative adolescents who attended a Governor's Institute for fifteen intensive days, where they wrote and performed operas, and participated in creative writing and printmaking. When the students arrived, I pretested them with the SOI Test of Creative Thinking (Meeker and Meeker, 1975), a test derived from the Guilford Tests. I administered Divergent Production of Figural Units (DFU), and also Divergent Production of Semantic Units (DMU). The day the creative adolescents left, I posttested them with the same two tests; each testing session took ten minutes. When I scored the DFU and DMU tests, and applied tests of significance to the results, I found that the students had improved in fluency to a significant degree. For the girls, the significance was $p < .001$ — about as significant as you can get — but that doesn't mean that the results are meaningful; it merely means that the results are likely not due to chance. In drawings, the results showed no significant changes. The two weeks of intensive creative work also did nothing for their transformational ability in drawing on paper. (I have a hunch that the transformation product of Guilford's model can be shown to be related to real-life creativity, a hunch that has never been tested and probably never will be, at least by me).

But what do those results really mean? The faculty and the boys also improved in fluency to the significance of $p < .05$, or a 95 percent likelihood that the results were not by chance. Can I measure what the Governor's Institute meant to fifty teenagers who wrote, thought, created, composed music, performed, and talked until 4:00 a.m., driving their resident assistants crazy with their creativity and humor, by giving the ten minutes of two divergent production tests? What does a significant difference in fluency mean? That these children became more creative? That the faculty became more creative as a group? One would certainly hope so, for the state granted us $40,000 to do that, but one would also have trouble believing that putting down a few more items on a five-minute test would actually prove it.

My small research study doesn't show much at all, even though when I presented the results at the state gifted education conference, people were impressed that I had found "significant" changes. It should be noted that about two-thirds of the students had a one-hour class daily where fluency, flexibility, elaboration, and originality were taught separately from the process they were going through. Upon testing, no differences were found between those who participated in this formal creativity training and those who did not take the creativity training class. That is, the ones who did not take creativity training improved in flexibility, fluency, and originality as much as those who took creativity training. They were a small control group.

But I didn't have a real control group. Thus, how can I say that these adolescents truly became more fluent? Even more to the point, why did they need to become more fluent? They came in, self-selected, highly creative already. Since the divergent production test measured fluency, I measured fluency. That's all. I didn't compare them with a randomly chosen matched group of adolescents and teachers, who were doing what adolescents usually do in August. If I had tested a matched group of adolescents and teachers, perhaps they, too, would have become as fluent as my experimental group of adolescents during that fifteen day period, without going to a Governor's Institute. I imagine my ideal control group playing in their summer band pratice sessions for the football games, or finishing up their summer work detasseling corn. And I imagine my faculty control group painting the houses they always seem to paint in the summer, or taking their children to swim, play ball, or just reading and gardening.

I didn't have a control group because it *was* summer, and the students came from thirty locations all over the state, and their high school counselors were not available to help me randomly select matching students at each school, and we didn't get the grant until the end of May, so I was trying to find students to attend the Institute and not students for a control group. So my "significant" results aren't significant at all, and even if they were, you shouldn't be very impressed that the students and faculty became more fluent. I suspect that the troubles with this study are quite common. My question is, so what? So what if there was an increase in fluency, flexibility, or originality?

What was the transfer of fluency, flexibility, and originality, and then, if it transferred, how did we measure it? Transfer means what one learns is applicable to real-life, or to another field. For example, what is the transfer of algebra? Some people would say there is no transfer. There-fore, they would say it is useless to study algebra. Others would say that algebra teaches one to think logically. Transfer is the main problem in discussions of both creative and critical thinking. Say a person practices separate skills, for example, being fluent, or being flexible; in what situation can the student use those skills? If one learns to add and subtract, those skills transfer when the person balances a checkbook. If a student learns to put down more answers in a short amount of time, where does that skill transfer? What did the people who underwent creativity training gain?

Torrance, in a 1987 essay called "Recent Trends in Teaching Children and Adults to Think Creatively," addressed that question, saying that continued opposition to creativity training had led to a decline in that training in the early 1980s, and that the measurement of real-life accomplishments was called for. Thus, he listed the real-life results that the researchers found as the transferred results of creativity training in elementary and secondary schools. Among these effects on the students were: (1) "increased satisfaction"; (2) evidence that academic achievement is not affected by creative performances; (3) writing more creatively in different genres — one student even wrote a novel; (4) growth in personality and the acquisition of a healthy self-concept; (5) improvement in attitudes toward mathematics; and (6) an openness to pursuing creative choices.

For adults, results of creativity training were that $60 per work hour profit was made by a company whose employees took CPS; a physician who received creative problem solving training used it with his patients; course subject matter knowledge was increased; and students wrote creativity policies. Torrance also noted that elderly people who took a creative art course reported that they felt healthier and more sociable.

A hard-nosed pessimist might wonder whether such tenuous results justify creativity training. But attitudinal and conceptual changes are difficult to measure, though they are vastly important in forming the necessary intrinsic motivation one needs to produce creative products. The students in our Governor's Institute learned, in a minimal way, how to write the libretto of an opera. They participated in the frustrating, lengthy, mind-filling creative process. They sat for hours at the piano in practice rooms composing, they acted, made costumes, wrote the story, rehearsed, collaborated, and sweated. Their journals showed us their attitudes changed, and the products they produced were novel, original; these works had never existed before.

I suspect the fluency the participants gained might have arisen partly because they felt comfortable, satisfied, and pleased with themselves after having been together in such an intensive effort for fifteen days. The point is this. We have a mystical belief in tests. If we would just sit back and look at the tests we've given, and stop investing them with magical powers, we'd realize that five or ten minutes of testing shows little, if anything. The students increased in creativity all right, but measuring their increase in terms of two ten-minute tests was ludicrous. Yet with accountability constraints, this is what educators are often asked to do. Let's take another example. Say a boy can throw a ball from center field to home plate with great and accurate force. Observation would dictate that he would probably do well as a center fielder. Is there any need to give him a paper and pencil test to see whether he has spatial ability?

A better indicator of the enhanced creativity of these adolescents was in the observational, or portfolio assessment we ended up with. We looked at what they had made during the Institute that had not existed before: many poems, short stories, prints, four rather polished operas, all shown on a videotape we made. These products were not judged or graded, for the emphasis was on the process they went through, and not on the quality of their products. An assessment of quality should come after many more poems, stories, operas, and prints are practiced. Whether or not the students became more creative is not the right question. To use a significant increase in fluency as a measure of whether or not they became more creative, or even more "divergent," is not the right answer to the question of whether they were creative. Asking people to increase their creativity as measured by numbers added up is the wrong question, altogether.

### The Normal Curve Assumption

Another issue with testing is the assumption that the scores obtained fall on a normal curve, with 68 percent in the middle, and about 16 percent on either end. Though one can derive a normal curve from any test, the underlying assumption that there is a normal curve of creativity, or, to put it another way, the underlying assumption that some people have a fuller cup of creativity than other people, has not been proven. Likewise, when some people talk about giftedness, their underlying assumption is that a person with a high IQ is gifted. The person has a fuller cup of giftedness than a person with a lower IQ. This assumption is an important issue when talking about creativity testing, for it assumes that the person taking the test has "more" creativity when she gets a higher score, and that a person has "less" creativity when she gets a lower score. This is nonsense, also.

When speaking about the creative person, we can say that the person is creative in something, or creative at something. We should never say that someone has more creativity or less creativity. But if you use a paper and pencil test and obtain a score, you'll be tempted to admit the highest scorers to the program for those who have creative potential. Many school districts establish a cutoff score, and say that everyone who scores above such and such a percentile gets into the creative thinking program. The assumption that people fall on a normal curve of creative thinking is operational here. Thus the person who is most fluent, or gives the most answers, will get a high score. If the test is measuring writing fluency, the person who spews out a lot of words will get a higher score than the careful, reticent, accurate poet who writes a few, but well-taken, words.

## Using Questionnaires

Other research we conducted at the Institute seems more promising than finding significant changes in fluency and flexibility. The work of Piechowski and his colleagues on Dabrowski's theory poses new questions about giftedness and creativity, and we wanted to explore them with our creative adolescents. We were interested in the intriguing possibility that creative people have certain patterns of "overexcitabilities." Dabrowski's theory of emotional development was explained by Piechowski, Silverman, and Falk in 1985. They defined an overexcitability as "enhanced and intensified mental activity distinguished by characteristic forms of expression which are above common and average." These forms of expression are: (1) psychomotor; (2) sensual; (3) intellectual; (4) imaginational; and (5) emotional.

We used the Dabrowski Overexcitability Questionnaire, (Piechowski and Cunningham, 1985) along with the Runco Quantity and Quality Questionnaire (Mark Runco, personal communication, July 1989), and it took each student about an hour and a half (minimum) to answer the questions. Then I, along with my colleague, David Kowalka, followed up with individual interviews, taking the students through the questionnaires, asking them to elaborate on what they had written. Coding the information was more difficult than counting fluency and flexibility on a divergent production questionnaire. We transcribed the interviews. Rendering the information into quantifiable form took much more training and at this writing is not yet complete. But we learned much more about the young people — about themselves, about their lives, about their thoughts.

Piechowski and Cunningham, in "Patterns of Overexcitability in a Group of Artists" (1985), postulated three distinct patterns of response in creative artists (as opposed to the intellectually gifted); each type of creative artist has different kinds of overexcitability. They found differences between creative people and intellectually gifted people, especially in the areas of imaginational overexcitability and emotional overexcitability. The creative artists thought with vivid imagery and associations and had a great capacity for metaphorical and animistic thinking. They had great depth and intensity in their emotional lives and were able to perceive subtleties in emotional experience. The authors also found the artists were quite similar to the intellectually gifted in intellectual overexcitability, which is characterized by curiosity and a thirst for knowledge.

Among the creative artists, pattern A were balanced and integrated, had childhoods without trauma, and demonstrated self-confidence. They felt free to express themselves and seemed emotionally balanced. Pattern B were emotionally vulnerable, and had "sensitivity, even oversensitivity, feelings of guilt, inadequacy, shame, shyness, or inhibition" and greater emotional overexcitability. They had experienced "criticism and rejection" in their childhoods and were prone to feelings of inadequacy, anxiety, and depression. The authors said these types could represent creative people such as Franz Kafka or Emily Dickinson. Pattern C seemed restless and rebellious and had flirted with danger during their youth. They were characterized by sensual, psychomotor, and imaginational overexcitabilities, and some came from fundamentalist backgrounds. All three patterns had high intellectual overexcitability, represented as intelligence, curiosity, love of learning, and thinking in both images and words. Such studies as these of how creative people respond to the world seemed much more interesting to us than the results of divergent production tests.

Here is the Overexcitability Questionnaire. I have included sample answers to questions 14 and 15 from a fifteen-year-old female creative writer. Space does not permit reproducing her full questionnaire responses.

## Overexcitability Questionnaire

1. Do you feel really high, ecstatic, or incredibly happy? Describe your feelings.

2. What has been your experience of the most intense pleasure?
3. What are your special daydreams and fantasies?
4. What kind of things get your mind going?
5. When do you feel the most energy and what do you do with it?
6. In what manner do you observe and analyze others?
7. How do you act when you get excited?
8. How precisely can you visualize events, real or imaginary?
9. What do you like to concentrate on the most?
10. What kind of physical activity (or inactivity) gives you the most satisfaction?
11. Is tasting something very special to you? Describe in what way it is special.
12. Do you ever catch yourself seeing, hearing, or imagining things that aren't really there? Give examples.
13. Do you ever think about your own thinking? Describe.
14. When do you feel the greatest urge to do something? Explain.
15. Does it ever appear to you that the things around you may have a life of their own, and that plants, animals, and all things in nature have their own feelings? Give examples.
16. If you come across a difficult idea or concept, how does it become clear to you? Describe what goes on in your head in this case.
17. Are you poetically inclined? If so, give an example of what comes to mind when you are in a poetic mood.
18. How often do you carry on arguments in your head? About what sorts of subjects are these arguments?
19. If you ask yourself "Who am I?" what is the answer?
20. When you read a book, what attracts your attention the most?
21. Describe what you do when you are just fooling around.

We also added another question that is not on the Overexcitability Questionnaire. (Piechowski has given permission to include this).

22. In what ways do your dreams influence you?

Here are one student's answers to questions 14 and 15, in which she expresses her reasons for writing: that writing is therapeutic and emotionally healing.

> I get the greatest urge to do something when I am depressed. Basically I don't like to express myself verbally and I don't talk to my mom. I don't talk to the

guidance counselor and my mom told me she was going to take me to a psychologist. I won't talk to psychologists. I don't waste my money cause I'll sit there and stare off into space and that's all I'll do. And so, I write, and I just write how I feel. And that's the time when I get into writing, when I have things on my mind that I can't really handle. Then I write it down. I feel the urge. I have to do it. And then it's like I don't know, it's automatic. I'll go to my room and reach for the pen and reach for the paper. I don't know. Just something clicks in my mind . . . Get some paper and write.

Here she expresses her vivid imagination.

This sounds really stupid, but when I was little I used to watch Raggedy Ann and Raggedy Andy, and the dolls, when the little girl would leave the room at night, the dolls would come alive and they would talk. So I used to be real nice to my dolls and buy them clothes and give them candy. Or act like they eat candy and stuff like that. And I would set candy bars and cookies on the tables at night because I thought they would get up and get some. And I didn't throw them or anything like that. I'd brush their hair and everything, real nice, because I didn't want them to get up in the night and talk about me real bad when they wake up. And sometimes I wonder what — if things could think, what would they think about. If this desk could think, what would he think about somebody sitting here and pressing down on his face and writing on him and things like that.

We decided, after interviewing several students and finding that they had imaginary playmates, to ask the rest of the students whether they had, also.

Interviewer: Did you ever have an imaginary playmate?

Yea. I had a guy named John Hutchins. I didn't have any brothers or sisters, and my mother and my father worked overtime, and so there was basically just me, me and my animals. I felt really dumb talking to the cat on the porch. But now that I think about it, talking to nobody that wasn't there isn't better than talking to the cat. So I was by myself all the time, so I invented this guy named John, and before we moved, we had this really big house. And there's a little corner in the dining room and right by it was a walk-in closet. And right there was where John lived, and he would come out and sit at my little table with me when I got my punishment. And he would protect me from everything and stuff. And I really believed in him. He wasn't imaginary to me. He was real. There was John. John was talking to me. And I thought he was naked, so my dad had to give him some pajamas and everything. And my mom had to wash the pajamas all the time, and he was John. John sat there at dinner with me, and John ate my liver for me. John didn't come up and get the liver, no he didn't. John ate my liver and stuff. There was really a John to me.

He was in my life until I was about nine or ten, when we were getting ready to move because I didn't like my stepdad, and I still don't like him. He still comes around, and I still hate him. I guess I don't hate him, but I don't like him very much. And I couldn't tell my mom because she loved him, and when you love somebody they don't do anything wrong. But he was wrong, because he was drunk all the time. He took my money and stuff. So I sat there and told John, and John was like my psychologist. I would tell him how I felt.

Our experience with administering this questionnaire was profoundly personal and informative. Our interviews with the students revealed more about the young creative personality than any creativity test or checklist could. The rigors of interrater scoring and rating preclude widespread use of such a questionnaire until the number of active researchers grows, but the anecdotal and personal knowledge that we gained seems at least as important. For example, one nonscientific observation we made after conducting the interviews was that the girls seemed to have had imaginary playmates at some time or another, and the boys seemed to hear voices calling them. Thus I was amused to read in Davis's article, "Testing for Creative Potential" (1989) that "Two virtually flawless biographical predictors of adult creativity are having had an imaginary playmate as a child and involvement in theater, for example, in high school."

## Creativity Training

A few colleges offer courses in creativity. McDonough and McDonough's "A Survey of American Colleges and Universities on the Conducting of Formal Courses in Creativity" (1987) found that only thirty states had colleges with formal courses in creativity. Of the 1,504 colleges surveyed, only 76 offered such courses in creativity. These courses were taught by diverse faculty in engineering, art, education, psychology, music, and philosophy.

### Creativity Studies Project

Parnes, in a 1987 essay called "The Creative Studies Project" recalled the history of the Creativity Studies Project at the State University of New York at Buffalo. Undertaken in 1957, this was a massive teaching effort to deliberately enhance the creative abilities of college students. Parnes said that this and other studies have shown "significant positive results when creative abilities are deliberately nurtured." He also noted, "a cluster of studies have evolved showing significant positive benefits for deliberate creative development in the 'real-life' arena — in industry, scientific achievement, and personal adjustment areas." He continued with "We now have convincing data showing that creativity-development programs work; what we need is similarly impressive data with 'real-life' criteria showing which parts or combinations of what programs are optimum for what type of person or situation."

With such glowing reports, I was anxious to look at how they had trained college students for four years in the Creativity Studies Project. Students learned the Creative Problem Solving Process, utilizing the intelligence theory of the Structure of the Intellect, combining convergent production with divergent production, in consultation with J. P. Guilford. After two years, students in the experimental group scored significantly better than the control group. They also did exercises in Noller's *Creative Action Book* (1976). Results indicated significant differences in students' scores on Guilford's divergent production of behavioral implications test, on his convergent production of semantic systems test, and on his cognition of semantic systems test.

Now the question is whether scoring well on these tests has predictive validity. Parnes pointed out that these tests "required considerable transfer from the kinds of exercises and materials the students used in the classes." When the students were compared with controls in English, they received the same grades as controls, even in writing themes which allowed creativity. No results were reported on math achievement, nor on nonacademic achievement, but at the end of two years, the experimental group seemed to be accomplishing more in such areas listed by the American College Survey as leadership, social participation, art, social service, etc.

Most interesting, though, is who dropped out of the creativity studies program. After lengthy analysis, including checked items on the pre-survey, and the Adjective Check List (Gough and Heilbrun, 1983), Parnes and Noller found that the students most likely to drop out were those with arts interests who had thought that the creativity studies project would feed those interests. Most of the students who signed up for the project were females, and those who dropped out were interested in music, entertainment, modeling, art, interior decorating, and journalism. Those who stayed in were interested in recreation leadership, mechanical activities, social service, sports, religious activities and office practice. Parnes said:

> Those lower in self-control and higher on "manic" tendencies (impulsivity, spontaneity, etc.) seemed to seek the quick answer, the novel experience, and when it no longer appeared to be novel and exciting, they tended to drop out of the picture. This pattern seems consistent with our experience in class with many of the dropouts. They would not work with the *Creative Behavior Workbook* . . . and with the structure of the program — repeated practice in the creative problem-solving process — but enjoyed greatly the ideation, the brainstorming, etc. (1987, p. 172)

Those educators who use the Creative Problem Solving Model and similar workbooks and materials must remember that Osborn, whose 1953 *Applied Imagination* started it all, was interested in increasing the creativity of business people. Parnes said that those who dropped out of the creativity studies program were those who might have "limited value in an organization." People who are creative with reference to staying in an organization are people who contribute to the profitability of that organization. They are looking for a reward, usually a monetary reward, for their creativity. The ones who stayed in the creativity studies program got increasingly better on Guilford's tests measuring evaluation ability. Again, there's some question about the predictive validity of these tests, though it would seem reasonable, especially to those who work in the area of thinking skills, that training in evaluation would help in real-life situations requiring evaluation. That is the whole premise of another training program, the Meekers' Structure of Intellect Institute. "Intelligence can be taught," is their motto, along with its corollary, "Creativity can be taught."

I have to admit that I nod out when I read creativity training books and programs. Perhaps I would also have been one who would have dropped out of the Creative Studies Program. It does seem that the people who dropped out had more interests that appear to be creative — music, entertainment, modelling, art, interior decorating, and journalism. I don't know. They may have felt they were creative enough already. I would rather someone cast me in a play, or go to choir practice, or write a poem or work on my novel, than fill in a workbook to enhance my creativity. I would rather go to our Sunday afternoon writers' group, and bring a new poem for my friends and me to discuss. Perhaps the value of creativity training books is that they help people who do not consider themselves to be creative to step into the stream.

### Creativity Training in the Schools

In the forty-odd years since Guilford's 1950 speech to the American Psychological Association about the concept of creativity, various people have asserted that creativity can be trained in young people and in adults. They have manufactured programs and exercises in divergent production to improve people's flexibility, fluency, originality, and their ability to elaborate and to make transformations. Other trends in creativity training have emphasized related aspects supposedly related to creativity. A brief listing follows.

1. Gordon's Synectics (1961). Synectics is putting unlike objects together to form a new object.

2. Meeker's (1973) divergent production exercises. Found in the *Sourcebooks,* there are basic and advanced levels that contain exercises in all of Guilford's divergent production factors.

3. Lozanov's Suggestopedia Technique (1978; Ostrander, 1979). This uses baroque music and relaxation to enhance memory and retention.

4. Torrance's research into the enhancement of divergent production (Torrance and Myers, 1970; Torrance, 1974, 1987). Torrance found the six most common types of creativity training to be: (1) teaching specific creative problem solving skills; (2) direct teaching of problem solving and pattern recognition; (3) using guided fantasy and imagery; (4) using thematic fantasy; (5) using creative writing; and (6) using Quality Circles.

5. Taylor's Multiple Talent teaching (1969). Taylor identified nine talent totem poles: academic, productive thinking, communicating, forecasting, decision-making, planning and designing, implementing, human relations, and discerning opportunities.

6. Williams's (1970) ideas for thinking and feeling. These exercises followed the Guilford divergent production aspects of fluency, flexibility, etc.

7. Samples's (1976) metaphorization. Samples created programs to help people form metaphors.

8. Eberle's (1982) visualization. Exercises in creative visualization were used.

9. Future Problem Solving (Torrance, Bruch, and Torrance, 1978) which is based on the Osborn-Parnes (1963, 1967) model of creative problem solving. Future Problem Solving is an international competitive program where students solve world problems.

10. Gourley's (1981) and Miklus's (1989) Odyssey of the Mind competitions. Odyssey of the Mind is an international competitive program where teams of students invent and create according to certain problems all have been given.

11. de Bono's coRT Lateral Thinking (1978). Lateral thinking is a packaged program used in thousands of schools internationally.

12. Davis's (1981) personal transformation. The Davis program emphasizes the affective as well as the cognitive aspects of creativity enhancement.

13. Bagely's and Hess's (1982) guided imagery. This popular book has many guided imagery scripts, useful in all curricular areas.

14. Crabbe's and Betts's (1990) emphasis on getting more creative people by means of creativity training. These are exercises designed in similar ways to those above.

15. Project Vanguard (1991). A two-year project in creativity training to help teachers be able to adequately identify children with creative potential. Teachers were trained in morphological analysis, synectics, metaphors, analogies, visualization, attribute listing, what if's, inferring, random input, forced input, criteria finding, and the creative problem solving process.

There are many others. As one graduate student said, it seems as if a new catalog of creative thinking materials arrives in the mail each week. Likewise, many popular books use various aspects of creative thinking, such as those by the former school superindendent, Bob Stanish.

I had to smile as I typed the list of techniques used in enhancing creativity, remembering that I took a Suggestopedia workshop in the Lozanov Technique in the late 1970s. Suggestopedia comes from Bulgaria and, simplistically stated, is the theory that people can learn during their sleep and absorb more when largo music is played. While not a theory of enhancing creativity, its use of relaxation and visualization foreshadows the creativity enhancing done in the 1980s. An administrator in special education who worked at a sheltered workshop with severely retarded adults asked me to share what I'd learned. The dedicated teachers of the retarded adults and I gathered on a Good Friday in Toledo, and I took them through the material covered in the workshop, and ideas from Ostrander's 1979 book *Superlearning*. The music at largo tempo was wonderfully relaxing, as they sprawled about on large, tattered easy chairs at the end of the warehouse that was their teacher's lounge. They had hoped the music would calm down their often violent charges, and hoped they could beam the music over the intercom while the adults shredded paper. I hope it helped. The book is still in print and quite popular, and the author cites studies that show that Suggestopedia worked.

Others, such as Torrance (1987), Torrance and Goff (1989), and Feldhusen and Clinkenbeard (1986) also have reviewed research results of over 2,000 studies of the Torrance Tests of Creative Thinking, as well as the studies using other measures such as the Purdue Creative Thinking Program, the creative problem-solving approach, the Productive Thinking Program, Imagi/Craft, and New Directions in Creativity. These tests and programs all measure and train divergent thinking. I have discussed the imprecise interpretation of results above. Nevertheless, the programs do work, if you are looking for results that may be nontransferable, or transferable in ways that may seem to be undistinguished.

## Creativity Training is Fun

Let's just admit it. Whether or not creativity training is even the province of the schools, creativity training enrichment is fun. The exercises produce laughter, humor, good feelings, and cohesiveness in a group. Even though I don't like to read the workbooks, I, like everyone, love being in a group and doing the training exercises. I remember teaching a group of teachers the Creative Problem Solving process on a dank November afternoon in Michigan. No one wanted to be at this required after school inservice, particularly since it was the week of the annual Ohio State-Michigan football game. Our "mess" was, "In what ways can we get tickets to the Ohio State-Michigan game?" By the end of our session, we were laughing, feeling good, and had invented a way to get tickets for the game. I still remember how we changed the size of the football field in order to add more seats to the stadium.

Many reading series and math series include creativity exercises in the teachers' manuals. Companies such as Good Apple and Trillium specialize in publishing books that help teachers to train divergent thinking. Training in divergent thinking includes such open-ended activities as brainstorming, making up stories, thinking of new and unusual uses for objects, and forcing relationships between unlike objects. In divergent thinking there are no wrong answers (unless you are scoring a divergent thinking test, and there it is always the fluent who get the highest scores), where in convergent thinking, there are right — and wrong — answers. Most school learning is concerned with convergent thinking, though Torrance and Goff in 1989 pointed out that "a quiet revolution" in the classrooms has been taking place, and more divergent thinking is being taught.

## Creativity Training as Differentiation for the Gifted

Gifted education programs often use creativity training as a means of differentiating the curriculum, a primary way of justifying education for the gifted. Years ago I heard such a rationale for using creativity training in gifted education from a famous speaker at a conference. She alleged that children with high IQs are rigid, prefer structure, and are uncomfortable when asked to do something that doesn't have a right answer. They are not risk-takers. Thus, they should be taught to be creative by having training in divergent thinking. I am not at all sure that children with high IQs are rigid and prefer structure; in my work with high IQ children at a school for the gifted in New York City, I found that children's personalities cannot be generalized. Kids are individuals; some are rigid and some are flexible. Their IQs did not presuppose rigidity or flexibility. However, this rationale is still heard as the justification for giving creativity training specifically to children with high IQs. The same suspect reasoning is also the case in asserting that children with high IQs learn best by the discovery method. Discovery learning is time-consuming and these children are rapid learners. A brilliant lecture and some challenging reading assignments might do much more good than constant discovery learning.

I don't believe that saying high-IQ kids are rigid is sufficient justification for using divergent production training, or that creativity training is the sole province of the education of the gifted. There is simply nothing in the training of fluency, flexibility, elaboration, and originality that justifies it as the special province of classes for high-IQ children. The fun, laughter, easy atmosphere, charged climate, and productivity that result from creativity training should be available to all children. The science of creativity training is not yet so perfected as to say that some children would benefit more than others. Frankly, it would seem that average and below-average children would benefit very much from discovery learning, especially guided discovery learning. When I said this to my students, some have replied that their entire written differentiated curriculum is based on creativity training, and it would be too difficult to give creativity training to all students. But I stand firm. (Teaching for creativity is discussed in Chapter 12).

### Teachers Get More Empathy with Creativity Training

Further, as one study showed, teachers also benefit from creativity training. In "The Effects of Group Creativity Training on Teachers' Empathy and Interactions with Students" (1985), McDonnell and LeCapitaine showed that thirteen teachers who received forty hours of group creativity training at Synectics, Inc., in Massachusetts, had statistically significant increases in empathy, in comparison with a control group. The teachers also reported that the training helped them to be more open with their students, and to listen intently to student responses and ideas. They gave students more reinforcement, and allowed more experimentation.

## Checklists

Checklists are very popular, except among those who review them for the *Mental Measurements Yearbook* (MMY). Two of the most popular checklists currently used to identify children with creative thinking ability are the Williams Creativity Assessment Packet (CAP) program, and the Renzulli-Hartman Creativity Scale in the *Scales for Rating the Behavioral Characteristics of Children.*

Again, the question arises whether what is being measured is actually related to creativity. Let's sample what the reviewers said.

### MMY Reviews of Williams CAP

Damarin, one reviewer of the Williams Creativity Assessment Packet (CAP) checklist in the 1985 MMY, emphasized that the manual was poorly written; the validation data were scanty and poorly documented, and he could find only one use for the checklist, which was to prove that, indeed, "creativity tests are measures of susceptibility to experimenter-demand characteristics." Damarin also pointed out that a creative child who is asked to sit down and "draw pictures in squares one at a time (no skipping around)" would probably do poorly, especially since the Williams tests penalize the child for skipping answers. A second reviewer, Rosen (1985), dismissed the CAP as containing "a technically uncertain set of instruments whose usefulness is limited by a lack of appropriate information as to validity and reliability," and said that Williams had made "exaggerated claims."

### MMY Reviews of Renzulli-Hartman Scales

Argulewicz, a 1985 reviewer of the whole *Scales* said: "The *SRBCSS* represents a significant advancement in the expansion of the methodology for identifying intellectually gifted, creative, or talented youth." Of the Creativity Scale, he noted that the validity was determined by comparison with the Torrance Tests of Creative Thinking, and that the Creativity Scale correlated with verbal subscales but not with nonverbal subscales. The other reviewer, Rust (1985), said the references in the manual seemed outdated, that concurrent validity was "untested," that face validity, stability, and retest reliability for fifth graders seemed acceptable. He said, "In summary, the scales' strengths include their conceptual formation and their ease of administration."

Nevertheless the average classroom teacher, being given the Renzulli-Hartman creativity behavioral checklist might experience some difficulty because of the number of questions asked in each item, called, in technical jargon, "the length of the stem."

Sample items on the Creativity portion of the *Scales for Rating the Behavioral Characteristics of Superior Students* are these:

> 5. Displays a good deal of intellectual playfulness: fantasizes; imagines ("I wonder what would happen if . . ."); manipulates ideas (i.e., changes, elaborates upon them); is often concerned with adapting, improving, and modifying institutions, objects, and systems.
>
> 6. Displays a keen sense of humor and sees humor in situations that may not appear to be humorous to others.
>
> 7. Is usually aware of his impulses and more open to the irrational in himself (freer expression of feminine interest for boys, greater than usual amount of independence for girls); shows emotional sensitivity.
>
> 10. Criticizes constructively; is willing to accept authoritarian pronouncements without critical examination.

### Mrs. Larson Fills Out a Checklist on Bobby

Remember Mrs. Larson? She was the teacher in Chapter 3 with the student who puzzled her. Suppose you are Mrs. Larson filling out Item 5 on this questionnaire about Bobby. Even though Bobby's school ability index was one point too low for the cutoff, Mrs. Larson requested a Renzulli-Hartman Creativity checklist to fill out. Well, Bobby displays intellectual playfulness all right, most of the time, but he doesn't seem to fantasize much; perhaps he does so at home, but Mrs. Larson doesn't know about it, so she can't mark it "sometimes."

Does he manipulate ideas? What does that mean? Changes or elaborates on ideas? Well, yes, sometimes. Is he often concerned with institutions and world change? Well, last week when they were talking about World Regions in third grade social studies, he asked about where Michelangelo came from; she just put that down to the Mutant Ninja Turtles on TV, but it could have been that he was interested in aesthetics and art.

Now Mrs. Larson notices that she has only four boxes from which to pick, and they are arranged Seldom or Never, Occasionally, Considerably, and Almost Always. Yet in this one item, number 5, she has been asked about eight different things about this child, Bobby. This illustrates one of the difficulties with the *Renzulli-Hartman Scale*. At item number 6, she checks Considerably, because Bobby does bring in those Calvin and Hobbes cartoons, but she'd never seen him frowning when other people are laughing, nor has she seen him giggling maniacally when the others are not laughing, and that's what she thinks that "sees humor in situations that may not appear to be humorous to others" means. (Sense of humor in creative people is discussed in more detail in Chapter 6).

Item number 7, "unusually aware of his impulses" could mean that he always asks to go to the bathroom, couldn't it? Or else it could mean that he is quite a conformist, buttoned-up, sanguine and shy. But then the item asks whether he's "open to the irrational in himself," which could mean that he's unaware of his impulses and acts out a lot. Then the item insinuates that Bobby could be quite feminine, a sissy boy, and Bobby certainly is not that. He's a roughhouser along with the rest of the third grade boys, and is always chosen first for games in the playground. Does he show "emotional sensitivity"? Well, yes, he does. He helps other children and he asked a question about that picture of a starving child in the *Weekly Reader* the other day.

Mrs. Larson, taking an unusual amount of time on this questionnaire because she really likes Bobby, and thinks there's "something there," as teacher lingo goes, has to check "occasionally" for this item. Mrs. Larson has anguished over the checklist, wondering, in Item 10, whether Bobby's criticism is really constructive or not, remembering the time he really got angry at the principal interrupting on the intercom just when he was going to do his demonstration of a duck call for show-and-tell, and she decides it is not, checking "occasionally."

The teacher and coordinator for gifted education, that cute young girl fresh out of college, Katherine Miller, picks up the checklists from Mrs. Larson, and adds up the scores. The checklist is weighted so that every item counts the same. Even though item 5 has been asking eight things, and item 4, "Is a high risk taker; is adventurous and speculative," has only been asking three things, every item is weighted the same. The total supposedly shows the *amount* (the number times the weight) of creativity characteristics a child has.

How can we evaluate whether these items predict the potential for creative behavior on the part of the student? Are they based on research into the characteristics of creative people as they were in their childhoods? And, in even more far-reaching terms, do the ten items on the checklist select for the potentially creative adult? For example, item 1, "Displays a great deal of curiosity about many things; is constantly asking questions about anything and everything," seems as appropriate for intellectual giftedness. The item is probably here on the creativity characteristics checklist because creative children are supposed to have a certain "amount" of intellectual giftedness, too. But do creative adults have curiosity, and did they as children, constantly ask questions about anything and everything? In a 1989 article, Davis called the Renzulli-Hartman traits "carefully selected and defended," but Renzulli in 1990 also told an audience that not a week passes that he and his colleagues don't get a letter or a phone call telling them how the caller has changed the checklist so that the stem is shorter. Renzulli and his colleagues have undertaken to do a substantial revision of the SRBCCSS (Renzulli and Westberg, 1990). This revision should be used by a school district if the *Scales* are to be used.

## GIFT, GIFFI, PRIDE

Another checklist or inventory is the 1982 Davis and Rimm GIFT and GIFFI I and II and PRIDE tests, which have been validated with children of all socioeconomic levels and races. These can be used with preschoolers through adults, and seem to measure traits often associated with creative people. Rimm in a 1990 speech was quite positive about the validation results being reported, and said that using these checklists is safe and predictive for a school district. However, they must be scored by the company, and are quite expensive, though an examination packet is available. The inventory is somewhat closely guarded, so I can show you no sample items.

### The Adjective Check List

Another commonly used checklist is Gough's 1952 Adjective Check List. This contains 300 words that the person checks as being self-descriptive. The Check List was not specifically designed to measure creative traits, but a thirty item scale within it was found to relate to personality characteristics of the people studied at the Institute for Personality Assessment and Research. Gough described that research in a 1979 article. (The research at the Institute for Personality Assessment and Research will be discussed in great detail in Part III). I administered the Adjective Check List to our adolescents and sure enough, they came out as being "creative personality (Cps)." Adjectives that describe a creative personality are "adventurous, ambitious, artistic, assertive, clever, complicated, curious, energetic, enterprising, imaginative, independent, initiative, intelligent, interests wide, inventive, original, progressive, resourceful, self-confident, temperamental, and versatile." Gough and Heilbrun used these terms in *The Adjective Check List Manual* (1983). Creative personality high scorers are "venturesome, aesthetically reactive, clever, and quick to respond." Intellectually, they have such characteristics as wide interests, mental ability, and fluency of ideas.

Our students also came out on the high end of the "Free Child" scale in Transactional Analysis. The person who scores high on this scale is "ebullient and enterprising, not at all inclined to exercise self-restraint or to postpone gratifications. Others are swept along whether they like it or not, in a rush toward enjoyment."

Another scale within the Adjective Check List is the Welsh Origence-Intellectence Scales, based on Welsh's 1975 monograph on creativity and intelligence as they relate to personality. Our students turned out high on the High Origence-High Intellectence Scale, A-2. Gough and Heilbrun said that high scorers on this scale are

> self-sufficient, strong-willed, original in thought and perceptions, aesthetically sensitive, indifferent to convention, and much annoyed by those who are uninsightful, intellectually maladroit, or lacking in perspicacity.

Despite many talents, the high-scorer on A-2 is

> scarcely more comfortable with his or her own needs and reactions than with those of other people. Intimacy based on candid sharing of emotionally significant feelings is sensed as dangerous and hence avoided (p. 25).

Our creatively gifted adolescents scored low on the Counseling Readiness Scale (CRS), another topical scale. The male who scores low on this scale is "less inhibited, more enterprising, and more confident of his ability to attain goals and gain satisfaction. Therefore, he is less likely to seek counseling or to feel he needs it," while the female who scores low is described as "not at odds with herself or with others, she feels little need for counseling nor would counseling serve much purpose." The comments of the girl on the Overexcitability Questionnaire would seem to corroborate this low need for counseling. However, the description of low-scoring females also said that such females are other-directed and gentle and not ambitious. That was certainly not true of our girls, as we observed them work, compose, write, do art, for two weeks.

While the checklist is among the best available, a careful person can see that there are some difficulties in using it to identify and select children for special programs. Checklists serve another purpose, however, and that is description. To use a checklist to select for a program is one thing; to use a checklist to describe a person is another. Whether or not one subscribes to the theory behind the checklist is also important, as exemplified in The Myers-Briggs Type Indicator. If one has doubts about the Jungian theory of personality types, the information gleaned from checklists on psychological tests about the personality of the person may not be seen as valuable information. The Adjective Check List is another example, as is the California Psychological Inventory and the Minnesota Multiphasic Psychological Inventory, the 16 Personality Factors Inventory, and many others. In the next few chapters, you will see that many of the major studies of creative people used these checklists, with varying results.

## Myers-Briggs Type Indicator

We administered our creative adolescents the Adjective Check List and they turned out to be "Creative" in personality. What a surprise, you might say. Yet, at the very least, this description confirmed our identification process throughout our state, for we came up with students who were recommended by their districts on the basis of their creative interests. We also administered the Myers-Briggs Type Indicator, and the students and faculty turned out to be overwhelmingly NFP (Intuitive, Feeling, Perceptive), with Introversion and Extraversion equally divided. Again, not a surprise, but a confirmation that these adolescents were like those studied by Myers and McCaulley for the Myers-Briggs Manual (1985) and were also like adult creative people.

## Cattell High School Personality Questionnaire

In a 1985 study of creative youth and intellectually gifted youth, Karnes, Chauvin and Trant administered the Cattell High School Personality Questionnaire, another checklist which also has an acceptable research base, to a group of intellectually gifted students, and to a group of students attending special schools for the fine and performing arts. The personality profiles of the young fine and performing artists showed them as "tender-minded, reflective, internally restrained, self-assured, but somewhat tense and driven"; the personality profiles of the intellectually gifted students showed them as "excitable, assertive, enthusiastic, and relaxed or composed."

## Promising Practices

Using personality checklists filled out by the students is entirely different from using behavior checklists filled out by the school system, supposedly showing that the student possesses certain researched characteristics and thus is potentially creative. Both our study and the Karnes et al. study took already identified students, and then described them, instead of selecting people for programs because of what the checklists added up to. As far as I am aware, no school district uses such well-researched, somewhat validated, and relatively reliable instruments as the Myers-Briggs, the Adjective Check List, the 16 PF, or the High School Personality Questionnaire to select children. These instruments would possibly be appropriate for high schools. But what is appropriate for elementary schools? The Myers-Briggs people have developed a similar form for children called the Murphy-Meisgeier. There is also an interesting questionnaire called the Wilson-Barber Inventory of Childhood Memories and Imaginings (Myers, 1983) that assesses fantasy and imagination in children. The problem of assessing young children is a universal one, and the challenges are being addressed increasingly by very well-qualified people.

Hennessey and Amabile in 1988 came up with yet another method, not using testing, that can be used to assess verbal creativity in elementary students, and that is storytelling. Children told stories that were rated by teachers. The procedure was simple. Children were asked to view a book with pictures, think up a story, and then tell the story aloud, telling one thing about each page. Three teachers with no special training then rated the tape-recorded stories on creativity, liking, novelty, imagination, logic, emotion, grammar, detail, vocabulary, and straightforwardness. Their ratings were very similar, giving high interrater reliability. The experiment had proper controls and the children's stories' results were compared relative to each other, so there was no confounding with IQ testing. Hennessey and Amabile said, "The storytelling technique of assessing children's creativity presents a number of practical advantages within a theoretically sound methodology." This shows there are many other ways to assess creativity than paper and pencil tests. Even so, writers such as Davis (1989) continue to feel that creativity testing is acceptable, and say, "In order to more accurately identify creative persons, for example, for participation in G/T programs, a recommended strategy is to use both types of tests, divergent thinking tests to evaluate some cognitive creative abilities and personality/biographical inventories to assess affective, motivational, and experiential factors."

Project Vanguard in 1991 was funded to prepare a Manual for the Identification of Creative Thinking. The researchers concluded that performance criteria should also be used along with divergent production tests and creativity checklists. They looked at the creativity components in such activities as Odyssey of the Mind, History Day, science fairs, Future Problem Solving, math contests, and writing contests, and recommended that schools who need to identify children with creative potential consider what the students are already doing in these arenas. They also recommended direct teaching for young children, with special teachers going from room to room, just as Wallach and Kogan recommended in 1965.

The assessment of creative potential has many pitfalls, but careful, thorough, and informed people, with proper attention, can sidestep these pitfalls.


## Summary

1. Behavioral checklists used to make decisions about students' lives are problematic.

2. Creativity test results used to make decisions about students' lives are problematic.

3. Weighting the items on creativity checklists might not be the best idea.

4. There is not necessarily a normal curve of creativity.

5. Even when the results of a study or program are "significant," you must ask, "significant in what?"

6. Creativity training has grown substantially in the schools in recent years. Many programs are available.

7. Creativity training, while fun, is not sufficient as a curriculum for gifted education.

8. All students should have an opportunity for creativity training.

9. Teachers can benefit from creativity training.

10. Personality checklists are better validated than behavior checklists.

11. Alternative methods of creativity testing, such as storytelling for verbal creativity, and performance assessment on aspects of already existing competitions, look promising.

# PART III

## TYPES OF CREATIVELY GIFTED

*As regards the question as to whether or not we can
clearly distinguish between the powers requisite
for scientific creation as opposed to artistic
creation, I don't think an answer is clearly forthcoming.
And if that is the case, then we might be wise waiting until
rather late before we make any classifying of children
into "likely scientists" or "likely artists" or
"likely neither" or "likely both." Indeed,
my own preference would be to wait until they
do it themselves.*

— Ian Winchester

*It's spring break, and Katherine has taken Brad to New York City to visit her beloved, eccentric and rich Aunt Margaret. A known supporter of the arts, Margaret is playing hostess to a wondrous mix of artists and thinkers that she has invited to her elegant Central Park West apartment in honor of Katherine's visit. She's invited writers, actors, artists, classical musicians, jazz musicians, choreographers, and dancers. She's invited a mathematician who will be bringing some colleagues in town for a conference. She's invited an evolutionary biologist who has recently written a provocative, but rather unreadable, book about the origins of humanity in offshore shale; his wife, a biologist and researcher, is coming too.*

*Margaret loves what happens when such diverse people get together. As the evening progresses, people who have stayed in their own groups begin to mix more. Someone proposes Charades. The actors love it; they shine. But when a round of Trivial Pursuit begins, the stars are the writers and scientists, who recall every detail that has ever passed through their brains. Then the men start talking about baseball. The dancers are bored with all this. They want to move. One of them finds a Chubby Checker album among Margaret's old records. They begin to twist, adding variations never seen in the sixties.*

*The visual artists think that baseball and trivia are all right, but Charades? They wouldn't be caught dead. They quietly head to the T.V. room for another game — Nintendo. With their hand-eye coordination and spatial ability, they are superb. The musicians are busy discussing the inadequacies of Margaret's sound system, and esoteric details of stereo equipment in general. One rock musician wanders off to dance.*

*At some late hour a group of writers gathers around the piano to sing show tunes while one of them plays by ear. They like this because they remember all the words. The dancers keep dancing, moving. The actors join the singing and really camp it up, with two of them throwing in absurd asides on every long note, in the form of favorite lines from Shakespearean tragedies they've performed. The loft artists are bored and leave early, making a stop at the Cedar Tavern in the Village.*

*Gradually, the party thins out. At 3:00 a.m. Margaret, exhausted, has retired. Brad, also exhausted, has gone to bed. But Katherine sits in the kitchen with a poet, drinking the last of the bourbon. She's wondering whether her kids at school will have the opportunities to become as successful as most of the people at the party. Her students seem so young, so in need of nurturing. More than she can give them.*

The poet reads Katherine a poem he's just written about the phony stiltedness of salons and cocktail parties.

Katherine listens, thinking how smug the poet is, and how ungrateful for her aunt's hospitality.

"Do you think you're creative?" she asks.

"Creative?" He seems taken aback. "Well, sure. I just created this poem, didn't I?"

She explains to him that she is supposed to teach creativity to gifted children, and he laughs.

"You can't teach creativity," he says. "A person is creative or not creative."

"But you can teach a creative person to be more creative, don't you think?" she says.

"Depends on what they make. A creative person has to make something, like I just made this poem."

"Of course!" Katherine says. "Of course. It's so simple. It's so clean. The creative person makes something that didn't exist before."

They go round and round, throwing out names — Martha Graham, Albert Einstein, Charles Darwin, Marlon Brando, Virginia Woolf.

They all made something. A theory, a character, a family of characters in a novel. It's so simple," Katherine says, more to herself than to the poet. "Thanks a lot."

"De rien," the poet says. "Glad to be of service." The bourbon is gone, and he makes an exaggerated sweeping bow and somewhat unsteadily goes out to the hallway. She presses the elevator button for him and sees him safely on.

Katherine giggles and goes to bed, wishing she had the energy to write it all down, the entire party. All those creative people, all together in one room.

If she had written it all down, she'd have a great deal of information about what dancers and scientists and poets are like. Maybe the creative act, that moment of fusion, or illumination, or realization is beyond definition or explanation, but creative people can be observed, and questions such as these can be answered. What are the intellectual and personality characteristics of various creative people? What is the relationship of measured IQ to creativity? How do the various types of creative people — writers, artists, actors, scientists, dancers, mathematicians — differ?

To put it simplistically, there are two ways to approach creativity. One is to judge a product "creative" and then to look at the person who has produced that product, to see what that person is like. The other is to *assess a child's ability through paper and pencil tests or through observation, pronounce him or her potentially or actually more creative than others, on a presumed normal curve of creativity, as a construct which supposed exists within everyone to some degree or another (explored in Part II).*

*Part III looks at studies of people who have produced creative products — visual artists, creative writers, creative mathematicians, creative scientists, performing artists, musicians, inventors. What are their backgrounds, their personalities, their ways of looking at the world?*

# Chapter 5

## Visual Artists

*What people can make with their hands is a lot better than they are themselves.*

— Joseph Brodsky

*That which fills my head and my heart must be expressed in drawings or pictures . . . Drawing becomes more and more a passion with me, and it is a passion just like that of a sailor for the sea.*

— Vincent Van Gogh

The stereotypic visual artist, with ragged jeans, dirty fingernails, and a cape or huge sweater, prowls the city streets. Or in a beret with palette in hand, on the banks of the Seine River, the artist paints a riverscape of Paris. But how much do these stereotypes reflect the truth?

From ancient times until recently, the artist was regarded as a craftsman, a solid worker who carved friezes or worked with tools to create useful decorations under the tutelage of a well-known artisan. The bohemian stereotype arose later, a result of the individualizing and personalizing of the romantic era, the late eighteenth and the nineteenth century.

The Industrial Revolution changed the perceived role of artists in society. Art became a romantic search for abstract "beauty," and artists were viewed as romantic figures, regardless of what their lives were really like. The ultimate romantic, Gauguin, who came to art late in life, was actually disdained by elite artists of France and Belgium as a Sunday painter. Having come under the influence of Pissarro, Manet, Monet, and Renoir in 1876, the artist finally got into his first show in 1880. There, Cezanne noticed Gaugin's work but considered him derivative, though talented, showing no obvious originality. However, Gauguin's "Study of a Nude" in 1881 finally impressed the key artists of his day, all of whom had devoted their lives to painting. Manet's statement that "No one is a painter unless he loves painting more than anything else" was a warning and a challenge to Gauguin. Even though he had been a banker for eleven years, was married, and had five children, Gauguin resigned his position at Bertin's banking house and in 1882 gave up his secure living to paint, exclusively. His wife never forgave him and the family never recovered financially.

From a time when many artists were anonymous — craftsmen under the patronage of the rich — to today, when the rebellious artist is an accepted stereotype, the fascination with artists' lives has continued. This chapter surveys biographical data as well as research on artists' personalities. In general its focus is on art students and adult visual artists rather than on children.

## Spatial Intelligence

Howard Gardner, in *Frames of Mind* (1983), made useful differentiations among kinds of intelligence. For example, he identified spatial intelligence as one of his seven "frames of mind," and stated that "the centrality of spatial thinking in the visual arts is self-evident." Spatial intelligence is the ability to see the world accurately, and to make and perceive changes and transformations in the physical world. Vincent Van Gogh, in Stone's *Dear Theo* (1937), described the importance to an artist of the talent for spatial visualization. He said, "It is at bottom fairly true that a painter as man is too much absorbed by what his eyes see, and is not sufficiently master of the rest of his life."

Spatial visualization is an area in which strong gender differences have been found, with men and boys outperforming women and girls. Male artists generally have scored higher than female artists in spatial visualization tasks. However, while few can be visual artists, everyone can cultivate his or her spatial intelligence and can learn to see the visual arts with the eye of a connoisseur.

## Early Signs of Visual Arts Talent

Artist Al Hurwitz, in *The Gifted and Talented in Art* (1983), identified certain behavioral and work characteristics that are common among visual arts-talented children. However, he also noted that while "No child, however talented, can reflect all of the characteristics . . . it is unlikely . . . that one who lacks all or most of them possesses special talent in art."

A key characteristic, according to Hurwitz, is that interest in visual arts begin early, emerging through drawing. Young visual artists often move through the stages of drawing rapidly, just as young musicians move through the mystery of music. Along with this precocious development, however, is a problematic corollary; when the child is between nine and eleven, she often becomes frustrated with her technical mastery as she unfavorably compares her efforts with images from mass media.

Another behavioral indication of potential of young visual artists is the ability to concentrate for a long period of time on an artistic problem, as well as a preference for being alone while doing art. The child is self-directed, creating on his own, away from the art room. Hurwitz noted that the person talented in the visual arts may not fit the common perception of creative people, especially regarding the personality aspect of risk-taking, for talented young people have "invested a great deal of themselves in developing mastery," and thus "they are unwilling or unable to experiment in new areas." The child may use art as a retreat, drawing for comfort.

There is also an indication of fluency in the talented young artist; that is, the child often has more ideas than there is time to enact. The work has details that other children miss. The child will often do multiple drawings and may use a drawing to illustrate a point, for drawing to the talented young visual artist is like talking or writing to the verbally gifted student.

The art work, itself, of visual arts-talented children also shows certain characteristics. Among those listed by Hurwitz are realistic representation, or verisimilitude. Talented young artists also are able to control their compositions, blending and mixing colors, consciously linking forms and experimenting. Junior and senior high school students will begin to surpass their teachers in realistic representation; they may draw detailed comic strips with narrative structure. Even young children who are talented exhibit extraordinary use of detail in drawings. They use their visual memories to enhance the art works they make. Their visual and kinesthetic memories show up at an early age, and they are able to use such recall in filling three-dimensional space. Talented young artists practice for hours and use a wide variety of media, not just pencil and paper. They are curious about the possibilities of other media. They often are doodlers, improvising with shapes and lines, seeing patterns that appear from negative space. As Hurwitz said, "Art functions as an extended conversation between form and imagination."

Hurwitz also differentiated between visual arts talent and critical sensitivity to the arts; the latter is also a visual perception talent, but relies more on verbal ability. Along with several other artists, he developed a way of identifying students who are critically sensitive to the visual arts. Their findings are detailed in his book, and assume particular importance in Hurwitz' view that the lack of critical sensitivity in the general public is due to the lack of arts appreciation study in the schools.

## Problem-Finding and Visual Artists

A particularly interesting study of visual artists is Getzels and Csikszentmihalyi's *The Creative Vision* (1976). Choosing 321 sophomore and junior student artists — 152 women (average age of 24) and 169 men (average age of 23) — studying at the Art Institute of Chicago, the researchers tried to determine what personality characteristics these students had as compared to students who were not studying art. About half had previous college experience, with about 10 percent having completed college in another institution. Their primary purpose was to determine how artists find problems: "By the careful observation of artists at work, we hoped to gain insights into the dynamics of this problem-finding approach, and perhaps to enlarge accepted ideas about the nature of thinking." Getzels and Csikszentmihalyi felt that problem-solving was not the crucial process in creative thinking, but rather finding the problem to solve.

The researchers studied the students for five years. They chose to follow up thirty-five men students, but none of the women students, because men are most often successful artists. Overall, the students were majors in fine art, industrial art, advertising art, and in art education, so the research also yielded some insights into the differences among personalities of students who chose various specialties. The students they followed, though, were fine arts majors.

## Characteristics of Art Students

Most of the students in the Getzels and Csikszentmihalyi study were from intact families, conventional in religious background. Over half had chosen art as a career between the ages of fourteen and nineteen, with more women than men deciding on art as a career before age ten. They chose art for self-discovery and self-knowledge, to gain an understanding of others, and to find out what's real and what's not. One young artist said, "I paint because it's necessary . . . it's something you have to say." Another said, "In other kinds of jobs, you rarely see the outcome of what you have been doing. I guess actually the drawing is me. There was charcoal, paint — but without me nothing would have happened." In other words, they chose art for intrinsic reasons that emphasized inner growth, self-discovery, and expression of feelings, rather than for extrinsic reasons that emphasize fame, recognition, and worldly gain.

In choosing art as a career, the students were realistic about their slim chances for financial reward. Older than other college students, many had chosen to go to art school after trying college or working for awhile. The parents of the men disapproved of this decision. One young man said that his father had supported him when he went to college, but now considered him a college dropout; he had to drive a cab to pay for his study at the Art Institute of Chicago. Frank Barron, in his 1972 study, *Artists in the Making,* similarly found that men artists had difficulty in being taken seriously by their families. The research revealed no clear childhood reasons for choosing the visual arts as a career. As Getzels and Csikszentmihalyi stated, "Instead of finding an inevitable destiny springing from a single source," there was "a higher complex formative process — innumerable events slowly building up to a final commitment."

Most of these artists had begun, as Hurwitz also showed, by copying cartoon characters as children do; and their drawings were often done when they experienced feelings of loneliness. This loneliness may have come from their mothers going to work or from the birth of a sibling. They discovered their talent, and that talent gave them a feeling of competence. The men artists remembered their mothers as being "warm and close," but their fathers were remembered as being "harsh." Getzels and Csikszentmihalyi said that ". . . when the young artists were adapting to the balance of forces in the family, they used art as a means of identifying with the mother and at the same time establishing their own competence and independence from the father." Their elementary years were remembered as being "bleak," but their high school years were a little better. The artists did not participate in athletics, but their artistic competence was beginning to show, and they designed stage sets, posters, and other art works that talented high school students usually do.

Among their young successful artists, Getzels and Csikszentmihalyi found that more of them were oldest sons. Many had not done well academically in school or college. They chose art because it was not a nine-to-five job. One artist had been a stutterer, and his skill in drawing gained him acceptance from peers. (Another stutterer was the writer John Updike, who is discussed in Chapter 7). One began to draw when a younger sibling was born. Another used drawing as a way to compete with older siblings. Getzels and Csikszentmihalyi pointed out that many young artists stick with drawing because they can control their environment better through drawing than through other means available to them. Their talent develops, and they get praise and recognition, so their motivation follows, and their values change as they come to realize that art has even more power than merely gaining them acceptance and praise; art has the power to interpret the meaning of life, and to help them resolve the problems of life.

The researchers used three main methods to study the young artists: (1) a biographical review, interviews, and observations; (2) school ratings such as grade point average, and ratings or originality and artistic potential; and (3) standardized instruments. The standardized tests fell into three categories: cognitive, perceptual, and personality.

What did all thest tests and inventories show about the artists? First, in their intelligence they were similar to college students, but they did less well when speed was required. As the authors said "quickness of response in standard intellectual tasks is not the forte of those who plan to become artists."

In perception, huge differences existed between the artists and regular college students. Not surprisingly, spatial perception was outstanding in both men and women, with women artists performing better than women college students. It is interesting to note, however, that the women artists still performed lower in spatial perception tests than the college men, while the men artists performed the highest of all.

In aesthetic judgment, both men and women art students scored twice as high as the college students. This was to be expected, even though the authors felt that aesthetic judgment does not have much to do with creativity. Aesthetic judgment is more an aspect of becoming a connoisseur or critic of art — becoming an art historian or a museum curator rather than an artist.

In their values, the arts students were quite "extreme," as the authors put it. Both women and men artists differed from college students in economic, aesthetic, social, and political values, and women artists differed from women college students on theoretical and religious values as well. Getzels and Csikszentmihalyi made the analogy that art students are committed to their profession in the way that the clergy are committed to their religions. Art students also apparently have very low economic and social values. Getzels and Csikszentmihalyi postulated that not caring much about society's opinions and not caring much about money are necessary for people who have careers "in which the only thing they can count on is economic insecurity," and where working alone in a studio constitutes the social milieu.

## Artists' Personalities

In personality, both the women and men artists were aloof, reserved, introspective, serious, and nonconforming to contemporary social values — that is, "standards of behavior and morality have little hold on them." Their personality measures had low scores in what is called "superego strength," or conscience. They were unconventional, subjective, intense, and imaginative. Independent, they preferred to make their own decisions, and their self-sufficiency was high. They were both radical and experimental. Indeed, the stereotype of the unconventional artist seems to have some basis if the results of this personality assessment are to be believed.

Artists also showed androgynous personalities. The women artists showed more masculine values than women college students of their age, and the men artists had more feminine personalities than men college students. Thus both genders have characteristics that have been traditionally associated with the opposite sex, and they could be considered to fall near the median on a masculinity-femininity continuum, where the extremes are the rigidly masculine Marlboro man or the rigidly feminine sweet young thing. The authors expressed this personality characteristic thus: "The psychology of creative men is a feminine psychology by comparison with less creative men; the psychology of creative women is a masculine psychology by comparison with less creative women."

A very interesting result was the uncovering of the artists' naiveté. The artists were not shrewd. Naiveté, in the sense of creativeness, is openness, and the artists were open to new ways of doing things, to see the old things in new ways. This enabled them to find creative problems to solve. They were not blasé about what they experienced; rather, they opened themselves to questioning with childlike wonder and awe. As discussed in Chapter 2, viewing the world with naiveté has been emphasized as a primary characteristic of the creative process. Ghiselin in his 1952 anthology, *The Creative Process,* noted that the creative person is always on the alert for "the alien, the dangerous," practicing "an imaginative surrender to every novelty that has even the most tenuous credentials." A look at the childlike yet sinister wonder with which the artist Maurice Sendak illustrates childhood fears is an example, as is the dreamwork of Paul Klee and Joan Miro and the circus of Calder. Red Grooms and Jonathan Borofsky also come to mind, in their ingenuous ways of looking at urban life.

Ideally, any work of art also teaches the perceiver to see old things in new ways. The artist approaches the world with newborn eyes, helping the jaded audience to see again. This is true in all the arts as well as the sciences. Magritte took naiveté to its essence. Suzi Gablik, in her 1976 book, *Magritte,* wrote, "For Magritte, paintings worth being painted or looked at have no reducible meaning: they *are* a meaning." Magritte said, "The mind loves the unknown. It loves images whose meaning is unknown, since the meaning of the mind itself is unknown."

*Differences Among Artists According to Specialty*

Getzels and Csikszentmihalyi found that students differed in their values, depending on the specialties they chose. Not surprisingly, fine arts majors cared less for economic things, and cared more for aesthetic things than the advertising and industrial arts majors. Again, not surprisingly, the advertising arts majors also had higher political values, and art education majors cared more for social issues. Fine arts majors were lowest of the art students in sociability, while the advertising arts majors scored highest. The fine arts majors were the most extreme, more naive, more imaginative, less conforming, and less conscientious than the other arts students.

## The Successful, High-Achieving Artists

The authors chose to follow thirty-five male fine arts students through the beginning of their careers. Women were not included because as late as the mid-1970s, women fine arts students were less likely to become well-known artists. Getzels and Csikszentmihalyi used teacher ratings to distinguish high and low achievers. The high achieving students seemed to become successful by the strength of their personalities, rather than by their perceptual or intellectual abilities. All the high achievers fitted the personality extremes described above: they were aloof, had low ego-strength, were introspective, sensitive, imaginative, self-sufficient, and nonconforming. They all had little care for the economic aspects of life.

Although women were not included in the follow-up, nevertheless their success was evaluated while in art school and showed findings that contrasted with those for the men. In fact, the most successful women students were dramatically different. Their high spatial visualization abilities had the closest relationship with how their teachers judged their success in art school. The authors evaluated the differences this way: art teachers seem to appraise a male student on the basis of long-range possibilities suggested by his personality, rather than on his perceptual aptitudes; they seem to appraise a female student on the basis of the perceptual skills she actually displayed. This may reflect a tacit belief that a man will develop his aptitudes with time, while a woman who does not initially have them will abandon her aspirations and settle for more traditional pursuits. This differential treatment by teachers may still be the case. In my article, "Why Are There So Few? (Creative Women: Artists, Mathematicians, Musicians)" (1991), I postulated that women's search for connectedness dominates their development during and just after their college years, to the detriment of their drive to succeed in their chosen field of creative endeavor.

## The Classic Experiment Regarding Problem-Finding in America

Getzels and Csikszentmihalyi went beyond the mere reporting of the results of tests and measurements of the cognitive, personality, and perceptual abilities of the students. They explored the students' abilities to find problems to solve via their art. In a studio were twenty-seven objects, for example, a feather, a mannequin, a bunch of grapes, a velvet hat, a glass prism. They asked each of their study group of male fine arts students to come into the studio, rearrange the objects, and then make a drawing. There were no time constraints, and the directions were that they could do anything they wanted with the objects, "so long as the drawing will be pleasing to you."

The artists were observed by expert artists and by trained psychologists. As the fine arts students formulated the artistic problem, the observers focused on three aspects: how many objects the students touched; how unique the objects were that were chosen for the arrangement; and what exploratory behavior the students exhibited. While the students were drawing, the observers focused on the process of how the problem was structured and on the behaviors of the students while they created the works of art. They then interviewed the students, asking them how concerned they had been in finding the right arrangement before, during, and after making the drawing.

The researchers then asked art teachers, artists, and business and mathematics students, to evaluate the works for originality and craftsmanship. From this information they devised a score for problem-finding. Who had been most original, and who had shown the most craftsmanship in manipulating the twenty-seven objects, in choosing which to focus on, and in making pleasing works of art? In this longitudinal study of successful and unsuccessful fine arts students, the researchers found that those with the highest problem-finding orientations were the most successful. Five years after the students had graduated, Getzels and Csikszentmihalyi contacted them again, to see who was successfully pursuing art as a career and who was not. About half, or fifteen of the young men, were in careers at least peripherally related to art and were still painting, about one-fourth had quit painting, and about one-fourth said they wanted to paint, but were not presently doing so.

Those who were most successful had the following attributes. The successful students had the best grades and ratings in their studio courses, though they may not have had good grades in their academic courses. In family background, both of their parents were likely to be professionals, and from higher socioeconomic backgrounds. The authors speculated that a higher socioeconomic status might encourage problem-finding behavior, because the artists have a family to financially help them if times get tough, freeing them to pursue a marginal career. Also, their early environments may have included "more sensory and intellectual stimulation." The personality characteristic that seemed most related to being a successful artist was low self-sentiment — that is lacking self-control, lacking a desire to conform to acceptable social behavior, and being unconcerned with social approval.

They also found that oldest sons were more likely than middle sons to experience success as artists. Oldest sons were also more likely to have had highly rated problems (in the experiment above), leading the authors to say that there may be "a peculiar constellation of experiences that firstborn sons undergo, alien especially to middle sons" that leads to a tendency to find the right problems and to be oriented to discovery, as well as to achieving success in art. The Goertzels (1962, 1978) and Simonton (1988) also found similar predominance of older children achieving success.

The study is still going on. Getzels, in a 1987 essay called "Creativity, Intelligence, and Problem-Finding," reported that the recent correlation of the "rankings of problem-finding with success and status of the professional artists, who have been followed from age twenty to mid-life, is now .35." This low correlation number, indicates only a small positive relationship between problem-finding and success as an artist, a finding which conflicts with earlier data. One reason that the correlation may not be higher may be the currency of the "artist of the moment" or the "in" artist, the artist whose work is popular but not necessarily the best. The quality of work of the truly talented artist, one who is high in problem-finding, may not be recognized until after his or her death. In fact, true success or eminence in any creative field often does not come during the artist's lifetime, but is based on the reputation his work gains after his death.

The Getzels and Csikszentmihalyi study is only one of the studies of visual artists. However, it is unique because of its exploration of problem-finding behavior. Other studies have looked at personality variables and factors contributing to success.

### Does Higher Socioeconomic Status Encourage Problem-Finding?

Pendarvis, Howley, and Howley, in *The Abilities of Gifted Children* (1990), observed that students in schools with higher socioeconomic-level families are treated differently by their teachers as well as their parents. Rather than directive teaching, as is found in lower socioeconomic level schools, students in more affluent schools are encouraged to explore, to think critically, to use judgment. A typical exchange in a lower socioeconomic level school may be "Now children, repeat after me the steps in the scientific method: first, form an hypothesis . . ." In a higher socioeconomic level school, it may be, "Let's discuss your hypothesis again, John. How are you going to set up an experiment to prove that?"

## The Importance of Luck and Other Social Factors for Success

Though problem-finding is important, so are other factors. Tannenbaum, in *Gifted Children* (1983), a seminal work on giftedness, pointed out that much of the realization of giftedness comes from factors that are other than personality or intellectual. Luck, for example, plays a large part in the realization of potential. The phenomenon of show-biz parents having show-biz kids (the Fondas, for example) is perhaps less a function of heredity than of the nearness of these children to movie making and to key powerful people. The fortune of birth has made many the film stars of today. Simonton, in *Scientific Genius* (1988), called it "proximity," which also exhibits itself in the very important step of choosing mentors. Getzels and Csikszentmihalyi called it the "social context of art."

Talent is not enough. For artists to be successful in realizing their creativity, they must engage in certain specific behaviors. Getzels and Csikszentmihalyi said they need to do four things:

1. Rent or buy a loft so the artist can socialize, show his work, and establish a reputation for being a serious artist — that is, one who has made the commitment by renting a working space.

2. Exhibit work in an art show. A group show is acceptable, but a one-person show sponsored by a private art gallery that represents one's work is preferable.

3. Move to New York City, for no artist is taken seriously as a major fine artist in the United States unless he or she has been validated by the New York City art scene. Tama Janowitz's 1986 novel, *Slaves of New York*, amply illustrates the art world among the young artists of New York in the 1980s. (Los Angeles artists would disagree, as would those who thrive in other art centers in the United States).

4. Relocate to a provincial art center. Though viewed as less desirable, a move for career visibility can be made to such popular centers as Taos in the southwest, or Provincetown in the northeast. Some artists also take the path of getting a master of fine arts degree from a univer-

sity or art school, and then teaching in the academy while doing their art on the side. This is considered a safety step, and the artist takes the risk of being isolated from the trend setters of the art world, and stagnating.

Such social necessities go against the personality grain of the creative visual artist, who is a loner, an iconoclast, difficult to get along with, valuing aesthetics far more than money. Getzels and Csikszentmihalyi said that many young men, when they moved, took two years to get back into the swing of producing art. Their art works changed in character, style, and size. They experienced depressions and frustrations, caused by the pressures of establishing themselves in different geographies than where they had begun their art. These conflicts affected them and their families. Several had spouses who worked or were rich. The necessity of the steady breadwinner cannot be overemphasized in the lives of creative artists whose work does not sell. Many turn to teaching, or to working for arts groups doing short residencies in elementary and secondary schools.

Robinson's 1989 biography, *Georgia O'Keeffe,* illustrates the career path of an artist with strong ties to New York City's "loft culture." O'Keeffe, a native of Sun Prairie, Wisconsin, arrived in New York City after studying for a year at the Art Institute of Chicago and taking classes at the University of Virginia with a visiting professor from Teacher's College of Columbia University. This teacher, Alon Bement, propounded the theories of Arthur Wesley Dow. O'Keeffe was taken by the theories and came to study with Dow at Columbia in 1914, at the age of twenty-seven. A year later she began taking classes at the Art Students League, and her group of friends began regularly visiting the Alfred Steiglitz gallery called "291." Later, O'Keeffe was granted a one-woman show by Steiglitz, who was shown her work by Anita Pollitzer, one of O'Keeffe's New York friends.

Although O'Keeffe didn't live in New York City at the time, her connections there were strong, and after her relationship with Steiglitz began, she spent many years in New York City exhibiting at Steiglitz's various galleries before establishing residency in New Mexico. Whether her work would have had its impact without her New York City "loft" cannot be known. Certainly Steiglitz's falling in love with her, moving in with her and eventually breaking up his marriage, as well as his dedication to the promotion of her work, did not harm O'Keeffe's visibility.

The artist Elizabeth Murray "lives in a loft in lower Manhattan, and her studio, a long bright room, occupies the front half," according to Deborah Solomon in a 1991 article called "Celebrating Paint." Murray grew up in Illinois in an eccentric family that Murray described as "unorthodox" and "goofball." While studying at the Art Institute of Chicago and Mills College, she "spent the whole time fantasizing about moving to New York." She taught in Buffalo for two years and arrived in New York in 1967, where she rented a loft. She married, had a son, and taught art at a private school, trying to do her own work at night. Her first one-woman show was in 1976, when she was thirty-six, and her fame began to grow within the New York art world. In addition to her son by her first marriage, she and her second husband had twin daughters when Murray was in her forties; however, by then her career was well-established. This phenomenon of career success/motherhood is consonant with Foley's 1986 work on the careers of artist mothers, which will be discussed later in this chapter. Murray, like O'Keeffe, also taught school to support herself while her career was being developed. (Although O'Keeffe wanted to have children, Steiglitz, who was much older than she, refused, saying that she would diffuse her passion for her work if they had children). Murray has been called "one of the few true talents to have risen out of the commercial hoopla of the 1980s." Again, the influence of the "loft culture" of New York City is evident in the path of her success.

## Other Studies of Visual Artists

Other studies of artists are presented in the upcoming section. One is Barron's well-known *The Making Of An Artist* (1972). Barron administered tests of intelligence, personality, and divergent production to students at the San Francisco Art Institute and the Rhode Island School of Design. To test divergent production, you will recall, is to give a paper and pencil measurement of how fluent, how flexible, how elaborative, and how original a person is. The Myers-Briggs Type Indicator has also been administered to artists, with interesting results. Anne Roe's 1975 study of artists who had already achieved will also be discussed. Sloane and Sosniak in 1985 conducted another study of accomplished sculptors in connection with Bloom's Development of Talent Research Project at the University of Chicago. Foley, in 1986, studied painters who were also mothers. Other biographical studies were done by the Goertzels in 1962 and 1978, by Shekerjian in 1990, and by Alice Miller in 1990.

## Roe's Findings

In "Painters and Painting" (1975), Anne Roe described her study of twenty-three successful male artists who averaged fifty one years of age — that is, they were long-time achievers. Fourteen were from the lower-middle and middle classes. Their fathers' occupations ranged from farmer to usher to brigadier general to businessman, and three of their fathers were themselves painters, with three others having connections with the art world. That is, 25 percent of them had fathers in the visual arts. Most had gone to art school, but only 12 percent were college graduates. Their fathers generally disapproved of their choices of professions because being an artist means being poor. Their mothers approved in the sense of wanting their sons to do what they wanted to do. However, the mothers who had suffered the economic deprivations of being themselves wives of artists disapproved.

In their relationships with their parents, Roe postulated that the artists had "unresolved oedipal problems." Roe also found that 25 percent of them had suffered rejection or social isolation or had serious childhood illnesses. Twenty-five percent of them also had lost a sibling or a parent through death. All of the artists were married or had been married, one of them four times. She administered the Rorschach ink blot test and the Thematic Apperception Test (TAT) to measure personality and personal dynamics. Because the artists objected to the inferior artistry of the stimulus pictures, administering the tests was difficult. When the results were sent to blind interraters, the results that came back were "so divergent in coverage, tone, and inference" that she could not use the results. Her experiences with administering personality tests to creative people are similar to what other psychologists have found — that creative people often looked askance and were sarcastic or even rebellious about being subjected to pencil and paper analysis.

## Barron Finds Gentleman Pirates

*Artists in the Making* (1972) described Barron's study of young artists at the San Francisco Art Institute and at the Rhode Island School of Design. Barron administered psychological and personality tests to the students and found patterns similar to those of the arts students in Chicago. They were not interested in making a good impression on other people and were not as well socialized as other students. Both women and men were similar. Though they cared little about social conformity, they had a high need to achieve success independently, on their own. They were more flexible in outlook and less cheerful than others. On the Minnesota Multiphasic Psychological Inventory, the art students, both men and women, scored in the "pathological" ranges on the various scales. This may indicate their low need for conformity. They differed from truly psychotic personalities, though, in that they were far less rigid. Barron described the men artists as "gentleman pirate" types, who showed "an independence of thought and unconventionality" which made their experiences and their conclusions unusual. The flair with which they lived their lives may account for the "pirate" description. Perhaps they swaggered when they walked, but they also paid attention to nuance and detail, and they were open to experiences, sensitive to the world around them, and were sensually tuned in.

The women also were unconventional, flexible, open, and independent, approaching life vigorously yet with sensitivity to details. Their patterns were different from the men artists in that they had less flamboyance, seemed more naive, and were more introverted. Remember, that's compared to the men artists. In the normal world, these women artists, compared with other women, would appear to be adventurous, independent, and very willful.

The art students had interests most closely resembling those of musicians, artists, author-journalists, advertisers and architects. They rejected such occupations as school superintendent, business education teacher, army officer, and other occupations which call for managing people physically and in practical ways. They were highly dedicated to their work and to their beliefs, and were very independent. They preferred working alone and often lost themselves in their work. They could visualize their emotional lives. In other studies by Barron, described in the 1968 book, *Creative and Personal Freedom*, he found that highly creative people tended to be pacifists, eschewing violence as a way of expression. He said that "pacifistic tendencies are related to personality development and are found most prominently in persons whose inner life and creativity are more highly developed." Perhaps this explains the passionate antiwar sentiments of many people in the arts. He also related these pacifistic tendencies to the androgyny of creative people, saying, "It is still the men and not the women among us who decide to go to war."

Barron also compared and differentiated among painters who were representational artists, abstract expressionists who used geometrical forms, and those who used dynamic color in their art. For example, those who painted representational art were often highly verbal, poor at judging the quality of mosaics, unoriginal in inkblot tests, and more concerned about social status. Their work was highly rated by the public and by the faculty. The abstract expressionists preferred asymmetry and complexity and were good at judging the quality of mosaics. They got good grades in drawing, but poor ratings from psychologists in originality. Highly geometrical painters did poorly in writing and drawing in school but were excellent in aesthetic judgment. They were also high in independence and autonomy. Painters who used dynamic colors in their work were rated as spontaneous and independent. They were good at judging the use of color in mosaic designs, but poor in judging the use of form.

### The MBTI Shows N and F

The Myers-Briggs Type Indicator (MBTI) has been used to indicate the Jungian-based personality types of many occupational groups, including scientists, artists, laborers, writers and counselors. Most creativity studies using the MBTI were done in conjunction with the Institute for Personality Assessment and Research, by Barron, MacKinnon, Gough, Helson, Crutchfield, and others. The Institute's subjects of study, chosen by peer nomination, included architects, mathematicians, scientists, and writers.

Simon (1979) conducted Myers-Briggs testing on 114 professional fine artists. The personality types, in descending order of frequency were:

> INFP (Introverted, Intuitive, Feeling, Perceiving)
> INFJ (Introverted, Intuitive, Feeling, Judging)
> ENFP (Extraverted, Intuitive, Feeling, Perceiving)
> ENFJ (Extraverted, Intuitive, Feeling, Judging)

The presence of the intuitive (N) and feeling (F) types stand out. The artists overwhelmingly preferred intuition as a mode of perception. Jung saw that people perceive the world in two ways, either sensing or intuiting. The person who uses the intuitive mode prefers to understand the world by the way of the unconscious. A sensing person may describe an orange as "juicy" and "orange," while an intuitive person may describe an orange as "Clockwork" or "Tequila Sunrise." Intuitive persons look towards possibilities and may not notice realities. They prefer to make decisions on what may not be seen and heard, but on what may come as a hunch or sudden insight.

Myers and McCaulley, in the MBTI manual, describe the INFP, INFJ, and ENFP personalities as follows:

> INFP: Full of enthusiasms and loyalties, but seldom talk of these until they know you well. Care about learning, ideas, language, and independent projects of their own. Tend to undertake too much, then somehow get it done. Friendly, but often too absorbed in what they are doing to be sociable. Little concerned with possessions and physical surroundings.
>
> INFJ: Succeed by perseverence, originality, and desire to do whatever is needed or wanted. Put their best efforts into their work. Quietly forceful, conscientious, concerned for others. Respected for their firm principles. Likely to be honored and followed for their clear convictions as to how best to serve the common good.
>
> ENFP: Warmly enthusiastic, high-spirited, ingenious, imaginative. Able to do almost anything that interests them. Quick with a solution for any difficulty and ready to help anyone with a problem. Often rely on their ability to improvise instead of preparing in advance. Can usually find compelling reasons for whatever they want.

The Myers-Briggs Type Indicator will be discussed in more detail. For now, it seems obvious that artists have definite personality type preferences in common. Please note that these are preferences, and as Myers and McCaulley said, "preferences are like handedness; one uses both hands, but reaches first with the preferred hand which is probably more adept."

## Goertzel, Goertzel, Goertzel and 700 Famous People

The Goertzel's studies, *Cradles of Eminence* (1962) and *Three Hundred Eminent Personalities* (1978) are two interesting biographical studies of eminent people, artists among them. In the 1962 study, 400 people were chosen about whom at least two books had been written, and in the 1978 study, they chose 300 people also about whom at least two books had been written. Common threads among them allowed conclusions to be drawn about their lives. The eminent were divided into four groups: the political, the literary, the artistic, and other. The artistic category included sculptors, painters, actors, composers, film directors, dancers, and performers. Of the 1978 group, 75 of 300 fell into this category.

Goertzel, Goertzel, and Goertzel found that those in the artistic category were less likely to have gone to college than others who had biographies written about them; as a corollary, the artistic people were not known as being good students in schools, and were not likely to be omnivorous readers. However, they were more likely to have had special schooling, perhaps because their precocity stood out early. Another interesting fact about the artistic group was that more of them were first and second generation immigrants than were the others.

Another observation they made was that artists are likely to come from families with other members who practiced the same art: "There are families who paint, families who sculpt, families who act, families who are musical." They also noted the families of Calder, Renoir, Wyeth, Picasso, Charles Aznavour, Charles Ives, Georgia O'Keeffe, Edith Piaf, Maurice Utrillo. They said that the family backgrounds and emphasis within the family upon the specific creative form did not uphold "the myth of the lonely, temperamental artist starving alone in a garret."

Another artistic family was that of the Van Goghs. Vincent served an apprenticeship in his uncle's gallery, as did his brother, Theo. Their sister also showed an interest in art, although Vincent did not believe she should pursue this interest.

> Our sister writes extremely well, and describes a landscape or a view of the town as it might have been in a page of a modern novel. I always urge her to occupy herself rather with household matters than with artistic things, for I know that she is too sensitive, and at her age she would find it difficult to develop herself artistically. I am very much afraid that she suffers from a thwarted artistic desire, but she is so full of vitality that she will get over it. (Stone, 1937, p. 466)

Germaine Greer, in her 1979 book, *The Obstacle Race,* about women visual artists through the ages, wrote that most women who were visual artists came from artistic dynasties, and if they did receive training in visual art, their work was often not signed. She also pointed out that easel painting has not been a preferred medium for women, and wondered why easel painting has gained such credibility as being the most prestigious way of doing graphic arts. Women such as Van Gogh's sister, if they did not work in art, would have been urged to make miniatures of their fathers' and brothers' works, or to design fabrics or gardens, or to be nurturing. Greer said, "Daughters were ruled by love and loyalty; they were more highly praised for virtue and sweetness than for their talent, and they devalued their talent accordingly."

### Having a Supportive Husband Helps

In 1986, Foley studied fifteen artists, all of whom were mothers of children ages three months to eight years, with regard to their ability to combine mothering and being painters. She found that though they were committed to their work, they experienced role conflicts. In order to do both, they used child care help in the home or at day-care centers, and they had husbands who were extremely supportive of their careers. The women were artists before they became mothers, and so were well-launched in their careers, having galleries to represent them and showing regularly in juried exhibits.

In their personalities they exhibited the same core traits as the artists elsewhere here described, and Foley said, "it cannot be said that women artists' commitment and motivation to becoming artists is any less than men's: rather, it appears to be more a difference in the timing of the commitment." The women artists were passionately committed to their careers, and to their families. Foley quoted one of them thus:

> Interviewer: What does it mean to you to be an artist?
> Artist: Almost everything! I mean it is me, it's what I actually am. I don't just make art. I am it. I live it out . . . I mean my whole life.

Another artist said,

> I think when you become a mother, you experience a kind of washing away of your identity. You're not sure

who you are anymore because you have this strange new relationship to these little people. And, I think because of that, because you end up wondering who the heck you are, that I went back with more vigor and determination into my art work in order to establish that identity and that anchor — that this is what I'm supposed to do and this is who I am and now I can deal with you guys.

Foley found, in her comparison group of mothers in professions such as law and business, that the conflicts were somewhat different. While the artist mothers wished that they had time to paint, the mothers in the other professions wished they had more time with their families. The artist mothers had more flexible schedules, often using the period from 9 a.m. to 3 p.m., when their children went to school, for their art. The other professional mothers were involved in careers with inflexible hours; according to Foley, "The problem for the professional mother was meeting, rather than defining, the demand."

The intrinsic rewards of creating made for a strong emotional well-being in the artist mothers. One of them said,

> The most gratifying internal — which is ultimately more important — is if I feel like I've answered a question. To me, each painting I do is like plunging into the abyss I never know if I'm going to swim out . . . by swim out of the abyss, of course, I mean solve the visual problems that painting has.

Here we see that the conflicts that arose with being a mother and an artist didn't diminish the rewards of doing the art. It should be noted that these women were in the middle and higher socioeconomic levels, did not have to struggle financially, had help with the children, and had supportive spouses.

## Sculptors Show Commitment

Sloane and Sosniak (1985) chose twelve men and eight women sculptors, under age forty, who had won either Guggenheim Fellowships or the Rome Award. Some had studied in the same schools with the same teachers, but none of them had studied with one another. Interviews revealed no outstanding demographic patterns. As many were first-borns as later-borns. Among the fathers, there were as many professionals as blue-collar workers. Among the mothers, as many worked outside the home as did not work, and there were as many professionals as nonprofessionals. There were as many sculptors from higher socioeconomic levels as from lower socioeconomic and middle levels.

For their elementary school years, the sculptors remembered, as do most artists, intense drawing and the emphasis on products, on making the drawings realistic and recognizable representations of what they were drawing. Their social life was normal, playing in the neighborhood with the other kids. Only one of their fathers was a commercial artist, though some of them came from families that went to museums, talked about art, and valued art.

The sculptors didn't remember elementary school art as challenging, or even as art. In out-of-school activities, they were more likely to take music lessons as art lessons. The authors speculated that this was because out-of-school art lessons are not as available as music lessons. It is also expected that art is a school subject in the elementary years, and that the students got art. However, in their elementary years, the sculptors did produce a lot of art — outside of school as well as in. The parents of the sculptors saved much of their work and displayed it to the researchers. This, in itself, is an indication that art was valued in the homes.

During high school the sculptors began to gain identity and recognition as artists. Several of them said that they were the best at drawing, or the best at building or welding. They were referred to in their yearbooks as "Rembrandt," or "the class artist." Several were honor students, good at everything they did, or had several other areas of expertise, such as athletics, music, or journalism. About half of the parents were actively helpful in finding teachers or in supplying equipment. The teenagers' work was also commented on positively, and displayed.

Taking art in high school was not universal among the sculptors, and some remembered art classes in high school as the class for "flunkies." In many high schools, if students are musicians and play in the band or orchestra, they can't take art classes, and vice versa. This may have precluded the sculptors from taking art, for group music such as band, orhestra, or chorus is a more social activity, and perhaps more socially accepted.

When they graduated from high school, these sculptors typically had no idea about what it took to make art a profession, and possessed no portfolios, perhaps no high school art classes on their transcripts, and perhaps no letters of recommendation from art professionals or teachers. But somehow they stumbled into four-year art degree programs, and three quarters of them went on to earn master of fine arts degrees.

They often transferred to programs designed for fine artists, not for art educators. The teachers they found were professional artists themselves, who worked in the field and had access to a network of other artists as well as connections to the art world. Even a short studio class with a professional artist had great impact. One said, "I mean, he was a very important person in the art world. And the fact that he was teaching at that school, it was the spirit of it or something." Another said, "Your teachers were professionals. We went to New York. We saw the shows. I knew what was going on." Another said, "If you don't have contact with someone who is doing good work, how do you know what's possible?"

As they took courses and studied, the competition and exposure to the other students increased in intensity. They all learned from each other. Almost all the sculptors went through a stage of imitating artists, trying to find the essence of what made a Henry Moore or a Jackson Pollock. But the breakthrough to finding their own styles, their own problems, eventually came. One said,

> In art you make up your own problems. And the art problems usually come from the immediate history . . . If on the walls of Fifty-seventh Street they're hanging abstract expressionist paintings, the [art student] will usually pick up from that point and say, "Now where do I take Jackson Pollock from here? What do I do next?" (p. 128)

The decision to become sculptors came as their works evolved. Often their works became progressively bigger and more three dimensional. Most were painters before becoming sculptors, probably because art education is very painting oriented. Some of them shifted to pottery before they shifted to sculpture.

The decision to commit their careers to making art — to being artists — came, as one sculptor said, "As a progressive or sequential revelation. It's nothing like a blinding flash. It didn't happen at any one time." When they did decide to commit their lives to making art, they did so "ferociously." For some that commitment didn't come for seven or eight years after art school. As one said, "Partially it had to do with really floundering around for personal identity as well as artistic identity." The artists who attained success often felt lucky, but some said that their luck was a matter of preparation. They had prepared themselves to be ready to take the chances that came into their paths. "I've had this uncanny luck at always being at the right place at the right time with the right people."

Even though they had reached forty, they were still viewed as young artists and the authors noted that the sculptors' commitment hadn't flagged; they still were doing what they wanted to do. One of the sculptors said, "Nobody calls me in the morning and says, 'Hey, it's time to mix that concrete, kid' . . . You do it because you want to do it."

## Recent Research

The vogue for large-scale psychological studies of artists' personality characteristics has passed. Large, expensive studies of groups of creatively gifted people are not being done. Instead, the focus is the case study or qualitative research on one or a small number of people, and assuming that the case is representative of the population. Quantitative research, by contrast, chooses a larger random sample of the population and generalizes from that. The biographical technique of historiometry as practiced by Simonton (*Scientific Genius*, 1988; *Genius, Creativity, and Leadership,* 1984) abstracts generalizations from historical populations such as musicians, writers, artists. For example, for the 1984 book Simonton examined the biographies of "2,012 philosophers, 690 classical composers, 38 American presidents, and 301 geniuses." Some of his findings are in Chapters 8 and 9. Now, however, we will look at two mainstream books on creativity, for most people read mainstream books.

### Pablo Picasso Was Influenced by an Earthquake

Compelling case studies have been done by the Swiss psychoanalyst Alice Miller; among her books is *The Drama of the Gifted Child* (1981), in which she conjectured that parental narcissism is a main difficulty that bright children have, for parents often put their own frustrated expectations upon their children. In *The Untouched Key* (1990), Miller postulated that the work of visual atrists such as Picasso is the result of childhood trauma. His *Guernica,* one of the most critiqued, lauded, and famous works of the twentieth century, details the beginning of the Spanish Civil War in 1936. Widely viewed as a representation of the cruelties of war, Miller saw in Picasso's painting the realization of repressed childhood trauma.

Studying Picasso's life, reading all the biographies extant about him, she noted that all glossed over his childhood, saying that he came from a happy family, his father an artist also. Instead, she found that at the age of three, he experienced the consequences of a devastating earthquake in which many villagers were killed. Three days after that earthquake his first sister was born. His second sister was born shortly before he began school, which he hated. Miller postulated that these two births caused him to paint angry portraits of women throughout his life. She said, "The three-year-old Picasso was painfully reminded of the trauma of his own birth by the horrors of the earthquake, the proximity of death, and the birth of his sister."

These shocks, however, were compensated for by his warm and happy home life. For instance, Picasso's indulgent parents permitted him to quit school early (he consequently never properly learned mathematics or reading) because he so protested going. Miller concluded that the severe shocks, along with nurturing at home, combined to make Picasso as creative as he was. She wrote that if his father had not carried him and made him feel safe in his fatherly strong arms, Picasso could perhaps have become psychotic, and in repressing these childhood traumas, "would have become an upstanding, compulsive functionary in Franco's Spain."

Miller's point in the book is that people respond to childhood trauma with creativity, or with destruction. They become creative if there is some warmth in the traumatic environment, and they become destructive if there is no warmth. Miller's attributing Picasso's creativity to his reaction to an early childhood earthquake and to the birth of sisters is an example of the psychoanalytic point of view of human behavior, that the one or two incidents are the "key" to a person's later behavior and personality.

### Robert Irwin Stares at a Line

Denise Shekerjian employed an interview approach to study creativity; her subjects, forty MacArthur Fellows, were described in her 1990 book, *Uncommon Genius*. Often called the "genius award" for creativity, the MacArthur award is a grant of from $30,000 to $70,000 per year for five years to continue doing what the recipient has been doing. People cannot apply for these awards but are chosen by an anonymous panel. Among those MacArthur Fellows interviewed were the lawyer Joan Abrahamson; the political scientist Robert Axelrod; the psychologist Howard Gardner; the cultural anthropologist Shelly Errington; the paleontologist Stephan Jay Gould; the filmmakers Frederick Wiseman and John Sayles; the poets Joseph Brodsky, Brad Leithauser, and John Ashbery; the educational administrator Deborah Meier; the conservationist Patrick Noonan; and one visual artist, Robert Irwin.

Robert Irwin's life in art could be called a prime example of problem-finding behavior. This designer of environmental sculptures came to his specialty through a long, hard process. He started in an art school and successfully exhibited as an abstract expressionist. Though he had the requisite shows, reviews, and awards, he became obsessed with the meaning of form and image. He took his art so seriously that he spent the years 1962 through 1964 in one room, painting the same painting over and over again so that he could discern exactly where to place two parallel lines, in order to begin again in understanding what art is.

While forming this philosophy, he would stare at the painting for hour after hour, not allowing his attention to waver. From that experience he formed a philosophy of art and creativity that caused him to move from the studio to the environment. He was "challenged," "excited," and "renewed" by his art, and he formulated his problems by looking deeply into the art itself. Shekerjian summarized Irwin's creativity by saying it is realized in the doing of the art itself. Irwin "got right down into the process and stayed there."

Shekerjian's and Miller's two books showed the visual artist to be much the same as revealed by earlier studies of larger numbers of artists. Visual art (as well as all arts) is learned in the doing, in the problem-finding, not the problem-solving, and the creative production is the result of motivation formed by childhood experiences. No massive psychological testing has indicated differently. The component of talent is essential in considering any of the various types of these creative people. Talent is necessary, but not sufficient, in the realization of creative production. The studies indicate that motivation and circumstances, as well as the historical and the personal milieu, also make a contribution. That inherited or acquired variable called talent would seem to be what divides the hobbyist from the careerist.

## Summary

1.  The visual artists showed independence, intellect, passion, persistence, and a rejection of conventional economic values.

2.  Their talent for art, though generally shown early in life, was often not formally developed until after high school.

3.  Gender differences were apparent in spatial ability and treatment by teachers.

4.  Though problem-finding abilities are important, chance, luck, and proximity to a loft culture were necessary in the realization of their promise.

5.  Visual artists were intuitive, and feeling.

6.  They sometimes experienced childhood trauma.

# Chapter 6

## Creative Writers

*A writer is someone born with a gift. An athlete can run. A painter can paint. A writer has a facility with words. A good writer can also think. Isn't that enough to define a writer by?*

— Cynthia Ozick

*If people only knew what lies at the heart of my novels! What a tumult of desires these carefully written pages conceal! I sometimes have a loathing for the furious cravings that gave me no peace except when I am working.*

— Julian Green

*I know my troubled nature and have tried to contain it along creative lines.*

— John Cheever

*A writer's self-consciousness, for which he is much scorned, is really a mode of interestedness, that inevitably turns outward.*

— John Updike

According to a recent survey of single people which asked what were the most desirable occupations for a mate, poet was near the top, as was novelist. In stating this preference for "writer as spouse," were these men and women choosing a fantasy? A stereotype that has little to do with reality? For the truth is that writers write. They write obsessively and at odd hours, and they require a solitude that excludes the spouse, along with everyone else. A poet, novelist, and playwright once told me that his wife left him, in part, because he spent so many hours all alone, writing, and she wanted him to be more sociable.

Perhaps those survey respondents thought marriage to a writer would be exciting. Imagine the thrill of sitting beside Coleridge as he wrote "Kubla Kahn," sprung full-blown from his unconscious, in a rush of opium-induced inspiration! But the truth, according to biographers, is that Coleridge had written several drafts of "Kubla Khan" before this reputed inspired visit of the Muse. And to watch a writer write is, well, boring. Most movies and plays about writers have focused on their personal lives, for seeing them do their work is not very exciting. The process of production of their art is solitary. Not romantic at all.

What leads one to choose such a profession? Creative writers — poets, playwrights, novelists, story writers, essayists — have definite personality characteristics. Not the least among them is an urge to communicate to the world what they think, as well as to discover, through writing, what they think. The reason someone becomes a writer, as Joyce Carol Oates said in *(Woman) Writer* (1988), is that the person needs to "verify experience by way of language." It is that simple. The writer needs to write, and "experience itself is not authentic," Oates said, "until it has been transcribed by way of language." In other words, the writer knows what she thinks only after she has written it down. Katherine Anne Porter in her *Paris Review* interview said, "This thing between me and my writing is the strongest bond I have ever had — stronger than any bond or any engagement with any human being or with any other work I've ever done."

Writers are different from one another, of course. Poets differ from novelists, essayists differ from playwrights. Simonton, in his 1986 article, "Biographical Typicality, Eminence and Achievement Styles," showed that writers and poets were apt to be from the city and have nonreligious, small families, with nonsupportive fathers and unhappy home environments; not surprisingly, the writers were voracious readers. Simonton calculated that poets reach their peaks of productivity at about age thirty-nine, while fiction and nonfiction writers peak at around age forty-three. In *Genius, Creativity, and Leadership* (1984) he wrote that "Twice as much of a poet's lifetime output comes from the twenties as is the case for novelists," but this may vary according to the type of work being written. Lyric poets (in addition to creative mathematicians) tend to peak early; many have died young. According to Simonton, "This youthfulness of poetic and mathematical creativity makes it feasible for poets and mathematicians to die at tragically early ages and still find a place in the annals of history."

Writers often write across genres. Is Tess Gallagher a poet or a short story writer? Was Raymond Carver a short story writer or a poet? John Updike is a prolific reviewer, essayist, and poet, as well as novelist and short story writer. So is Joyce Carol Oates, whose yearly production of novels, poetry, short stories, nonfiction, and essays is nothing short of frightening to less productive writers. (Yet some writers stick to their niche. A case in point is the poet David Citino, who told me that everything he tries to write comes out as a poem). The ability to cross genres is an example of what Gruber called a "network of enterprises," all feeding each other. Gruber used this term in regard to the scientist Charles Darwin, referring to his related projects, but it applies equally well to writers.

Linguistic intelligence is listed by Gardner, in *Frames of Mind,* as one of the seven types of intelligence. In discussing different kinds of writers, he asserted that the poet composes in the most difficult verbal art, one that requires the greatest verbal or linguistic intelligence. The poet must have these language talents: (1) an ability to sense the several meanings of words; (2) an ability to position the words so that their meanings resonate with words on other lines, or a spatial ability with words; and (3) an ability to catch, in an imagistic way, the feelings that made the poet want to make the poem.

Gardner further differentiated among various types of creative writers. The novelist wants to "wrest the essence, the real truth," from life. The writer of narratives wants to show the reader what he has experienced or envisioned. Translation is possible for plays, novels, and essays, but not for poems. Poetry is untranslatable, as Frost said.

Who are the poets and writers of today? A *Directory of American Poets and Fiction Writers* lists names and addresses of contemporary poets and fiction writers who have published at least one novel, or three short stories, or twelve poems in at least three different literary publications, or they must have won literary awards, or any combination of these. About 6,600 American writers have met these qualifications. There is a lively literary world in America, even with the consolidation and commercialization of major publishing houses. While the sensational aspects of the lives of poets and writers will always draw attention, these and the others who are writing, alone in their rooms, collecting rejection letters, are the real story of the creative writer.

## Barron's and Other Studies of Creative Writers

Donald MacKinnon, in *In Search of Human Effectiveness* (1978), described the work of the Institute for Personality Assessment and Research (IPAR), at the University of California at Berkeley. The purpose of IPAR, begun in 1949 with funds from the Rockefeller Foundation, was to determine which people were most highly effective in their chosen professions and to define what made them that way. Writers, architects, engineering students, women mathematicians, inventors, and research scientists, all chosen by peer nomination, were studied. Researchers at IPAR included Barron, MacKinnon, Gough, Helson, and Crutchfield, among others.

IPAR's study of writers was described by Barron in *Creativity and Personal Freedom* (1968). Literature and drama professors at the University of California were asked to submit names of the most creative outstanding contemporary writers. Their list of sixty-six authors included Truman Capote, Frank O'Connor, Norman Mailer, Muriel Rukeyser, and Kenneth Rexroth. After extensive testing and interviewing of these writers, some qualities of writers emerged. Not surprisingly, they scored extremely high in verbal intelligence, averaging 156 on the Terman Concept Mastery Test. Compare this to the average of 137 scored by the gifted population Terman observed in his famous longitudinal study, begun in 1922 and carried on by Stanford University after his death. Captains in the Air Force scored 60, and the general population scored lower than that. In addition to possessing striking verbal intelligence, the writers were found to be independent and unconventional, possessing traits which seem to be core characteristics of most creative people, not only writers. For instance, Getzels and Csikszentmihalyi found that visual artists, like writers, were independent and unconventional. The writers were interested in all the arts and felt strong reactions to various media. Allen Ginsberg, according to Barry Miles' 1989 biography of him, visited museums whenever he visited a new city and took detailed notes about the works of art.

Additionally, many creative people have talent in several fields: for example, musicians often are painters, writers often musicians. In particular, writers seem to have a fondness for late night singing of old songs, and of course, they also seem to be able to remember all the words. When I was chair of the literature panel of the Ohio Arts Council, other panel members, all writers, brought their guitars, banjos, and harmonicas to our annual meetings in Columbus, and we regularly sang late into the night. Several played professionally. Root-Bernstein, in "Tools of Thought" (1987), called this aspect of giftedness and creativity "correlative talents." Another term for one who crosses over into other talent areas is "polymath." Many, if not most, talented people are talented in several areas. Some examples of artists with correlative talents: William Carlos Williams and Anton Chekhov were doctors; Einstein, Max Plank, Paul Klee, and Aldous Huxley were musicians; Michelangelo, Galileo, Margaret Mead, and George Washington Carver were poets; Saint-Saens, M. C. Escher, and Edna St. Vincent Millay were fascinated with mathematics, as is Steven Sondheim.

What constitutes writing talent is most often a matter of peer judgment, although there is a large popular following for many writers who would not be judged talented by other writers. The writers studied by Barron aspired to fame, to recognition by the public as well as by their peers. However, peer recognition is more important than public recognition. (This also characterizes other creative producers). The "loft culture" of artists described by Getzels and Csikszentmihalyi also exists in the writing world; writers keep in touch with one another and often seek to establish themselves through public readings, which unfortunately are frequently attended only by other writers.

Ironically, while writers obviously need other writers, they are also threatened by other writers. The ambition needed to survive is often relentlessly ignored by the general and publishing public and seems to be accompanied by envy and insecurity in the face of others' success. T. Coraghessan Boyle, according to a 1990 interview in *The New York Times Magazine*, aspires to be "the most famous writer alive and the greatest writer ever." (Note that this ambition combines both public and peer, both present and future, recognition). But the other side of this extraordinarily confident man is glimpsed in his novel *East Is East* (1990), for he modeled his character Ruth after himself, giving her the same anxieties and "petty jealousies" that he felt as a young writer studying at the famous Iowa Writer's Workshop.

Writers' workshops and conferences do engender jealousy and anxiety among the participants, who often see each other as rivals. In addition to this inherent competition, writers also face a caste system in many workshops. For instance, at the Bread Loaf Writer's Conference, a two-week conference held in Vermont every August, writers are divided into ranked divisions, with "Auditors" (those who do not have manuscripts) and "Contributors" (those who will have manuscript conferences with a writer who is featured as a teacher) at the bottom. These struggling writers are not permitted to socialize with the Fellows, Associates, and Senior writers, all of whom have their parties in a certain cabin. Sometimes a Contributor or Auditor may have an affair with someone on a higher rung, and be invited to this cabin. Rumor has it that one struggling young poet had such a violent reaction to the social tensions at this conference that he chained himself to a tree and tried to commit suicide. Social stratification exists in all professions, of course, but at the Bread Loaf Writer's Conference this class difference, enforced from above, is especially apparent. However, despite all the tension apparent at Bread Loaf, opportunities nonetheless exist. For example, it was there that I had the chance to study with Toni Morrison and to hear her read from *Song of Solomon;* I heard Irving's *Garp,* O'Brien's *Cacciato,* and Gardner's *On Moral Fiction* in manuscript. My roommate had a chance to study with Maxine Kumin.

In addition to the need/fear relationships among writers, Barron also observed that writers value productivity. As in any creative profession, writers must be productive to achieve the "senior" ranks. *East Is East,* Boyle's seventh book, was published when he was only forty-two. According to his wife, Boyle is "more like a workhorse than a thoroughbred," writing seven days a week for four hours a day. Glance at a list of your favorite author's published books, and you may see many titles you've never heard of. Most famous poets are famous for only one or two poems that keep getting anthologized, but their collected poems include hundreds, perhaps thousands, of other works.

In fact, the sheer volume of a successful writer's output is often an important aspect of his or her success, for it indicates that the writer has simply kept writing. Brad Leithauser, interviewed by Shekerjian for her book on the MacArthur Fellows, commented on the drive and resilience that writers need to persist despite the world's disinterest. He has many projects going simultaneously, and when he can't stand to work on his novel, he writes poems. When he can't work on poems, he composes an essay or review, making good use of the "network of enterprises" described by Gruber. In the 1980s, Leithauser wrote five books: novels, poems, and nonfiction. He planned eight for the 1990s.

John Sayles is an amazing example of a productive writer. Sending a short story blind to *The Atlantic,* he caught the attention of the editor; he later turned the story into his first novel, *Pride of the Bimbos.* A second novel followed: *Union Dues,* which was nominated for a National Book Award and the National Book Critics Circle Award. After receiving two O'Henry Awards for his short stories, collected into *The Anarchists' Convention,* he set to work writing a play, over two dozen screenplays, and making films. He has written rock videos for Bruce Springsteen as well as a third novel, *Los Gusanos.* His film *Return of the Sacaucus Seven* is a cult favorite. Other films include *Lianna, Brother from a Small Planet, Matewan, Eight Men Out,* and *Baby, It's You.* David Stathearn, a quintessential Sayles actor who has played, among other characters, the sheriff in *Matewan,* described the writer as a kind, workaholic genius (personal communication, New York City, May, 1988). Sayles has raised money for his films by writing and revising other people's screenplays for more commercial projects. At this writing, he is in his early forties.

The writers studied by Barron at the University of California were typically concerned with the meaning of life and with the search for truth and beauty, and they furthermore were particularly concerned about behaving in an ethically consistent fashion. That the writers searched for truth and beauty is not surprising, since that supposedly is the lofty purpose of literature. From Shelley's "beauty is truth, truth beauty" to John Gardner's *On Moral Fiction,* it has been put forth that literature can explain, analyze and uphold human values. This is not to say, however, that literature is written expressly to set forth doctrines, for any such literature would, and does, seem dogmatic. (And teachers who insist that students come up with the "one true meaning" of a literary composition are just as dogmatic). For the writer's act of writing is, itself, a search for meaning. As John Gardner said,

> Art is as original and important as it is precisely because it does not start out with clear knowledge of what it means to say. Out of the artist's imagination, as out of nature's inexhaustible well, pours one thing after another. The artist composes, writes, or paints just as he dreams, seizing whatever swims close to his net. This, not the world seen directly, is his raw material.

> This shimmering mess of loves and hates — fishing trips taken long ago with Uncle Ralph, a 1940 green Chevrolet, a war, a vague sense of what makes a novel, a symphony, a photograph — this is the clay the artist must shape into an object worthy of our attention; that is, our tears, our laughter, our thought. (p. 13)

Barron, in observing that the writer is independent in thought and judgment, and frank and "candid in dealings with others," implied that the writer may value freedom of expression more than others. Indeed, writers throughout the world have often been the first to be thrown into jail or sent into exile for what they have written and said. Solzhenitsyn and Brodsky were sent to Siberia for their writings. The British writer Salman Rushdie, sentenced to death by the Ayatollah Khomeini of Iran for his novel *Satanic Verses,* had to go into hiding in 1989. The writer's organization, PEN, has a Freedom To Write Committee, a watchdog group concerned about writers throughout the world being persecuted for expressing themselves. In 1990, nine of the eleven panelists on the National Endowment of the Arts literature panel resigned in protest over the antiobscenity pledge the U.S. government was threatening to require grant awardees to sign. (Congress eventually voted that awardees would not be required to sign such pledges). At a less lofty level, young creative writers often publish frank underground newspapers that are the bane of their teachers and school administrators.

But it is perhaps precisely because of their ability to say what they think that writers attract the interest of others. I once ran into a best-selling author from my home town, Robert Traver (*Anatomy of a Murder,* 1955), outside the university library. The best-known citizen of Ishpeming, Michigan, by then in his eighties, was as opinionated as ever. He talked about the evils of the city and the beauties of the wilderness of the Upper Peninsula. As he held forth on the timeless tranquilities of nature and the filth and noisiness of the city, he sounded for all that summer's day like Wordsworth proclaiming "the world is too much with us." The grizzled old man was almost blind, but he still read avidly, and still wrote.

With his straightforwardness and adamance, Traver was much like the writers in the Barron study, who were found to be frank people who needed to communicate and were likely to take risks in doing so. Through psychological testing the study also found that the writers showed a desire to achieve through their own work rather than through conformity to a social group. They had presence, they wanted to achieve social status, and they liked themselves.

Barron's team of researchers divided the writers into three groups: (1) distinguished writers, (2) student writers, and (3) representative writers (those who had achieved financial success and popular recognition but were not considered distinguished). In independence of judgment, the distinguished writers scored well above the general population. Interestingly, the student writers also scored above the representative writers. Perhaps this indicates that to become a commercially successful writer, as opposed to a distinguished writer, one must be more like the general population. In this, popular writers are like popular elected officials, for studies have shown that leaders chosen by the people generally are a little more intelligent than the general population, but not so intelligent that the populace cannot identify with them.

In flexibility, student writers scored higher than distinguished writers, who in turn scored higher than the representative, or commercially successful, writers. That student writers were more like distinguished writers in this quality may be attributed to identification and life-style imitation, Barron postulated, since distinguished writers retain their independence and flexibility.

### Creative Writers and Deviance

According to Barron, creative writers were "markedly deviant" from the general population. In particular, distinguished writers tended to be schizoid, depressive, hysterical, or psychopathic, and not to have rigid sex role expectations. Barron said,

> In brief, if one is to take these test results seriously, the writers appear to be both sicker and healthier psychologically than people in general. Or, to put it another way, they are much more troubled psychologically, but they also have far greater resources with which to deal with their troubles. This jibes rather well with their social behavior . . . They are clearly effective people who handle themselves with pride and distinctiveness,

but the face they turn to the world is sometimes one of pain, often of protest, sometimes of distance and withdrawal, and certainly they are emotional. (Barron, 1968, p. 244)

Psychoanalysts and psychologists have often stated that writers write because of deep-seated pathologies. Freud, in "Creative Writers and Day-Dreaming" (1908), theorized that writers use their personal childhood fantasies. Ernst Kris wrote, in *Psychoanalytic Explorations in Art* (1964), that writers write because of "regression in service of the ego." More recently, Rothenberg has dealt with the mind of the writer in *The Emerging Goddess* (1976) and *Creativity and Madness* (1990). Psychologists and psychiatrists have analyzed writers, searching for the "key" that will unlock the mystery of their creativity. According to Alice Miller, in *The Untouched Key* (already discussed with reference to her theories on Picasso's creativity), the writer and philosopher Friedrich Nietzsche experienced the death of his father and brother as a child and grew up as the only male in a house full of women who taught him self-denial and who silenced his curiosity. Miller wrote, "Friedrich Nietzsche needed his entire philosophy to shield himself from knowing and telling what really happened to him." Miller said that for years she has been trying to tell the world that poets, writers, and painters tell the "encoded" stories of childhood trauma in their works, but that no one will listen to her. She believes that the denial of evidence is due in part to the revelation of the "forbidden knowledge" of the idealization that children put upon their parents — in other words, the lies children tell themselves about their parents, to compensate for the parents' failings.

In 1988, in *The Literary Mind,* psychologist Leo Schneiderman proposed that Faulkner wrote because of ego defects, including low self-esteem caused by an overprotective mother and a rejecting father. Schneiderman also said that Lillian Hellman wrote out of narcissistic "chronic rage" that resulted from "maternal deprivation"; Tennessee Williams wrote to compensate for his incestuous feelings towards his mother and sister; Flannery O'Connor wrote out of guilt for getting ill with lupus in her late twenties and being dependent on her mother during adulthood; John Cheever wrote because of "early withdrawal of parental empathy"; Vladimir Nabokov wrote out of a longing for his presexual days; Jorge Luis Borges wrote because of oncoming blindness and his shame after a series of crises in his family's fortunes in Buenos Aires; Samuel Beckett wrote out of a "character disorder marked by extreme rigidity and self-centeredness"; and the playwright Harold Pinter writes out of "regression to a past that was as emotionally deprived as is the present." Schneiderman said, "Great literary art is a synthesis of technical skill with tremendous fear, rage, or other powerful emotions, and . . . the fundamental character of great writers reveals significant failure along developmental lines, that is, a basic lack of maturity."

## The Myers-Briggs and Writers

In conjunction with other studies of writers at the Institute for Personality Assessment and Research were those using the Myers-Briggs, a personality type indicator that has been used to examine the characteristics of scientists, artists, laborers, writers, counselors, and many more. Writers tested with the Myers-Briggs were found overwhelmingly to be introverted, intuitive, feeling, and perceptive — INFP, in Myers-Briggs jargon. These findings, consonant with other studies of writers done by the Myers group, showed writers to be similar to artists. Most striking was that writers much preferred to use their intuitive and perceptive powers over their sensing and judging capabilities. This was true whether they were classified as thinking or feeling, introverted or extroverted. Such persons who prefer introversion, intuition, feeling and perception, according to Myers and McCaulley, show inner strength, especially with regard to their personal values, and are reserved. They look for a type of job that provides satisfaction rather than money, and they can be perfectionistic about their work. They are interested in ideas, often reflecting on the disparities between ideals and realities. Extroverts in this category are more outgoing and can be persuasive about their passions, while their preference for intuition and feeling allows them to tune in to and trust inner selves.

Barron's study also noted that creative writers are not good cooperators or committee members; they do not have a great need for harmony, nor do they seek easy praise. Indeed, anyone who submits manuscripts time after time after time — and most writers have this experience — must be patient, resilient, and stubborn.

# The Biographical Approaches

While the Barron study combined testing and interviews, there are other approaches that have been used to study writers, such as the case study approach. Another is Simonton's historiometric approach. The first would be to take a few random biographies of writers, which could be called case studies (though not in the strict psychological sense). The other would be to take many biographies and extrapolate from them, as the Goertzels did, or to apply statistical techniques to their analysis — the technique called historiometry, as Simonton did — and see what researchers have found.

*Cradles of Eminence* (1962) and *Three Hundred Eminent Personalities* (1978) document the Goertzels' studies of seven hundred eminent persons who had at least two books written about them. The 1978 study included eighty-two literary people: forty-seven fiction and drama writers, twelve nonfiction writers, thirteen poets, and ten editors and publishers.

The Goertzels found more only children among writers than among artists, politicians, or others in the study. The writers, not surprisingly, were voracious early readers. About half the writers hated school, teachers, and school curricula. (See Chapter 11 for a survey of what writers thought of school). Literary people were twice as likely to attempt, or to commit, suicide than other subjects of biographies. Also, literary people were less likely to come from literary families than were artistic, business, or political people to come from families established in their respective areas. Two-thirds of the writers described their childhood home life as unhappy, while less than half of the other eminent people so described their early years. Literary people were also more likely to have alcoholic parents.

An aspect of family life not mentioned by the Goertzels but noted by playwright Arthur Miller, in his 1987 autobiography, *Timebends*, is that many writers have had ineffectual fathers. He said, "It would strike me years later how many male writers had fathers who had actually failed or whom the sons had perceived as failures." He listed, for example, Faulkner, Fitzgerald, Hemingway, Wolfe, Poe, Steinbeck, Melville, Whitman, Chekhov, Hawthorne, Strindberg, and Dostoyevsky, and said, "The list is too long to consign the phenomenon to idiosyncratic accident."

This aspect of the writer's life, Miller thought, led the American writer to seek to create a new order, springing "as though from the ground itself," of self-made men "quite like the businessmen they despise," and he called the American male writers, "fatherless men abandoned by a past that they in turn reject, and better to write not the Great American Novel or Play, but verily the First." The writer T. Coraghessan Boyle said about his father, "I tried to understand him, but he was usually extremely morose and insensibly drunk, like his father before him." Boyle's grandfather had put his father into an orphanage. In a 1990 article about Boyle, Friend said that Boyle's recent novels "featured a foredoomed search for a missing father." The poet Robert Bly said at the 1991 James Wright Poetry Festival that it took him years to put the word "stagger" in a poem about his father, whose alcoholism filled Bly with shame.

The Goertzels observed yet another aspect of an unhappy home life among writers; more literary people had marriages that ended in divorce than others in the study, and yet more of the writers never married in the first place. Perhaps the twin phenomena of fewer marriages and more divorces have something to do with sexual divergence; of the twenty-one people identified as sexually divergent in the Goertzels' study, twenty were literary people. In addition, the writers were often ill as children, or handicapped, or "homely." The Goertzels noted that "Their photographs as children and adults are less attractive than those of politicians, athletes, and performers." Their childhoods and adult lives were judged to be more "lonely, unhappy, and difficult" than others'. On the positive side, they were as children very sensuous, reacting profoundly to visual, olfactory and tactile sensations. But even this sensitivity worked against them; writers as small children "were intensely responsive to the emotional climate in their homes" and were "acute observers of the family dramas being played out before their eyes." (Overexcitability and the Dabrowski theory are discussed in Chapter 4).

Tobias Wolff's 1989 memoir, *This Boy's Life,* detailed his early life with his mother, the two of them "on the road" until his mother married a very uncongenial stepfather. Their life in a northwest town was described in vivid detail by Wolff, who almost became an Eagle scout, yet ran with a gang who stole, drank, and did drugs. Wolff, realizing he had to get out, faked his credentials on an application to a prep school in the East. Once there, he flunked out. Meanwhile, his real father, a con man who pretended to come from a blue-blood eastern family, and his brother Geoffrey, who also became a writer, were living in comparative ease in the East, ignoring the traumas Tobias was enduring. Tobias had tended to forgive his father's neglect, rationalizing that he must have been very busy, until he himself held his own newborn son in his arms; he then felt overwhelming anger toward the man.

The Goertzels noted that writers as children often retreated from the world by reading and fantasizing, and that they didn't need as much companionship as other children. One of the young writers who studied at the aforementioned summer Governor's Institute in 1989 described his reading behavior as compulsive and constant. "If my friends knew how I behave when I read, they would be surprised." Often reading in the woods under a tree, he would imagine himself a character in the book, even talking out loud, "No, don't do that! You'll get killed!" Also, he rewarded himself for doing some homework by reading a chapter of a novel, then doing more homework, then reading a chapter, then doing more homework. This behavior, uncovered by the Dabrowski Over-excitabilities Questionnaire, revealed an intense imaginational and intellectual reaction to the written word.

The Goertzels found that writers weren't popular with their peers. In fact, they often provoked dislike and rejection from peers, adults and teachers. Although peaceful children, they had to be pushed into doing physical activities or studying subjects they didn't like, such as math and science. The writers also were not joiners of social causes, and were content to be alone much of the time, though they did like to socialize with other writers occasionally.

## Midcentury Writers: The Academicians

Other biographies bear interesting witness to the lives of creative writers. The psychotherapist Eileen Simpson's 1982 memoir, *Poets in Their Youth,* which included stories about several of the United States' foremost modern poets (Simpson was married to John Berryman), gave interesting insight into the social lives of poets and novelists. Berryman, Caroline Gordon, Robert Lowell, Jean Stafford, Delmore Schwartz, R. P. Blackmur, Mark Van Doren, Randall Jarrell, Allen Tate, Theodore Roethke, Saul Bellow, Robert Fitzgerald, Edmund Wilson, and others crossed paths in the 1940s and 1950s. Simpson's documentation showed that even for these prestigious college-educated poets, the way was tough.

Applying for grants, living on one-year appointments at various universities, hoping to win contests or to get manuscripts published by major houses, the poets described by Simpson were in the 1950s like other poets are now. How many people today have read books by these famous poets or novelists? Or by the poets writing today? Being published does not ensure being read. Poets have an especially rough time in the United States, where poetry is not popular. Recently on a plane I sat next to a well-educated radio commentator. When we got to talking about modern poetry, he looked at me strangely and said, "I bet I can't name one contemporary poet alive today. I remember Shelley and Keats from high school, but that's all."

Several of the poets described by Simpson had major bouts with mental illness. Lowell was institutionalized often for manic-depression (before the use of Lithium). Schwartz was diagnosed as a paranoid schizophrenic. Tate was rumored to be a philanderer. Stafford was institutionalized for alcoholism; Roethke, for mental illness and alcoholism. Berryman himself was an alcoholic depressive who, after several suicide attempts, died in 1972 after jumping off a high bridge into the Mississippi River. Jarrell also was alleged to have committed suicide by jumping in front of a car on a lonely road one dark night.

Alcohol was a major part of the social lives of these writers; indeed, addiction to alcohol figures in the lives of many creative writers, artists, and performers, but whether there is more alcohol addiction here than in the overall population is not known. A struggling young musician, talking about excessive drinking among his artistic friends, claimed that "Alcohol is at least as important as love." But the writers studied by Simpson were established as the elite of the nation. Praised by the academy, they were the heirs of Eliot and Yeats, the founders and editors and writers for the most prestigious literary and political journals: *The Nation, The Partisan Review, The Sewanee Review, The Kenyon Review.* They were the inventors and purveyors of the New Criticism. If there were any accolades to be given to poets and novelists, they received them. They sat on the Library of Congress advisory committees and dedicated themselves to lives of thought and writing. Yet their personal lives were anything but pleasant, anything but happy.

Schwartz, Lowell, and Berryman all had strong mothers who were hard to please, and absent, dead, or ineffectual fathers. Berryman's father committed suicide at the age of thirty-nine. To get his mother's attention, John would often feign fainting spells or leap onto a parapet and threaten suicide. Delmore Schwartz's mother was a strong Jewish traditionalist. When her younger son married a non-Jewish woman, she said he would be "better off dead." Delmore also married a woman who was not Jewish; Simpson wrote, "Anticipating an hysterical attack, Delmore might well not have told her." Robert Lowell's mother was the only one he would let rescue him when he was thrown into jail during a manic bout he suffered while visiting his old Kenyon College roommate from Indiana. She came and collected him and committed him to an institution back home in Massachusetts.

## Midcentury Writers: The Beats

While these writers produced that which was accepted by academics in the 1940s, '50s and '60s, the Beats were writing rebellious poetry and prose with a jazz beat and a downtown air. Kerouac, Cassady, Ginsberg, Ferlinghetti, and Burroughs shocked and thrilled the youth of the age. They wrote about jazz and heroin and addiction and being free, on the road in automobiles and motorcycles, and about the decline of America. Ginsberg's landmark poem, "Howl," published by City Lights in 1956, began the San Francisco renaissance. Barry Miles' biography of the poet, *Ginsberg,* tells of the profound influence Ginsberg had on a whole generation of youth and writers in America, and throughout the world. Ginsberg's revolutionary "saxophone line" style, his call for the legalization of marijuana and for stopping discrimination against homosexuals echoed throughout the 1960s, and blended with the anti-Vietnam War movement.

Ginsberg crossed paths with many of the great writers of the world beginning at Columbia University, where he studied under Mark Van Doren and Lionel Trilling. Later, exiled to Paterson, New Jersey, after his hospitalization for mental illness, he came under the tutelage of William Carlos Williams. Then came his residence in various apartments in Manhattan, where the Beat generation began to formulate its theories of art. He hung around with theater people such as Judith Malina and Julian Beck at the San Remo Bar in Greenwich Village, where the term "beat" was first applied. Miles wrote about the group:

> They explored the sinister, the criminal, and the forbidden. They rejected the conformist, consumer society of America in the late forties but were not thinking in terms of rebelling against it. The Beat Generation began with

personal exploration. "It wasn't a political or social rebellion," Ginsberg said. "Everybody had some form of break in their consciousness or an experience or a taste of a large consciousness or 'sator.'" They had all read Spengler's *Decline of the West,* and took it for granted that civilization was collapsing around them. The atomic bomb had just been dropped on Japan and that, to them, was proof enough. The early Beats had no hope of trying to change society. (Miles, 1989, p. 73)

Ginsberg hobnobbed with Bob Dylan, the Rolling Stones, and the Beatles. He founded a literary movement and was kicked out of Cuba and Czechoslovakia for his advocacy of homosexuality and his frank diaries. He lived in Mexico, Tangier and India. He was decried for writing obscenity. He was in Dr. Timothy Leary's LSD experiments and had experimented with many other drugs as well, especially the hallucinogens. He had meditated naked, chanting "Om" in public places, had met Ezra Pound, and had marched in many antiwar protests. He had tried to levitate the Pentagon. He became a Buddhist and helped to found a Buddhist poetry center in Boulder, Colorado. He gave readings all over the world.

Ginsberg also spent a few years working in advertising promotion, an educational experience which enabled him to effectively, tirelessly and ceaselessly promote his own works, and those of his friends. Self-promotion, or promotion by friends, is necessary to the realization of the creative writer's hope to have an audience for what is written, and promotion is often undervalued in the realization of creative writing talent. As Getzels and Csikszentmihalyi (1976) wrote, the loft is important in the socialization and professionalizing of the visual artist. For creative writers, the literary agent and a group of connected friends is equally as important. Many literary works are first published by small presses, and many books of poetry are published by one friend for another. Where self-publication is looked down on in academic fields, it often occurs in literary fields. Ferlinghetti founded the printing press City Lights expressly to publish his own, Ginsberg's, and other Beats' work. Ginsberg loyally continued with City Lights, even when he could have made much more money publishing with mainstream publishers.

I, myself, was publisher and editor of a small literary press in the late 1970s and early 1980s. I published poems, with illustrations, by many poets, among them Nick Muska, Larry Smith, Robert Fox, Howard McCord, Peg Lauber, Linda Hasselstrom, Judith Lindenau, Joel Lipman, Bruce Severy, Carol Pierman, David Shevin. Dorothy Linden illustrated many of the poems. I solicited poems from poets who were my friends, and also accepted poems sent to me by submission. And why not publish good poets who were my friends? In a 1990 essay on the Scribner's publishing house, called "I Who Knew Nothing, Was In Charge," Charles Scribner, Jr. said that throughout its early years, Scribner's was "a staunch Princeton house." It is quite a sport among literary people to watch how connections and friendships bloom into publications and contracts, and in fact, *Esquire* published a tongue-in-cheek family tree on just that subject a few years ago. *Spy* magazine has a column called "Logrolling," featuring blurbs by one friend for another and the corresponding jacket blurb by the second friend, for the first friend.

## Midcentury Writers: The Women

The 1960s also found the U.S. poetic world with two suicidal women poets, called "confessional" by their male detractors (though confession was the mode of discourse in poetry long before them). Anne Sexton and Sylvia Plath wrote their longing lyrics and the literary world waited, breath bated, as they played out their sad destinies. Sylvia Plath died by putting her head in an oven in 1963, and Anne Sexton gassed herself in her garage.

Their works often spoke of the typical conflict experienced by women. As Foley found in her 1986 study of artist mothers, and as Belenky, et al. (1986), and Gilligan (1990) found, women with children experience great conflict in finding time, inclination, support, and social approval for the strenuous effort of a successful writing career and maintaining a family. Both Margaret Drabble and Tillie Olsen told of writing in the middle of the night before the children got up.

Such writers as Adrienne Rich, Margaret Atwood, Joyce Carol Oates and Anne Tyler demonstrate that productivity, persistence, and prolificness are of crucial importance in maintaining the writer's vision. Both Atwood and Oates were rumored to be candidates for the Nobel Prize in 1990. Oates, in her 1988 essay called "(Woman) Writer," noted that most women writers write because they have to, and do not view themselves as "woman writers." Virginia Woolf, in her 1954 *A Writer's Diary*, described the hard work of getting it right:

> I write two pages of arrant nonsense, after straining; I write variations of every sentence; compromises; bad shots; possibilities; till my writing book is like a lunatic's dream. Then I trust to some inspiration on re-reading; and pencil them into some sense. Still, I am not satisfied. (Woolf, p. 147)

Women as well as men put down one sentence after another, writing toward completion. Woolf wrote, "I have just finished, with this very nib-ful of ink, the last sentence of *The Waves*. Yes, it was the greatest stretch of mind I ever knew."

## MacArthur Fellows

Denise Shekerjian (1990) interviewed several MacArthur Fellows who are poets and writers. Among them: John Ashbery, Pulitzer Prize winning poet; Joseph Brodsky, exiled Russian poet, Nobel Prize winner, and U.S. Poet Laureate for 1992; Robert Coles, Pulitzer Prize-winning writer and poet; Douglas Crase, poet; Brad Leithauser, poet, novelist, and essayist; Ved Mehta, writer and editor at *The New Yorker;* John Sayles, novelist, playwright, short story writer, filmmaker; and Derek Walcott, poet and playwright. On the writer's concentration and drive, Mehta said:

> What does it mean to succeed as a writer, if you really think about it . . . But for a writer, you could give him a Mercedes, chateaux to live in, every earthly thing, and still he wouldn't be comfortable. There's something in the nature of the craft that will always set him apart. Tolstoy. What did Tolstoy really want or need? Here was a man who denounced *War and Peace* and *Anna Karenina* as false books not worth reading. He had children. He had marriage. He had genius. It wasn't enough. Why? It's the discomfort of genius — I don't know how else to put it. A writer can never be satisfied with an idea of success. Writers may have something in common with nymphomaniacs — they have to keep going. More and more and more. (Shekerjian, 1990, pp. 143-44)

# Writers and Depression

In early 1990 the Pulitzer Prize-winning author William Styron wrote an op-ed piece for *The New York Times* about the cavalier treatment of the suicide of Primo Levi, the Italian writer. In this letter, Styron confessed to having been suicidal himself, and from this grew one of the major bestsellers of 1990, Styron's account of depression, *Darkness Visible: A Memoir of Madness.* Styron wrote that in his early sixties he had fallen into deep depression after stopping drinking. He was hospitalized for his mental condition, but it was not until later that he realized his psychiatrist had over-prescribed medication, thereby exacerbating the very condition being treated.

Styron named other writers and artists who had suffered from debilitating depression: Albert Camus, Romain Gary, Jean Seberg, Randall Jarrell, among others. Styron wrote that although it was denied by biographers and family, Jarrell "almost certainly killed himself. He did so not because he was a coward, nor out of any moral feebleness, but because he was afflicted with a depression that was so devastating that he could no longer endure the pain of it." Others who suffered depression were poet Hart Crane, Vincent Van Gogh, Virginia Woolf, abstract expressionist Mark Rothko, photographer Diane Arbus, playwright William Inge, and humorist Art Buchwald. Of the origins of such depression, Styron wrote:

> When one thinks of these doomed and splendidly creative men and women, one is drawn to contemplate their childhoods, where, to the best of anyone's knowledge, the seeds of the illness take strong root; could any of them have had a hint, then, of the psyche's perishability, its exquisite fragility? And why were they destroyed, while others — similarly stricken — struggled through? (Styron, 1990, p. 36)

Styron pointed to the childhood roots of his own depression. His mother died when he was thirteen, and he had not mourned her fully. He described the night he had finally decided to commit suicide. He was sitting in his living room listening to classical music when he heard a Bach tune his mother had hummed. In an extremely distraught state of excitement and emotion, Styron woke his wife and begged her to take him to the hospital. He began his recovery upon hearing a song which unleashed his feelings.

Woolf, in her Diary, wrote often of her "black moods" being lifted through writing. Writing *To the Lighthouse* was therapeutic because of the hold her parents had on her:

> November 28, 1928. Father's birthday. He would have been 96, 96, yes, today; and could have been 96, like other people one has known: but mercifully was not. His life would have entirely ended mine. What would have happened? No writing; not books; — inconceivable. I used to think of him and mother daily; but writing the Lighthouse laid them in my mind. And now he comes back sometimes, but differently. (I believe this to be true — that I was obsessed by them both, unhealthily; and writing of him was a necessary act). (Woolf, 1954, p. 135)

Miles, in his biography of Allen Ginsberg, wrote that a study in the early 1980s conducted at Oxford University by UCLA showed that creative people — artists, poets, and writers — were "35 times more likely to seek treatment for serious mood disorders than the average person, and of these three groups, poets suffered the severest forms of disturbance." The British poets studied were winners of the Queen's Gold Medal, "a very conservative group," Miles said, but 20 percent of them had one episode of manic-depression serious enough to cause them to be hospitalized, and over half of them had received treatment for either mania, or depression. Miles wrote that "Clearly Ginsberg was in a dangerous profession." Indeed, at one point Ginsberg, suffering extreme self-doubt and almost arrested for burglary, checked himself into the New York Psychiatric Institute. (Incidentally, tests given at this time showed Ginsberg's IQ to be "near genius level," according to Miles).

Ginsberg's childhood in New Jersey had been odd, to say the least. His mother was a paranoid schizophrenic who was often institutionalized; Allen himself had to take her to the institution once. At home, she liked to be "natural," often striding around the house in the nude. Ginsberg's father was the well-known poet Louis Ginsberg, a teacher who tried to keep life somewhat normal for Allen and his brother. Ginsberg's moving 1961 poem "Kaddish" is an artistic revelation of his family's trials, an anguished expression of regret that when his mother died insane in a mental hospital, they were not able to summon ten Jewish men to say the Jewish prayer for the dead, Kaddish.

Such revelations, whether in diaries, memoirs, or biographies, provide insights into what writers are like. The diaries of Etta Hillesum from 1941 to 1942 (published in English in 1985) are illustrative of the struggle that writers, or perhaps any artists, go through:

> There are moments in which it is suddenly brought home to me why creative artists take to drink, become dissipated, lose their way . . . The artist really needs a very strong character if he is not to go to pieces morally, not to lose his bearings . . . I feel it very strongly in myself at certain moments. All my tenderness, all my emotions, this whole swirling soul-lake, soul-sea, soul-ocean . . . wants to pour out then, to be allowed to flow forth into just one short poem, but I also feel, if only I could, like flinging myself headlong into an abyss, losing myself in drink. After each creative act one has to be sustained by one's strength of character, by a moral sense, by I don't know why, lest one tumble, God knows how far. And pushed by what dark impulse? I sense it inside me; even in my most fruitful and most creative inner moments, there are raging demons and self-destructive forces. (Hillesum, 1985, p. 94)

John Cheever struggled also, and wrote in the diaries published posthumously in *The New Yorker* (January 28, 1991):

> I must convince myself that writing is not, for a man of my disposition, a self-destructive vocation. I hope and think it is not, but I am not genuinely sure. It has given me money and renown, but I suspect that it may have something to do with my drinking habits. The excitement of alcohol and the excitement of fantasy are very similar. (p. 52)

The 1991 suicide of the Pulitzer Prize-winning novelist Jerzy Kosinsky prompted this letter from the playwright Kenneth Brown:

> Jerzy Kosinsky was a friend of mine, hence the enclosed poem. He committed suicide recently by pulling a plastic bag over his head and sitting in a hot tub and suffocating. It was a great shock to me. We used to sit in the saloons late at night and talk about his childhood. The Nazis

killed his family when he was about eight years old, and he became a street urchin for awhile. Have you read *The Painted Bird*? He adored the SS troops because they were tall and clean and handsome with shiny boots and black uniforms. It haunted him all his life; he had enormous guilt about his success and his survival, worried about having become a Nazi equivalent through his fame and fortune. I tried to reassure him that his work was a weapon against fascism. Alas, what I said was not enough. I guess nothing would have been enough. (personal communication, May 15, 1991)

Highly verbal, highly conceptual, highly opinionated, often nonconforming, frank, highly driven, writers are prone to self-abusive and self-destructive behavior even as they are enriching the lives of their readers. But this is not always the case, and there are many writers whose lives are not lived so tragically, those who have, as Styron said, "struggled through."

The picture that emerges can perhaps be summarized in the words of E. L. Doctorow, who said in the 1988 interview with George Plimpton for *Paris Review,* "A writer's life is so hazardous that anything he does is bad for him. Anything that happens to him is bad: failure's bad, success is bad; impoverishment is bad, money is very, very bad. Nothing good can happen." Plimpton responded to Doctorow's statement with: "Except the act of writing itself." Doctorow replied:

Except the act of writing. So if he shoots birds and animals and anything else he can find, you've got to give him that. And if he/she drinks, you give him/her that too, unless the work is affected. For all of us, there's an intimate connection between the struggle to write and the ability to survive on a daily basis as a human being. So we have a high rate of self-destruction. Do you mean to punish ourselves for writing? For the transgression? I don't know. (p. 315-16)

"Except the act of writing itself." This statement perhaps illustrates the intrinsic nature of writing giftedness. The writer does not know what he or she thinks until it's written down. There is something in the very act itself that is healing, relieves frustration, and satisfies the need for communication, for self-expression.

Like visual artists, writers write because they must, and not because they think it would be fun to be a writer. The high incidence of depression would seem to be an indication of the intense sensitivity with which creative people apprehend the world. It is as if the senses were tuned louder, stronger, higher, and so the task becomes to communicate the experience of both pain and joy. The creative person's products become consumable commodities for the public, but these very products are stuff of life for the creative person. What John Gardner called a "fishing trip with Uncle Ralph" becomes the epitome of fishing trips, and "Big Two-Hearted River" is born, at the expense of excruciating pain for the writer, the pain of self-revelation, and of immense power and joy, the power and joy of saying something that makes people say, "Yes, that's true. That's true."

## A Sense of Humor

I am including a discussion of sense of humor within this chapter on creative writers, because essentially the giftedness is the same: verbal giftedness. While there are those humorists who are physical humorists such as Jerry Lewis or the Three Stooges, they are actors, using their bodies; actors and dancers, the physically gifted, are covered in Chapter 10.

Most checklists for giftedness and creativity include "Shows a sense of humor." Teachers are asked to check whether a potentially creatively or intellectually gifted child has a sense of humor. This is a ridiculously phrased screening point, since every child has a sense of humor, a sort of compass that points out what's funny. (And every adult has a sense of humor, too). What the checklists seem to be getting at is whether or not the child has a highly developed sense of humor, or a sense of humor that is more mature than that of others of the same age.

Humor is developmental and cultural. What we laugh at in our society is not what is laughed at in another society, and if we went to a comedy club in Japan or India, we would probably not laugh; we would miss the point, even if we could understand the language, for humor, especially stand-up comedy or written humor, often relies on idioms of the language. When we learn a foreign language, the idioms are the most difficult to master. Any society's humorists are often not understood in another country or society, even if there is a common language. Miles Kington of Great

Britain, in an 1990 review in *The New York Times*, wrote, "Calvin Trillin is almost completely unknown in Europe. There's nothing odd about that; most American humor columnists are unknown over here, and most of ours are unknown in America. That's the way humor works."

When we say that a mark of giftedness is having a sense of humor, we probably mean that the child has advanced verbal development and can appreciate and understand humor that older children understand. Members of Mensa, at their Regional Gatherings, have joke-offs, where people tell jokes that have a high abstraction level — puns, analogies, puzzles, riddles. Having a high IQ, which of course all members of Mensa do, means having a high level of verbal ability, for IQ tests are largely constructed to elicit verbal responses. A group of writers that included John Ciardi and Isaac Asimov exchanged off-color limericks in the mail for years (personal communication, John Ciardi, July 1976). These intellectually gifted and creative people share a love of humor — but a certain type of humor, primarily verbal.

Children appreciate certain types of humor at certain ages (Owens and Hogan, 1983; Bernstein, 1986; Fabrizi and Pollio, 1987; Bariaud, 1988; McGhee, 1988). Bariaud suggested that children appreciate humor that matches their cognitive level. Bernstein pointed out that while early appreciation is of nonlinguistic humor, the older children get, the more they understand linguistic humor. Thus the precocious child would appreciate humor that is enjoyed by older children and would stand out as having "a sense of humor." Fabrizi and Pollio, in a 1987 article called "Are Funny Teenagers Creative?" showed that seventh graders use humor in a different, more accommodating, less verbal way than do eleventh graders. They noted that a child who tries to make his friends laugh during early adolescence often is silly, is acting out, or is anti-authority. Later on in adolescence, "making one's peers laugh is a more complex matter and there is some requirement to be original."

Many of the most admired humorists in our society have been writers, even if they also performed as comedians: Mark Twain, James Thurber, E. B. White, Tom Wolfe, Damon Runyon, Groucho Marx, Kurt Vonnegut Jr., Dave Barry, Joseph Heller, Roy Blount Jr., Calvin Trillin, Garrison Keillor, Erma Bombeck, Steve Allen and Woody Allen are examples. Comedians who have not been writers have hired writers to make their humor come alive in language.

Humor, distinguishable from jokes and comedy, is what helps people cope with incongruities, and maintain balance in situations that are threatening and dangerous. According to Chafe in his 1987 article, "Humor as a Disabling Mechanism," humor disables in two ways. First, the very act of laughter disables us, for we are unable to do anything else while laughing — we can't do push-ups and we can't run and we can't read and we can't talk. The act of laughing is so pleasurable that we seek it out by attending shows where funny people perform, or we go to movies starring our favorite funny people, or watch television sitcoms. We enjoy being around people who make us laugh.

The types of humor we prefer differ. Some people like joke-cracking, physical humor, while others like witty satire. We have preferences in jokes. I sometimes stand helplessly trapped while the office "joker" tells me a story that "rolled 'em on the floor" at the Elks Club. I giggle politely and leave. Later, curled up with a Thurber anthology, I choke with laughter over the story about the banquet speaker.

Chafe pointed out that humor helps us deal with taboo topics in a socially acceptable way, thereby disabling us in a second way. Humor disrupts the schema we have for certain topics. That is why stand-up comics often talk about sex or other topics that would offend us if spoken about seriously, but which we enjoy and don't find offensive when spoken of in the schema-shattering manner of humor. Humor disables us mentally. Jokes make explicit the contexts and definitions of words and symbols, and help us to see the ambiguities. To "get" a joke in any culture demands a dense schema, a high ability to play with meanings of words. That is perhaps why "sense of humor" appears on checklists. We have noticed the verbal ability of young gifted children, and "sense of humor" is another way to emphasize the verbal content of most of the standardized tests we give, verbal content that discriminates against children whose cultural background hasn't provided them with rich schemata possessed by children whose cultural background has been so enriched.

Therefore, I propose we take "sense of humor" off our creativity checklists, and substitute something more specific. For example, "has dense verbal schema and so can make puns, jokes, analogies, that are humorous." Or, "Has a sense of humor that is verbally advanced for his age."

### Summary

This is what we know about creative writers:
1. They are often early readers.

2. They have often experienced childhood trauma and may suffer from depression.

3. They used early reading and writing to escape.

4. They have high conceptual and verbal intelligence.

5. They are independent, nonconforming, and not interested in joining groups.

6. They value self-expression and are productive.

7. They are often driven, able to take rejection, and like to work alone for long periods of time.

8. They often have difficulty with alcohol.

9. They prefer writing as their mode of expression of emotions and feelings.

10. They often have an advanced verbal sense of humor.

# Chapter 7

## Creative Writers: Children with Extraordinary Writing Talent

*Sweet aromas fill the stallion's heart*
*Eyes of blue, hide of white*
*Glimmering with its sweat*
*On the run, under burning sun.*
*As quick as a shimmering, sunny stream.*
*Panting wildly, wildly panting*
*Suede rabbit hops in its way.*

— nine-year-old girl

*Music . . . the most amazing thing about music is that you can't describe the tonal quality of a sound. Before you say anything, make sure you're not giving me any of that scientific stuff about waveforms, attacks, decays, sustains, and releases. A sound is relative to the ear, and those words are relative to an idea a computer showed a bunch of scientists who don't even know how to carry a tune . . .*

— eleven-year-old boy

This chapter continues the study of writers, but with an emphasis on children. Little work has been done on the juvenilia of eminent writers, and in fact little work has been done on the quality of youthful creative production in most of the arts. In particular, there appears to have been little analysis or study of what makes children's writing good, with the consequence that much excellent work goes unmarked as such. Parents or teachers may say to a youngster, "Oh, that's a very nice poem!" without knowing or appreciating the aspects of the writing that make it truly remarkable. Hence I believe that writing prodigy occurs more frequently than is commonly thought.

The material presented in this chapter comes from two areas of study. The first is my examination of the writings, partially presented here, of seven children: (1) four were selected from 400 students in a Manhattan school for gifted children where the mean IQ was 140+; and (2) three were brought to my attention by professional writers, parents, and administrators. From these writers, as well as from many years' observations, I have generated sixteen characteristics of quality juvenile writing. Secondly, I have also studied childhood biographies of well-known adult writers, to determine, if possible, the early situational factors that lead to success as an adult writer. Parts of this study have been published (Piirto, 1989a, 1989b; 1991c).

What exactly is a child prodigy? In *Nature's Gambit* (1986), David Feldman asserted that the youthful talents of child prodigies emerge with the "fortuitous convergence of highly specific individual proclivities with specific environmental receptivity." In other words, a child prodigy gets that way through the extremely lucky combination of a very strong inner impulse toward an activity, and an environment that is supportive. For his six case studies, Feldman defined "prodigy" as a child of ten or younger who produced work on the level of an adult professional. A conflicting definition is proposed by Radford in *Child Prodigies and Exceptional Early Achievers* (1990): prodigies may be older than ten and their achievements need not have "lasting merit." He said, "Indeed, if the work of children is always to be measured against the highest adult standards, there would probably be none who could be called prodigies at all." However, *The Random House Dictionary of English Language* defines a prodigy simply as "a child or young person having extraordinary talent or ability."

For Feldman, with his emphasis on environment and the fortuitous, the prodigy phenomenon is obviously more than just an effect of high-IQ or of special neurological makeup, as in the case of *idiots savants*; rather, prodigies are those who manifest high ability in one specialized field of intellectual development. The three disciplines in which prodigies most frequently occur are mathematics, chess, and music. Most prodigies are found in music and in chess, fewer in mathematics, fewer still in art, and very few in writing. Feldman, who studied only one writing prodigy, asserted that

> For the most part, writing is not a domain where prodigious achievement occurs. Serious child writers are uncommon for at least two reasons. The field itself has few organized supports or strategies for instruction in the craft . . . [and] child writers may be rare because children normally lack the kind of experience, insight, and understanding that writers are expected to convey in their works. (p.44)

However, my personally-gathered data conflicts with Feldman's: there are more children than Feldman thought who write at an adult level of competence. I have come into contact with such children in the course of my work in the schools, as have many of my colleagues, both writers and teachers. The following poem was written by a nine-year-old girl enrolled in a school for gifted children, but her ability far surpassed those of her peers. A letter from her mother in 1990 said that she was in high school, now writing novels.

> Sweet aromas fill the stallion's heart
> Eyes of blue, hide of white
> Glimmering with its sweat
> On the run, under burning sun.
> As quick as a shimmering, sunny stream.
> Panting wildly, wildly panting
> Suede rabbit hops in its way.

This poem illustrates unusual linguistic precociousness in the repetition of consonant and vowel sounds (assonance and consonance), the sophisticated rhythms ("Eyes of blue, hide of white"/ "on the run, under burning sun"; "Panting wildly, wildly panting"; the improbable images "suede"). "Sweet aromas" in the horse's heart creates an initial paradox. It is not logical that there would be aromas in a horse's heart, but this young poet pays no attention to logic. The second line uses the repetitive device of parallel structure to create a rhythm. The third line sets up a visual image that is answered in line five — "glimmering" and "shimmering." In the fourth line, the letters r, y, u, and n are repeated in various melodic combinations: "run," "under," "burning"; then "run" is resolved into "sun," which is repeated in the next line, in an alliterative phrase, "shimmering sunny stream." The urgency of the reversed phrases in the fifth line, "panting wildly, wildly panting," keeps up the excitement of the poem. Then, when a suede rabbit hops, we can feel the danger inherent in that ordinary situation. The unusual adjective "suede" is far from any cliche that a child or adult might use to describe a rabbit.

After looking at such writing by children, I have defined sixteen qualities their writing often shows:

1. The use of paradox
2. The use of a parallel structure
3. The use of rhythm
4. The use of visual imagery
5. Unusual melodic combinations
6. Unusual use of figures of speech — alliteration, personification, assonance
7. Confidence with reverse structure
8. Unusual adjectives and adverbs
9. A feeling of movement
10. Uncanny wisdom
11. Sophisticated syntax — hyphens, parentheses, appositives
12. Prose lyricism
13. A natural ear for the rhythm and sounds of language
14. Sense of humor
15. Philosophical or moral bent
16. A playfulness with words

Here are six haikus, three by an adult professional and the rest by a sixth grade girl. Can you tell whose is whose? The young poet was featured on an episode of *Nova* called "Child's Play" in 1984 when she was eight years old and in second grade. The adult professional is Bernard Einbond, who in 1988 won the Japan Airlines Haiku contest over thousands of entries. His haikus below are taken from *The Coming Indoors and Other Poems* (1979).

Treading glory lane      Delectable crumb —
To see it end in flood     the quickness of a sparrow —
Or go up in flame.       indignant pigeon.

At day's end, straying
the ocean's edge, tang
on my lips.

Tides of the ocean long
serving the moon's every whim of
leaving skeletons.

In the crowded train,
two women seated apart
who must be sisters.

Words without meaning
Rebel without a cause
Constant paradox.

Let's take a few more examples from children in New York City, Ohio, Michigan, and New Jersey. Some of the writings were sent to me, some I discovered, and some were shown to me by teachers, parents, and professional writers. The children were Caucasian, Asian, Hispanic, and African American, girls and boys, though mostly girls. Interestingly, while girls' writings are more often brought to my attention than boys', Feldman asserts that "boys have more frequently been identified as prodigies" in all areas of endeavor, possibly because a crucial element in the making of a prodigy — environmental receptivity — is more available to boys.

The following poem was written by a six-year-old girl while riding in a car during a rainstorm.

### Ripples of Liquid Caterpillars

Ripples of liquid caterpillars
Roll down my window
They travel slowly
Shedding old transparent skins
How sad
They will not stop long enough
To want to see
Their winged reflections
In the sunshine.

This poignant phrasing, with its automatic repetitions of the letters i, l, r, s, t, and o, uses paradox. Note that it is not that they won't see their winged reflections, but that they will not want to. And how did caterpillars turn into butterflies in just the length of a rainstorm? Again, the freedom from the need to be logical is a strong point. Note also the meditative, almost Buddhist quality of the poem.

The following was written by our young Haiku artist when she was nine.

## Star Poem

I am picked up by a star
And flung on to Saturn's turning ring
The star begins to throb
And turns bright red.
All the heavenly bodies turn to fire.
They are rejoicing in the birth of a sunset.
The stars toss me into the sunset.
It is a joy,
It contains all the dreams
People will dream tonight.
A sunset is a dream keeper.

The movement in this poem — the flinging, tossing, turning, throbbing, picking up — is immediately evident. The attributing to the star of the ability to pick someone up is rare: usually children's personification takes the form of animals becoming people. Rings and stars and heavenly bodies and sunsets are evocative of the dream being portrayed here. The progression from beginning to end of this work, from being picked up by a star, flung onto a ring of Saturn, witnessing a sunset being born, and then being tossed into that sunset which paradoxically keeps the dreams of people, is reminiscent of the wisdom of the psalmists.

The next two examples, submitted by a writer from Teachers and Writers Collaborative in New York City, were written by a junior high school boy from a poverty-stricken area in the South Bronx.

## Expression

A comedy of errors,
throughout changing time
you live. Die all in one maze
you run, hide still it all ends
the same. Life is an everchanging
play that blossoms and closes
then dies.
Just a comedy of errors,
Forever a comedy.

## Sin-Eater

A clear pure soul of simple logic.
You milk the moment,
Taking a deliberate pace of time.
You don't seem to quit as
You pull the trigger.
He's dead. You're glad. It's
over. You touch him.
Blood smears your fingers.
Running crazy, you feel a sharp pain.
It skips through your mind,
You forget. You're in a war.
You're dead. Simple, isn't it?

These poems show a sense of music and rhythm, of heard phrases turned upon themselves in different contexts, of macabre details (common among junior high boys), perhaps a reflection of the circumstances in which the boy finds himself in his neighborhood. But talent is evident: "clear pure soul of simple logic" stands out as a measured musical phrase. The use of "a deliberate pace" in reference to time and not to walking shows that the writer has absorbed and heard the common language and is able to put it into an artistic context. The echo of Shakespeare's "a poor player that struts and frets his hour upon the stage" is heard in the writer's "Life is an everchanging / play that blossoms and closes / then dies." Above all, these poems show a natural ear for language that makes this boy's poetry stand out as exceptional in the context of his classmates, whose lesser poems in the anthology are more typical of children's poems.

Here is another example by an eight-year-old girl.

## Colorful Wildlife

Colorful wildlife is a beautiful violet sun
covering the earth with warm rays.
Wild sweet music all at once.
It is really Phasiphe.
Love, love all around.
Phasiphe Phasiphe Phasiphe
All Phasiphe

This poem was written spontaneously, in response to a jar in the Metropolitan Museum of Art. The child demonstrates a playfulness with her repetition of a word that intrigues her, "Phasiphe." The willingness to play with words and a joy in pure sound is a mark of all good writers, especially poets. This girl shows such joy — and a fearlessness. She doesn't know what Phasiphe means, but she is willing to ascribe adjectival powers to the word.

## Prose Talent

What about prose? Does extraordinary talent exist among child writers of prose? If so, what are the characteristics of such writing? On my first day on the job as a coordinator for gifted programs, a principal came to me with the following composition and asked that most common question, "Do you think this child is truly gifted?" I did indeed. This reminiscence was written by an eight-year-old from a small rural town in Northwest Ohio.

### The Dog Who Stayed With Me

Jimmy, me, and Carol were excited today. It was time to meet under my apple tree. We often, after we met, played in the empty house next door (which was for sale), and brought Teddy to play too. It was one Sunday morning, a chilly one, too. We hardly met that day. But we met inside my house instead of under the frozen, cold apple-tree, pale blue frozen sky, cold icicles of sun falling on us. We were very chilly as we instead went into the empty house with Teddy, who was kept over- night by Carol. "Rudy!" Ma yelled at me, "Get away. Here comes the moving truck." I didn't have time to ask questions. I just ran in to get Teddy if dad meant moving in the empty house. Carol said, "Rudy! Look!" A little setter, just a baby, leaped out of the car (behind the moving truck) and ran to my arms. "Why, hello, there!" Carol said, scratching the setter puppy's red-shining back, "Rudy, ball time!" I chattered my teeth, as another sun-icicle fell on my head. The wind furiously blew, and almost knocked the puppy out of my arms. "Come on, puppy!" and I tried to run without jolting the puppy. But I was so cold I couldn't help it. "Rudalas, come!" Dad yelled, and he saw the puppy. "Bring it in, but hurry!" I flung open the door and put the setter down upstairs in my warm bedroom. I ran downstairs, and the puppy followed. I got some meat scraps and a small, low bowl of milk. I teased him and held out the meat. He didn't need teasing, though. He followed me anyway. "Come on, Caboose." I began to call him Caboose. "Little Red Caboose," I often said. He followed me like a caboose and was fed. I went to bed, and below my bed I heard Caboose lapping up the milk and snapping the meat. I fell asleep at last, for Caboose's lullaby of panting was wonderful. His panting was like a lullaby. Next morning was school. I flung up my coat, and caught it. Last of all, I patted Caboose. But every time I turned my back, he whined. He leaped up and followed me. I didn't even know until I entered the school, for the marble-tile on the halls made Caboose's claws go click, click. When I got to school, Mrs. Dainty, my fourth grade teacher, just about died. "Don't you ever bring pets to school without my permission," she said.

This piece displays remarkable use of syntax. "We often, after we met" shows an understanding of grammatical apposition. The use of the parentheses is unusual, as is the use of the hyphen in several two-word phrases: "apple-tree," "red-shining back," "marble-tile." While such hyphenation for these words may not be common usage, its presence suggests sophistication, for it would seem that the writer has read prose works where the hyphen, as well as the parenthesis and the use of apposition, is common. Perhaps nineteenth century or early twentieth-century novels? The lyricism of the child — "under the frozen, cold apple-tree, pale blue frozen sky, cold icicles of sun falling on us," and "lullaby of panting" — is adult in quality. Many adult professional writers strive for such lyricism, whereas this child, composing the piece after church and before dinner, effortlessly wrote this way. "I chattered my teeth" suggests that the writer knows that teeth chatter, but not that they do so involuntarily. The "lapping" and "snapping" of the dog show a sense of parallel structure and prose rhyme.

The next prose piece is mature in subject matter and shows a remarkable sophistication. An entire third grade class of gifted students wrote novels, but this nine-year-old girl's stood out. When I asked her for permission to use her story in this book, she assented, with reservations: she thought this piece was too childish. I disagreed.

Petrova Polinski was a thirty-seven year old Russian immigrant to America. She was poor and depressed. She had black hair and eyes and wasn't really short or tall. There were always rings of weariness from hard work under her eyes. Her situation was like that of a tiny weather beaten rowboat in the middle of a raging storm, far from any help. Her pathetic sighs of self pity made you feel very sorry for her and her family.

Now that she, Petrova Polinski, had actually COME to America, she wished she was back in Russia. Everybody back home had said that in America the streets were paved with gold. Instead they were paved with sweat, hard work, and poverty. She hardly spoke her language and didn't read or write it either. She could only pin her hopes of a better life on her children, of whom there were five. She sighed and then her baby cried. Then she sank into a shabby chair with stuffing protruding from beneath the cover and closed her eyes.

The baby wailed again. Suddenly she jumped up and went over to the cupboard, took out the last crust of bread, threw it at the baby and screamed, "THERE! Now eat it!" She walked back to her chair, sank down and began to reflect on her situation again. Why was it that some people, no matter how hard they worked, never had any money? Why was it that people who never worked were so rich? If He (God) was really there, then why didn't He give them a good life? She was beginning not to believe in Him. It wasn't fair. She never had a moment to rest. And why didn't her husband at least DO something?

Then came the voice of her six-year-old daughter Olga. "Mama, Papa's coming home. Let me help you get dinner. Papa'll be hungry."

This story goes on about Petrova and her family, but already, in its first few lines, one can see the maturity of the writer, in both style and substance: "Her situation was like that of a tiny weather-beaten rowboat in the middle of a raging storm, far from any help. Her pathetic sighs of self pity . . ." And again, in the narrator's wondering about why some people are poor and some are rich, and why hard work doesn't pay, the nine-year-old author is asking questions great novelists have struggled with, from Tolstoy to Roth. This child's work shows the frankness and concern with moral questions that writers are known for, so it was no surprise when she was chosen to be a child reporter during the 1988 Presidential campaign. I turned on my TV one Saturday and saw her on national television addressing Dan Quayle: "You mean that if my father raped me and I got pregnant, you wouldn't let me get an abortion?" Quayle sputtered in amazement.

There is another characteristic of good literature that is most difficult for children: wisdom, especially uncanny wisdom. This is the quality that we look for in the literature that we read, and its presumed absence is why we don't give much credence to literature by children. What wisdom can children have? What can a child know about life? Wisdom is acquired by experience. The subject matter of the poems and stories by children is usually childlike, with predictable plots: space ships for the boys and mysteries for the girls, and monsters and fantasies all around. And poems are usually about the concerns of the children writing them. However, the maturity of vision that we call wisdom is essential to quality writing.

Sometimes children display wisdom not won by age, as the excerpts from this essay by an eleven-year-old boy show. Observe that extraordinary talent in writing shows itself not only in poetry and fiction, but in nonfiction. This sixth-grader's gift as an extraordinary writer had been recognized by his teachers since second grade. A polymath, he is also a talented composer and musician. (Incidentally, he says he has changed some of his opinions since he wrote this.)

## Philosophy

If I could put a Bronx cheer on paper, I would. Philosophy is a fake. It's just a bunch of ordinary people capitalizing words and writing theories about things they know nothing about. Sometimes I make up theories. I spend a lot of time with them and play around with them, but I keep forgetting them and they will never get on paper.

Actually, I do remember one faintly, about the universe as a constantly changing picture God wants to frame in his living room. When everybody in the whole universe is doing the right thing, the picture will stop moving, and God will go and buy a frame, and put it upon his wall. If you find this theory interesting, you are probably the kind of person who sits in his or her room and reads German epic poetry.

## Music

Music . . . the most amazing thing about music is that you can't describe the tonal quality of a sound. Before you say anything, make sure you're not giving me any of that scientific stuff about waveforms, attacks, decays, sustains, and releases. A sound is relative to the ear, and those words are relative to an idea a computer showed a bunch of scientists who don't even know how to carry a tune . . .

## Lyrics

Before I tell you anything, I have to tell you something. From where I see it, there are two kinds of writing. The first is the kind I like, which is in fact writing as if you were speaking. The second kind would be prose or verse following a rigid structure, using fancy words and stuff. Lyrics are the other kind of writing in its extreme form and in verse. I admire good lyricists because I cannot write verse at all, let alone using fancy words . . .

Good lyrics depend on the type of music they are sung to. For example, if I was commissioned to write lyrics for a country or folk tune, I'd write simple-minded lyrics.

Sometimes wonderful lyrics are ruined by the type of music they are sung to: Here's a song everybody knows: "Row, row, row your boat / Gently down the stream / Merrily, merrily, merrily, merrily / Life is but a dream."

Now take a closer look at these lyrics and absorb what they mean. See what I mean? They are beautiful lyrics. It's the music that makes them corny . . .

### Bugs

Bugs are the most annoying things on the face of this earth. Sometimes I think bugs just spend the winter thinking of gross things they can do to me. Once when I was about $5.33333333\frac{1}{3}$, I was walking near my country house or someplace that had a lot of bugs. Without warning, those disgusting tiny green aphids or gnats or something made a beeline for my eyes and I was rubbing them out for the rest of the week. I used to have brown eyes. I'm not kidding . . . Since God made more insects than humans in this world, we can conclude that He meant for them to be the dominant species. Therefore, I believe that we should honor the bugs by giving them the entire turnip and spinach crop every year.

These extraordinary diary entries show not only wisdom, but humor. A sense of humor is one of the marks of the verbally advanced child, as discussed in Chapter 6.

## Characteristics of Children with Writing Talent

What characteristics do children with such talent have in common? I have surveyed adult published poets and young unpublished poets about their youth (Piirto, 1987), and found that (1) they read early; (2) they all read — a lot; (3) their parents read to them — a lot; (4) they admired words and expressions by words. One nine-year-old girl said that writing "is a sometimes better way to express feelings than words and actions. It also helps me to think logically." Another of the girls, age nine, said that her mother was now reading Shakespeare with her — "the real stuff, not watered down." Research on early readers has shown that they have parents who answer questions, who spend much time reading to the child, and who were readers themselves (Roedell, Jackson, and Robinson, 1980).

I believe that further examination of the Dabrowski theory of over-excitability by Piechowski and his colleagues (1985) will show that writers engage the written word with an intensity that is often interactive, almost physical. One such example is a young writer in our study of creative adolescents, who spoke out loud to the characters when reading an exciting book. Another example is from Green's *Diary* (1961), in which he described Andre Gide reading from Solugub: "His voice reminds one of a bird of prey; it suddenly pounces on a word, swoops off with it, and feasts on it. Then he lowers his book and smiles as though he had really eaten something delicious."

Whether or not these young writers will become well-known novelists, poets, or essayists is impossible to say. Few well-known child prodigies become adult geniuses. Chance plays a large part in the flowering of creativity, as well as the honoring and rewarding of it. It is precisely because we cannot predict which child will be of great benefit to society as an adult artist that we must nurture the talents of all gifted children.

Bloom, in *Developing Talent in Young People,* noted that talented children who become successful adult professionals study their field to the point of "automaticity" (Bloom, 1985, 1986). Musicians practice, athletes practice, mathematicians practice, chess players practice, all to acquire higher and higher levels of performance that is automatic. The notion that prodigy springs full-blown without specific practice in the field is false. Idiot savantism may do so, but not prodigy. However, the practice must come from interest, engagement, and motivation on the part of the young talented person. Being forced to practice only works until the practice of practicing takes hold. This is true in other fields as well: the tennis champion Andre Agassiz's father, a tennis coach, insisted that Agassiz serve thousands of balls per day, seven days per week. Perhaps writers practice the use of words and thus develop automaticity when they read as well as when they write.

On the other hand, Chomsky, Jung, and Bloom have postulated that prodigies' early mastery is a knowledge of form that comes about through intuition, through archetypal or innate knowledge, or even through reincarnation. In their adolescent years, spontaneity in young writers often gives way to conformity. But, as studies from Galton's *Hereditary Genius* (1869) to the present have shown, some writers come from "eminent" families who themselves are erudite, extremely literate, and encouraging, or at least tolerant of the voluminous reading these writers did in childhood. It is also true that some writers came from unerudite families, and in fact, the Goertzels (1972, 1978) found that only one adult poet who had a biography written about him had a parent who was a poet.

Allen Ginsberg would have been another; Ginsberg's father was the poet Louis Ginsberg, who was also a high school teacher.

In adolescence, potential writers should acquire the knowledge that they need. Although generally "divergent producers," they now become the necessary "convergent producers" (Piirto, 1989a). In youngsters with writing talent, complusive reading usually continues, and the study of literary works becomes more formalized as they approach adulthood. Young adult writers become older adult writers, and their wisdom and experience become part of the literature they create. That is the good thing about literary talent. Precocity or prodigy is not necessary for adult achievement, since most literary achievers continue writing throughout their lives, though precocity or prodigy is often predictive, as the biographies of writers tell us.

## Famous Writers as Children

*I do not remember when I could not read.*
— Benjamin Franklin

*There were books in the study, books in the drawing room, books in the cloakroom, books (two deep) in the great bookcase on the landing, books in the bedroom, books piled as high as my shoulder in the cistern attic, books of all kinds reflecting every transient stage of my parents' interest, books readable and unreadable, books suitable for a child and books most emphatically not. Nothing was forbidden me.*
— C. S. Lewis

While we cannot know who among our youth will "make it," we can observe similarities between them and successful, established writers. A look at the juvenilia and childhood of a sample of prominent writers reveals that they wrote and read avidly and early.

### George Eliot

In *George Eliot's Life as Related in Her Letters and Journals,* Cross (1903) described the father, a strong, powerful man, sitting in his leather chair with his six-year-old daughter. "The child turns over the book with pictures that she wishes her father to explain to her — or perhaps she prefers explaining to him." There was little children's literature in their home, but Mary Ann Evans (George Eliot) devoured with "passionate delight and total absorption" a copy of *Aesop's Fables,* ". . . the possession of which had opened new worlds to her imagination." At eight, now at school, "she read everything she could lay hands on, greatly troubling the soul of her mother by the consumption of candles as well as of eyesight in her bedroom." When a book had to be returned before she could finish it, she wrote out the rest of the story for herself. This is but one example of the delight that young writers take in the act of reading.

### Stephen Crane

Stephen Crane began writing as a journalist at the age of fifteen, writing legibly and fast because the salary of a compositor depended upon it. Berryman, in his 1950 biography, *Stephen Crane,* notes that Crane's mother "encouraged the boy's reading with worthy narratives like the Rev. James Dixon's *Tour of America,*" while his sister, a schoolteacher, gave him a more "rakish" book called *Sir Wilfred's Seven Flights.* She had a great desire to write, and encouraged Stephen to. "From his dissertation at eight on Little Goodie Brighteyes she followed his stories and verses with pride for four years." Crane devoured westerns, war books and other paperbacks, leading his gang in play based on the stories he read. He attended college for only one year. According to Berryman, the extent and breadth of his reading has been "understated" by his critics.

### Jane Austen

Jane Austen, unlike most children in Georgian England, grew up in a home that held no restrictions on reading material or subjects of conversations. With her earliest writings, which were parodies and satires, she developed a slant that would pervade all of her later works. According to Halperin, in *The Life of Jane Austen* (1987), her juvenilia totaled about 90,000 words, written mostly to amuse her brothers. Her writing illustrates that Austen was, even as a young girl, well-read. "Richardson was her favourite novelist, and she knew his works intimately, but she read all the fiction she could get her hands on."

## Sinclair Lewis

Sinclair Lewis was the son of a doctor in Minnesota. Schorer's biography, *Sinclair Lewis* (1961), revealed that there were about 300 books in the house by such authors as Scott, Dickens, Goethe, Milton, Beattie, Collins, Gray, and Young. These books "formed the boy's earliest literary preferences and the subjects for his reverie." Lewis, graduating seventeenth in a class of eighteen grammar-school students, was a poor speller with horrible handwriting. But by his junior year in high school, he had started his diaries and was an "omnivorous, unsystematic reader." He opened the diary with a list of books, about fifty, that he had read during the summer, works by Kipling, Thackeray, George Eliot, Victor Hugo, as well as "trash." He read "continually and often guiltily ('Wasted a lot of time reading tonight' is a kind of refrain in the diary during the high-school years)."

## Dylan Thomas

Dylan Thomas taught himself to read from comic books, according to Fitzgibbon, in *The Life of Dylan Thomas* (1965). When he was four, his father, a schoolteacher, read Shakespeare to him, reasoning, "He'll understand it. It'll be just the same as if I were reading ordinary things."

His sister: "He wrote a poem, a most interesting little poem, about the kitchen sink. And then another about an onion. That kind of thing."

## Thomas Wolfe

In *Thomas Wolfe* (1960), Nowell records that Wolfe attributed his becoming a writer to an undeniable urge within, an urge that was nurtured by his father, a stonecutter, who had "great respect and veneration for literature." (Once again, observe the prodigy-producing phenomenon of "highly specific individual proclivities with specific environmental receptivity" described by Feldman.) His father had a very good memory, reciting such works as Hamlet's soliloquy, Mark Antony's funeral oration, and Gray's "Elegy." Wolfe was also a great reader as a child. Between five and eleven he read every book in the public library of their small town.

## Virgina Woolf

When she was a child of nine, Virginia wrote and produced a newspaper, *The Hyde Park Gate News,* illustrated by her sister Vanessa. The two Stephens sisters read books aloud to each other, then reviewed the books in the newspaper; with childlike fascination they included in their reviews the number of deaths in each story. Their reading material included Thackeray, Richardson, Eliot, and most of the Victorian writers. Virginia was avid for praise from her parents; their "Rather clever, I think" overjoyed her. The children produced this newspaper well into their teenage years. But by then, "the charm and fun of the earlier numbers has evaporated. Occasionally a phrase, a joke, a turn of speech anticipates her adult style; but the general impression is rather flat," according to Bell, in *Virginia Woolf* (1972). Bell noted that Virginia changed as she entered adolescence: "She is still writing for an adult audience; but now she reached a self-conscious age and plays for safety."

This adolescent need for safety has been discussed by Bamberger in "Cognitive Issues in the Development of Musically Gifted Children" (1986). She observed a self-conscious stage in adolescence, a "midlife crisis" from which young musicians must pass if they are to progress from "early prodigiousness to adult artistry." This is over-sensitization to what others think, a state of mind which seems "to go with the gig" of being a teen, is probably true for young writers as well. (For example, the young Haiku artist wrote me that she wasn't writing much poetry as a teen but was reading fantasy and science fiction and co-editing her high school's fantasy/science fiction journal.) Fortunately for the English-speaking and -reading world, Virginia Woolf safely made it through this rite of passage.

### Tennessee Williams

According to Spoto in *The Kindness of Strangers* (1985), Tennessee Williams' mother read stories and plays to her children, acted out tall tales, recited Scottish and English ballads, told stories about folk heroes such as Annie Oakley and Davy Crockett, and sang hymns. Bible tales were told by neighbors, and the black maid sang spirituals, hymns, and lullabies. He soon began making up his own stories. Small and sickly and teased by the children at school, he took refuge in solitary reading. By the time he was nine, he had read at least two of Dickens' books, some of Scott's Waverly novels, and some Shakespeare. A few years later his mother bought him a typewriter and he began to write poems, stories, and articles, many of which were published in his junior high school newspaper. He also contributed to his high school newspaper and yearbook. His grades were average, but at this time he was already entering literary contests.

## The Bronte Family

Emily, Charlotte, and their less famous brother and sister, Quentin and Vanessa, created tiny books, written beneath magnifying glasses in an invented language known only to them. These long sagas were themselves fantasies, a genre always of interest to children. The Brontes all became adult writers of various degrees of success. Their early interest in books and writing seems typical of writers, as does their intense interest in reading.

## Harry Crews

The book by which Harry Crews, a poor sharecropper's child, was formed was the Sears Roebuck catalogue. He would look at the "Wish Book" and make up stories about the "perfect" people there, telling the stories to his cousin. In the anthology *American Childhoods* (1987), Crews wrote that "fabrication became a way of life." The stories helped him to comprehend his family's mode of living and to form a defense against harsh difficulties. His childhood story-telling "was no doubt the first step in a life devoted primarily to men and women and children who never lived anywhere but in my imagination. I have found in them infinitely more order and beauty and satisfaction than I ever have in the people who move about me in the real world."

## John Updike and C.S. Lewis

Besides a childhood environment filled with books and words, health factors can affect whether a person becomes a writer. The prolific novelist, essayist, reviewer, and poet John Updike suffered as a child from psoriasis and stuttering. He was an only child, the son of a high school teacher (many creative adults have been the children of teachers) and a writer mother whose typewriter clacking in the living room was one of the sounds of his childhood. Of the influence of the psoriasis, Updike wrote in his 1989 memoir *Self-Consciousness*:

> Only psoriasis could have taken a very average little boy,
> and furthermore, a boy who loved the average, the daily,

the safely hidden, and made him into a prolific, adaptable, ruthless-enough writer. What was my creativity, my relentless need to produce, but a parody of my skin's embarrassing overproduction? Was not my thick literary skin, which shrugged off rejection slips and patronizing reviews by the sheaf, a superior version of my poor vulnerable own, and my shamelessness on the page a distraction from my real name? (p. 75)

The stuttering made him careful of his spoken words, and so he poured his thoughts out on paper. He called his stuttering "this anxious guilty blockage of the throat," and said that despite the impediment, he has "managed to maneuver several millions of words around it." He won the Pulitzer Prize for *Rabbit at Rest* (1990).

C. S. Lewis also suffered from a physical disability. In his memoir, *Surprised by Joy* (1955), he wrote:

> What drove me to write was the extreme manual clumsiness from which I have always suffered. I attribute it to a physical defect which my brother and I both inherit from our father; we have only one joint in the thumb . . . With pencil and pen I was handy enough . . . but with a tool or a bat or a gun, a sleeve link or corkscrew, I have always been unteachable. It was this that forced me to write. I longed to make things, ships, houses, engines. Many sheets of cardboard and pairs of scissors I spoiled, only to turn from my hopeless failures in tears. As a last resource . . . I was driven to write stories instead; little dreaming to what a world of happiness I was being admitted. You can do more with a castle in a story than with the best cardboard castle that ever stood on a nursery table. (p. 12)

Another reason that young writers write was pointed out by Updike, who said that the thought of his words in print motivated him: "To be in print was to be saved." Updike, like most young writers, spent "dreamless endless solitary afternoons" reading nineteenth century novels, books of humor, and mysteries. He did not recall that his reading interfered with his social or academic life, and he graduated president of his small town Pennsylvania high school class with a scholarship to Harvard, even with the stuttering and the psoriasis. Lewis also spent "endless rainy afternoons" reading, taking "volume after volume from the shelves. I had always the same certainty of finding a book that was new to me as a man who walks into a field has of finding a new blade of grass."

## Graham Greene

Graham Greene's childhood is a good illustration of the high emotionality and strong imagination that incipient writers show. He liked to be sick, as his biographer, Norman Sherry, in *The Life of Graham Greene* (1989), revealed: "Minor ailments pleased him, for they confined him to bed and brought him a sense of peace, endless time, and a night-light burning in his bedroom, a feeling of security." He had fears of darkness, of bats, of the footsteps of strangers, of drowning, and of touching the feathers of birds, all of which appear in his novels. This "sensitivity toward animate and inanimate nature was apparent when Greene was only four years old."

Even though he grew up in a large family with older brothers, younger sisters, and relatives and servants about, Greene as a child stayed a loner; he was a secretive child who kept his terrors to himself. When he was seven, he discovered he could read *Dixon Breet, Detective,* a book his parents did not approve of because it wasn't a basal reader. So he went to the attic to read in secret, and he read from then on "with absorption and intelligence." He claimed that an advantage of being the headmaster's son was being able to read from the many books in the school library during holidays.

Greene theorized that only in childhood does reading have a "powerful influence." He recalled "the missed heartbeat, the appalled glee" he experienced when he first read Dracula: "the memory is salt with the taste of blood, for I had picked my lip while reading and it wouldn't stop bleeding." But he said that reading had other importance apart from providing excitement, fear and escape: "In childhood all books are books of divination, telling us about the future, and like the fortune-teller who sees a long journey in the cards or death by water they influence the future." Greene expressed his belief that early reading has more influence on conduct than any religious teaching, and said that the books for children in the early twentieth century (he was born in 1904) not only provided adventure and excitement and the strangeness of foreign lands, they instilled standards of heroism, idealism, courage and self-sacrifice.

At age ten, when he moved from prep school to the junior school, he realized the world was not as he had gathered from his reading. While the loss of innocence and childhood illusions is part of the normal process of maturing, in Greene's case the abruptness of his awakening to reality was traumatic and yet, even at an early age, there was a strangeness about him. As a child Greene invented a language of his own called the "lollabobble dialect." Schoolmates thought he was "very different and perhaps a bit bonkers." He early demonstrated a great sympathy for people that would make him weep. He was quoted as saying, "I remember the fear I felt that my mother would read us a story about some children who were sent into a forest by a wicked uncle to be murdered, but the murderer repented and left them to die of exposure and afterwards the birds covered their bodies with leaves. I dreaded the story because I was afraid of weeping." His biographer said that this "imaginative sympathy with the predicaments of others helped to make him a novelist," and even until his death in 1991 he would weep at a sad movie.

Greene shed some light on the life of a young boy who is about to become a world-class writer in an essay in the *Spectator:*

> Against the background of visits to grandparents, of examinations and lessons and children's parties, the tragic drama of childhood is played, the attempt to understand what is happening, to cut through adult lies, which are not regarded as lies simply because they are spoken to a child, to piece together the scraps of conversation, the hints through open doors, the clues on dressing-tables, to understand. Your whole future is threatened by these lowered voices, these consultations . . . the quarrels in the neighboring room, but you are told nothing, you are patted on the head and scolded, kissed and lied to and sent to bed (June, 1933, p. 22).

### Summary

Gifted young writers, like children gifted in any other field of endeavor, need recognition and nurturing of their talents. The necessary library cards, the quiet places in which to write, the supportive and not overly evaluative atmosphere, the reading aloud and discussing of literature together (perhaps the turning off of the TV), and honest delight in the written word — all of these can help young children with potential to write truly and confidently.

1. Young talented writers may appear more often than some researchers have shown.

2. This talent seems to occur in all socioeconomic and ethnic groups.

3. There are at least sixteen qualities found in the writing of talented young writers.

4. A look at the childhood of writers who became well-known as adults shows that they often were early readers, and they read a lot.

5. Talented children often go through a developmental crisis in adolescence.

# Chapter 8

## Creative Scientists, Mathematicians, and Inventors

*I still can't get over it that you can sit at your desk and noodle around with equations and try out ideas and put together physical principles that may or may not be right, and every once in a while, you can say something about the real world. You can predict the result of an experiment, or a new particle, or say something about the forces of nature or about the way the universe evolves and all out of pure thought.*

— Steven Weinberg

*My life is what I have done, my scientific work; the one is inseparable from the other. The work is the expression of my inner development, for commitment to the contents of the unconscious forms the man and produces his transformations. My works can be regarded as stations along life's way. All my writings may be considered tasks imposed from within; their source was a fateful compulsion. What I wrote were things that assailed me from within myself.*

— Carl Jung

There he is, immortalized in many teenage movies — the nerd. His shirt pocket lined with a plastic pen holder, his glasses held with an elastic band around the back of his head, in his high-water pants and clumsy shoes, his plaid shirt, his floppy leather belt clasped just below his breast, and with an earnest gaze through thick glasses, he is a whiz at math or science or computers. But the last thing a gifted teen wants to be called is a nerd. Often such students avoid the gifted program because of that stereotype.

Roe, in the essay "Psychological Approaches to Creativity in the Sciences" (1963), observed that among the personal problems of young scientists are: (1) the lack of in-groups, or groups where they will be accepted; (2) the conflict between students' values and family values, if parents and siblings devalue science; (3) the development of verbal abilities in the early grades; and (4) the attitudes of the schools, where teachers often dismiss "off-the-wall" and non-conforming ideas. These problems are similar to those that any creative youth suffers.

And what about the girl who is a whiz, a creative young scientist or mathematician? She is thought to be so rare, unless she is Asian, that she is not even stereotyped. Brody, reporting in 1989 on Johns Hopkins University's Study of Mathematically Precocious Youth (see also Stanley and Benbow, 1986), showed that those few girls who qualified for radical acceleration (the ratio is 20 boys to one girl) had mothers with Ph.D.'s who didn't work outside the home. She also found that these girls were predominantly Asian.

People who are good in mathematics and science have what Gardner (1983) called "logical-mathematical intelligence," one of his seven frames of mind, while Kruteskii, in *The Psychology of Mathematical Abilities in Schoolchildren* (1976), called it a "mathematical cast of mind." Gardner said they have: (1) a good memory for mathematics and science and the ability to solve problems in their heads, often intuitively skipping steps to come up with the right answers; (2) the ability to perceive a process of mathematical reasoning and to recreate it; and (3) the ability to make new problems and solve them. The ability to be creative in mathematics is, Gardner said, the ability to be "absolutely rigorous and perennially skeptical: no fact can be accepted unless it has been proved rigorously by steps that are derived from universally accepted first principles."

Scientists, on the other hand, don't deal with such abstractions as mathematicians do; they use mathematics as a tool. Mathematicians find joy and fulfillment in the beauty of mathematics for its own sake, while scientists find joy and fulfillment in considering the true nature of physical reality. Scientists want to unlock the secrets of nature, and they are motivated by their beliefs in underlying universal themes or patterns in nature. Gardner went so far as to say that "science itself is virtually a religion, a set of beliefs that scientists embrace with a zealot's conviction." Scientists, equipped with mathematical understanding, observational powers, and technical knowledge, are often motivated by the hope or even mystical conviction that their theories will be proven right as they perform their experiments on the physical world.

## Psychological Studies of Scientists and Mathematicians

What have psychologists and biographers discovered about creative scientists and mathematicians? What is the creative scientist or mathematician really like? Fortunately, many psychologists studying the creative personality have focused on scientists, and many studies have used both tests, and a biographical approach. We now know much about the personalities of scientists. Drevdahl and Cattell (1958; Cattell and Drevdahl, 1955) in their research using the 16 Personality Factor Questionnaire, found that creative artists and writers had personalities similar to those of creative scientists, except that the scientists had more emotional stability than had the writers.

In 1968, almost a thousand teenage scientists competing in a national science talent search were compared with some two hundred adult writers, architects, mathematicians, and scientists who had been studied at the Berkeley Institute for Personality Assessment and Research (IPAR). The study was called "Personality Characteristics Which Differentiate Creative Male Adolescents and Adults" (Parloff, Datta, Kleman, and Handlon, 1968). The researchers compared scores on the California Psychological Inventory and found that the young scientists scored highest on "Disciplined Effectiveness," a measure of self-control; in making a good impression; in having a sense of well-being; in achieving by way of conforming; in being tolerant; and in being sociable, responsible, and intellectually efficient.

The creative adult scientists, however, were not apt to be so conforming or dependable, and the authors posited that this difference between adolescent scientists and creative adult scientists was a practical adaptation used by the adolescents to get on in the world. A creative adult scientist who is eccentric and demanding is treated with more tolerance than is the "brash, unrecognized adolescent." They also asserted that the job of the adolescent creative scientist is to have the discipline to "learn principles, heuristics, and basic information, which he may then proceed to reintegrate and reorganize in a constructively creative fashion."

MacKinnon, in *In Search of Human Effectiveness* (1978), pointed out that this picture of the self-controlled science student was not that of the stereotyped bohemian creative adolescent. However, while young scientists may be conforming and disciplined, they also have been found early on to incorporate their interest in science into their play. As children, they have been found to have had collections of rocks, insects, spiders and the like; to have had a parent, relative, family friend, or teacher who encouraged them and who talked to them about their interests; and to have had a sense of wonder about nature and its manifestations. A case in point is the description of early family fun by Jonathan Weiner, a science writer, who wrote in *The Next One Hundred Years* (1990):

> Not long ago, trying to fathom Gaia, I remembered a game that my father, my brother, and I once played. It sounds incredible, but we built a computer out of Dixie cups and pieces of shirt cardboard, and the contraption quickly got smart enough to outwit the three of us at a game of strategy. I still recall our delight as we sat around the kitchen table and watched the Dixie cup computer making better and better moves until by the end of the evening it trounced us every time. (Evenings like this are not for everyone.) (p. 203)

Vera John-Steiner, in her *Notebooks of the Mind* (1985), which contains a discussion of scientific thinking as revealed by interviews, biographies, autobiographies and the notebooks of scientists, said that young scientists have "informal apprenticeships of the mind." For example, Einstein hated the discipline of the gymnasium (i.e. school), preferring instead to read and think and talk with people such as his Uncle Jakob, a sound engineer who played algebraic games with his young nephew and who made mathematics fun. Uncle Jakob called $x$ "a little animal whose name we don't know." (Clark, 1971)

The childhoods of Einstein and of scientist Edward Teller were remarkably similar. Einstein was born in 1879 in Germany and grew up there; Teller, born in 1908, grew up in Hungary. Teller, like Einstein, was thought at first to be mentally slow. Einstein did not speak well until about age six, and Teller did not speak well until about age three. However, by the time Teller was four, "The words gushed forth in polysyllables, understandable phrases, complete sentences," according to his biographers, Blumberg and Panos, in *Edward Teller: Giant of the Golden Age of Physics* (1990). Before age 6, Teller showed his precocity in mathematics by putting himself to sleep with multiplication problems, asking himself the number of seconds in a minute, hour, day, week, and year. However, a few years later, he was bored in math class: "His keen interest in mathematics had propelled him into the realm of basic algebra, and he was so far ahead of the class that he seemed apathetic." His grade school teacher ignored him when he tried to answer questions, for Teller was so advanced that the teacher assumed he was repeating the class and hence knew all the answers. Similarly, Einstein was demonstrating precocity in mathematics by the age of nine.

But the boys were interested in other subjects as well. Both were readers, Teller especially liking Jules Verne's science fiction. Both began musical instruction at age six, Einstein the violin and Teller the piano. Before long, Teller was playing so well that his mother, a talented musician, had hopes that he would become a concert pianist. As a young teen he would often become "engrossed for hours at a time in the sonatas and fugues of Bach, Beethoven, and Mozart." Interestingly, Einstein was roughly the same age, fourteen, when he discovered the mathematical structure of music through the works of Mozart. And at fourteen Teller was plunging into Einstein's book on relativity.

It is an odd fact that there were several other Hungarians who grew up along the same river valley in Hungary at the same time, an era of political unrest. These boys didn't know each other then, and when they met later, they said they all must have come from Mars. These were Eugene Wigner, a 1963 Nobel Laureate; Leon Szilard, who in 1942 with Fermi produced the world's first controlled nuclear reaction; Theodor von Karmann, an aeronautical engineer; and John Von Neumann, considered one of the finest mathematicians in the world. All came from close families who valued education and provided a stimulating intellectual atmosphere in the home.

Both Teller and Einstein had the influence of a university mentor. Einstein's parents took in a boarder, Max Talmey, a medical student. Talmey called the Einstein home "happy, comfortable and cheerful" and wrote a book on his impressions of the twelve-year-old Einstein. Max gave the child Bernstein's books on physical science, Buchner's *Force and Matter,* and Spieker's *Geometry,* a textbook. Einstein would show Max the problems he had solved. Talmey said,

> After a short time, a few months, he had worked through the whole book of Spieker. He thereupon devoted himself to higher mathematics, studying all by himself Lubsen's excellent works on the subject . . . Soon the flight of his mathematical genius was so high that I could no longer follow. Thereafter philosophy was often a subject of our conversations. I recommended to him the reading of Kant. At that time he was still a child, only thirteen years old, yet Kant's works, incomprehensible to ordinary mortals, seemed to be clear to him. (Clark, p. 16)

Teller often helped his older sister with her mathematics homework; Einstein did likewise with his younger sister. Both men stayed extremely close to their sisters throughout their lives. Einstein called his sister Maja his "constant companion and unfailing confidant." Both boys wanted to be physicists but their fathers were afraid they wouldn't be able to make a living, and so they persuaded them to enroll in engineering school. Both were from Jewish backgrounds that were not particularly religious. Both fled the Nazis to come to the United States during World War II. Both boys, strong in mathematics, chose to become theoretical physicists.

## What Are Scientists Like?

Why did Einstein and Teller choose science as opposed to mathematics? Is there some disposition of personality toward one or the other? Research has found that young mathematicians and young scientists do differ (Tannenbaum, 1983; Bloom, 1985); however, both need a certain threshold of general intelligence. According to Tannenbaum, in *Gifted Children:* "After the scientist's first job, IQ influences positional recognition directly, regardless of first job prestige, educational background, and scholarly performance." Simonton said that people in the physical sciences have the highest IQs, with the physics Ph.D.'s having IQs of about 140. People in the biological sciences have "somewhat less Olympian minds," and those in the social sciences are lower in IQ. He said that merely learning what is essential in the physical sciences requires high intelligence. For instance, Einstein's field, theoretical physics, requires more basic intelligence than Freud's field of psychoanalysis. Simonton, in *Genius, Creativity, and Leadership* (1984) said:

> Thus it is not utterly preposterous to suggest that Einstein and Oppenheimer may have been equally bright and that both were the intellectual superiors of Freud. Both Einstein and Freud were revolutionaries, but Freud revolutionized a field that requires less intrinsic intelligence. Oppenheimer may have surpassed Freud in raw brain power, but the field of physics demands more, so Freud is a revolutionary, Oppenheimer is only an advancer. (p. 76)

You are probably feeling a little intimidated right about now, whether you know your IQ or not. You may believe that you have been predestined to achieve according to your IQ. But remember that Simonton didn't say which IQ test was used, nor what it measured. And please stay tuned for the test scores of innovative inventors. IQ tests were made by scientists, for scientists. Do not ascribe mystical properties to pencil and paper tests.

Young scientists also showed early differences, according to specialty, with biologists preferring hobbies and books related to nature. For example, a plant geneticist I know had gardens in his family's backyard from an early age. Young physical scientists often like to work with mechanical toys and gadgets, and young social scientists are often spellbound readers. Terman's follow-up studies confirmed that scientists had what Tannenbaum called "an early and persistent interest in science." Science students were interested in the cause of things, were daydreamers, liked to solve mental puzzles, and liked art that was symbolic and music that had classical structures. They liked to read science books, to build models, and to take walks in nature. Often solitary, their interests in high school tended to emphasize science clubs and science experiments, and they liked to solve scientific problems. Science teachers often had great influence on them. Brandwein (1955) studied about a thousand New York City high school science students and found that they had high IQs, were predisposed to like science, and had teachers who inspired them. These teachers were themselves science achievers, active professionals in their learned societies, active also in curriculum writing; they had hobbies associated with science, such as memberships in hiking clubs or birdwatching societies.

Young mathematicians also display their talent early, and they also have high IQs, high spatial visualization ability, and high verbal ability. Krutetskii (1976) studied 200 children and found that the able and very able students had six characteristics which surfaced early. These were: (1) the ability to grasp the structure of a problem, separating extraneous information from essential information; (2) the ability to easily find abstract principles within problems; (3) the ability to skip steps in the process of solving problems and still come out with the right answer; (4) the ability to appreciate elegant mathematical solutions; (5) the ability to be flexible and to solve the same problem in many ways; and (6) the ability to remember essential features of problems, even many months later. A young mathematician might exclaim in the middle of a solution, "Oh, we had this problem last summer!"

Krutetskii also found that mathematical talent comes in four varieties: the analytic, the geometric, and two types of harmonic abilities. Young mathematicians with analytic talent have stronger verbal-logical abilities and weaker spatial abilities. Those with geometric talent have stronger spatial visualization abilities and weaker verbal-logical abilities. Both types of harmonic ability math students have strong verbal, logical, and spatial visualization abilities. Krutetskii emphasized that the ability to calculate is not a prerequisite for strong mathematical talent. However, analytic ability is a prerequisite for strong mathematical talent, for mathematics requires the ability to think abstractly.

*Gruber on Darwin*

The seminal psychological study in the field of creativity in science is Howard Gruber's (1974) study of Charles Darwin, *Darwin on Man*. In it, Gruber asserted that the detailed study of one life was necessary to uncover the essence of scientific creativity. Gruber studied the development of Darwin's theory of evolution, utilizing Darwin's notebooks of 1837 to 1838, written after his famous voyage to the Galapagos on the *Beagle* in 1831-1836. Gruber wrote that scientific creativity takes courage, "brave and patient struggle under conditions of adversity," and that it does not come about through a few moments of insight, but from a long and laborious process of thinking, revising, and reformulating.

Darwin waited until 1859, when he published his *Origin of Species,* to make public his belief that natural selection through the survival of the fittest had operated to transmute species. Alfred Wallace had written Darwin a letter in 1858 about his field observations in the South Sea islands. This precipitated Darwin's writing, finally, of the book, for Darwin was well aware of the social consequences of coming out with such a theory. Wallace's work caused Darwin to try to act first. Wallace was also influenced by Malthus's work, and the Linnaean Society gave both men credit at the same time for publishing the theory of natural selection. (However, Wallace stopped short of saying that human intelligence had evolved through natural selection.) Gruber called Darwin's delay in publishing his theory a "grand detour" of twenty-three years, a delay that was illustrative of the psychological process of creativity in people.

For example, a scientist is taught to use the scientific method, to gather data and to form a hypothesis and to construct an experiment to prove or disprove that hypothesis. Gruber called this view of the scientific process "the rationalist myth," explaining that a person who takes hold of one theory or one point of view discovers hypotheses "with difficulty." Darwin's notebooks showed that he worked differently, for while the hypothesis was in the air, so to speak, certain events in his life were necessary before the hypothesis could be formed. Darwin had written in his notebooks about natural selection, but through a long growth process encompassing both the forming of a dense schema (or much data gathering) and the process of coming to equilibration, Darwin didn't fully realize what he had found until much later. Gruber said that "novel ideas can be forgotten until the structure of which they are to become a part is sufficiently complete to stabilize them." Another way of stating this could be found in the popular saying that when the student is ready the teacher will come, implying that people take in much but don't fully remember it or utilize it until they are ready.

Gruber also spoke about a "network of enterprises" contributing to the formulation of a scientific theory, or of any theory. (I mentioned the "network of enterprises" in Chapter 6, in regard to writing across genres.) While Darwin was delaying in publishing his *Origin of Species,* he spent eight years studying barnacles; he wrote many articles and papers; he continued to accumulate geological and biological information. He delayed also in publishing his second major theoretical work, *The Descent of Man* (1871), for he was fully aware that his theory that man also had evolved would be explosive, invoking the ire of the Church.

And so between 1859 and 1871 he published many works, accumulated more evidence, and wrote and thought and spoke on related topics. He lived his life and continued to consider. His theories did not spring instantaneously, but came to fruition after many related projects brought them into being as a "network of enterprises."

Gruber concluded that creativity, or creative thought, is the "work of purposeful beings." Those who say that creative thought arises from chance or Zeitgeist, or accident, are only partially correct, as are those who say that creative thought arises from unconscious processes and from internal, hence not rational, mechanisms such as night dreams and daydreams. He said that while both of these are necessary and important, the scientific creator is "governed by a ruling passion" that informs all of his activities. When Darwin went to the zoo, he found behavior that informed his theory; when he went to the opera, he did the same. Darwin was seeing everything in the context of the theory he was hatching. However, since he was working on this theory over a long period of time, he was able to take such events not as "proof" of his theory, but as part of the fabric. According to Gruber, Darwin was able to scrap useless information without scrapping everything.

> Darwin's work was divided into a number of separate enterprises, each with a life of its own. This type of organization has several constructive functions. It permits the thinker to change his ideas in one domain without scrapping everything he believes. In this way he can go on working purposefully on a broad range of subjects without the disruptive effects that would ensue if every new idea and even every doubt immediately required a reorganization of the whole system of thought. (p. 251)

A scientist combines personal imagery (for example, Darwin's image of the irregularly branching tree, and of the wedge) that has been developed through intense exposure to the natural world, with empirical data-gathering. Gruber said that this intense gathering of knowledge must be "private and personal, even when the desired end product is the public knowledge of science." A density of personal experience is necessary; the scientist develops his theory as a means to put coherence to the enormous amount of information that is coming in.

Darwin claimed that his schooling was not important, but upon examining his school life, Gruber found that Darwin had been informally exposed to the germs of what he would later propose as theories. Darwin's grandfather, Erasmus, was also part of his development. The family itself was interested and involved in science. At Cambridge, "informal contact with some of his professors and some fellow students was the most important part of his education. Has it ever been otherwise?" The foundations were laid, and Darwin himself had as a mentor or idealized role model Alexander von Humboldt, who had sailed to the Tenebrides.

When Darwin took on the post of naturalist on the *Beagle,* he was already well-prepared by his family milieu and his school interests. Then he undertook the five-year task of taking notes, collecting specimens, making sketches. Sailing on the *Beagle* was not chance or luck, but what Gruber called "the exploitation of an opportunity that fitted in perfectly with his own well-developed purposes." Darwin began as a geologist and ended as an evolutionist. During this process he went through many phases, and he ended up challenging the strong beliefs of society about the origins of biological systems. He did not do this through a moment of insight or a rigorous application of the five steps of the scientific process, but through the process of a life-long creative production.

### Simonton's Historiometric Studies

Other interesting and comprehensive work in the area of scientific creativity has been that of Simonton (1988). He has been working in the field of historiometry, or the mathematical translation of biographical information. With the Goertzels' 1962 and 1978 data, and with other data from people like Roe and Cox, he is helping to define what constitutes genius in creativity, as in his book, *Genius, Leadership, and Creativity* (1984). Simonton has developed what he called the chance-configuration theory of the development of creativity in science. Briefly stated, there are two steps in the creative process in science. First is the making of a theory, or a configuration. This step is inner, intuitive, associative, meditative, and more likely generated in solitude than through group brainstorming. The second step is more public, more secondary, changing this subconscious idea into something that can be communicated or published.

Simonton held that on one personality dimension, all creative scientists are alike: they are devoted to work. That is, their motivation — their task commitment — differentiates them from others. And if someone is devoted to his life's work, huge productivity is more likely. In *Scientific*

*Genius* (1988), Simonton reported that Darwin could claim 119 publications by the close of his career; Einstein, 248; and, in psychology, Galton, 227; Binet, 277; James, 307; Freud, 330; and Maslow, 165. Edison may be best known for his phonograph and incandescent light bulb, but all told he held 1,093 patents — still the record in the United States Patent Office. However, it would seem that all creative people are devoted to work, not only scientists, as we have seen already with visual artists and writers, and as we shall see with musicians, actors, and dancers. Furthermore, Piechowski (personal communication, December, 1990) said that this view of scientific productivity as a mark of genius may be particularly American; that is, "productivity may be a by-product of genius but is not its fundamental characteristic."

Simonton's data lead him to conclude that scientific productivity has an age curve, beginning in the scientist's twenties, reaching its highest point in the late thirties or early forties, and then tapering off. Botanists and disease specialists are most productive in their early thirties. Bacteriologists, physiologists, pathologists, and general medical scientists are more productive in their late thirties. Chemists peak in their late twenties. Mathematicians and physicists peak in their early thirties. Geologists and astronomers reach their peak productivity in their late thirties. Theoretical mathematicians and physicists, if they have not made their contributions by the time they are in their late twenties, will probably never do so. Simonton's putting these age constraints on scientists' peaks of productivity is frightening to some people, but he derived them from statistical analyses of the lives of world-class scientists. Individual cases differ. Simonton further wrote that this characteristic of early productivity holds true for other creative people as well, including artists, writers, and musicians.

But Simonton's age curve may not be a good predictor of later productivity. For example, Gruber's work on Darwin's delay in publicly announcing his theory points out that this age curve may be misleading. Furthermore, Darwin once advised a colleague to hold a theory he was pursuing in mind but not to publish it until the data he had gathered supported the theory. The age curves shown by extant biographies may be misleading for women, also. Women may be prevented from producing at such young ages by their dual concern for childbearing and career development. While the timeline may hold true for men, women may have a different career pattern, peaking in productivity later than men tend to.

And yet Simonton also wrote that "Early productivity is one of the single best predictors of later productivity in all domains of creativity." Those who begin their productivity early often continue in it. They refuse to acknowledge retirement and retain their enthusiasm for scientific research, as well as the publication of their research, much later than less creative scientists. They are more likely to have their careers ended by illness or death than by a lack of ideas. Simonton said that those who publish more, also publish the most high-quality papers, just as those who submit the most grant proposals get the most grants. In other words, quantity is needed for success and recognition. Simonton called this the "constant-probability-of-success model" and applied it also to careers of those in literature and music.

## Family and Educational Factors

Simonton's search through the biographies yielded an odd fact: many creative people have lost a parent. Simonton called this "the orphanhood effect." Of course, one must take into account that the subjects of these biographies often lived at a time when life span was not as long as it is now. But orphanhood also comes about through parental absence caused by disease, alcoholism, divorce, or abandonment.

Why do some people become creative in the absence of a parent and others destructive? Factors to consider are the child's intellectual capacity, the cultural enrichment in the home environment, the birth order, role models, formal education, and the Zeitgeist of the times. As we have already noted, Alice Miller has asserted that whether an adult will be creative or destructive is determined by how childhood trauma was received and dealt with. Creative scientists and mathematicians, though, seem to have had more stable homes than artists, especially writers.

Choice of college is important to potential scientists and mathematicians. If the student attends a college that is not elite, not demanding, located in a backwater away from the action, the chances that the young scientist will make major achievements in science are slight. This is important, and illustrates that counseling for scientifically talented students is necessary (Subotnik and Steiner, in press). How much education is enough for scientific creativity? The attainment of the Ph.D. at a young age is almost *de rigeur*, although many of the scientifically creative made their contributions before they attained their Ph.D.s, including

Einstein. If the student qualifies to get into a highly competitive college and does not pursue that school because of finances, counselors should advise that admission is the important thing, and that the money may follow once admission is achieved.

Firstborns make up more than half of active scientists; this figure includes only children, who are somewhat different from firstborns. The reasons for the achievement of only children and firstborns are obvious: the child is exposed to exclusive adult care, whereas subsequent children have to deal with a more complex family environment from the moment of birth. Of the second-borns and other younger siblings, there is more of a chance to achieve if the birth order is spaced at about five years between children. Later children who have lost an older sibling are also more likely to achieve creatively than those who have intact families. Research on the achievement of firstborns often makes middle children angry, for they achieve also; note that the first sentence of this paragraph implies that almost half of active scientists are born second or later.

Researchers have found that scientists and mathematicians more often come from stable homes, with stronger father influences, than do other creative types. Another positive benefit is that the parents of the scientific achievers allowed the child to be present when adults were around and to interact with those adults. In fact, the young people met professionals in the fields in which they would achieve in the home. This was as true of musicians and writers as of scientists. Middle class and professional homes were most likely to have these cultural environments. The existence of such casual role models is important for young creative scientists.

More formal ones are also needed. Subotnik et al. (in press), in a longitudinal study of Westinghouse winners, found that the mentor is extremely crucial to the full development of scientific talent. Simonton described the structuring of such role-model relationships. In science, an apprenticeship, which is a form of role-modeling, is necessary. For example, Nobel Prize winners have studied under other Nobel Prize winners, thereby enhancing their opportunities of winning the Prize. Simonton said that the scientist mentor should be about twenty years older, but never less than ten years older. The mentor should still be in the "intuitive" stage of creativity, not in the "analytic" stage that comes in later years. Instructive as the role model is, however, there is a danger if the student becomes too imitative of the mentor and does not strike out on her own.

A note to school counselors; the influence of the right school, the right mentor, the right environment for the nurturing of scientific creativity is crucial, and such placement should be a priority of school counselors. Unfortunately, counselors are often content to advise bright creative scientists to attend the local community college or state university rather than seek scholarships at more competitive institutions. Many worthy students from rural areas are deterred by the myth that they can't afford a competitive college, but frequently, where there's a will, there's a way. For instance, when one scientifically gifted young man from a small town was accepted to M.I.T., the gifted coordinator at the high school contacted the M.I.T. alumni group in the region and money was found.

What is the role of religion in the lives of scientists? The least they could say was they didn't object to it, though very few scientists have come from dogmatic, fundamentalist, rules-filled denominations. It may be that requiring the scientifically creative to attend church, wear a tie, and join activities hampers the creative instincts of the young man or woman.

Schools, of course, can also suppress. Again, as Brandwein showed, teachers should emphasize inquiry rather than rote learning, should encourage independent reading and study, and should recognize the importance of self-instruction. Perhaps the reason that both Einstein and Darwin disclaimed the influence of formal education in their lives was that lecture was the primary method of discourse in German gymnasiums and British public schools.

A factor contributing to scientific creativity is what Simonton called "marginality," one of the meanings of which is to live in two cultures. Significant numbers of creative people have been first or second generation immigrants, able to straddle two cultures and to see things in new ways. Simonton concluded that "The disproportional representation among notable scientists of those with Jewish backgrounds illustrates this point." However, Abba Eban proposed another theory for the preponderance of Jewish scientists: "The Hebrew mind has been obsessed for centuries by a concept of order and harmony in universal design" (Clark, quoting Eban in *Einstein*, 1971). Eban continued: "The search for laws hitherto unknown which govern cosmic forces; the doctrine of a relative harmony in nature; the idea of a calculable relationship between matter and energy" have all contributed to Jewish interest in science.

Simonton noted that professional marginality, or being skilled in two professions, can also lead to greater creativity. In fact, many contributions to science have been made by people who have switched fields. This would seem to be evidence against a theory of "the earlier the better," for when one switches fields, one is older, past one's early bloom, yet switching fields permits people to see and to combine in new ways, perhaps becoming younger mentally. However, a third type of marginality, geographical marginality, operates against creativity rather than for it. Being away from the action, so to speak, does not contribute to either aesthetic or scientific creativity, because such creators have little access to those who can help them along.

## The Right Time

The researchers and thinkers about creativity and giftedness also postulate that certain times and places are better, historically, for scientific creativity. For example, Simonton wrote in 1985 that great advances in biological knowledge take place the generation after advances in medicine, chemistry, and geology. Politically, a sense of nationalism enhances creative production, while large empires do not. One generation after the overthrow of an empire, though, scientific creativity is on the upswing. This is because diversity increases the number of ingredients or ideas that go into a scientific discovery. However, great upheavals such as that found in the Middle East or in Africa, with revolts, shootings, rebellions, and terrorist activities, do not produce the climate for scientific innovation.

The best proof of the power of the Zeitgeist is given when multiple inventions happen — when two or more scientists come up with the same invention or creation. Simonton cited the near-simultaneous invention of calculus by Newton and by Leibniz, and the manufacture of oxygen by Priestley and Scheele; Gruber discussed the proposing of the theory of evolution by both Wallace and Darwin. Gardner (1988), Feldman (1988), Gruber (1988), and Tannenbaum (1983) all discussed the importance of the social and political climate, the very time in history, the progression of inventions, making it necessary for these discoveries to be made. It is as if they are inevitable, and thus proof that scientific creativity is not chance, but destiny.

Csikszentmihalyi (1988) argued the same point, saying, "We cannot study creativity by isolating individuals and their works from the social and historical milieu in which their actions are carried out." Gardner

(1988), in a case study of Freud's career as a creative person, argued that his work could not have been done without the milieu of Vienna at that time in history, the early twentieth century. Likewise, the period of the Renaissance in Florence is often cited as being especially fertile for creativity. Simonton argued, though, that in all cases of multiple discoveries, one of them is always more completely designed and described than the others that come during the same time period. For instance, many people tried to invent photography, but only one came upon the daguerreotype, the perfect and, at the time, complete working design.

The production of multiples in the sciences is often used to suggest a higher level of creativity in the arts, for the artistic product cannot be duplicated. There is only one Michelangelo, and only he could have created that particular Sistine Chapel ceiling. There was only one Faulkner, and only he could have created his Yoknapatawpha County in Mississippi. There was only one Beethoven, and the Fifth Symphony could not have been created by anyone else. These works of art would not exist if their creators had not existed. Did the world first need a ceiling, a county, four notes that resonated throughout ensuing history? We have these creations because of the inner visions and even inner needs of their creators.

This is not to say that artists do not participate in the Zeitgeist, the creative milieu, the progression of invention. They do. As Van Gogh wrote to his brother Theo,

> Do you know what I think of pretty often? That if I do not succeed, all the same what I have worked on will be carried on; not directly, but one isn't alone in believing in things that are true. And what does it matter personally then? I feel so strongly that it is with people as it is with corn; if you are not sown in the earth to spring there, what does it matter? You are ground between the millstones to become bread. (p. 452)

However, it is quite clear that the world did need a polio vaccine, a phonograph, a steam engine, a theory of evolution. The world needed geometry, calculus, and quantum theory. The world needed space travel and will need time travel. Scientific creativity has invented these when they were needed. Buckminster Fuller's timeline of inventions in *Critical Path* (1981) is a case in point. Fuller showed the "Chronology of Scientific Discoveries and Artifacts" and the "Chronological Inventory of Prominent Scientific, Technological, Economic, and Political World Events,

1895 to Date," placing his own inventions and discoveries in chronological order with the Zeitgeist of the times and places. He showed the rapid acceleration of inventions and their impingement on world history, using his own life span as an example. Fuller said that there is a lag of twenty-two years between the invention of a needed product and public use of that product; it is because of this need/use gap that we are on a critical path. In his last book, *Grunch of Giants* (1983), Fuller advanced the hope that there would be "bloodless socioeconomic reorientation" between nations brought about by young business people in pin-striped suits, straddling continents as they propound international technological sharing and commerce. He said the question is: Can it be successfully accomplished before the only-instinctively-operating fear and ignorance preclude success, by one individual, authorized or unauthorized, pushing the first button of chain-reacting, all-buttons-pushing, atomic, race-irradiated suicide?

We still ask the same question today. The existence of nuclear capabilities in so many countries with histories of instability and revolution comes to mind. The cavalier setting on fire of oil fields in Kuwait comes to mind. The careless burning of Amazonian forests comes to mind. Will the benevolent use of the inventions and discoveries of creative mathematicians and scientists get to all the peoples of the world in time?

## Helson's Study of Creative Women Mathematicians

With the preponderance of male subjects in studies of creative people, it is refreshing to discuss Ravenna Helson's study of creative women mathematicians, "Creative Mathematicians" (1983). Helson found that her subjects were essentially like other creative people, especially women and men creative writers.

Forty-four female mathematicians were studied at the IPAR Project at the University of California at Berkeley. They had been nominated by peers and were listed in directories of Ph.D.s who had completed their degrees between 1950 and 1960. The criterion for labeling these women "creative" was the quality of their work. Calling them "marginal" in the profession of mathematics, Helson noted that several of them did not hold academic posts or positions in research institutions, but did their work at home. Their average age was forty-one, one-third were Jewish, and foreign cultural influence (European and Canadian) was strong, as it is with male mathematicians. They were administered tests such as the California Psychological Inventory and the Minnesota Multiphasic Psychological Inventory.

The mathematicians had superior intellect and great perseverence. They were adaptive and sensitive to the new and the unforeseen. Their temperaments were subdued but still individualistic. A clinical Q-sort revealed still more characteristics descriptive of the creative mathematicians. They were independent and autonomous, taking pride in their objectivity and rationality while still being able to form associations and think in new ways. They were seen as dramatic personalities, even "histrionic," and as moody and nonconforming rebels.

In addition, a comparison study was done between the creative women mathematicians and other women mathematicians. The creative women were found to be performing in a manner superior to the others in that they received their Ph.D.s earlier, they submitted papers for publication before receiving their Ph.D.s, and they received more fellowships and grants after graduate school. The creative women were higher in flexibility and lower in achievement orientation and in cooperation, showing that they preferred to make their own ways of doing things. They did not enjoy the routine details of working in a highly structured environment. The creative women mathematicians seemed to be preoccupied with themselves, showed more autonomy, and could be described as temperamental.

Self-descriptions showed that they were more involved in research than the comparison women mathematicians, and their thought processes seemed to be less overtly conscious. They described themselves as "inventive and ingenious" and were less interested in salary, promotion, and teaching. In their leisure time, the creative women had intellectual pursuits such as listening to classical music, taking nature walks, going to the theater, and reading. They seem to have simplified their lives and they did the few things they cared about greatly. Homemaking and research occupied most of their time, while the comparison women spent much time in administrative duties, teaching, political activity, and community work. Creative subjects scored higher on the Terman Concept Mastery Test than the comparison group. Their average score was 144. (The Stanford gifted subjects scored 137, industrial research scientists scored 118, and military officers scored 60.) Creative male mathematicians scored 148. In mechanical reasoning, the creative and comparison women did not differ, and they both scored lower than men.

Helson noted that these women seemed to be more identified with their professional fathers than the comparison group of women. Both groups often came from families of girls, and the creative women, especially, seemed to have few brothers. She said, "A number of the women mathematicians seem to have been adopted as the 'son' of an intellectual father."

The creative women mathematicians differed from the creative men mathematicians studied. The creative men were higher on social ascendancy, or a desire to rise on the social ladder, as well as intellectual efficiency, or how fast and clearly they could express themselves. Interestingly enough, the comparison men and women were quite similar. The staff saw different patterns in the creative men and women mathematicians also. Helson said,

> The creative men described themselves as having confidence, initiative, ambition, impact on the environment, and intellectual balance and soundness. In contrast, the creative women described themselves as nonadventurous and inner-focused. In the work style of the creative women the self is totally committed, unconscious as well as conscious process are involved in the creative effort, and emphasis is directed toward developing what is within rather than toward exploring or mastering the environment. (p. 317)

The fact that this is a late-1960s study of people who received their Ph.D.s in the 1950s and 1940s may explain the large differences between creative men and creative women mathematicians. Women who have grown up in today's less gender-restrictive society may be more similar to men in confidence about mastering the environment. Attitudes toward women's potential for success in math have much power in shaping a young girl's self-image. Eccles (1985; 1991) and her colleagues have shown that attitudes in the family contribute to women achieving less in mathematics, with mothers' attitudes towards the probability of mathematical success being of crucial importance. It would seem that mothers who say to their daughters, "Well, I was never good in math either," and to their sons, "Boys have math ability," wield much power, both negatively and positively.

Helson theorized that there may be biological or societal causes for the gender differences. Through a study comparing creative women writers and creative women mathematicians, she found that the two groups of creative women were remarkably similar. Interestingly enough, she also found that the creative male writers were more like the creative female mathematicians and female writers than they were like the creative male mathematicians. This led to Helson's describing the creative male mathematicians as people who stood alone. "They [creative male mathematicians] have a personality in which there is relatively more social assurance and assertiveness and less conflict with conventional channels of expression and achievement."

The men writers, like the women, paid more attention to unconscious processes than to mastery and initiative. However, the male mathematicians and writers both emphasized their ambition to a greater extent than the creative women, who emphasized that they would be willing to put aside other things in order to write or do mathematics. Helson did further studies and came up with the hypothesis that there are two creative styles: (1) high in ego-assertiveness, or the need to push oneself in the world; and (2) low in ego-assertiveness. Women creators seem to be the latter, while men may be either.

The creative women mathematicians worked at home, did not have prestigious academic posts, did not teach graduate students. In fact, their life-styles were more similar to those of the writers than of their male mathematical counterparts. The low ego-assertiveness style does not publish many papers, nor is it productive in the way that Simonton said creative scientists must be. Helson said that the creative women mathematicians may have been more productive, but the institutions had trouble with their ambivalent and aloof personalities. She said that "Understanding and experiment are needed on both the institutional side and the individual side." These glaring differences between creative female mathematicians and creative male mathematicians speak to the continuing difficulty for women to achieve in creative fields because of their double bind, the continuing expectation that they work the second shift at home as well as the first shift at their creative work. Unfortunately, as of this writing, little seems to have changed.

## Mathematically Creative Boys

Keating studied for their creative potential 72 junior high school boys who were in the Johns Hopkins Study of Mathematically Precocious

Youth; his findings are published in Albert's anthology of 1983. (Note: at the time, only 4 girls qualified, making analysis by gender impossible.)

The students were administered the Allport-Vernon-Lindzey Scale of Values. Like other creative scientists who have been so studied, these young mathematicians showed a high regard for theoretical values. They were low in aesthetic values, but Keating expected that these values would grow during college. Like creative scientists, the mathematically creative boys had little regard for religious values.

## Studies of Inventors

The work of two researchers who have studied inventors, MacKinnon and Colangelo, will be presented here. Donald MacKinnon was head of the famous Institute for Personality Assessment at the University of California at Berkeley, which sponsored many of the studies described in this book. MacKinnon's specialties were the study of inventors and of architects.

Inventors have spatial intelligence, in Gardner's terms, or figural intelligence, in Guilford's terms. This type of intelligence is the ability to manipulate objects in space, from parallel-parking a bus to figuring out gears, levers, and the drawings that accompany children's toys on Christmas Eve. Mary Meeker (personal communication, 1977) said that most job titles in the U.S. government's directory require figural intelligence as opposed to semantic or symbolic intelligence, but that figural intelligence is not as valued as semantic intelligence in our society. We send students who have figural intelligence to vocational school.

MacKinnon, in *In Search of Human Effectiveness* (1978), said there are three major types of inventors. First are those who are employed by business and industry, working as researchers, who are known as "captive" inventors. Second are the "independent" inventors, those who work on their own. This latter type may be self-employed as inventors, or may invent in their spare time, after working for money at another job. In this, independent inventors are similar to creative people in the arts, who are often unable to find employment or to support themselves with their art — e.g., poets, novelists, actors, visual artists, musicians. A third type of inventor is the "basic" inventor, who creates "truly radical" new things such as telecommunications, printing, or explosives.

Of the forty-five research scientists who were studied at IPAR, twenty-seven were inventors. To be designated an inventor, the research scientist had to have obtained or applied for a patent or to have made a disclosure. The independent inventors numbered fourteen; the captive, thirteen. No basic inventors were found. A major difference in the two groups represented was that all of the captive inventors were highly educated, most with Ph.D.s, with fathers who were professionals or semi-professionals, while the independent inventors had fewer fathers in professions and more fathers in the skilled trades. Only three independent inventors had completed a bachelor's degree, and only half had completed high school.

They were administered the Terman Concept Mastery Test, which does not reveal spatial (or figural) intelligence. The captive inventors had a mean score of 119, while the independent inventors scored a mean of 51, the lowest score among the groups tested. However, there was little difference between the groups in the number of patents held. This was surprising, since people specifically employed by corporations to be inventors presumably know the ropes better, and would be expected to go through the formal channels of obtaining patents more often than people who invent in their spare time. In fact, who held the most patents? It was not a research scientist with a Ph.D.; rather, it was an independent inventor. This great discrepancy between people who achieve as inventors and people who score well on a verbal test illustrates the great harm done to figurally intelligent people by evaluating their intelligence only via verbal IQ tests.

MacKinnon's group analyzed the two types of inventors according to personality and preference and came up with eight categories of industrial research scientists. These men were described as Type I, The Zealot; Type II, The Initiator; Type III, The Diagnostician; Type IV, The Scholar; Type V, The Artificer; Type VI, The Aesthetician; Type VII, The Methodologist; Type VIII, The Independent. They concluded that the research scientists who were inventors were mainly Initiators and Diagnosticians, as were the independent inventors. The Initiators were described thus:

> This man reacts quickly to research problems and begins at once to generate ideas; he is stimulating to others and gives freely of his own time; he sees himself as being relatively free of doctrinaire bias — methodological or substantive — and as being a good "team" man.

Observers describe him as ambitious, well-organized, industrious, a good leader, and efficient. (p. 98)

Here is how the Diagnosticians were described:

This man sees himself as a good evaluator, able to diagnose strong and weak points in a program quickly and accurately and as having a knack for improvising quick solutions in research trouble spots. He does not have strong methodological preferences and biases, and tends not to be harsh or disparaging towards others' mistakes and errors. Observers see him as forceful and self-assured in manner, and as unselfish and free from self-seeking and narcissistic striving. (p. 98)

Independent inventors, not surprisingly, had high self-confidence, high self-esteem, and a willingness to troubleshoot and plunge in. MacKinnon theorized that this personality aggressiveness contributed to their low test scores on the Terman, since they guessed wrong answers as often as right answers. The captive inventors, while less cautious than their colleagues who are employed by industry but who don't invent, were much more cautious than independent inventors in taking the tests, and they didn't guess as often.

Another analysis of inventors was done by Colangelo, who studied mechanical inventiveness and inventors and presented his findings in "The Development of a Scale to Identify Mechanical Inventiveness" (1991). His group was made up of thirty-four patent-holding inventors who ranged in age from forty-four to eighty-two years. These inventors had certain patterns in their lives: (1) They had extremely happy childhoods and came from intact homes. Ninety-five percent of them viewed their families as very close. (2) They had very strong religious ties. (3) During their childhoods, they all had some area to tinker in, and about two-thirds of them came from farming backgrounds. (4) Many of their inventions came about as ways to cut down on time done in chores. (5) Many were married to wives who were very supportive of their work. (6) They had few outside hobbies, viewing their work as their fun. Their inventions were always on their minds. (7) They were conservative in many areas — family, religion, politics, dress — yet were risk-takers as inventors. (8) They were strongly independent.

Colangelo and his colleagues undertook a study comparing these inventors, students who had attended a summer inventions workshop, and students who had scored high on the American College Test. They found that the students who had attended the summer inventions workshop and the inventors were equally innovative, and both groups were more inventive than the high-scoring, academically-achieving students. The inventors believed that too much schooling would ruin a person's good ideas. Also, they cautioned young inventors to keep their ideas to themselves, for two reasons: to avoid theft, and to avoid society's sometimes dampening effect, for most inventors had difficulties in realizing or selling their ideas.

## Summary

1. As a general rule, scientists and mathematicians have more formal education than people in the arts.

2. They demonstrated an early aptitude and love for the field.

3. They are motivated less by external concerns than by internal concerns, or the desire to know.

4. They were encouraged by parents or by teachers.

5. They began producing early and produced in quantity.

6. Their personalities varied from reserved to aggressive.

7. Their family environments were happier than those who pursued the arts and literature.

8. Women were underemployed and had to do their work in less than ideal conditions.

9. Young scientists and mathematicians were more conforming than older scientists and mathematicians.

10. There was a need for supportive and connected mentors.

11. The societally-recognized creativeness of their work depended on the historical milieu, or Zeitgeist. Were they in the right place at the right time?

12. Inventors are mostly male, and often come from rural and conservative backgrounds.

# Chapter 9

## Musicians and Composers

*Of music so delicate, soft, and intense*
*It was felt like an odor within the sense . . .*
— Shelley

What comes to mind when you picture a musician? Do you see a young boy, forced to practice his piano lesson, who plays a tape recording of himself so he can escape to play baseball? Or a young girl lugging her cello to school for orchestra rehearsal or down the street for her private lesson? Or a garage band practicing at all hours of the night, waking you up and inspiring you to call the police? Or do you see young Van Cliburn wowing them in Moscow, making the evening news?

Whatever you see, it is probably an image that includes practice and study. Musicians practice. They take private lessons. They play alone. They play in groups. Even if they are in school groups — choirs, bands, orchestras — they must take private lessons in order to further themselves in their music. Schools have the responsibility to identify students who are musically gifted, and the responsibility to serve them in music programs, but no child who has musical talent will proceed very far unless he has private teachers. While this could be said of visual-arts talent as well, few young talented visual artists take private lessons. Few young talented creative writers take private lessons. Few young talented scientists and mathematicians take private lessons, but all young people who are talented in music must, if they are to succeed.

Much has been written on musical talent, especially in the genres of autobiography and biography. Musical intelligence, another of Gardner's seven "frames of mind," is characterized by acute hearing ability, or audition, as well as the ability to understand the organization of rhythms. Many have likened musical intelligence to mathematical intelligence, but Gardner pointed out that this ignores the emotional aspect of music and the musically talented person's ability to understand and express that emotion.

He also noted that musical illiteracy is acceptable in our society, and that little training in music, beyond basic singing and reading of notes in elementary school, happens: "Music occupies a relatively low niche in our culture, and so musical illiteracy is acceptable." I once asked a group of about one hundred educators of the gifted how many could read music, and five raised their hands. Four of these were music teachers. The rest could not read music, even though many of them were elementary teachers who had taken a mandatory course in music. Our knowledge of classical music is also poor.

However, the power of music to move us cannot be disputed. I once wrote a newspaper column on what makes us spontaneously weep, and most people questioned said they got tears in their eyes upon hearing children sing, hearing an old love song, singing the national anthem, or singing a favorite hymn.

## Identifying Musical Talent

Musical talent often shows up early, and if a family has a keyboard instrument, the musically talented child will probably be picking out tunes at a young age. Musical prodigy, or a child's ability to perform at an adult professional level, shows itself as more complex and more advanced at a young age than simple musical talent. In Great Britain, the Gulbenkian Foundation's 1978 report about training young musicians adopted several definitions of musical talent. Gifted children are those who have the potential to become performers; among them are those who can become stars, termed "outstandingly gifted." Britain distinguishes between degrees of musical talent, with the school taking a role in identification when musical talent isn't identified by parents and friends, just as in the United States.

There are crosscultural differences in attitudes toward talent. In Japan, for example, talent is not thought of as arising in a child; talent is trained. Suzuki, in *Nurtured by Love* (1983), advocated musical training from early infancy in a system of talent education called The Suzuki Method. He wasn't interested in definitions of talent, claiming that any child who learns to speak can learn music. Repetition of the correct, as in learning a foreign language, is necessary: he said, "ability is one thing we have to produce (or work for) ourselves. That means to repeat and repeat an action until it becomes a part of ourselves." Tone-deaf children are not hopeless, either, as is commonly thought in the United States. Suzuki wrote:

> Most tone-deaf children cannot produce the first four notes of the scale, do, re, mi, fa, without making the semitone interval, fa, a little too high. That is, they have already acquired the habit of making fa too high. This "pre-education" cannot be changed, as I found out. Then what does one do? I found out that one has to teach them a new fa. If they have learned the wrong fa by hearing it five thousand times, one must make them listen to the right fa six thousand or seven thousand times. At first there are no results, but after hearing the right fa three thousand, then four thousand times, and when the number reaches five and six thousand times, the ability to produce the correct fa acquired by listening to it six thousand times begins to take precedence over the ability to produce the wrong fa that was acquired by listening only five thousand times. A new function has been developed . . . the right fa became easier and more natural for that child, so in the end he always produces it. The result is that he is no longer tone deaf. It takes six or seven months to achieve this with a child of six. (p. 90)

With the Suzuki method, a parent, usually the mother, works closely with the child in the acquisition of the rudimentary musical skills necessary to playing the violin. (Suzuki instruction on piano and cello is also available.) In one application of the technique, mothers of infants are first taught to play one piece on a tiny violin that is actually sized perfectly to the child. The child listens to recordings of the piece but does not play at first; training begins when the child asks for the violin. The more the child practices, the better she gets. The first song is a set of variations on "Twinkle, Twinkle Little Star." This, it is to be emphasized, is a training method, and follows the philosophy that musical intelligence can be taught. Asian education utilizes drill and practice to the point of mastery, and Westerners often wonder whether such education creates automatons or maestros.

Gardner, in a 1989 article called "Learning Chinese Style," shared his observations of art education in China. He noted that young students were taught calligraphy, repeating over and over certain patterns and figures. The differences between U.S. education and its emphasis on early exploratory activities in art and early Chinese art education were so great, he wondered whether the Chinese children would be able to transfer their training in calligraphy to freehand drawings, so he asked them to draw a portrait of him with their calligraphy brushes. They were able to do so, with several of the ten-year-olds making recognizable portraits. Gardner said, "Chinese children were not simply tied to schemata. They can depart from a formula when so requested."

## Standardized Tests

Schools should never use IQ tests as a screen in identifying music talent; rather, they should use the musical aptitude measures that have been validated over the years. These can be used to identify talent in youth from musically deprived families, where the school is the only agency that identifies the child. In the United States and Great Britain, standardized tests have been developed to identify music talent in young people. There are such tests as the Seashore Measures, which were developed for the Eastman School of Music in 1919, the Gordon Primary Measures of Music Audition (PMMA) developed in 1979, and the Gordon Intermediate Measures of Music Audition (IMMA) developed in 1982.

## Developmental Research

Bamberger (1986) said that young musically talented children go through a "midlife crisis" in their adolescent years. Prior to this period, younger musically talented children approach music holistically, using many strategies quite naturally as they approach music. Bamberger said, "For these younger children, internal representations of musical structure are not yet fixed in their attachments to the conventional meanings associated with external notation systems." The crisis comes when the child comes to consciousness, becomes more self-critical and reflective about music. This time is a "period of serious cognitive reorganization." She said that "there can be neither return to imitation and the unreflective, spontaneous 'intuitions' of childhood, nor a simple 'fix-up.'"

Lorin Hollander presented a classic case of the spontaneous child musician becoming the reorganized youth in a 1987 article, "Music, the Creative Process, and the Path of Enlightenment." Hollander, who described himself as a child prodigy, related that when he was three, his violinist father handed him a violin, but Lorin rebelled, smashing it "coldly and empirically." He then began to play on the piano only those notes that his father couldn't reach on the violin, F# below middle C and lower. He gave his first concert in kindergarten, for a pageant called "Circus," and at eleven, he played Carnegie Hall for the first time. Hollander said, "Following [Erik] Erikson's nicely laid out cycles, while continuing to perform I have three or four times undergone profound changes in my personality and, I believe, in the actual dynamics of my nervous system."

This transition from the promise of prodigy to the artistry of the adult musical artist is developmental, and Bamberger likened it to Piaget's concept of disequilibrium falling to equilibration and then to a reorganizing of schemata. She said that the mid-life crisis is a process of reorganizing, during which the child learns to analyze and synthesize musical knowledge.

### Choosing a Career in Music

While there are many people who are highly accomplished in music, it takes a special breed of person to face the stiff competition that a career in music necessitates throughout one's professional life. A career in music performance means that one must practice, take lessons from ever more advanced teachers, audition, and win over all entrants, only to receive what is often a low salary. And like creative writers who take jobs in university writing departments and visual artists who teach in art, musicians often become music teachers in order to support themselves. Hence many performers "moonlight" during the day, as typists or underwriters or waiters, while school music teachers often gig in orchestras or bands at night. Many of us know musicians of many trades by day (including teaching) whose weekend nights end at 3:00 a.m., after the bars close. Their families barely see them, but the supplementary salary helps them stay in a profession that feeds the soul more efficiently than it does the body. In addition, the classically-trained musician frequently must take any job that comes along, auditioning for faraway symphonies and obscure chamber groups. A friend of mine plays the flute in a symphony orchestra in underdeveloped Latin America. Young and fresh out of music school, she could find work in music only with this faraway symphony.

Perhaps all of this indicates that we have trained too many musicians, or that our conservatories and music departments are turning out students who are unemployable. But perhaps the real problem is a lack of appreciation and employment for highly-trained musicians because as a society we are musically illiterate. A flip through the radio stations in any urban or rural area will illustrate the types of music and musicians our society supports. Depending on geography, rock 'n' roll, golden oldies, soft rock, hard rock, Top 40 or country music will be prevalent. The lower end of the dial will have perhaps one jazz station and one public radio station that plays the chestnuts of classical music. Little new symphonic music hits the airways. Nor does much innovative music of any genre. My point is that as listeners we are untrained, even lazy, and unable to appreciate what our countless fine musicians would like to play for us.

When a young person chooses any of the arts as a career, it is often with the knowledge that our society does not really support its artists. In 1990, during the furor over the funding for the National Endowment for the Arts, some nationally syndicated columnists asked why the government should even have a National Endowment for the Arts, expressing the view that if a young person wants to be an artist, he or she should just do it. Yet these same commentators would probably not dispute the necessity for the government to support young scientists with scholarships and grants and research jobs. In some ways, young creative artists are less valued by our society than young scientists and mathematicians are. This is not necessarily true in other countries. While traveling in Finland, for example, I met the director of the regional theater in Lahti. His theater, subsidized by the government, employed forty full-time actors.

The arts, all of them, are necessary for human well-being. The pleasure and knowledge of ourselves that we get from the arts cannot be duplicated in any other human enterprise. A person who does not get pleasure from the arts has an impoverished soul. The arts feed our spirituality, speak to our humanness and our universal similarity, and bridge continents and languages. Many times the arts are the first programs to be cut in schools, because they are viewed as extraneous to the school experience. Yet when children remember what they have learned, often they remember what they learned in arts experience — projects they did, concerts they sang in, plays they participated in, physical performances they gave in sports, editorials they wrote for the school newspaper.

## Personality Studies of Musicians

Kemp, in "The Personality Structure of the Musician" (1981a, 1981b, 1982a, 1982b), studied performers and composers in Great Britain as well as students of music. In his study of music performers, he administered the High School Personality Questionnaire (Cattell and Cattell, 1989) to 496 musicians aged thirteen to seventeen. He also gave the 16 Personality Factor Questionnaire (1968 Anglicized Edition) to 688 music students, aged eighteen to twenty-five, from conservatories in Britain. A third group of 202 professional musicians, aged twenty-four to seventy, was also administered the 16 PF. Suitable control groups of nonmusicians were also tested.

Secondary school musicians were found to be significantly different from nonmusicians in these personality factors: they were more intelligent, more dominant, more conscientious, more individualistic, more self-sufficient, and more controlled. They were less emotionally stable, less happy-go-lucky, and less outgoing. The more talented musicians who were attending conservatories were less outgoing and less adventerous than secondary school musicians. The more talented musicians were also more excitable as well as being more individualistic and more apprehensive.

Adult professional musicians contrasted with the control group of nonmusicians in that they were more outgoing, more intelligent, more individualistic, more imaginative, more forthright, and more self-sufficient. Male musicians were shown to be less emotionally stable than male nonmusicians. They also were more suspicious and radical. Why this was so is not spelled out, but perhaps it is because professional musicians have had to weather great competition from peers, always checking to see who might be "gaining on them," and they also need great personal drive and passion for their music. Women professional music performers were found to be more dominant and more tense than the control females. Again, drive and passion are needed for success in musical performance, and the women would need to be more like men performers than like other females.

## Intelligence of Musicians

Kemp (1981a), noting the higher IQs of music students, said that although earlier researchers had reported no consistent relationship between intelligence and musical aptitude, later studies showed that "even when the music students were compared with the undergraduate norms, their level [of intelligence] was marginally higher." These data suggested to him that music students "choose to pursue music in preference to other academic studies because of a strong motivation towards music rather than any lack of intellectual capacity." In other words, their intelligence indicated that the musicians were capable of entering other professions, but they chose music because they wanted it. (Incidentally, Kemp also said that many adult musicians use their intelligence to leave music for more lucrative professions.) In fact, there is a basic assumption in schools that music students tend to be smart. When the band director addressed parents of fifth graders at my son's school, he said that an advantage of playing in the band is that a child's peers are the kids who are often on the honor roll.

When people ask me how to get their children through junior high school intact, I often advise them to get their children into the band; the entire school schedule will be such that they'll be in classes with good students. A high school band director told me that the grade point average of the students in all his bands is 3.2 on a 4-point scale. Whether bright students join music groups because they are good at it or whether they join music groups because their parents make them is not known. However, since it is well-known that a high IQ is positively related to earning high grades, these observations would seem to support Kemp's study.

## Personalities of Music Teachers and Composers

Kemp (1982b) also did a most interesting study of music teachers and performers, using the 16 PF Questionnaire for comparison. Musicians who were studying to be teachers were more extraverted and outgoing and less sensitive to criticism than those who wanted to be performers. The music teachers also found conforming to be easier. Kemp said, "This movement away from the high levels of introversion and sensitivity known to characterize the music student allows the student teacher to withstand the rough and tumble of classroom existence." People who become music teachers showed their conservatism in their tendency to "cling to the well-worn methods of music teaching embedded within their own music education." The necessity for teachers to be outgoing, more outgoing than performers, may be a problem for those who have spent many hours alone in practice rooms training for performance. Kemp wrote that:

> Music teachers who, over several years, will have spent long periods in the solitary confinement of the practice room focusing on their own personal musical development, may find it difficult to readjust to the interests and learning difficulties of others. As the earlier research has shown, musicians are characterized by a rich, colourful and imaginative inner mental life which renders them self-sufficient and detached from others, and, therefore, apparently not naturally suited to the business of class management. On the other hand, teaching may offer exactly the right opening for individuals who may be poorly adjusted to the demands which performance makes on them. (p. 73)

Composers also differed from performers and teachers (Kemp, 1981b). Kemp studied student composers (thirty-six men from conservatories and university music departments) and used as a comparison group fifty male music students who didn't compose music and weren't interested in doing so. He also administered the 16 PF Questionnaire to twenty-eight men and ten women, members of the Composers Guild of Great Britain, comparing them with men and women professional musicians who did not do any composing. Male professional and student composers were found to be more aloof, dominant, sensitive, and controlled. They were imaginative and self-sufficient. The only difference between the students and the professionals was that the professionals had higher IQs. Female professional composers were also dominant and self-sufficient. Composers were the most extreme in all the personality factors.

## Sosniak's Study of Concert Pianists

Results of The Development of Talent Research Project, centered at the University of Chicago, were edited by Benjamin Bloom and published in *Developing Talent in Young People* (1985). "Talent was defined as high-level demonstrated ability, rather than as natural aptitude"; the most outstanding young (under age forty) creative producers in several fields were asked to participate. The Project sought to answer these questions:

> How were the outstanding persons in art and music, in athletics, in various fields of scholarship, and in industry, government, and other areas of human endeavor discovered, developed, and encouraged? Do these very talented individuals achieve because of innate and rare qualities and/or as the result of special training and encouragement? (p. 5)

Sosniak's contribution to the project was her study of twenty-one concert pianists under the age of forty who had received international recognition in piano competitions. The study focused on three phases in the development of talent in piano: the early years, the middle years, and the adult years. The group had no outstanding physical characteristics or interests; they were as likely to go hiking in their free time as to read romantic novels. Sixteen of them were male, and all were Caucasian. They were mostly only or older children, mostly also from middle-class families; 80 percent of them had parents who were professional or white-collar. (This means that 20 percent of them came from homes that were not professional or white-collar.) Half were from urban areas, half from small towns and middle-sized towns from around the country. Their families appreciated music and music was in the home, though their parents may or may not have played an instrument. Their families thought music lessons were a good thing for children to have.

However, most families think that music lessons are good. According to Market Surveys of 1974, Sosniak pointed out that 69 percent of all families thought that learning a musical instrument was good for children to do, 79 percent of all families had a habit of listening to music, and 44 percent of families had at least one amateur musician. This made the families of these future concert pianists almost indistinguishable from the normal families. What explained the achievements of these young pianists?

## The Early Years

What did the early years show about the development of the talent of these pianists?

1. They came from homes where music was respected, even valued, and often there were amateur players in the household.

2. Music lessons were considered a necessary part of growing up, and the children were expected to take lessons. Their parents scheduled lessons for the children, and the children went.

3. The teachers were such that the children liked going to music lessons. The families chose teachers who were good teachers, and who conveyed a love of music to their students.

4. The families expected the young musicians to practice, to spend time in preparing their piano lessons. It was part of the family script, the family ethos. Other children of their ages spent a lot less time at lessons. The students also liked the piano and liked practicing. Often siblings were also given music lessons, but the ones with the most drive were the ones who achieved the most.

5. The lessons began early enough that the routine of practice had been made part of the family schedule before the other activities normal to young children came up, before the scout troops and the sports teams and the other lessons. Their practice was already a set part of their days.

6. The young pianists were called such, and got the label of "pianist" by their friends, by adults in the community, and by audiences, even before they were teenagers.

Sosniak pointed out the importance of these early years in developing habits of motivation, discipline, and self-concept in the young pianists. Their aspirations to become pianists had a foundation in the family commitment to the playing of the piano as worthwhile and valuable, and in the family's physical and financial and psychological support of that commitment.

## The Middle Years of Talent Development

As the young pianists reached adolescence, the playing of the piano became the playing of music with the piano as the instrument for the music. In other words, aesthetic appreciation of music itself was beginning.

1. The young pianists' practice sessions and music lessons were now part of daily and weekly habit.

2. About twenty hours or more a week were spent in practicing, lessons, and other activities in learning to be musicians. Sosniak said that this was "at least equivalent to a half-time job."

3. The young pianists were engaged and involved in their playing.

4. Music lessons took place at least once a week, and their teachers were also dedicated and knew a lot about music. The teachers pushed the students to have precision in their playing, and they also encouraged the students to learn more than the mechanics.

5. During this time, options were narrowed and decisions made that focused on music. Families making long-distance moves to be near the best learning environment and choosing for the young musician a limited general education, in order to focus more on music, were two dramatic examples of such narrowing of options.

6. The whole family was affected by the budding career of the young pianists. Perhaps other children in the family were negatively affected by this intense commitment of the family's time, of the family's monetary resources, and of the family's change in life-style.

7. The student moved into the world of music from the world of the family: the teacher became even more important, as did the competition of peers for motivating the student and for providing feedback as to his/her worth as a pianist.


### The Musician as Adult

Finding a master teacher and being accepted as a student by this master teacher were crucial steps in the development of adult piano talent. Such teachers don't advertise for students, operating instead within informal networks of lesser teachers. I often use the 1989 movie *Madame Sousatzka* in my classes as a classic illustration of this pattern of talent development in musicians — and in other top youthful performers. Madame Sousatzka, a middle-level piano teacher, struggled to keep her prize pupils, who moved on to other teachers when they felt ready. The movie explored the teacher's emotional difficulties and those of her students as they made their transitions.

Sosniak's study found that being a student of a master teacher meant more than just taking lessons; it meant adopting a style as well as a certain repertoire, and a raising in standards of musicianship and performance. The master teachers expected discipline and commitment.

The students were expected to practice at least four and as many as seven hours per day between lessons. Because the master teachers were often on tour, lessons lasted longer than an hour, and could be as far apart as three weeks or a month. The master teachers did not tolerate excuses or sloppy preparation. The students had moved from their parents' sacrifices and the expectations of their homes to the world of music professionals. Having closed their other options of study, they were in select music conservatories or schools where their teachers were located.

A final step in talent development, the teachers then themselves became lesser gods to the mature young pianists, and were seen as "coaches" as the students began to pursue their own careers, aggressively seeking the correct venues and contests and awards in order to enhance their visbility as musicians. Many continued to take lessons as well as to give lessons.

## Biographical Studies

The memoir, the case study, and the historiometric study of biography all provide qualitative and quantitative illustrations that illuminate musical giftedness and genius. Several examples follow.

### John-Steiner's Work on Musicians

Vera John-Steiner interviewed musicians and studied their biographies and autobiographies; her findings, published in *Notebooks of the Mind* (1985), confirmed the Bloom group's data concerning the education of talented young musicians. She noted that musicians serve apprenticeships through their families, their family friends, and their teachers. Jean Bamberger, a musician and a psychologist who studies musical prodigies, told John-Steiner that the pattern of the family giving up many things for the sake of the musical talent of the child is quite common. Bamberger also validated that young musicians practice before school, after school, on weekends. Understandably, the conflict between the need for much practice and the need to live a normal life presents difficulties for young musicians and my lead to their giving up music during adolescence. Burt Bacharach said he quit music from ages twelve to sixteen, but his mother's encouragement and his early rigorous training brought him back to composing and playing. Another conflict cited by John-Steiner occurs when the young musician tries to balance a broad general education with professional music education.

These researchers have shown that mentors, teachers, and other supporters are crucial to musical development. The cellist Pablo Casals throughout his life was grateful to his mother for her devotion to his musical talent; she was instrumental in his attending music school in Barcelona, far away from the tiny Spanish village where the family lived. Composer and conductor Leonard Bernstein studied with Serge Koussevitzsky, Fritz Reiner, Heinrich Gebhard, Isabella Vengerova, Aaron Copland. The successful conductor and composer, like the successful scientist, depends much on mentors.

The role of imitation and duplication of others' works in composing was also discussed by the musicians John-Steiner studied. Beethoven's composing career has been divided by musicologists into three periods: (1) the imitative period; (2) the heroic period; and (3) the introspective period. The first works by even the greatest composers came from practice, imitation, and learning what had gone before in order to free the composers for the great works they would make in their more mature compositions. Thus, musical ideas are transmitted from one generation to the next.

### Simonton's Studies of Composers

Simonton, using historiometry, studied 696 classical composers, and his findings were published in *Genius, Creativity, and Leadership* (1984). Simonton found that the composers studied tended to compose their best-known melodies between their thirty-third and forty-third years, peaking in production of famous tunes at about age thirty-nine. However, their most melodically original works appeared later, for the influence of the Zeitgeist, or historical milieu, upon their works tended to diminish as composers aged. They felt more free to go against the temperament of the times, creating their most musically innovative works after age fifty-six. Bach's "Art of the Fugue" and the increasingly abstract, less classically-structured music Beethoven composed in his Third Period (the last five piano sonatas, the *Missa Solemnis*, and the Ninth Symphony, among others) are examples.

Simonton also pointed out that longevity pays off for long-lasting classical musical fame: "The most famous composers of Western classical music tend to have the longest productive careers, to be the most prolific, and to have been born long ago rather than recently." Like scientists, composers who attained the most eminence tended to begin their productivity earlier, tended to produce more, and tended to have long careers. Within those long careers, however, quality of life had a direct influence on quality of composition. When Simonton studied ten of the most famous composers, examining the aesthetic merit of their compositions, he found that the most artistically original music was composed "during those periods in which they were facing the most intense life challenges — the death of family members, job changes, geographical dislocations, marriages, legal hassles, and the like." Hence the composers' life circumstances and emotional stresses influenced their melodies.

## Kogan's Memoir

Judith Kogan, in a 1987 memoir called *Nothing but the Best: The Struggle for Perfection at the Julliard School,* described the education of the world's finest young musicians studying at New York City's Julliard School at Lincoln Center. Julliard students believe they are the elite young players of the world: according to Kogan, Julliard students and administration "seem to think that students at any other conservatory (except, maybe, the Curtis Institute of Music in Philadelphia) couldn't get into Juilliard and therefore can't play." For its students, Juilliard is the universe. Its windows sealed, Juilliard is cut off from the world even physically. The tie that binds is music, and the force that creates order is ability. Some invisible hand ranks people. Ability loosely corresponds to technical proficiency. In some ways, the focus on ability blinds people to music itself: music is appreciated not as something beautiful but as a tool of commerce. Professional motivation is more important than artistic, the glamour of personality more important than the art of music.

The 750 talented musicians then enrolled in Juilliard fought for the eighty-four practice rooms, where they practiced eight to ten hours a day, confining their social lives "to those who do the same thing at the same level of proficiency." Students at Juilliard knew each other by the instruments they played, by how well they played the instruments, and by who their teachers were. They practiced, practiced, practiced. Kogan said,

Practicing is an integral part of living for them, different from eating and breathing only in that they ate and breathed before they walked. They practice because practice gives them security. A passage practiced thirty times feels more secure than one practiced twenty. The cost of not practicing can be enormous . . . Practicing enables the students to tune out the world: the hassles of life in New York City, the agony of adolescence and young adulthood, the pain of a shaky or battered ego, the unpredictability of a course in an unstable profession, where one can pick up the instrument and sound heavenly one day and hellish the next. And they practice because if they leave — even for a bathroom break — they never know whether the room will be empty when they return. (p. 59)

After the competitions, the rivalries, the hours in the cafeteria, the required ear training and chorus classes, and the egos of the temperamental teachers, the students graduated and found that those who were their rivals were now their friends, for they had all come through, and now they only had to put "Juilliard" on their resumes in order to have people take notice.

But it is still not easy for graduates of one of the best schools in the world. The students joined, then, the "thousands of musicians" living in the neighborhood of Lincoln Center. Kogan said:

Hardly anyone ends up with a solo career. Some earn spots in orchestras, some in principal seats. Some teach, some free-lance and some do both. Some leave music entirely. Some reach the top and are disenchanted. Some drift into new careers and find contentment . . . The musician who wants a solo career must make a new commitment once out in the real world. The rest of life will be ruled by excessive discipline. The commitment must be seen as something one has chosen. The musicians who sees the commitment as a sacrifice will always be bitter. (p. 232)

Despite her frank description of the demands of music, Kogan, who ended up in another profession, found that the ultimate discovery in a talented musician's life is a personal, even spiritual one. The musician ultimately discovers that he loves the music. He discovers that it was all worth it, for the music.

## Improvisation and Composition

But, you may be asking, all of this describes the development of talent, not of creativity. Isn't creativity more loose, more free? All that Sosniak's study described was continual practice, competition, and striving in an effort to learn how to use the musical instrument. How is this creativity? How is this giftedness? Many musicians and devoted listeners would insist that the instrumentalist who has mastered the technique so that the soul of the music can come through is as creative as the person who puts the notes down on the page, just as the actor would insist he is as creative as the playwright. However, without entering the debate of who is more creative, we will now take a look at composers and improvisators, who clearly do go through what we have conventionally called the creative process.

The difference between improvisation and composing can be illustrated through scenes from the life of composer and conductor Andre Previn. Previn's done it all. He's been a successful composer of scores for movies; he was a successful jazz pianist with his own trio; he has been a songwriter; he has risen through the ranks of orchestral conductors to lead world class orchestras. Born in Berlin in 1929, Previn was the son of an enthusiastic amateur musician who took his child to concerts. Previn felt pure joy in hearing a symphony at the age of five, and from then on he pursued music as a career. In *Andre Previn,* Bookspan and Yodkey's 1981 biography, he said of his childhood:

> I think we musicians have always had rather selfish childhoods. The luxury of having a unilateral talent, which makes one's future life inevitable, is wonderful, but it also makes you selfish. It makes you insular and your perspective tends to be quite narrow. I, myself, was always so concerned with being a musician, with becoming a good musician, with becoming a better musician, with learning this and with learning that, that even my areas of amusement and leisure time, even my play time

seemed to be connected inevitably with music. As a result, I never really bothered to look around me to see what else was going on in the world, as someone else might have done, someone whose interests were more divergent. (p. 31)

Previn was so classically trained that he couldn't improvise. Early in his life, fleeing Hitler, the family moved to Los Angeles, where Previn came under the influence of American pop culture, especially jazz. At fourteen he heard a scratchy recording of "Sweet Lorraine" by blind black pianist Art Tatum, and he "just fell apart. It was unbelievable." Previn scoured the stores for sheet music to "Sweet Lorraine" and found that it was just a "pleasant, folksy little tune." Wondering where all the notes on the record came from, he realized that Tatum himself had added them. "He'd taken that puerile thirty-two-bar melody and made ingenious music out of it."

Previn then became "very interested." He played the entire Tatum album over and over, painstakingly recording on paper each song from the record, note by note, using up several packs of needles:

> The process was a long and a painstaking one, for Tatum's playing was crammed with fists full of notes and harmonic changes that might look like mistakes on paper if you hadn't heard them first. Here was a musical magician whose illusions remain to this day something of a mystery to his fellows. No less a jazz pianist than Oscar Peterson . . . tells of being stunned by his first hearing of a Tatum record; Peterson at first refused to believe anything but that he'd heard two pianists and a bass player, not just one man on one piano. (p. 103)

Previn finally finished notating the music. Sometimes just a few bars would take a page or more of notation. Then he began to practice the music, "like you'd learn a composition of Mozart's."

> I simply didn't understand what jazz was all about. I figured this was the way it was done . . . Finally I learned to play Tatum's pieces and I practiced them for hours on end. Slowly it began to dawn on me: the trick was not to play this stuff but to make it up as Tatum had done. A jazz player had to be his own composer and play not

premeditatively but make up his music on the spot. Improvisation. That's what jazz was all about. (p. 104)

Is formal study of the medium, or achieving a basic level of expertise in the medium, necessary for truly creative products to be produced? The British aesthetician Robert Abbs would say yes, even though many of the world's jazz lovers would disagree. Abbs believes that only those who are trained in their fields can be receptive to the ideas that come to them and can transform these ideas into useable symbols. In his 1989 book *A is for Aesthetic* Abbs writes:

> Originality . . . can only have meaning in terms of the origin of the debt, adaptations and transformations made possible by the material of the received culture . . . If we return to consider . . . Stravinsky, Tippett and Wagner . . . we can see that these gifts from the unconscious came to individuals who were highly accomplished in musical composition and who were already consciously engaged with a particular problem. Only someone who formally understood musical chords could actually hear "the pure triad of E flat major" and only someone who had mastered the art of composition in his own culture could musically record it. (pp. 20-21)

Abb's comments imply that there is some music that is of a higher form than other music and that true originality comes in creating so-called classical music. Others would assert that true creativity is having no notes in front of you, only a melody in your head, and transforming that melody into jazz. The improvisational musician Stephen Nachmanivitch begins his 1990 book, *Free Play*, with these words:

> I am a musician. One of the things I love best is to give totally improvised solo concerts on violin and viola. There is something energizing and challenging about being one-to-one with the audience and creating a piece of work that has both the freshness of the fleeting moment and — when everything is working — the structural tautness and symmetry of a living organism. It can be a remarkable and often moving experience in direct communication. (p. 4)

# Why Are There So Few Women Composers?

In an interview for a book called *The Creative Experience* (Rosner and Abt, 1970), Aaron Copland discussed creativity in composing. Copland spoke of music as a language that expresses emotions at all times, but the composer only becomes aware that he is feeling such an emotion when he begins singing or playing a sad song, for example, and he wonders then why he is feeling sad. The lack of awareness in the mind of the composer about his feelings creates an abstractness. A person cannot compose when he is too depressed, because creating art is a positive statement, and the composer has to feel that he is accomplishing something. If a composer composes when he is moderately depressed, he then becomes elated as he expresses his depression. A composer might also compose to get rid of repressed anger. To create a chord that is fortissimo and dissonant is an expression of anger. Copland went on:

> One of the reasons why cultivated music is one of the glories of mankind, one of the real achievements of mankind, is that we are dealing in amorphous, highly abstract material without any specific thought content. Incidentally it's one of the mysteries of music that there have been no great women composers. There have been great women singers, pianists, violinists, who interpret marvelously well, but for some reason or other, no outstanding composers. People have made an analogy between the fact that there have been no great women mathematicians and no great women composers. Perhaps it's the inability to handle abstract material that defeats them. (p. 275)

(Incidentally, of all the people interviewed by Rosner and Abt in their book, only one was a woman, fashion designer Bonnie Cashin. All of those interviewed were from New York City or the New York City area. The book also contained no interviews with minority scientists or minority artists, male or female. Yet despite its unbalanced representation, this book is widely quoted by experts on creativity.)

Women in music, except for the necessary sopranos, mezzos and contraltos, have been relegated in the past to the role of helpmates and muses, even those who were rigorously educated in music. Alma Mahler, wife of Gustav Mahler, was classically trained in Vienna at the turn of the century, a prime time for creativity (cf. Gardner, 1988). A serious composer, she studied with other composers there. But she is described by Monson, her biographer, as a "muse," an inspiration to male creatives (1983). "She might have become an important composer; had she been born a century later, she could have been a conductor. As it was, she devoted her life to men whom she considered to be geniuses." After Gustav Mahler died, Alma married Walter Gropius, who founded the Bauhaus, and later she married Franz Werfel, a writer. She also had long affairs with the composer Alexander von Zemlinsky, Arnold Schoenberg's teacher; with Ossip Gabrilowitsch, a pianist; and with the artist Oscar Kokoschka.

Creative women musicians are allowed now to see themselves as more than muses, to dare to be more than helpmates, and while one last male bestion in music exists — conducting — women composers can be found. Copland may have been surprised that the 1991 Pulitzer Prize for conducting was won by a woman, Shulamit Ran, for her Symphony. Ran, a professor at the University of Chicago, has said, "I think music must reflect life, or at least life as the composer sees it," and "I want my music to challenge both the mind and the heart, and to do so in equal fashion" (Kozinn, 1991).

## Marilyn Shrude

Marilyn Shrude, an Associate Professor of Music and Director of the Mid-American Center for Contemporary Music at Bowling Green State University in Ohio, is another successful woman composer. She has a doctorate in music from Northwestern University and is in her early forties, mid-career, at the time of this writing. She has composed music for large and small ensembles, and her music has been performed in almost every state in the U.S. Performances of her music have also taken place in Korea, Switzerland, Germany, the Soviet Union, Canada, Belgium, the Netherlands, France, Japan, and Australia. She has received two Individual Artist Fellowships from the Ohio Arts Council and has been active in the American Women Composers Group. She has received a Kennedy Center Freidheim Award and been named a Woman of Achievement by Women In The Communications Industry (WICI).

In an interview, Marilyn described that she grew up in an ethnic Catholic Polish and Lebanese family in Chicago and entered the convent as a high school student at age fifteen. She always composed music, though it wasn't particularly valued or noticed. Shrude's career as a composer began formally during her graduate work at Northwestern University, when she took a course in composition. She was the only woman in the composition class at the time, the late sixties. Her middle and late adolescence were times of concentrated effort in music. She took lessons on three instruments, and since she was in a convent and had decided to become a music teacher, she had intensive study — more intensive than if she had been in a regular high school with all its distractions. She practiced all three instruments and also spent a lot of time singing. She had been playing the organ for Masses since the age of eleven. The simultaneous and intensive training in religion and music led her to doubt her talent, because humility was required of a religious girl and she could never think that her work was good. When she emerged from the convent, she had to work through many feelings so that she could accept her talent. Though many of her teachers and mentors were supportive, the years in the convent had given her a poor self-concept. Composing was not encouraged because it was vain, and women were not to be proud.

Shrude said, "I always had the urge to write music, and did so since the age of ten; I did it on my own, mostly for school programs. People knew I did it, but it was never encouraged. They rarely looked at it. I had very little professional feedback on it whatsoever" (M. Shrude, personal communication, September 1990). She taught music in a high school for a few years after she left the convent. Then she found herself accepted to graduate school at Northwestern, where she met her husband, saxophonist John Sampen.

She was in residency at Northwestern for one year while she got her master's degree, and then she went back to teaching school. She and John married and moved to Kansas, where Marilyn found herself without a composition teacher. For three years in Kansas she taught herself composition by listening to contemporary works. She views this as an exploratory period wherein she gained literacy by trying out ideas and imitating. She sometimes studied with a good friend on faculty at the university where her husband was teaching, but she was essentially on her own. When the couple then returned to Northwestern to pursue doctorates, she found that her relationship to her mentor on the composition faculty had changed. She had grown. She was not as needful as she had been. She began to strike out on her own.

Shrude talked about the necessity for a composer to know people who perform music. Many of the strides she had made as a composer were the result of having good performers to write for. She also discussed what for her is now the main struggle, that of time, for she and John have two children.

Like Copland, Marilyn Shrude expresses her emotions through her compositions. Even when she has started a composition ostensibly to solve a technical problem, she finds later that the music essentially turns out to have expressed what she has been struggling with emotionally. I think that most creative artists would agree with that assessment.

Most of her pieces are narratives, even though the story is not apparent. The form of "A Window Always Open on the Sea," composed early in 1990, is shaped by lines from a poem by Michael Mott. Michael and his wife were neighbors and good friends of Shrude and Sampen when Michael's wife was dying of cancer. Shrude's father had recently died, and Shrude's sister-in-law was dying of cancer. This piece turned out to be "a working out of all these deaths." She dated the piece the day her sister-in-law died. For Shrude, composing is the expression of emotions, no matter how the piece starts out.

She doesn't compose on a computer or on a piano, but at her table. She tries things on the piano, but "you get to a point where you know how things work. I can hear the sounds in my head." She works in the lengthiest blocks of time she can get. Like most artists in any genre, she composes "because I have to." She often uses poetic texts in her compositions. Howard McCord's "Arctic Desert" (1979) was one; "Lines from Tennyson" and "I Wandered Lonely as a Cloud" were others. Other works include "Psalms for David" (1983); "Genesis: Notes to the Unborn" (1975); "Four Meditations; To a Mother and Her Firstborn" (1975); "Solidarnosc" (1982); "Drifting Over a Red Place" (1982); "Interior Spaces" (1987); and "Renewing the Myth" (1988).

In the past few years she has been composing mainly on commission and has recently written the score for a public television show. She rarely submits her pieces to competitions or blindly to publishing houses. She has a network of fellow musicians all over the country. "I know a lot of people all over and they're helpful. They sometimes give you favors that you don't even expect." As co-director of the New Music and Art Festival, she annually listens to each of the five hundred submissions that the Festival attracts, from all over the world. Twenty compositions are chosen for performance. She agrees that it can be difficult and costly for composers, especially for younger people, to have their work performed well. Often a composer must find some performers, hire them, and organize a studio performance, but it's worth the effort, for a good tape can open doors to festivals, contests, and the like.

Marilyn Shrude is a mother, which has put her on a timeline different from other composers'. Like the artist mothers in Foley's study (1986), Shrude has had to make modifications in order to combine parenting with composing. The value of a supportive husband cannot be underestimated, for their children "have always come first. We've done pretty well at trying to accommodate each others' schedules, even with young children, though it's been difficult." Whether or not having children has stymied her career doesn't matter to Shrude. She can't imagine not having children. "I love having children. It's so enriching. If I didn't have children I'd be more reclusive. I wouldn't have to schedule myself to cook, to take them to places. When I'm alone, I let my duties go and don't seek out social contacts." She has never thought that she would have been better off childless, nor has she resented the interference in her creative work with the demands of motherhood.

To return to the question of whether improvisation is more or less creative than composing, Shrude believes many improvisational artists can "speak but not read and write. To be able to read the music and to write it down is to know the full language of music. Music is a language. Some people read and some people write and some people do all of it."

Shrude considers herself competitive but not cutthroat. There are things she "should" go for but doesn't. One of her ambitions as a composer is to receive recognition from her peers; while she has a certain amount of recognition now, she's not a "top dog." Peer recognition is important to her, as it is to any producing artist of any field. To have work performed by a major orchestra such as the Chicago Symphony or the New York Philharmonic would be a zenith representing peer recognition from the world of "serious Western art music."

Shrude, in the middle of her career, does not exhibit the anxiety or drive that Kemp (1981b) observed in composers. Perhaps the balance she has achieved comes as a result of being a mother. The serenity with which she views her life and her accomplishments seems to reflect an aspect of the creative female personality that hasn't been explored in research.

Foley's 1986 study showed that the artist mothers, while they were often in a frenzy trying to get everything done, felt an enormous serenity in doing their work. Foley contrasted the artists with professional women who worked in law, medicine, and business, and found that the artists, perhaps because they were able to express their emotions through their art work, seemed to have less emotional stress. In fact, their emotional stress came from having their responsibilities as mothers interfere with their emotional need to work in their art. One of the artist-mothers was not able to work for ten months because of a complicated pregnancy, and she said, "Honestly, I'm sort of tearing my hair out about not having painted for that length of time." One of the professional mothers spoke of "going nuts" when she was at home with her children for too long, and of escaping into her workplace where the demands were predictable and appointed. The professionals, who had been high academic achievers, felt accomplishment in achieving a product, a sale, or a contract. By contrast, the artists valued the "process" of painting, which provided "escape and relief of tension and the return of mental tranquility." The artist, no matter what genre he works in, uses his art as an expression of emotion, and when he is deprived of that expression, he feels conflict and tension.

## Summary

1. The development of musical giftedness and creativity comes after long work and hard training.

2. There are crosscultural differencess in talent development. Asians, for example, emphasize repetition, drill, and training, and Americans emphasize inspiration and improvisation.

3. The whole family is affected in the development of great musical talent. The family may move to better teachers, and siblings may be affected by the emphasis on developing one child's talent.

4. Young talented musicians often undergo a midlife crisis in adolescence as they move from natural expression to learning the structure and mechanics of music.

5. Musicians are similar in personality to other creative people, with slight variations among types of musicians. Composers have the most extreme personalities.

6. Improvisation and formal composition require different skills.

7. Musicians find practice healing and fulfilling, not drudgery, as non-musicians do. This practice often leads to immense joy and freedom and wholeness of expressing emotions through music. Performers and composers alike feel this joy.

# Chapter 10

## Actors and Dancers

*The qualities above all necessary to a great actor: in my view he must
have a great deal of judgement. He must have in himself an unmoved and
disinterested onlooker.*

— Diderot

*I know a woman, lovely in her bones,
When small birds sighed, she would sigh back at them;
Ah, when she moved, she moved more ways than one.*
— Theodore Roethke

She is so dramatic about everything. Even the least bit of criticism sends
her into a tirade. She talks to her dolls and makes up elaborate scenarios
of distant lands, and she takes all the parts. And him! He can't stop
moving. Teachers get angry and call him hyperactive. They say he has
a lot of energy. When the chorus sings, he moves to the music, even
in church.

Are these children creative? For children like this are incipient actors
or dancers or athletes. And as such, they are interpreters, like music
performers. Some questions asked in the previous chapter arise in
regard to these performers, too: are choreographers and playwrights
the creative ones, while actors and dancers are merely the tools of the
words and patterns? Let's investigate.

Two of Gardner's frames of intelligence, kinesthetic and intrapersonal intelligence, are what actors and dancers exhibit. Athletes display kinesthetic intelligence also, but the intrapersonal intelligence is what enables actors and dancers to interpret the world through their bodily actions. Kinesthetic intelligence is the "skilled use of the body" that has evolved in humans over millions of years. Westerners have divorced the mental from the physical and have spoken of the body as separate from the soul or heart. Recent thought has attempted to reconcile the two, as people have been urged to exercise and research has shown that physical activity is positively related to longevity.

## Actors

The most admired and highest-paid creative people in our society are movie stars, some of whom command millions of dollars for a few scenes. Yet one of these super-stars, Marlon Brando, thinks acting is not a profession worthy of a man (Schickel, 1986). However, others have been more eloquent about the mental and physical artistry that comprises acting. Like singers, they are dependent upon their instruments, their voices and their bodies, but unlike singers, their material is other people, not notes on a page.

The MacArthur Award-winning actor Bill Irwin was trained as a clown. In describing one of the classes Irwin taught, Shekerjian (1990) said,

> The first students arrive and from a distance try to copy his motions. They fail miserably. Irwin's too good to be casually imitated. Every inch of him understands movement and exactly how much can fit in the space of a split second. His gestures are lean, tight, targeted, spare. He wastes nothing. His concepts are neat, not epic. And when you're not laughing at his antic behavior, you are dazzled by its elegance. (p. 158)

Irwin begins by observing people's behavior. The shuffle of a bag lady, or the quick moves of the hustler with shells, or the waiter who gives the specials of the day, are all material for the actor. He stores these motions "in some remote but active corner of the mind," and practices at home in front of a mirror.

The comedian Buster Keaton earned his living, and got his laughs, by keeping completely silent, no matter what was done to him; he would be beaten up on stage and never show expression. Keaton's early life was spent on stage with his vaudeville parents. His father would actually beat the young Keaton on stage, and Keaton's act was to show no reaction. Keaton lost his ability to smile for the camera: "If something tickled me and I started to grin, the old man would hiss, 'Face! Face!' That meant freeze the puss. The longer I held it, why, if we got a laugh the blank pan or the puzzled pose would double it. He kept after me, never let up, and in a few years it was automatic. Then when I'd step on stage or in front of a camera, I couldn't smile. Still can't." (quoted in Miller, 1990, p. 40)

Stanislavski, one of the founders of the Moscow Art Theater, described his training as an actor in the turn-of-the-century Moscow in *An Actor Prepares* (1936). His tenets of acting came to be known as the Stanislavski Method, later shortened to "The Method" when Lee Strasberg began his Actors Theater in New York City. Now Stanislavski's technique is simply called "Method acting." Stanislavski detailed the processes by which acting is made an art; in these processes, one can see the great influence of psychoanalysis on the acting profession.

1. Acting is made an art through the use of the subconscious.

2. Acting is made an art through the actions that the actor takes in even something as simple as taking a seat on a chair.

3. Acting is made an art through the actor's use of imagination to turn the words of the playwright into believable reality, for the playwright cannot put into directions all that the actor must do.

4. Acting is made an art through the actor's so concentrating his attention that he is unaware of the audience; also through observation and paying attention to how people act in real life.

5. Acting is made an art through rigorous physical training, such as muscle relaxation and conditioning.

6. Acting is made an art through breaking a piece to be acted into its units and its objectives, marked by buoys in a "channel" that "points the true course of creativeness."

7. Acting is made an art through a process of inner probing into the psyche with a sense of faith that the performance will be as true as it can be at this stage of the actor's life. Stanislavski spoke of truth related to the actor's inner vision:

What we mean by truth in the theater is the scenic truth which an actor must make use of in his moments of creativeness. Try always to begin by working from the inside both on the factual and imaginary parts of a play and its setting. Put life into all the imagined circumstances and actions until you have completely satisfied your sense of truth, and until you have awakened a sense of faith in the reality of your sensations. This process is what we call justification of a part. (p. 129)

8. Stanislavski said that the actor must use emotion memory, recapturing within himself feelings he has had, in order to interpret the character at hand, but always acting as an artist, in his own person. The actor plays himself, but "in an infinite variety of combinations . . . which have been smelted in the furnace" of the emotion memory.

9. Acting is made an art through communion with the inner self and communion with the other actors on stage. This is not communication, but deeper connection, almost spiritual. (Perhaps this aspect of the actor's creativity is evidenced by the reputedly large numbers of love affairs between actors during rehearsals or filmimg or the run of the play, and the quick breaking up thereafter.)

10. Acting is made an art through adaptation to each circumstance, so that manipulation of the situation can take place. For example, an actor who wants to get the part of a bully will not appear recessive at any moment of the audition, and the actor who must attract the attention of a character supposedly across the street will project her voice, even though the person is not really across the street but across the stage.

After all these aspects of the actor's art, Stanislavski said there is still one more, and that is the most important one:

11. Acting is made an art through the "inner motive" to play the instrument that the actor has developed of himself. Furthermore, three aspects of the character being portrayed must be balanced: the emotions, the will, and the intellect. To strive for balance among these three is the inner goal of the actor, who must then create an "unbroken line" between audience and the stage, by being that character in balance from morning until night in all aspects of his life, thus never wavering from the inner concentration that playing requires.

Stanislavski called this the "inner creative state," and warned that even playing a familiar part, the actor must prepare himself to act with renewed fervor.

> The inner preparation for a part is as follows: instead of rushing into his dressing-room at the last moment, an actor should (especially if he has a big part) arrive there two hours ahead of his entrance and begin to get himself in form. You know that a sculptor kneads his clay before he begins to use it, and a singer warms up his voice before his concert. We need to do something similar to tune our inner strings, to test the keys, the pedals and the stops. (p. 265-66)

In all works that she performs, the actor must always look for the super-objective that the work projects. Great authors such as Dostoyevsky, Tolstoy, and Chekhov write about human themes, and these themes are the "main artery" of the work, "providing nourishment both to it and the actors." In bad plays or lesser works the actor must still try to find the super-objective and to make it "deeper and sharper."

The actor cannot always have the inspiration or instinct to play a part, and that's where discipline and training come in. How to get inspiration was described this way:

> Therefore put your thought on what arouses your inner motive forces, what makes for your inner creative mood. Think of your super-objective and the thought line of action that leads up to it. In short, have in your mind everything that can be consciously controlled and that will lead you to the subconscious. That is the best possible preparation for inspiration. But never try for a direct approach to inspiration for its own sake. It will result in physical contortion and the opposite of everything you desire. (p. 292)

That, to the Moscow Art Theater, was the summary of creativity in acting. As it was later interpreted by the New York acting studios, Stanislavski's Method became the ultimate expression of the true inner self. Psychoanalysis and the belief that the actor was a true artist, not merely a skilled imitator or charming mimic, began to influence theater just as such a romantic shift was taking place in other arts. By the 1950s

Method acting, with its dictate that to be a true artist one had to suffer and to bare one's soul, had become a great influence on many actors. Marlon Brando's portrayal of Stanley Kowalski in Tennessee Williams' *A Streetcar Named Desire* became, to many, the epitome of the achievement of the Method actor. Richard Schickel, in his 1986 critique of the cult of celebrity, *Intimate Strangers,* said that Brando "brought the spirit of modernism over from literature and painting (where, increasingly, the subject of the work was the work itself) and brought it to performance."

Here's a telling but perhaps apocryphal story about Sir Laurence Oliver and Dustin Hoffman filming *Marathon Man.* Hoffman stayed up all night running himself into exhaustion in preparation for the shoot the next day, immersing himself in the actual physical experience of the character. The day after the shoot, Hoffman collapsed exhausted in a chair, bleary-eyed and rubbery-muscled. Olivier came over to him and said, "You know, there's an easier way. It's called acting." This illustrates the basic controversy within the acting profession of emotional reality versus technique. Brando and Hoffman, DeNiro and Streep are reputed to search for the emotional reality of the character in their preparation for their roles. Actors such as Cary Grant and Laurence Olivier relied on technique and training. British actors are known for the latter, while American actors are known for the former.

Following are some comments made by actors on acting in the anthology of the same title.

## Actors on Acting

### *Laurence Olivier*

In an interview in 1967, Sir Laurence Olivier called acting "the art of persuasion (Cole and Chinoy, 1970). When asked about communicating a sense of danger to the audience, Olivier said that he was not very conscious of how this "caged animal" feeling that he gave to audiences and other actors worked, but that the particular play he was in had a lot to do with it. He said, "*Othello,* of course, screams for it." He also said he watched other actors for ideas. He imitated Sid Field for his comedic sense, borrowing "freely and unashamedly," and admired all his colleagues for their differences. He learned "stern professionalism" from Noel Coward, timing from Rex Harrison, and naturalistic acting from Alfred Lunt. Olivier said, "I think the most interesting thing to see is that an actor is the most successful when not only all his virtues but all his disadvantages come into useful play in a part." Olivier thought he flung his hands about too much while he acted and he tried to control them, but he said that sometimes he just had to let go.

### Michael Redgrave

The British actor Michael Redgrave, whose daughters Vanessa and Lynn and son Colin are also actors, wrote in 1946 a piece called "The Stanislavski Myth" (Cole and Chinoy, 1970). The Stanislavski myth was the religious fervor that had grown up throughout the world whenever Stanislavski was mentioned. Speaking of the immense impact that Stanislavski — "that thunder-clap of a name" — had on the theatrical world, Redgrave said that any actor reading Stanislavski's book would be filled with self-doubt; however, the book would also bring the actor into reconciliation with his own necessary exhibitionism.

Stanislavski urged actors to seek their characters in themselves and to do away with cliche. The temptation of the actor to act with cliche is great, and audiences often want cliche. "Do not a great many audiences prefer, or at least feel more comfortable when witnessing, the artifices and cliches to which they are accustomed? Of the two types of acting in vogue in 40s England, the one where the "effect springs from the cause," and the other which "begins with effect and which rarely . . . seeks the cause," Redgrave said that the latter was more popular. He noted, "It is very seldom that we see a production in which more than a few actors are faithful to the author, the director, and their artistic conscience." Without this commitment, actors become "casual laborers" and not artists.

### Stella Adler

Before the Actors Theater, there was the Group Theater in the 1930s in New York City. The Group Theater modified the Stanislavski system. Besides emphasis on the actor's self-awareness and preparation in his craft, the Group Theater brought together the whole company. One of it's founders, Stella Adler, said,

This theater demanded a basic understanding of a complex artistic principle; that all people connected with this theater, the actor, designer, playwright, director, etc., had of necessity to arrive at a single point of view which the theme of the play also expressed . . . Each of the artists would best express that point of view through his individual craftsmanship. (Cole and Chinoy, 1970, p. 603)

The influence of psychoanalysis can be seen in another aspect of Adler's theater: the actor was viewed as having personal problems that the whole group could help solve. As the actor got immersed in the whole process of the theater, he was sometimes re-educated and "clarified," a buzz-word of that day. By 1934 the Group Theater had modified Stanislavski's system to emphasize the actor's clarity of actions rather than the actor's inner life. Adler said, "Now emphasis was put on the circumstances of the play and a much stronger use of the actor's need to find greater justification in the use of these circumstances and a more conscious use of them." Even if an actor was insufficiently aware of his unconscious feelings, for acting was considered a process of bringing up the unconscious and making it conscious so it can be used, and the actor could be freed emotionally, the Group Theater process of rehearsing scenes would help him: "Each scene was given an architectural solidity which was difficult for anyone to break down, and no matter what their individual acting problems were, they nevertheless helped enormously to achieve the ensemble excellence."

The Group Theater was built on the idea of "ensemble"; that is, no one actor was more important than another actor, but all were essential cogs in the machine, parts of the whole, members of the collective. This idea coincided with the worldwide rise of socialism as a political system. The presence at this time of the left wing attraction to communism is evident in the theories of the Group Theater; they felt that the whole company must live together in a communelike existence. In fact, many of them were later accused and blacklisted during the infamous McCarthy hearings of the House UnAmerican Activities Committee in the 1950s.

## Judith Malina

By the 1960s, Judith Malina and Julian Beck had founded The Living Theater. Malina and Beck modified the purpose of the theater to include dramatic social consciousness. They believed that theater transformed the participants as well as the audience, and many of the plays were staged with students, factory workers, school children, and other nonactors, as well as the members of the company. The actor's technique was subsumed to the social message of the play. The public outcry after they produced Kenneth Brown's *The Brig* in 1963, a raw and disturbing portrait of life in Marine Corps prisons, may have contributed to social changes in the Marines (Brown, 1990). One of Malina's diaries, written at the age of twenty-one, in 1947, indicated that even early she was not a Stanislavskian:

> For years I have refuted Stanislavski's sense memory theory . . . I played the last scene of *Iphigenia in Aulis* in a conscious attempt to demonstrate that I could play the famous tearful plea with my mind empty of all but the most prosaic thoughts. I said: A painter does not weep when he paints a weeping figure. Yet I exploited my own emotional turmoil when I played Cassandra. And in the role of Mildred Luce, driven mad by the loss of two sons in the war. What alternatives can I find to the sense memories of grief? Does the actor exhibit his peculiar emotion the way the freak exhibits his distorted physique? (Malpede, 1983, p. 201)

In a later note, Malina wrote that she was not protesting realism, but was protesting the "fake mimicry" that is acting falsely. Actors in the Living Theater spoke of being changed utterly by their work there. The emotional impact of the plays was often so strong that the audience joined the actors in protest, marching out of the theater with them. The lines between stage and audience became blurred. In one play performed in Brazil, where Malina and Beck were in prison for three months, an actor was hung from a parrot perch and given electric shock. Malpede, in *Women in Theatre* (1983), said of the Living Theater productions, "The scene is a brutally naturalistic moment in an otherwise imagistic play; Judith says it is meant to wake us from our trance and make us face the reality of daily torture in prisons throughout the world." Malina saw the actor's art as showing the audience that he really believes what he's saying, in order that they listen very carefully, "to see whether they are in accord with it."

## Peter Brook

Peter Brook was called a Wunderkind when he was young. Born in Great Britain, he went at the age of seventeen to Oxford, and became a film and stage director of international repute. He and Paul Scofield founded the Theater of Cruelty. In 1987 I was privileged to sit through all twelve hours of his *Mahabarata* at the Brooklyn Academy of Music; the next day, I wrote this: "I woke up this morning to dreams of Ganesh and the mythological characters of Hinduism, they became so real to me yesterday at the production. I was talking with the Elephant King and rooting for Vishnu. I have not been so moved by a production since I saw Sam Shepard's *Buried Child* at the Pittsburgh Public Theater years ago." (In 1991, Brook released a shortened movie of *Mahabarata,* only six hours long.)

That spring I went again to the Brooklyn Academy of Music to see Brook's production of Chekhov's *The Cherry Orchard.* Sitting three feet from where Academy Award-winner Linda Hunt entered, I saw her gather herself for the entrance. She focused her attention, took a deep breath, closed her eyes into a squint, opened them wide, and burst onto the stage. As the doors closed in the final scene, we the audience, were locked in. We sat sadly and breathlessly listening to the axes chop, chop, chop their way to progress. The genius of the playwright, the genius of the director, the genius of the actor all came together.

The Theater of Cruelty emphasizes improvisation and the collective lives of the actors in company. Brook's company for *The Mahabarata* included actors of every ethnicity possible. In *Actors on Acting* (1970) Brook wrote: "Acting begins with a tiny inner movement so slight that it is almost completely invisible." He went on to say that stage actors have an awareness of this tiny inner movement because they must amplify it in order to convey it to a live audience, but film actors have as an audience the camera, which is able to pick up the inner impulse much more acutely than a live audience is. This is why stage actors can be film actors, but film actors often have difficulty becoming stage actors.

Brook said that this flicker, this tiny movement, is often present instinctually in young actors. Child actors "can give subtle and complex incarnations that are the despair of those who have evolved their skill over the years." Then something happens, and later on, the child actors "build up their barriers to themselves" and find that touching the essential is difficult if not impossible. This is similar to Bamberger's developmental theory of music talent fulfillment and the presence of the "mid-life crisis" in adolescent performers, as discussed in Chapters 7 and 9.

Brook also criticized the Method actor, claiming that his spontaneity is not truly spontaneous when he bases his actions on observations of others: "his observations of behavior are often observations of projections of himself." For Brook this means that the Method actor cannot draw on "any deep creativity." The creativity of acting comes from improvisation. In improvisation, the actor can come up against "his own barriers, to the points where in place of a new-found truth he normally substitutes a lie." Creativity in acting comes through rehearsals in which improvisational exercises are faithfully done. The mediocre actor builds his character during rehearsals, Brook said. But the really creative actor comes to the opening night in terror, because during the rehearsals he has only been exploring partial aspects of the character he is playing. Even at the last rehearsal, the creative actor will be willing, if necessary, to "discard the hardened shells of his work" in order to come to a resolution. The creative actor will undergo "the trauma of appearing in front of an audience, naked and unprepared."

When a show goes into a long run, discarding hardened shells and appearing naked unprepared before the audience gets to be impossible. This is when the actor must begin to rely on technique. The actor's most difficult job is to be "sincere yet detached." Brook compared the actor's creation with that of the painter and the pianist:

> With any of the other arts, however deep one plunges into the act of creating, it is always possible to step away and look at the result. As the painter steps back from his canvas other faculties can spring into play and warn him at once of his excesses. The trained pianist's head is physically less involved than his fingers and so however "carried away" he is by the music, his ear carries its own degree of detachment and objective control. Acting is in many ways unique in its difficulties because the artist has to use the treacherous, changeable and mysterious material of himself as his medium. He is called upon to be completely involved while distanced — detached without detachment. He must be sincere, he must be insincere: he must practice how to be insincere with sincerity, and how to lie truthfully. (p. 428)

In summary, the actor's creativity is rewarded in the emotional and nonverbal responses of audiences to the skills the actor has been able to use in order to portray human behavior, gestures, personalities. The actor's body, observational powers, memory of emotions, and prior experiences all enter into the creativity that is expressed when the actor acts.

## Psychological Studies of Actors

Unlike visual artists, actors, despite all the value we attribute to them by paying a few of them their huge salaries, by writing about their loves and lives in many popular magazines and gossip columns, have attracted little scientific curiosity as to their personality characteristics. A few psychometric studies do exist, however. In the *Myers-Briggs Type Indicator Technical Manual,* a sample of sixty-two actors was found to be among the top five professions exhibiting ENFJ personality tendencies (extraversion, intuition, feeling, and judgment). Also showing this configuration were clergy, home economists, priests and monks, and health teachers, as well as writers, artists, entertainers, and agents. (Myers and McCaulley, 1985). The ENFJ personality combines intuition with extraversion; they are change agents; they have broad interests and like new relationships and new patterns. FJs prefer to use feeling in the behavior they outwardly show, and, as would be necessary for actors, they are very observant, especially about the needs of people. They are "expressive leaders" and "spend energy in making people happy and in bringing harmony into relationships." The bibliography in the *Manual* showed that this study of actors, though, was of theater majors in a college, in an unpublished study presented at a regional conference.

Two other studies using the Myers-Briggs Type Indicator were of people who choose to be psychodramatists (Buchanan and Bandy, 1984; Buchanan and Taylor, 1986). The 1984 study administered the MBTI to thirty-seven prospective psychodramatists, and the ten successful psychodrama applicants were found to be ENFP (extraverted, intuitive, feeling, and perceiving); they were innovative people who were not conservative. In a study of 170 certified psychodramatists (Buchanan and Taylor, 1986), nine out of ten certified psychodramatists were intuitive (N) types, and only one fourth of psychodramatists were extraverts. The psychodramatists were more like experiential psychologists and least like psychoanalytic therapists. The authors suggested that creativity and spontaneity are essential to psychodrama.

Successful actors are among the most highly paid creative people in our society, but they are among the least studied. The biographies studied by Goertzel, Goertzel, and Goertzel (1968 and 1976) included those of many actors, but many of the biographies themselves do not in fact reveal much of the inner substance of their subjects but are instead merely puffery, a list of famous people met, a catalog of performances with little introspection about the art of those performances.

## Dancers

Almost every little girl wants to be a dancer at some time in her life. She imagines herself as Isadora Duncan, rebellious and so very artistic in her bare feet, swinging her scarves around, or as Pavlova, Margot Fonteyn, Suzanne Farrell, or Moira Shearer in *The Red Shoes,* dancing a pas de deux with Nureyev, Diaghilev, Nijinsky, or Jacques D'Amboise. Or she imagines herself the daughter of Shirley Maclaine in *The Turning Point,* having a romance with Baryshnikov. If her body doesn't meet the ballet standard, she may imagine herself a modern dancer, one of the kids of *The Chorus Line,* or hoofing it with Fred Astaire in an old black and white movie, gliding in a frothy white dress as Ginger Rogers or Cyd Charisse, or as *Flashdance*'s heroine, coming up the hard way from welder to dancer.

The career of the ballet dancer is brief, a flame ignited before adolescence, at the age of eight or nine, and extinguished in her twenties or thirties, when, if she has had any success at all, she goes back home to the Midwest and opens a ballet school in her hometown, to teach hopeful children with the same dreams she had. Of course, there have been exceptions, such as Martha Graham, who didn't dance until she was in her twenties. Modern dancers seem to have longer professional lives than classical ballet dancers. Some continue dancing through their forties and into their fifties.

The creativity of dance is a creativity of the body in motion to the sound of music. Dance is the province not only of the highly-trained ballet dancer, but also of the folk dancer, the tribal dancer, the dancer as ritualist from time immemorial. Whirling dervishes danced themselves into trances of ecstasy. All primitive cultures used dance in religious ceremonies. Dance, movement to music, induces ritualistic behavior, and, coupled with substances such as alcohol or peyote, bestows a feeling of well-being and of communion with the other dancers. Ballroom dancing, disco dancing, rock 'n' roll and hip-hop dancing, slow dancing, jitterbug, the frug, the twist, the mashed potato, the slam dance, the tango and the waltz, have been praticed by people in our culture as a means of entertainment. Dance is an immensely pleasurable form of creativity, both in the watching and the doing.

It is also painful. Professional dancers are notorious for having injuries, and dance aficionados know the disappointment of coming to a performance and finding a substitute because the featured performer was injured. Readers of dance criticism are just as likely as readers of the sports pages to be regaled with litanies of pulled ligaments, twisted shoulders, overworked knees.

### The Aesthetics of Dance

What are the aesthetics of dance? H'Doubler (1968) said that the dancer uses bodily tension and disciplined movement to communicate meaning. However, the dancer is always distant from that meaning, using her body as a tool. Yet the dancer must be inspired by emotion and, through concentration on her body, convey that emotion to the audience. H'Doubler wrote, "Thus dance may be considered a neural projection of inner thought and feeling into movement, rhythm being the mold through which the creative life flows in giving its meaning form."

Walter Terry, for many years *The New York Times* dance critic, in *Dance in America* (1971) called dance an art of danger in which we, as spectators, participate vicariously. The aesthetic of dance is kinesthetic, and we "journey with the dancer along the paths of adventure created by the choreographer." The philosopher Susanne Langer, in *Form and Feeling* (1953), called dance a phenomenological art, an art that exists in the moment, that is apprehended in the moment. Dance provides an illusion of force through the skill of the dancer, who uses her body to implicitly provide that force. Even more than the actor, who has voice and speech, the dancer must rely on gesture, extension, and physical being to tell a story. The music is the framework, but the dancer is the frame.

The movement of the dancer has four dimensions or qualities which Maxine Sheets described in *The Phenomenology of Dance* (1966). First is the tension that the body of the dancer shows. Second is the linear quality of the dancer's extensions. Third is the shape or range of the force in the dancer's body and in the form of the movements the dancer makes upon the stage area. Fourth is what is projected by the dancer. These projections can be abrupt, sustained, or explosive (ballistic). In all of these, what the dancer is conveying is abstract, not real but a simulation of the real, communicated through gesture and subject to the training and perfection of form that the dancer has attained.

The ballet, begun in the sixteenth century, is the most formal expression of dance in the Western world. The dancer needs a classic body, a certain shape of neck and curve of the arch of the foot. The dancer must not be too tall or too short, though currently those limits are being stretched. In 1988, Peter Martins defended his use of the short dancer, Gen Hogiuchi, who was criticized by dance critic Arlene Croce for being offensively diminutive (Gruen, 1988).

Throughout ballet's history, Russian ballet became the standard for other countries' ballet. In the United States, the New York City Ballet, founded by George Balanchine, preserved the Russian standard, while according to Agnes de Mille in *America Dance* (1980) the American Ballet Theater, under Michel Fokine, began to drift from that standard.

The American Ballet Theater incorporated the techniques of the modern, or Martha Graham, style of dance. De Mille said, "The ballet dancer now on occasion droops and convulses, falls to the floor, spins on a nonvertical or changing spiral axis, beats and jumps off beat." Balanchine, who danced with Diaghilev's company before it closed in the 1920s, was asked by two young Harvard graduates, Lincoln Kirstein and Edward Warburg, to start an American ballet in the Russian style. Balanchine preserved Russian classical ballet, but gave it an American flavor (Buckle, 1988). Among his many accomplishments, Balanchine choreographed the works of his fellow Russian, the composer Igor Stravinsky.

While the more avant-garde modern dance draws upon the rigid ballet dancing of its dancers, it is choreographed to music that is less formal than typical ballet music. Agnes de Mille's use of roping and riding in *Oklahoma* and of fantasy and dream in *Carousel,* Twyla Tharp's variations on Sinatra's music, Pina Bausch's abstractions of dance hall behavior, Pilobolus' athletic and not ascetic geometries of gymnastics done to rock 'n' roll, Mark Morris' explorations of form and space done to the music of the Violent Femmes, Merce Cunningham's silent and still interpretations of John Cage's four minutes of silence — all of these creations have extended dance far beyond the classical standard, yet all have been created by dancers who began in classical training

Again, in our consideration of creativity, we come to the word "training." Or "practice." This is the key element in all considerations of the creative product. The product of the actor is a role. The product of the dancer is a role. The product of the musician is the performance of a piece. The role, in order to be enacted with perfection, demands that the person enacting it be trained.

Dance is an ephemeral art, and many dances have not been written down. The Lee Theodore American Dance Machine Company has as its aim the reconstruction of the dances of the American theater, the dances of such choreographers as Jerome Robbins and Bob Fosse. The oridinal dancers of such classics of modern dance are asked to remember and to record the dances. Theodore, quoted in Gruen's *People Who Dance* (1988), said, "On one number alone, there might be five or six of them, because what happens is that one person will come in and remember the first sixteen bars, and the next person will remember what happened afterwards, and so on, down the line." Of the dances that have been written down, many of the choreographer's notes are indecipherable, or the dance was changed so much in performance that the choreographer's notes are useless. This, to me, illustrates the non-literary quality of dance and the lack of interest many dancers have in the written word. Dancers prefer movement over the static drudgery of documentation.

### Suzanne Farrell

As with actors, the biographies of dancers are often puff pieces, chronicles of who danced what when, and who met whom where, with little insight given as to the process of dance in the dancer's mind. But Suzanne Farrell's 1990 autobiography, *Holding On to the Air,* is a notable exception.

Farrell was the premier ballerina for Balanchine's New York City Ballet from the mid-1960s until the mid-1980s. Mark Morris called her work "perpetually astonishing" (Gruen, 1988). "I learn things just by watching Suzanne Farrell dance . . . She has a spontaneity that I can't believe . . . She dances with the speed of thought."

Farrell, born and reared in Cincinnati, grew up in a family of women. Her grandmother was divorced, her aunts were divorced, her mother was divorced. In her 1990 autobiography, Farrell described her life with her two older sisters as that of a daring tomboy who lived in a small four-room house and who, for play, would walk the beams and pipes of the construction site of a nearby subdivision. Like most active girls, Farrell had a childhood of scrapes and bruises, of scabs on knees and elbows, but this was the childhood of a girl slated to become one of America's premier ballerinas.

Suzanne and her sisters studied dance at the Cincinnati Conservatory. Her mother was good at getting her daughters scholarships, and so the girls went to school at Ursuline Academy, near the Conservatory, so they could go to their lessons easily. The three girls shared a bedroom, and one of their favorite games was called "Ballet," with one sister being the teacher, one the mother, and one — Suzanne — the student.

What she liked about her early ballet lessons were the acrobatics they did for the first fifteen minutes and the tap dancing for the last fifteen minutes. Farrell said that early on she "loved the way the clicks and the rhythms overtook my body and made it move." The only reading she remembered doing while she was growing up was looking at the picture books of ballet that she found in the Cincinnati Public Library. She also had a girlfriend who was as obsessed about dance as she. The two girls would call each other up on the phone and give each other combinations to do, writing them down in the dark, using flashlights: "Glissade, jete, glissade, jete, pirouette . . . and then we'd both put the receiver down and get up and slide, jump, slide, jump, turn before reconvening on the phone to discuss the difficulties and changes necessary."

School was not her favorite activity: "I wasn't stupid, but I had a hard time sitting still in class and was always being reprimanded for fidgeting. Nonphysical concentration was simply boring." Suzanne's talent was apparent early on; she was chosen to be Clara in *The Nutcracker.*

Farrell was discovered in Cincinnati by a scout, Diana Adams, who had been sent by the New York City Ballet throughout the country after the Ballet received a Ford Foundation grant. Adams spotted Suzanne, advising her that if she ever got to New York, she should audition. That was enough for Suzanne's mother, and within weeks, in July of 1960, the family moved to New York City. Suzanne had an audition with Balanchine himself. Diana Adams had told Balanchine that Suzanne had one flat foot, injured when a horse had kicked it. During the audition, Balanchine examined the foot, pressing it hard to test for resilience. When

Suzanne's foot successfully passed the test, Balanchine arranged a scholarship for her to study with the company. Suzanne also attended two high schools, but her dance schedule at the New York City Ballet was so strenuous and the tour schedules so demanding that she never did graduate from high school.

While she credited her mother for the opportunity to go to New York City, she said that her mother, a nurse, was not a stage mother. She had made lessons available to the girls, but she didn't watch the classes and never stayed outside the room commenting on their progress with the other mothers. Her mother had to work, and "She had been lonely as a child, and perhaps she knew that if you have the arts in your life you will never be lonely. I have often been alone, but I never felt lonely when I was dancing, even dancing by myself." Her father was absent and never came to the Farrell sisters' recitals; said Farrell, "It mattered to me that he didn't seem to care."

Within two years after the family arrived in New York, Balanchine, then in his sixties, was making ballets based on the eighteen-year-old Suzanne, sending her love poems, and treating her as a real ballerina. By 1964, she had danced sixteen new ballets. This progress was unusual, and she said she "skipped through the natural hierarchy of the profession" because "Balanchine felt there wasn't time." Whether or not Balanchine was infatuated with her is not important. What is important was that Balanchine, as the foremost choreographer of the land, felt that she could do the dances he created better than anyone else:

> He obviously had already chosen to commit himself to
> me, and he had plans, serious plans, for what he might
> do with me. But he had already lived a hundred different
> lives in the ballets he had choreographed before I was
> even born, and for us to continue forward together I
> had to pass through his past. And his past, even his
> loves and personal passions, were in his ballets. All those
> movements, all those pirouettes, all that music, all those
> stories and styles, all that romance, all that beauty and
> joy and heartbreak, all of that was who he was. I am
> convinced that he wanted me to catch up to him. (p. 101)

Farrell married another dancer, Paul Mejia, in 1969, when she was twenty-three. Her mother was so upset she stopped speaking to her, and Balanchine was so upset that he dropped her and her new husband from the New York City Ballet. "I was now a Balanchine dancer without Balanchine," Farrell said. Occasionally, she was asked to guest-star with such companies as the National Ballet of Canada, and finally, she and Paul were asked to join the Ballet of the Twentieth Century in Brussels, Belgium. The company, more avant-garde than Balanchine's company, did more world touring than the New York City Ballet, and Farrell got rave reviews.

In 1975, she wrote to Balanchine, asking to dance with him again. He took her back — but not her husband Paul. In 1977, the Company performed on the Corporation for Public Broadcasting "Dance in America" series. Farrell said, about the filming of her dancing, that the results were not representative of either her dancing or of the ballets, for the editing and splicing took their toll and the immediacy of the performance was lost as "videotape seemed to spread an even sheen over the nuances of any movement." She said that she would lock up any filmed performances of hers, if she had her way. "I certainly don't relish the idea of future generations watching a film and thinking that that is how I danced, because it is not." This again illustrates the transitory nature of dance, of choreography, of the creativity that goes into the performance. It also illustrates that dancers are not as concerned with historical preservation as they are with the moment's mastery of movement.

Farrell, like many creative people, suffered a deep depression just when everything seemed to be going well. "I couldn't understand why I was so depressed at such a wonderful time in my life — I had come back to the company, I was dancing, and Mr. B. was making new ballets." The incidence of depression in creative people was discussed with reference to writers, but creative people of all types have been prone to depression.

Mikhail Baryshnikov joined the company in 1979, but Farrell didn't work with him because of the great difference in their heights. Balanchine had suffered heart attacks. Her husband, Paul, was in Chicago working with one of Balanchine's five ex-wives, Maria Tallchief, choreographing for the Chicago City Ballet. Balanchine died in 1983. By 1985, when she was forty, Farrell had developed a hip problem that prevented her rehearsing for the long hours necessary. The hip degeneration continued. "I could find no relief. I could hear clicking and grinding inside my hip where the cartilage was completely gone. Bone was gnawing bone, and I was visibly limping." In 1987, a hip operation, a plastic hip, and a reunion with her father after thirty years occurred. She performed again in 1988. Her last performance was on November 26, 1989, with Peter Martins. She then retired to teach at her school in the Adirondacks and to teach as a guest with other ballets.

Farrell's life as a ballet dancer was typical of that of many. The concentration and dedication necessary must come early. The biography of any dancer reads like a medical report, at times, as well as a list of dances performed and people met. But physical problems for dancers are always present.

## Physical Repercussions of Dancing

Dancers' lives are constantly filled with practice. Along with the practice comes an ethic of self-denial. Researchers have found that dancers suffer not only from physical injuries, but from physical maladies, among them eating disorders, trouble with menstrual periods, and wounded self-concepts.

### Eating Disorders

The rigorous demands on the body and the continuous pressures to meet the body standard of ballet often produce eating disorders in young dancers. In one study of forty-five dancers and forty-four nondancers, Braisted, Mellin, Gong, and Irwin (1985) found that adolescent ballet dancers exhibited the characteristics of anorexia nervosa significantly more often than did the nondancers. These characteristics were underweight, distorted body image, amenorrhea, and binge eating. The dancers also used frequent strategies to reduce their weight, such as fasting and purging. They also used vitamin C more and were not prone to eat carbohydrates. Lowenkopf and Vincent (1982), in a study of fifty-five female student ballet dancers, found that most of them weighed significantly below national norms and had the eating and hyperactivity patterns of people with anorexia nervosa. The girls were obsessed with food and weight. They also experienced delayed menstruation, were likely to be virgins, and did not date. Their "bizarre eating habits" were reinforced by the dance world in which they were immersed. Their concern with their dancing ability went along with their rejection of their bodies.

Dancers, figure skaters, and swimmers were studied by Brooks-Gunn, Burrow, and Warren (1988). This study confirmed the earlier studies, showing that dancers and skaters were leaner and lighter than swimmers, were more likely to have delayed menarche, and that they had more negative eating habits than swimmers. Suzanne Farrell insisted that Balanchine did not encourage the symptoms of anorexia in his dancers, but Buckle's 1988 biography of Balanchine indicated that he would often speak to his dancers about being light, about being easy to lift, about being thin. Farrell spoke about "the endless diet," and said that the object of her diet was not to overcome obesity, but "to attain the ideal shape for a dancer." Farrell herself failed to recognize that she was pregnant, because she was so used to the irregularity of her menstrual periods. "I was having a miscarriage, but I didn't know it because I didn't know I was pregnant. Like many dancers, I had irregular cycles, and skipping a month or two had never been cause for alarm."

## Delayed Menarche and Physical Injuries

In a 1985 study of 345 adolescent dancers' and nondancers' times of maturation, Brooks-Gunn and Warren found that more dancers were late maturers (having menarcheal age after fourteen years). These late maturers weighed less, were leaner, and had higher oral control scores and lower diet scores than the girls who matured on time (eleven-and-a-half to fourteen years). Those dancers who matured on time had higher psychopathology, perfection, and bulimia scores than the late maturers. They also had lower body image scores. Brooks-Gunn, Warren, and Hamilton (1987) surveyed fifty-five adult dancers in four dance companies in the U.S. and Western Europe. They found that 56 percent of these adult dancers had delayed menarche (age 14 or later), and 19 percent of these had not had a menstrual period for the preceding five months. One third of these dancers self-reported that they had eating difficulties resembling anorexia nervosa or bulimia. The researchers found that amenorrhea and eating problems were related, and that 50 percent of the dancers who reported anorexia nervosa, also were not having menstrual periods. The dancers were dieting at the time, and this was found to be significantly related to their amenorrhea.

Besides these eating and menstrual disorders, dancers are also prone to physical injury. Common dance conditions include ingrown toenails and other great toe injuries from being en pointe; stress, compression, and friction injuries; calluses; metatarsal arch and other foot injuries. Strains, sprains, dislocations, and fractures are also prevalent (Arnheim, 1975).

## Personality Studies of Dancers

Dancers have personalities that are a little different from those of visual artists, creative writers, musicians, scientists, and actors. They are more similar to athletes than any other creative people, except for their tendency to have low self-esteem.

The presence of eating disorders in such a large number of dancers would indicate a low self-concept; this was confirmed by Bakker (1988). Two groups of young dancers, aged eleven to twelve and fifteen to sixteen, were compared with control groups, and the results showed that though the leisure activities of the dancers and nondancers differed only slightly, the dancers had less favorable attitudes in physical self-esteem and self-concept, especially in the older group. Dancers were more introverted, also.

### The Relationship Between Dancers and Other Creative People

Brennan (studies in 1982, 1985) attempted to relate the creativity of dance to Guilford's Structure of the Intellect, using figural or kinesthetic dimensions. She made movement tests using divergent production and scored them for fluency, flexibility, and originality. She also used a checklist and questionnaire to identify visual artists and scientists, and found that the personalities of creative dancers were more like those of the athletes than they were of creative people in other fields. She concluded in her 1982 study that "Creativity is multifaceted and not easily nor consistently identified by different types of tests purporting to measure its presence or predisposition." She also postulated that "creative people in dance do not display to the same degree, the characteristics found in other creative persons." Paper and pencil tests seem inadequate to measure the creativity of the dancer, whose memory and intellectual sense are more physical than verbal or visual. (For instance, sometimes dancers cannot remember a particular dance until they actually begin to dance it. It is as though their memory is stored in their muscles and movement.)

A study by Zakrajsek and colleagues in 1984 describing and comparing the learning styles of dancers and physical education majors found that there were no significant differences between the two groups, and that both preferred to learn in concrete ways. There were also no gender differences. (Zakrajsek et al., 1984). The researchers used the Kolb Learning Style Inventory. The women tended to be concrete, or dependent, learners, needing personalized feedback and preferring to work with others. They were not interested in self-directed learning through printed materials or books. This would indicate that teachers of dance and of physical education should include concrete experience and few lectures.

Another study by Predock-Linnell (1987) sought to prove that dancers, musicians, and artists are alike in preferring abstract, asymmetrical, and complex designs on the Barron-Welsh Revised Art Scale, and that dancers who studied modern and jazz dance would prefer these more than ballet and flamenco dance majors. However, Predock-Linnell reported that "The creativity measure was disappointing." She found no significant differences among the three artistic groups and the control group, and somewhat disappointedly concluded, "It is likely that even a limited aspect of creativity calls upon unconscious motivations, specialized cognitions and variations in approaches to learning and problem-solving." She also concluded that the Barron-Welsh Art Scale may not have been the proper test to use to try to discover abstract-thinking preferences. This again illustrates the difficulty, or perhaps the folly, of using paper and pencil tests to assess creativity.

And that is the problem with assessing the creativity of dancers and actors. The results of the training of their talent into the end result, creativity, is seen in the audience's reaction — the audience being moved, suffering, laughing, ooing, and ahing. The critics rejoicing and grousing. When a friend and I saw Dustin Hoffman in *Death of a Salesman,* we left the theater speechless, went to a restaurant speechless, and sat there speechless. Hoffman defined the role for us, for all time, and we were so struck we were unable to discuss how he had moved us. That is the result of the actor's art. When Pavlova performed the Dying Swan, crowds all over the world cheered and cried. Are actors and dancers artistic creators? Of course. Can we find their talent early? Yes. But not by giving them tests of abstract designs; instead we should ask experts in the field to conduct auditions. We should evaluate children by means of their emotional intelligence and bodily intelligence. We should attend performances and do the myriad practical, useful, and time-consuming things that experts have been doing for years in order to determine which of the young actors and dancers have potential.

## Summary

1. Dancers and actors are similar to other creative people in that they master complicated tasks in order to perform their art.

2. They have kinesthetic and emotional intelligence.

3. The actor's art has been influenced by Stanislavski, The Actors Theater, The Living Theater, The Theater of Cruelty. All have reacted to what Stanislavski wrote and taught.

4. Actors are observant and use what they have observed in the characters they create.

5. Dancers are interested in movement from early ages.

6. To study dance is painful and a career is often ephemeral.

7. Young dancers and professional dancers often have suffered from eating disorders and delayed or missed menstrual periods.

8. Dancers often have permanent physical injuries, just as other athletes do.

# PART IV

## HOW TO ENHANCE CREATIVITY DURING CHILDHOOD

*It is the middle of October. Katherine and Brad were married in August, and, after the honeymoon spent at a nature camp in a national park, Katherine has come back to work, a new bride, a teacher of the gifted with one year's experience. The year is going well. Katherine feels she has some control over what she is doing and isn't just reacting. She actually has a long-term curriculum plan. Long-term until Christmas, that is.*

*One morning Katherine feels nauseous. Luckily, her preparation time is first period and she doesn't have to teach just yet. She barely makes it to the faculty room. Within a few days she knows; she and Brad are to become parents. She begins the healthful diet regime of well-educated, modern, savvy mothers-to-be. She stops all caffeine, all alcohol. She has never smoked, so that is no problem. She takes vitamins and goes to bed early. She and Brad know that their baby is going to be the healthiest, strongest, most intelligent and creative baby of all time, and she knows that a healthy pregnancy is crucial.*

*With what she has learned during her first year of teaching about the childhoods of creative people, she feels a little confused, for it seems that some of the most creative people had awful childhoods. She and Brad love each other, never fight, have good jobs, and want to be parents. Didn't some of the most creative people have parents who were teachers? But then, maybe she shouldn't work while the baby is young. Maybe she should quit her job. But she loves her job and her kids at school and is getting to be very good at what she does. Maybe Brad should quit his job. Well, the baby will be born in July and she'll have some time before school starts. But what if the baby turns out to be creative? Does she want a creative child? What good is being creative if it requires a childhood that is full of trouble?*

●

# Chapter 11

## Encouraging Creativity:
## Teaching and Parenting

*Our schools demand far too little of the best or the worst. And too many bright young people are encouraged to regard their playful fantasies and emotional effusions as "creativity" . . . Marianne Moore meant it when she said, "There are things that are important beyond all this fiddle."*
— Howard McCord

How does one become a creative adult? Can creativity be taught? Do we even want more creative people? Where do creativity and discipline intersect? What have we learned about how creative adults have become creative? Is it the place of the schools to encourage creativity? What happens when we stifle creativity? Can we stifle creativity? What is the place of trauma in the enhancement of creativity?

In reading many biographies and accounts of the childhoods of creative people to research this book, I have been awed and dismayed. Often, the childhoods of creative people had sad elements; some of these creative people experienced literal orphanhood, while others had clearly dysfunctional families. This makes it difficult to write a chapter on how to enhance creativity. While writing this book, I have shared the process with my students, as each week they ask me whom I've been reading about this week, and what their childhoods were like. I have begun joking that in these last chapters about teaching and parenting for creativity, I will give just a few words of advice and be done with it. For teachers, these words are the following: Try to be the teacher that the creative child will remember as encouraging, not as discouraging. For parents, these words — only partially tongue-in-cheek — might be: To enhance your child's creativity, get divorced, or die.

The jokes fade, but the questions remain. Does family trauma automatically yield creative genius? Do not all the biographical reports point to this? Or is Alice Miller (1990) right, that creative people experience trauma in their childhoods, but they also have some warm person to be close to, while destructive persons experience trauma in their childhoods without that warm person being there? Of course, nowadays it is the fashion to come from a dysfunctional family. Everyone is codependent, addicted, and messed up. We can all blame our mothers and fathers for our problems. If the ideal family ever did exist, no one today came from one, if the television talk shows are to be believed. Then why isn't everyone creative?

Many creative people have little or nothing good to say about their families or their schools, and many creative people certainly have had family lives with early trauma, including moving often, the death of a parent, sickness, the absence of a parent through divorce or substance abuse, childhood abuse and neglect. You name it, creative people have experienced it during their childhoods.

## What Creative Writers Said About Their Schooling

In 1978 I surveyed published poets and novelists who worked in the old National Endowment for the Arts — Poets in the Schools program. These were writers listed in a *A Directory of American Poets & Writers,* meeting the criteria for listing. To be eligible for listing, a writer must have accumulated twelve points of credits based on previous publications. For example, a published novel is worth twelve points, as is a published chapbook or book of poetry. A short story in a journal is worth four points, and a published poem is worth one point. Most of these authors are still writing, publishing novels, poetry, essays, and critiques. Most still chose to list themselves in the 1990 poets and writers directory.

Here is a sampling of what twenty-six contemporary American writers said about their own childhoods and school experiences in answer to the question: How did your own experiences as a child in school help or hinder your creativity?

*Writer 1:* I was given responsibility and allowed to fail, but I was also allowed to see myself grow and was given recognition. I was also given the sense that there are forces working through us that help us grow and do worthwhile work, and I have ever since believed in these forces.

*Writer 2:* I was lucky enough to have teachers who told me to get started, praised what I did, and encouraged me to continue. They also insisted I learn much of what is my craft, the skill of using the tools and rules of the trade. My family also, being creative and artistic, encouraged and admonished me, believing it to be not unusual but ordinary to do such things well. They were often my best critics.

*Writer 3:* My artistic life is a negative response to the negativity of this world to my well-being. I think it is therefore very positive in its energy flow. I've never quit being the daydreaming nonconformist I was at eighteen.

*Writer 4:* Hard to remember — I was always full of "chutzpah." I always loved school even when I had awful teachers, the way Francie, in *A Tree Grows in Brooklyn,* loved the library. You must understand that no creativity can occur in uptight, tense places. Kids must feel good in themselves. That's the first job.

*Writer 5:* It is tempting to say that they hindered it. But not all. In my day when a quick child was finished before the rest of the class, he was asked to do a report, or sometimes write a story. What began as busy work sometimes became the best part of any day. But all too often the different answer was crushed, the need to question what seemed too pat was seen as insolence, a novel approach or use of materials was disallowed automatically without a trial. An abiding horror from grade one on was the objective test in which no possible answer was really right, and my desperate need to explain why could not be met. Under the pressure one's creativity soon gets put to figuring out what might have been in the the test maker's mind, so one can guess what the test maker expects. The best thing was learning, in high school, to put a textbook in front of me, to look up from time to time with an interested expression as if I were taking notes, while I wrote my stories in class after class and refined them in study hall. Aside from two excellent high school teachers who continually challenged our imaginations and abilities, virtually nothing in my schooling helped much.

*Writer 6:* We had "dramatics" for thirty minutes each Tuesday, and we were required to recite — with prescibed gestures — a poem. God, how dreadful! Art class was a reward if the whole class was good the whole week and if the teacher had a project she liked, and if there were materials (which our parents paid for in September but we never saw except as a handout of one sheet of manila paper at a time), this on Friday afternoon. Music wasn't much more. What helped my creativity was having a place of my own in the attic that even my brothers, even my mother, couldn't invade, and where I could even spill ink or paint (not to mention tears) without being punished.

*Writer 7:* I had the benefit of encouragement by a fine teacher — fine teachers, I should say — my parents, especially my father; and much luck. Most of what gets done in school and most of what gets encouraged in school does not contribute to creativity. When I feel I'm dealing with my own experiences at something like their true value — however this is brought about by those around me and my environment — I feel capable of doing things. I learned perseverance working in the fields; I learned about persons and nature in those same fields. Having operated a commercial garden and orchard for some thirty years I've had reasons to cultivate the habit of observation and reflection. Schools have helped in that regard, I think.

*Writer 8:* As a child in a small town school in a high Colorado valley my teachers let me express my feelings for the earth, my horse, and how I hated leaving the ranch to come to town. The influence before that was the limited far-from-town library of three books — *The Bible,* the poetry of Robert Burns, the *The Diseases of Cattle.* The latter book first made me want to write poetry. I came across the words *hemorrhagic septicemia.* When my father pronounced them for me and told me what they meant I heard the words sing and saw the tragic death of cattle.

*Writer 9:*  totally terrible
       depressing
        & self-destructive
    made me develop a "closet"
    personality & a disdain
    for mass society at large

*Writer 10:* My "creative writing" teacher in high school was certifiably senile; I switched out of the class, an honors one, to a regular English class with a teacher who loved grammar. I hated grammar, but I learned there to love learning, precision with words. Other memorable teachers were so only because they loved what they taught; thus I, who cannot draw a straight line with a ruler, recall the electricity and excitement of geometry class; I have a lot of buried knowledge and continuing fanaticism about Alexander the Great, because of an ex-jockey-turned-history-teacher whose love of that period of history sent me to the most obscure and advanced of resources, gave me a knowledge of library sources that has served me since, and gave me an absolute adoration of the whole process of knowledge: from the atmosphere in libraries to love of books for their bindings and type as well as for their contents. It was not, I emphasize, WHAT these people taught, but HOW that worked the miracles — and I try to remember that every day I go into a classroom.

*Writer 11:* I was a bookworm and read for escape; I was also paranoid and persecuted by other kids through fifth grade or so. After that, I eventually went to a school for gifted children that was better socially — I wasn't so weird. High school was an utter waste and that was one of the country's supposedly best school systems. My creativity? Growing up outside New York and having access to Manhattan's cultural life was my salvation. Also sympathetic parents.

*Writer 12:* Even though teachers encouraged us to draw, and even though some of my own paintings and pastel drawings were given special honor and hung in the hall outside the principal's office, I lost all interest in visual art by the fifth grade. Art projects were too structured (so that teachers wouldn't fail, I imagine). But then too, in those days, imagination wasn't much of a priority.

*Writer 13:* Since I was an only child and my parents were divorced, I grew up in a fairly lonely environment. I think this fostered my reading and my work habits. Writing is a lonely profession. So, I was prepared.

*Writer 14:* School must have helped — but who knows, finally, where the lyric impulse comes from? Some aestheticians believe the creative impulse begins with an experience bordering on the traumatic. But certainly my reading — which was intense and wide — helped. Otherwise I might believe that schooling plays a very minor part in kindling the creative fires. But I know many poets who never read a book until their late teens and who were uniformly poor in school.

*Writer 15:* I had a wonderful language/literature teacher through junior/high school; sheer encouragement there as far as anything in early life helping or hindering my urge & ability to write; experiences as a child at home, certainly, the far greater factors.

*Writer 16:* I got F in conduct in junior high. That helped a lot. I had fun in class. My father was pissed. But I don't mean badness, cruelty, hoody behavior. I mean acting up wittily, that glee that shakes up a long school day. My father and I get along fine now, but in those days he must have imagined that I was being mean and foul or something — to get that F. I was being, simply, irreverent and spontaneous. I was finding my own way to like school while the teacher was going over and over stuff. And I know that's elitism. Some of the kids needed all that drill — and I was in the way with my whispering and chortling. But I kept it up. Irrepressible. A pain. Guilt tormented me when I lay awake thinking how much the teachers resented my ways. Next day I'd do it all again. Well, I was, luckily for me, intellectually quick, and they might have had some way of endorsing that. The "quick" kid is often discriminated against by the necessities of disciplined mass education. Something in me was addicted to rebellion in this matter.

*Writer 17:* I would say that most of my school experiences were godawful. However, I was a very rebellious student, and often learned things of value by default. For example, at thirteen I was subjected to the first "teaching" of Shakespeare *(The Merchant of Venice)*. I immediately responded to W.S., and realized that the teaching had nothing to do with the poetry. Accordingly, and with full recognition of what I was doing, I read all of Shakespeare on my own. I did not wish to have it spoiled. One old classics master was an amateur botanist, and he sparked a lifelong interest in me, on walks in the woods which got me out of competitive sports. Probably the most positive of any of my school experiences.

*Writer 18:* A dual language background and a large dose of ethnicity helped. I was, for the most part, discouraged rather than encouraged by my teachers.

*Writer 19:* For the most part I was lucky. I ran into several teachers who encouraged me to write as much as I wanted to and rewarded me with kind words. Also my classmates seemed to enjoy my efforts. God bless them all. In college however I was not so lucky. I could not and would not write a standard paper. One idiot actually asked me if I would mind writing a more conventional paper the next time. And I did mind, and that's why I dropped out. I'm getting mad right now just thinking about it — and also this other idiot in teachers' college, who took us to visit a classroom — where, by coincidence, this incredible woman was doing a creative writing class. I wrote an essay on whatever it was we were supposed to report from that visit, but I went on to report on the creative writing aspects — and this nut marked me down for going beyond the limits of his assignment. Shame on him. He is the reason I seriously question the creative capacity of anyone who graduates from a teachers college. In fact, my college experience was so bitter, so anti-creative, I have my doubts about anyone who graduates. Period.

*Writer 20:* I remember school as a struggle to slant my paper in the same direction as the right-handed kids. School generally is carefully constructed to eliminate sensitivity, assertion, intelligence, and guts. The question is, if I didn't get the creative impulse from school, where did it come from? Certainly not from middle-class parents. Not from my genes. I think it came from the fact that I was fat, repressed, left out of the social scene. And when you've got that many strikes, you've got to be creative to survive. Creativity, then, was a survival option — and survival is the synonym of public education and of middle-class, middle-Ohio parents.

*Writer 21:* I think my experience hindered my creativity in the sense that there was no structured openness. We would write an occasional poem (in rhyme, of course) for a holiday or for some kind of Catholic school competition, but there was no joy or interest in the process of the poem, only a dogged persistence until a certain result was achieved. There were no "arts" taught, no music, and so I think it might be fair to say that creativity was neglected rather than hindered. Real hindrance and destruction did not begin until college where no one made any bones about women's inability to create anything but babies.

*Writer 22:* I certainly go back to moments of childhood often. I think I give a special place to "creative/ephiphany" experiences. I'm not sure any specific "creative projects" were important in their own right. But if you listen and respect someone who fascinates you with the ability to perceive what you can't quite (and I think a creative artist should do this naturally) and offers you an opportunity to pierce the veil of the mysteries, I think this becomes the route to creative experiences of your child's own. Creative experiences are not planned — that's an opposition of concepts.

*Writer 23:* I was somewhat self-willed. Schools did not hinder or help. They simply functioned. I was the one with the motivation and it was outside of their sphere.

*Writer 24:* Creativity was a secondary, perhaps even tertiary, priority in my schooling, hence, even though my creative output was exemplary it did not truly flower until college. Curriculum designers need to develop creative tracks in the same way that academic and business tracks are defined, to isolate students with creative talent and to model their studies to develop and refine this talent. This is not to say that the minimally creative student should be ignored; every student should be exposed to creative endeavors and encouraged to foster, if not their own creative output, at least an appreciation and understanding of the arts.

*Writer 25:* My school experiences were hindered, thwarted, denigrated, ignored by insensitive, dull prejudiced elementary school teachers on the one hand, but freed up, encouraged, praised, and shown off by loving, caring, talented teachers in junior high school on the other.

*Writer 26:* I didn't get help from school until I was in college. I started to write a lot in Latin, where I was bored silly, and to avoid getting bad citizenship marks, I wrote and kept my mouth shut. It was a great place for "reverie." An hour where no one could interrupt me (except to translate an occasional sentence). College classes were even better because in lectures I wouldn't be called on.

From these comments can be seen that some writers liked school and others hated it; some were openly rebellious and others sneakily rebellious. Some hated and others liked college. But they all had a strong reaction to their schooling, and praise for good teachers and encouraging parents. Perhaps the personality traits that Barron (1968) and his group found were already taking hold; the independence of judgment, the nonconformity, the challenging of authority, the search for truth, the uncompromising verbal intelligence that saw fools for what they were and called them that. Personal attention from teachers, encouragement, and love for the subject matter being taught — all influenced these writers. Writers are probably not much different from other creative people in their reactions to school, though one would suppose that writers would get better grades, since so much of the school curriculum is verbally oriented.

## Motivating Creative Behavior

Should we do nothing special, but just what we are doing now, and then the truly creative ones will emerge through rebellion? If so, the next generation, our children, should be very creative, for 50 percent of them have been children of divorce, victims of the excesses of us — parents who grew up in the 1950s and had children in the 1960s and 1970s.

### Emotion as a Motivator

I remember talking with five college-aged people who attended select eastern colleges. Every one of them had parents who had divorced; as youth they had all experienced trauma and the emotional consequences were still clearly evident in their unconventionality. Actually, their dress was conforming, but conforming to current styles of rebelliousness. They wore black, dyed their hair black or had it bleached blond in spots. The boys wore spiked hair and earrings in the proper ear for their preferences. I remember saying, "What will happen when you begin writing your novels?" The pointed statement in reply was, "We are just beginning to deal with our anger."

A few years have passed, and these youth, graduated from their colleges, are settling into careers. They have gravitated towards the arts, publishing, theatre, music. One began as a physics major but switched to music composition, transferring from engineering to a liberal arts school. I have no doubt that emotion played a great part in their career choices as well as in their motivations to be creative.

With regard to emotion as a motivator, we parents had already parented for creativity, but we didn't even know it. Even so, it remains important when working with children to try to create an atmosphere that permits relatively free expression of emotion within the structures of school and home. But besides this, what are some specific processes or techniques that may be helpful in enhancing the creative process?

## Close Your Eyes

In a 1979 article for *Gifted Child Quarterly,* I detailed the creative process I used as an Arts in Education poet in the schools (Navarre, J. Piirto, 1979). It was a rather naive article, but it did describe helping students with the creative process through the use of preparation, guided fantasy, and, most important, having them close their eyes. This technique is used quite often in the schools (see Chapter 2), and many books have described using guided fantasy, breathing, and imagery. My approach was a little more directive, though:

> I knew I would have to put them in the mood to write, if they were to produce any inspirations, or random thoughts written down which some teachers call poems. I had some gestalt training when I was a school counselor, and have found the fantasy work in gestalt helpful to my own writing. This technique combines relaxation and suggestion in order to facilitate what could be called a "creative response" in the participant.
>
> My objective was to have them explore their teenage desire for privacy, for a place to go where they could be alone and be themselves. I talked to them a little about this need, and I read them a few short poems. I used a soft voice and spoke slowly, and with a smile. One of the characteristics of high school students, especially boys, is that they never have pencils or paper, and must borrow from the girls, thereby having a chance to flirt a little, and so I had made sure, before starting the exercise, that they had pencils and paper, so that they knew they were going to be asked to write.
>
> "What a weirdo," one boy said. "I can't think of anything to write about. I just took this class for easy English credit."
>
> Undaunted, I asked them to close their eyes, after I felt they were with me, and I asked them to get into their own private spaces, to forget the presence of their

friends, to focus on themselves and on their breathing. I took my time. There were, at first, protests and giggles, but soon they were all quiet, and listening to me.

I asked them, after a few moments, to think about their bedrooms at home, to imagine themselves behind a full-length mirror, looking into their bedrooms: "How does your room look right now, empty, with no one there? Pretend you are a stranger, seeing the room for the first time. What details do you see that will tell you who the person who sleeps in this room really is? [I took a version of this from Talarico, 1975.] It could be the dusty rock collection on top of the dresser, or the dried flowers pinned up on the bulletin board, or the hubcap in the middle of the floor, or the beer can collection on the shelf, or the dirty clothes under the bed." I paced this slowly, and then paused, asking them to focus on these details.

Soon I asked them to open their eyes, and in the same soft voice I asked them to write about their room, to show the reader, by use of specific objects, who the owner of that bedroom really is. I gave them about fifteen minutes, and I suggested that they write at least ten lines. The time and space limit helped to focus them, to give their reverie some structure.

I said that I would collect the poems after they were done with this initial draft, and would read them aloud, so the whole group could share; if they were shy about this, they could make up a nom de plume. Adolescents are usually very shy about having their work read; little children clamor for the privilege. Perhaps this speaks to the inculcation, within the schools, of a fear of spontaneous expression, as children grow older. (p. 796)

Then I included in the article some of the poems the recalcitrant teenagers wrote, and concluded:

Perhaps parents and teachers of gifted children should pay more attention to allowing daydreams and reverie into the lives of their children. Who ever heard a parent or teacher say, "Go and think awhile. Go and daydream"? Perhaps we should send them out into the woods to sit under the trees and contemplate. Perhaps we should give some thought to creating conditions and situations conducive to incubation. (p. 799)

I thought about the structured lives children seem to lead, and was beginning to wonder when they could be free, to experience creative solitude.

### Escaping and Getting the Giggles

When I was the principal of a school in New York City, I would take my little writing group of six talented boys and girls to the Metropolitan Museum of Art for our "poets' lunches." We would walk down Fifth Avenue to the Museum, jotting down details with our newly sharpened pencils as we walked. Then we would go to the Museum and settle in a room, picked by one of the kids, and we would each write a poem or two about an object in the room.

Sometimes I invited other writer friends along; sometimes not. But uniformly, by the time we got back to the school, where I had to resume being a principal again, we were all filled with giggles from a feeling of freedom and having escaped to do something secret. When my schedule didn't allow time for visiting the museum, the kids would bring their lunches to my office, and would tape a sign, "Poets at Work" to my door. While eating our lunches, we would talk, write, giggle. I certainly felt creative then, and I think the kids did, too. We had fun. Those moments with the kids stand out as high points in otherwise pressured, over-scheduled days.

The secret feeling of escape, the free feeling of release from duty, the relaxed feeling of being able to giggle, all contributed to our sense of being creative. We were participating in a safe way of breaking the rules, just for an hour. Teachers and parents can do this with small gestures; I have seen classrooms where children sit on beanbags under work tables during reading — they are quietly escaping momentarily. Parents may take each child out alone, without siblings, for spontaneous special times together, to fly paper kites or to attend a recital.

*Creativity as Adventures*

A friend, whose two boys have turned out to be art majors like their mother, said that she encouraged their art by springing "adventures" on them when they were little. On a particularly boring Saturday when the boys were lolling around on the living room floor watching cartoons, she would announce: "All right, up! It's time to go and have an adventure!" With their sketchbooks, they all would pile into the car, and go to some nearby site to sketch. Then they would stop off at the restaurant widely known as having the best ice cream cones in town to have double dips. Her boys grew up loving the impromptu "adventures" as special opportunities to do art. Of course their home was also alive with art, art books and discussions of the latest show at the Toledo Museum. But again, the primary framework for doing their art was as play, not work.

Perhaps we can extrapolate from these stories three hints for enhancing creativity in children. First, creative production is motivated by emotion. Second, creative production even in a classroom can happen after quiet reverie and closed eyes. Third, creative production is escape from the mundane, is special, secret, and delicious.

## Intrinsic Motivation for Creativity

Theresa Amabile, a social psychologist, has done some of the major work on motivation for creativity. Six terms used in the field of social psychology are "intrinsic motivation" and "extrinsic motivation"; "field dependence" and "field independence"; and "inner locus of control" and "outer locus of control." People who produce the most creative works, according to the work Amabile and her colleagues have done, have "intrinsic motivation," are "field independent," and have "inner loci control." To have intrinsic motivation is to proceed in the work for love of the work itself, and not for fame or glory. To have field independence is to proceed with confidence and individuality rather than with wanting to be liked and wanting to please. To have an inner locus of control is to do what you do because you need, or want, to do it, and not because someone else has given you an assignment to do it. A person who is field independent sings "Climb Every Mountain." A person who is field dependent sings "Raindrops Keep Falling On My Head."

Amabile's studies have been published throughout the creativity literature, as she and her colleagues try one experiment after another that all seem to show that intrinsic motivation produces the most creative responses, and that extrinsic motivation actually hinders creative responses. Her 1983 book, *The Social Psychology of Creativity,* detailed earlier studies, and her 1989 book for parents and teachers, *Growing Up Creative,* is about the best book I can recommend for learning how to enhance intrinsic motivation in children.

Amabile said that motivation is an important key to creativity, and gave suggestions for enhancing motivation towards creative ends. She said, "Intrinsic motivation, too, may be inborn to some extent. But it also depends very heavily on social environment. This motivation to be creative has been so neglected that you might call it creativity's missing link." Amabile came up with a Venn diagram similar to Renzulli's three-ringed definition of creativity (see Chapters 1 and 4), and said that creativity takes place where these three intersect: domain skills, creative thinking and working skills, and intrinsic motivation.

Domain skills are those necessary for functioning in the specific area of creativity; for example, a painter needs to know how to paint, and a composer must be able to read music. Creative thinking and working skills are those practical habits we develop as we grow up. Intrinsic motivation is the inner drive necessary for achievement. Amabile said we should never speak of creativity without speaking of creativity in some domain or other, for example, creativity in science, creativity in writing, creativity in drawing.

### Rewards

To enhance intrinsic motivation, parents and teachers need to rethink how they are interacting with children. Under what circumstances do we give rewards? Behavioral psychologists advocated token systems as rewards, but cognitive psychologists said that these were extrinsic, and did not produce the joy for learning that is needed for intrinsic motivation. External rewards do not enhance intrinsic motivation. When the child comes home from school with the report card, what is the parent's response? No matter what the grade is, does the parent say, "What did you learn?" Or does he say, "Only a B? Why didn't you get an A?" Rewards should be given as rewards for quality of performance, and for trying, and not just because the child completed the chore.

Hamachek, in his basic education psychology textbook (1990), in discussing extrinsic and intrinsic motivation research, said:

(1) both types of motivation are important in the everyday operations of classroom work; extrinsic motivators get things started when interest is lacking, and intrinsic motivation sustains learning itself, and (2) tangible rewards (gold stars, bonus points, and the like) are important extrinsic motivators, but a teacher's oral or written acknowledgements of a good job or fine effort are more likely to be incorporated in students' own feelings of satisfaction. This has the effect of encouraging the self-perpetuating energy behind intrinsic motivation. (p. 268)

We can extrapolate, as parents and teachers, from the educational psychologists' and social psychologists' work on "reward." The most enhancing rewards for creative endeavor are in the pleasure the creator takes in doing the work itself and in achieving the result, not from the pay or the prize. Even painters who don't have galleries, musicians who don't have audiences, writers who aren't published, actors who act in community theatre, dancers who dance alone, scientists and mathematicians who spread the table with arcane formulas to solve personally challenging problems, do not stop doing. While some may say that creative people need a killer instinct, and need to be so driven that they would do anything for fame, recognition, or validation, continued creative production derives from less cruel motives. The work itself is intrinsically interesting.

## Summary

1. Although the creative adult has often had childhood trauma, there are other ways to enhance creativity in children.

2. Writers had very specific reactions to their schooling, and very specific suggestions for how that schooling could have been improved.

3. Setting a creative tone and valuing creative expression are essential in enhancing creativity.

4. Creating a feeling of escape, of adventure, of play and fun are important in enhancing creativity.

5. Creative expression comes from the need to express emotion and from an inner drive.

# Chapter 12

## How Parents and Teachers Can Help Nurture Creativity

*childhood's glut of moments*
*ticking away like the furnace*
*just before the blower comes on*
— David Citino

In 1990 I was asked to write an article about the creative adolescents described in Chapter 3. After I submitted the article, Linda Silverman, the editor of *Understanding Our Gifted,* said that one thing was missing: concrete suggestions for her readers. Did I have any? Though I had thought that those suggestions were easily deduced from the stories I was telling, apparently that wasn't true. So I sat and pondered. Could I make such a list? I could. Here it is. Feel free to add or subtract.

## Provide a Private Place for Creative Work to be Done

### For Parents

Does your child have his or her own space? A corner in the basement? A desk in the apartment? Is the child permitted to be messy? Writer 6 especially talked about her secret place in the attic. One of my son's friends lived in two houses as a result of a custody agreement. At his father's house he had to be neat, orderly, clean, do his homework, not watch television, and be a good student. He kept all his materials and treasures in a small cigar box beneath his bed. His stepmother, a therapist, gave him a ledger for Christmas, so he could keep his accounts in order. However, at his mother's house, he was permitted to spread out, cut, paste, build, draw, play music, and feel free, be messy. He had a hammock in his room at his mother's house, and shelves for all the many books he was always reading. His stepfather played in a rock and roll band and musicians filled the house. His father was a college administrator and his mother was an artist. At which house do you think he was creating anything?

When my children were growing up, we lived for awhile in South Dakota. I noticed all the forts that were around the house, and I wrote this poem:

### Forts

there's one beneath the basement steps
carpeted with a crib mattress
closed off with a worn out bedspread

there's one in the attic
secret in the junk and jumble
small hollow under caving boxes

there's one in the garage
where this week's neighborhood club
exchanges officers
"No Grils Allowed"

there's one this rainy Sunday
hung from the television
over chair and stool one quilt's

drooping width to the beanbags
holes shut with towels
corners pegged with books,

the cat slips in to visit
reclining brother and sister
covered inside a warm soft roof

whispering and bickering
in the world of the marxes
three stooges

they told me
when I peeked
I'm too big to fit

I've used this poem in my work as a poet in the schools, in conducting writing workshops with children. I ask the children to describe their favorite fort. I've only run into one child who never had a fort, a secret place, used for hiding, for getting away from adults. The kids know exactly what I mean, and describe that secret, safe, and protected feeling they get beneath the roofs of their forts. One described how her father helped her and her friends build a snow fort that didn't melt for two weeks! He got the hose out in the middle of winter and sprayed it for them. What a good father. He understood the need for forts. Children need privacy, freedom to run freely and to pretend, away from the supervision and planning of adults. Organized play is not creative play.

One of the tragedies, I felt, for the parents I knew when I lived in New York City, especially for parents in Manhattan, was that children were always being watched. They had to be, for safety's sake. We conducted assemblies for kindergartners and their parents on "street-proofing your child." One parent said that her child became so dependent on the presence of adults that even when they went to the country in the summer, the child played within sight of her parents and wouldn't even go into the backyard, out of sight. I used to watch children play, supervising them, as the principal, and some of the more disturbed children were the ones always asking the teacher or their parent to watch them, to help them, to see them climb. The children who were able to play and forget that there were adults watching seemed more creative.

When I work with adults in writing, I have also asked them to recall their childhoods, and to describe a time in their childhoods when they were so involved in the world of play that they forgot time. Grown men have described elaborate war games played in dappled grottos, and grown women have described galloping pretend horses in the morning mist. One of the most fantastic things about my growing up was our neighborhood, with a bluff across the street and woods in the backyard. My friends and I would range for hours, not coming in except for meals and at dusk, playing jungle girls, pretty ladies, and cowgirls, losing track of time and the watchful demands of adults, fantasizing and pretending.

## For Teachers

Elementary school teachers often have a corner in their rooms for private reading, thinking, hiding away. As the grades get higher, the spaces for such activities disappear. The difference between elementary school, middle school, and high school classrooms reflect the differences in teacher-centered learning. Middle schools used to be run as mini-high schools, but that is changing, and so are middle school classrooms becoming less teacher-centered. Few high school classrooms are conducive to student-centered work, unless it is in the laboratories, the art rooms, band rooms, the home economics and chemistry work spaces. As the grades get higher, the teacher becomes more important. High school teachers lecture, stand in the front of the room, and point a lot. Elementary school teachers move around, sit on small chairs, and have less need to be the center of all activity. Which environments provide the most encouragement for creativity?

## Provide Materials (e.g., Musical Instruments, Sketchbooks)

### For Parents

Yes, it costs a lot and takes a year or two to pay it off, those time payments for the piano, the trumpet, the saxophone, but do it. No one started to be creative during adulthood without having some thread for that creativity leading back to childhood. My son, who decided to major in visual arts during his sophomore year in college, had never taken an art course because he was in band, and at his high school, you couldn't be in art if you were in music. This is not uncommon due to the scheduling requirements of high schools.

But he had always had sketchbooks, and he would go to his room and spend hours drawing and sketching. His thirst for the visual arts can be traced to his earliest childhood. When we went to museums, he would remember the paintings in great detail as we discussed them on the way home. His trumpet is on the shelf now, though he says he will never sell it, and his BFA degree in visual arts provides his living as a professional photographer.

Let the kids hang out at your house. Junior high school boys who are creative often get involved with fantasy games such as *Dungeons and Dragons,* though these do not seem to appeal as much to girls. My son's D & D group lasted from junior high until about their junior year, when social lives with girlfriends seem to take over. They often played at our house, probably because I was a single mother and a little more permissive than some of the other parents. Having a houseful of teenage boys in sleeping bags on the living room floor after playing D and D all night is one of my most pleasant parenting memories; I was happy to make breakfast for them and to see them devour stacks of pancakes, listening to them talk and occasionally observing the game they were conducting in their minds. I also got a short story from the experience, which I called "D & D."

If as a parent you really don't take pleasure in having gangs of kids around, don't try to fake it. Kids can tell. Just remember to provide supplies, private places, and encouragement.

*For Teachers*

Does your room have supplies, and are children encouraged to be free with those supplies, or do you, as Writer 6 in Chapter 11 reported, parsimoniously hand out the paper one manila sheet at a time? Many teachers are notorious scroungers of supplies, recyclers of containers, beggars for friends' leftover scraps of cloth, oatmeal cartons, discarded clothing. These will be used for their costume boxes, craft projects, and science fairs. I have worked in many schools, and I can always tell a good one by the art work displayed, and whether or not there is an easel inside or outside the early childhood education rooms.

Do you give three triangles and a circle and tell the children to make a person? Or do you encourage free expression? Do you have the children copy your master drawing, or do you suggest but not require that they do what you have modeled for them? Is you room filled with books, music, posters, and other stuff? Do you enthusiastically enter into the art, music, and writing endeavors, or do you take a break and go to the teacher's lounge and let the visiting artist take the kids for awhile?

Does your school value the arts and have special teachers to help you help children with creative expression? I have served on state and national arts in education panels, and have been struck at the cavalier treatment of arts specialists by schools. The presence of trained specialists is not questioned when schools talk about coaches for teams, but when budget cuts are made, the art specialists are the first to go. Someone on one of these panels said that the professional arts organizations — the theaters, the operas, the symphonies — themselves might be in jeopardy even in New York City, because the audiences for the arts haven't been developed, since New York City's Board of Education cut art and music specialists as nonessentials during the budget crunches of the late 1970s.

## Encourage and Display the Child's Creative Work, But Avoid Overly Evaluating It

### For Parents

So what if it doesn't look like a horse? Do you say that to your children when they come to you with their attempts to draw a horse? I have a theory that many children stop drawing forever when they can't draw a horse that looks like a horse. The child knows her horse doesn't look like a horse. You don't have to tell her. Is your refrigerator door filled with children's work? How about the walls of the kitchen? The doors? Their rooms? Do you need to have control over your house, and are you such a neatnik that you allow only a small place, a cigar box under the bed, for your child's treasures?

Along the same lines, does your child's practicing of his musical instrument drive you nuts? My sister's violin practice used to do that to me. But she had to practice. That was a rule in our house. She was so rebellious about having to practice both violin and piano that our mother finally let her quit the piano before the requisite five years. Now she says our mother should have made her continue. Among the most musically talented families I know is one where you are invited to hear the latest piano or violin piece when you come to visit. It's just part of the milieu of the home. When you visit Suzanne and John, you ask the children to play for you. And do they ever play well! John, a college professor, was the one who sat with each child for an hour at night, listening to them play their music lessons. It provided not only quality time for the children with their father, but it provided a household atmosphere that said that music was important.

*For Teachers*

Do you as a teacher know what creative talents your students have, and do you praise them for themselves; or are you in the dark, like Mrs. Larson in Chapter 3? Many a child has stopped singing because of a teacher's or other students' sarcastic comments. We all know people — and perhaps we are among them — who, in giving a speech or demonstration, say, when illustrating something on the blackboard, "I'm not an artist, but . . ." They make the drawing anyway, and most often we can tell what it is. The self-deprecating statement reflects on some past perceived failure in drawing. Look back at your childhood in school for a moment. What did a teacher or a peer say to you that made you stop singing, stop drawing? Are you that same teacher, making remarks to children? Your remarks will live forever in those children's minds. I have a friend who was told he couldn't sing, and so he always mouthed the words. Then he told the choir director at our church. The choir director knew that everyone can sing, and challenged my friend. It turned out my friend thought he was a baritone, but he was a tenor. He's been in the choir for ten years, and recently started singing in a barbershop chorus. Some teacher had arrested his singing development for thirty years.

## Do Your Own Creative Work, and Let the Child See You Doing It

*For Parents*

The writer Lucia Nevai lives in a small apartment in New York City with her husband, stepchildren, and her two sons. She won the Iowa Short Fiction Award in the late 1980s. When she writes, she goes to her room and puts this sign on the door: "Lucia's writing." The message machine on her telephone has this message. "Lucia's writing. She'll get back to you later. Leave a message." One of her sons attends the Rhode Island School of Design, in filmmaking. The other wants to be a writer, too. Of course. She values her own creativity, and her sons value creativity also.

This is especially difficult for women to do. Loeb (1975) called it the "If I haven't dusted the furniture do I have the right to begin carving?" syndrome. We think that we have to sneak our creative work, and not tell anyone that we're doing it. When my children were young, I wrote while the children were outside playing or after they went to bed. I would be all alone in the living room, or in the small office in our home, working on poems, my husband and kids long asleep. It was the only time I had, as a working mother, to be alone, to be private. But everyone knew I was doing it, as the rejection letters and a few acceptances arrived regularly.

Here is a poem I wrote in the early 1970s.

### POETMOTHER

the afternoon is calm
silence time to write
the paper is green
like the summer

the mind floats into
itself like distanced
birdsong with images
bright as the kitchen sink

the polished coffee table
slowly right there
the words twist
from the images and

the fingers take dictation
fast and willing
then the back door
slaps

and his feet in dirty
sneakers tramp
and the voice begins

"Mom where are you?
I can't find
anyone to play with
Where's the juice?

(Mom I want)
(Mom I own you)

"You can't catch me!"
and the front door crashes
and a little girl runs
shrieks laughing through

the twisting words
and out again
the back door slams
on my resentment

a child's voice yells
"Bye, Mom!"
I sit up and try again
for stillness

Now I write in the morning. For me, such morning writing time is a joyous luxury. The point is that people must make space and time for their creative work.

## For Teachers

So what if you're a math teacher? Do your students know you are also a cabinetmaker? A painter? A writer? That you sew, or knit, or design boats? The wee bit of humanizing that such information about you does for you with your students can make a big difference in their feelings of freedom of expression with you. Try it. When I conduct workshops with teachers, I often ask them to write briefly and then to share how they are creative. Many of them say they aren't creative, but when I push them, it turns out that their creativity comes out in their hobbies, what they do when they are not teaching school. The cooking, the crafts, the building, the refinishing of furniture, the running of marathons, all emerge in these teachers' descriptions as times when they feel creative.

## Set a Creative Tone

When I was a principal, I tried administratively to set the tone of the school as one of valuing creativity. When the long-awaited, six-months-late first copy of my novel arrived from my publisher one afternoon just before an assembly, I was so thrilled to see it, I jumped up and down and shouted, "Yes! Yes!" As the assembly began, one of the teachers announced to the kids why I was behaving so strangely. Everyone applauded and laughed. They recognized that I was a struggling writer as well as a principal.

When I left the school a few years later, one of the kids in a goodbye speech described me as a writer as well as a principal and said he would remember me because I encouraged the kids to write a lot of poems and stories. Besides hiring professional writers to work with the students, through Teachers and Writers Collaborative, I myself wrote for them. Each year in the yearbook, for my Principal's Message, I would tell a story because Principal's Messages are usually such dull reading for the students. For example, I once wrote about the neighborhood characters where I grew up, and exhorted the readers to "read my story, and then write your own about your neighborhood characters." Then I told them about Mrs. Ollikainen, who made rag rugs and dolls out of hollyhocks, and Old Joe, who had a bull that we used to tease, Mr. Nelson, who yelled for his kids all the time, Brandon, who had a mysterious past and walked downtown all the time, and Bulltop, who drove old cars into the mine pit. Many of the children subsequently did write about their neighborhoods. It seems important to have someone in authority be a model for the risk-taking involved.

Many of the teachers in that school likewise set examples of creativity, and it showed in their rooms. The halls were filled with art work; the bulletin boards were replete with children's efforts. The rooms were filled with learning centers, and every week there was a performance or a class project.

The point I am trying to make is that the atmosphere was creative. The teacher's lounge talk was often of movies, plays, books and musical performances, with opinions freely given about the latest pan by Frank Rich. The teachers traveled, too, even on their teachers' salaries, to Europe, Asia, and Africa. Many had never been to Yellowstone Park, but they had been to the Louvre. The teachers were interesting people, interested in creative things, and it showed in their teaching.

## Value the Creative Work of Others

*For Parents*

Is your house filled with books? Do you subscribe to any magazines? Do your children subscribe to any magazines? Do you visit the public library? Does your child have a library card? When was the last time you went to a museum? A live performance of theatre or music?

You say you live in South Dakota and have two radio stations on the dial, both of them country-western? Photographer James Mackay grew up in Pollock, South Dakota, and managed his family's newspaper there for many years. He is among the most creative people I know. His collection of blues albums taught me almost all I know about the blues. My late friend, the poet and novelist Peggy Simpson Curry (Writer No. 8), grew up miles from any town on a ranch in Wyoming, and she was among the least provincial people I knew.

In fact, as James Thurber said, "The most provincial people I ever met were the ones I met in New York City." When we moved to New York where my daughter attended La Guardia High School for the Performing Arts, one of her friends asked if there were drugstores in Ohio. (Yes, this is a true story.)

Once I was stuck in traffic on my way from my apartment in Brooklyn to my work in Manhattan. A radio station was giving away two tickets to Broadway shows. A person from Queens, five miles from Broadway, won them. She said it was her first Broadway show, and she was forty years old. Provincialism is a state of mind, not of geography.

## What Is Your Family Script?

*For Parents*

What I like to call your family mythology, or your family script, is important. "In our family, we — ." "In our family we value the arts, and talk about art." "In our family we go to college." "In our family we read books." "In our family we go to museums." When parents ask me how to get their kids to do certain things, I ask them what their family mythology is. In my family I knew I was going to college from kindergarten, even though my parents were children of Finnish immigrants and neither had been to college. In fact, my parents couldn't speak English when they went to kindergarten. But in our family mythology, we went to college. On my paternal side, eighteen of my first cousins went; only two, both female, did not. My younger sisters and I formed only one of very few families in our mining town neighborhood, Cleveland Location (we called our neighborhoods "locations"), who went to college. In our high school class of 130, a friend and myself are the only ones with Ph.D.s. One of our classmates is a dentist and one has an MSW. But that is all the terminal degrees we have, though a lot of us got bachelor's degrees and master's degrees — more of us than our parents' generation.

What family mythology made all my cousins, my sisters, and me believe we could go to college? I suspect it had to do with our grandmother, educated only to second grade in Finland. Once when my father wanted to drop out of high school, his father said he would have to work harder then, and put him shoveling manure all day long (they had cows and delivered milk before school). My father said he went back to high school rather than do that, and he graduated. Ten of his eleven brothers and sisters had some education beyond high school, mostly trade education, but there were two teachers, a dentist and a nurse there, too.

The motivation of immigrant families is not new, and my family's story may be similar to your family's. The story is still happening. Asian families in particular have succeeded, by and large, in our present school structure. Taylor (1990) in a "Commentary" in *Education Week,* said that 43 percent of Asian Americans had learned a first language other than English, and still they outperformed other ethnic groups. Taylor said that it was parents who made the difference:

— Parents who value their children's education so much that they inculcate the centrality of that education into every aspect of their everyday lives.
— Parents who actively monitor and supplement what the schools teach their children.
— Parents, and therefore children, who believe that academic effort and hard work are rewarded with accomplishment.
— Parents, and therefore students, who support the schools.
— Parents, and therefore students, who believe in taking the most challenging courses.

One may argue that the increased necessity for both parents to work, as well as the great rise in single-parent families, most of which are headed by overburdened mothers, preclude this parental involvement. But if parents are aware of their great importance to their children's education, and schools become welcoming places for parents, with planned outreach efforts such as personal telephone calls to share good news in addition to bad news, parents might overcome their great fear of school. Schools must remember that parents often retain some of their childhood intimidations regarding school. As a Wall Street broker parent said, "Even though I've been out of school twenty years, when I go back, I feel as if I'm without my hall pass and the principal will call me on the carpet." Looking back on the many studies detailed in this book, the influence of parents on creative people is apparent.

## For Teachers

If your students don't have a family mythology that encourages cultural activities such as museums, concerts, or books, then your role is crucial. Field trips are a bother, yes, and busy school administrators often discourage efforts to take students to cultural events; but this should be a priority and a necessity, not a burden. Even if there is no encouraging atmosphere for field trips, videos of cultural events can be used. However, students are television-sated, so videos can be both a blessing and a curse. A rule of thumb is that doing is better than passive viewing.

At the very minimum, each student should have a public library card, and each classroom should have a set of encyclopedias. As teachers, you can make sure that this happens. And model for your students that research and learning are part of your life, as well. Remember what Writer 10 said about about it not being what her teachers taught, but how they taught.

## Avoid Emphasizing Sex-role Stereotypes

### For Parents

I'll bet the Marlboro Man and the Sweet Young Thing aren't very creative, for they represent the extremes of masculinity and femininity. If you recall the studies described earlier in this book, creative men and women were more androgynous than noncreative men and women. On a continuum of masculinity-femininity, with the most masculine and most feminine at either end, creative children and adults are more towards the middle. The humorist and screenwriter Nora Ephron (1983), in her essay "Breasts," described her childhood thus: "I did not feel at all like a girl. I was boyish. I was athletic, ambitious, outspoken, competitive, noisy, rambunctious. I had scabs on my knees and my socks slid down into my loafers and I could throw a football."

The emphasizing of sex-role stereotypes by parents and teachers makes for rigid, rules-filled environments, where boys don't cry and girls don't climb. The rigidity and the rules are what stifle creativity. By the age of five, children are strongly identified with their genders and whatever the family environment, they understand that boys are firemen and girls are ballet dancers. The creative home and school environment softens these expectations, and children can come to understand that girls can be firemen and boys can be ballet dancers.

There is a strong element of homophobia in our society. A teacher once told me that when she noticed one of her gifted students was a great actor, she told the parents about their son's talent. The mother said, "We don't want him to act in any more plays. Actors are homosexual." Perhaps she had forgotten John Wayne. A softening of gender role expectations does not lead to homosexuality, for most people are heterosexual. The presence of gays in many creative fields may represent the attitudes of creative people, who seem more tolerant of differences and more accepting of people whose beliefs are freer. Androgyny is the key word. Or to put it another way, creative people seem to have both yin and yang.

### For Teachers

Many people who are homosexuals, regardless of gender, seem to have always known this about themselves, though some repress the knowledge. A book about how a gifted boy discovered his homosexuality is the cult classic, *Best Little Boy in the World,* by John Reed. The works of the prize-winning fiction writer David Leavitt are also instructive in the description of coming to awareness of one's homosexuality. Whether homosexuals are more creative than other people is not known; it would seem that creative fields are more open to sexual divergence.

But the point is not that there is a risk of homosexuality in being creative; the point is that following rigid sex-role stereotyping limits creativity. In order to succeed in the world of visual arts, for example, a female artist needs to be willing to exhibit what are typically called masculine characteristics. The profession of artist demands an extraordinary commitment in terms of willingness to take rejection, to live in poverty, and to be field-independent. Those are typical traits of committed males, but not of committed females, who often choose careers as art educators and not as artists. Girls' problems come when they try to reconcile the stereotypical paradox of the nurturing, recessive, motherly female with that of the unconventional artist. Boys' problems come when they try to reconcile the stereotypical paradox of the six-shootin', muscle-flexing "real" man with that of the sensitive, perceptive, and insightful artist. [Further in-depth discussion of the problems of creative women can be found in "Why Are There So Few? (Creative Women: Visual Artists, Mathematicians, Musicians)" (Piirto, 1991b).]

There is no evidence that creative people are more often homosexual than people in other fields, such as teaching, politics, the military, or athletics. In the field of fashion, however, the recent deaths of homosexual males from AIDS has decimated the industry, according to a segment in October 1990 on the popular television show *20/20*; reporter John Stosill and Barbara Walters wondering aloud whether the fashion industry attracted homosexuals more than other fields.

The Goertzels, in their studies of biographies, found that writers were more likely to live in *menage a trois* arrangements than other eminent people. These *menage* arrangements seemed more often to be two females and a male, as depicted in the 1990 movie, *Henry and June*, about Henry Miller, his wife June, and Anais Nin.

## Provide Private Lessons and Special Classes

*For Parents*

Most schools, unless they are special schools for the arts or sciences, are not going to provide all of what your child needs to truly develop the talents she has, and so you must be the one to do so. This means lessons as well as materials. Even if your child plays in the band, the orchestra, jazz band, or string ensemble, if your school is fortunate enough to have such groups, your child also needs private lessons in order to develop musically. This is usually understood in the field of music and dance, but is less understood in writing, visual arts, and theatre. Few children who have talents and desire to learn get private lessons or tutoring in these fields, and this is a terrible shame.

The Development of Talent Project (Bloom, 1985), discussed in Chapters 5 and 9, documented well the sacrifices and provisions that parents went through for their talented children. Parents are the first and most important influences on their children's talent development.

If there are special schools for the arts or sciences in your area, they should be considered. We don't know whether students accepted into these special schools have had prior creativity training funded by their parents, but we do know that they demonstrate potential in the particular domains they are studying. Students can be accepted as a result of their concrete performance on tests, auditions, in portfolios and with assessment by professionals. Curricula in such special schools may not include formal creativity training, either. Instead, a typical eight-period day at the La Guardia High School in New York City contains three or four periods of intensive study of the art (for example, an instrumental music student studies music theory, has an ensemble period, and then has one or two periods of band or orchestra), as well as four periods of general academic study. Most schools for the arts have similar curricula.

The gifted adolescents are chosen for these schools on the basis of their creative products, and not for their success on paper and pencil tests that measure divergent production. While they attend the school, they practice. Talented children who become successful adult professionals, as mentioned before, study skills of their field to the point of automaticity. The notion that creativity is separate from what is produced by the gifted adolescent, that it springs from exposure to general exercises in fluency, flexibility, brainstorming, and elaboration, without specific nurturing in the field in which the creativity is exhibited, seems not to have influenced, at this time, the curricula of special schools for gifted adolescents. Whether such activities would enhance the adolescents' creativity, or whether such activities are desirable as curricular options is, as shown in Chapters 3 and 4, doubtful.

Actually, the role of parents and specialized teachers in these adolescents' talent development seems more important than whatever structured creativity training they have had. Parents often nurture and direct their children in the fields in which the parents themselves have interest and talent. The talented child is then taught by a teacher, who passes on what knowledge he or she can, and then the teacher passes the child to another, more masterful, teacher. That is the path of creative adult production. In the very depth of their special training, these children are developing automaticity.

In their adolescent years, spontaneity in young creatively gifted students often gives way to conformity. Residential schools for young artists make special provision to deny the stereotypes that young artists are interested in drugs, rock 'n' roll, and sex. In an interview, an administrator at the North Carolina School of the Arts said, "Peer pressures with our students are more intense than with other students. We try to create an atmosphere for them where they can pursue academic and artistic pursuits without undue pressure." (R. Ussery, personal communication, July, 1989). Parents who don't have proximity to special schools should send their talented students to special summer and Saturday programs, such as the Governor's Institute discussed in Chapter 4.

## For Teachers

The value of mentors is often spoken of in the literature for the gifted. Researchers such as Simonton and Zuckerman have gone so far as to say that a person will not reach eminence in science without apprenticing himself to a mentor scientist, without studying with the right teacher. Kogan (1988) also discussed the importance of having the right teacher, who will have access to the right connections.

The classroom teacher and the gifted education specialist also have a role, and that is to provide the child and the parents with information about suitable mentors. A few years ago a grant project in Minnesota was established where schools found practicing creative writers to work one-to-one with talented children, to work one-to-one outside of school. The talented child thus had an expert writer with whom to share works-in-progress. This should happen as well in other fields, such as the visual arts or invention.

Schools must also play a part in the development of talent, helping find private teachers and mentors for talented children from families without financial resources. Petitioning local clubs and organizations to pay for lessons for a struggling but talented child can best be done by the school (anonymously, of course). A teacher paid for the room and board of one of our students at the Governor's Institute in 1989. She did it so quietly that I never learned her name, but the child's life was changed by the experience.

The black Caribbean poet, Derek Walcott, a MacArthur Fellow, in an interview in the "Writers at Work" series in the *Paris Review* (Plimpton, 1988), told this story about growing up in the Caribbean country of St. Lucia, having the good fortune to come under the influence of the visual artist, Harry Simmons:

Harry taught us. He had paints, he had music in his studio, and he was evidently a good friend of my father's. When he found out that we liked painting, he invited about four or five of us to come up to his studio and sit out on his veranda. He gave us equipment and told us to draw. Now that may seem very ordinary in a city, in another place, but in a very small, poor country like St. Lucia it was extraordinary. He encouraged us to spend our Saturday afternoons painting; he surrounded us with examples of his own painting. Just to let us be there and to have the ambience of his books, his music, his own supervision, and the stillness and dedication that this life meant in that studio was a terrific example. The influence was not so much technical. Of course I picked up a few things from him in terms of technique; how to do a good sky, how to water the paper, how to circle it, how to draw properly and concentrate on it, and all of that. But there were other things apart from the drawing. Mostly, it was the model of the man as a professional artist that was the example. (p. 271)

Harry Simmons might not have had a teacher's certificate, but he was certainly a mentor and a teacher.

## If Hardship Comes into Your Life, Use It Positively to Teach the Child Expression Through the Arts

*For Parents*

This book has described how childhood hardship often leads to creativity. So if you or your family experience hardship in your lives, try to make something of it. Writer and storyteller Marie Vogl Gery told of her yearlong residency at a junior high school where the mother of one of the boys she worked with committed suicide. This boy demonstrated talent and expressed his feelings through poetry that didn't specifically refer to the suicide, but that permitted him indirectly to defuse his feelings of sorrow, confusion, and sadness.

Release of emotion through the arts is often indirect, thus more therapeutic than therapy itself. There are branches of therapy called music therapy, art therapy, poetry therapy, and dance therapy that recognize the positive effects that the arts can have when a person has experienced trauma or emotional upheaval. However, the child should also have a right to privacy. Snooping in private journals, asking for detailed explanations of what may seem to be weird artistic endeavors, is against the rules. The expression is itself enough. Remember the life of Christy Brown as shown in the movie, *My Left Foot*? Brown's family refused to let him be institutionalized for his profound handicaps and provided him with materials, company, support, and a neighborhood full of loving friends.

## For Teachers

Try to notice and be sensitive to the situations of the children you teach. Ban the term "broken home" from your vocabulary. Don't be under the impression that a child will not be creative because he is poor or dishevelled. A student of mine, a bilingual Spanish-English teacher, discovered the creativity of a boy living in extreme poverty because he was always reading. She took photographs of him reading in the bus line, in the lunchroom, in the hallways, in math class, on the playground. She then identified him as having potential writing talent by asking him to write stories, which were extraordinary blends of Mexican and Central American mythological characters. She recommended him to the gifted education specialists in his district, even though his IQ scores did not meet the threshold cutoff.

## Emphasize that Talent is Only a Small Part of Creative Production, and that Discipline and Practice Are Important

### For Parents

Talent is necessary but not sufficient. True realization of creativity comes through hard work. That has been emphasized repeatedly through studies of creative people and their interactions with their domains of creativity. A child gradually realizes that talent comes through habits of hard work. Bamberger's work on the development of musical talent is important to remember. She said that there are two stages in the development of talent, and that the first stage is the natural stage, where everything seems to come easily; during the second stage the adolescent learns the formal aspects of the discipline — the talent becomes consciously developed. The world is full of talented people, but fully creative people do a lot of hard work.

Does that mean you should make your child practice the piano? Use your own judgment. The key is to realize that discipline and practice are important. No creative adult in any field got to be successful without first having had many fits and starts and having spent many hours in conscious practice. How many times did Edison try, before he came up with a successful electric light bulb?

### For Teachers

Teachers of the gifted especially must realize that talented children are often overly praised and rewarded just for possessing talent. Teachers of the artistic disciplines, the visual arts, writing, music, dance, theatre, know what it takes to realize that talent, but talented students are often not given special help by the school. They are instead thrown in with far less talented students in art, music, math, and science. This would never happen in athletics, where gifted students are permitted to advance according to their abilities, competing with people at their own levels of expertise. Accurate and qualified feedback is important in the development of talent, and the child should have access to people who have some expertise. Thus, mentoring is important.

Talented people often are talented in many dimensions, and it is hard to choose which field to pursue. Art? Music? Acting? Helping talented children to make these choices without closing down options is a challenge.

Another challenge is not to counter-identify, as Sylvia Rimm said in her book, *The Underachievement Syndrome* (1986). Often the teachers of talented students are almost as jealous and anxious as parents are. Such teachers hesitate to lose the student to other, more advanced teachers. They feel horrible when the student doesn't perform or when the child makes a mistake. They are as narcissistic as the parents described by Miller in *The Drama of the Gifted Child* (1981). This is particularly difficult when the teaching relationship becomes a coaching relationship. Teachers can be temperamental and cruel, pushing hard until the students hate the field. A former swimmer once told me that he would never swim again, never go near a pool, because his college coach demanded that he swim seven hours a day in order to improve his time a few seconds. Swimming will never again be a pleasure for him. Kogan (1988) also spoke to this difficulty while describing the idiosyncratic Juilliard teachers, when she said that the greatest discovery for a student of music who has spent her life practicing is that of the pleasure of music. Often musicians are so technically oriented that they have difficulty listening to music without analyzing it unduly.

## Allow the Child to be "Odd"; Avoid Emphasizing Socialization at the Expense of Creative Expression

*For Parents*

So your daughter didn't get to be Clara and had to settle for being a soldier in *The Nutcracker*. So your son didn't get his brilliant short story in that magazine of children's writing. Is this the end of the world? Is it your child's or your own ego that is hurt? Alice Miller wrote about parental narcissism — that is, parents investing so much of themselves in their children's successes and failures that they lose sight of the purpose of the practice, and the children are harmed. In the high-powered world of national children's chess, parents have become so involved in their children's chess tournaments that fathers came to blows, and the chess association finally had to ban parents from the chess arenas at the primary levels.

We all know the phenomenon of the Little League parent. This syndrome is found in the creative world as well. Sometimes these parents are called stage mothers. Sylvia Rimm (1986) wrote about the necessity for children, especially talented children, to be able to take the second lead in the play, or second chair in the band. She said when children work for their achievements they learn how to fail, and thus appreciate their achievements more.

Other parents either deny that their children have talent, seemingly fearful of what might be the implications for their future development, or they don't see their children's talent as important. Or, like the mother of the talented young actor, they see actors as odd. But the need to get along with others is not paramount in creative people, as the research has shown repeatedly. Most creative people weren't president of the club or queen of the prom or the one voted most likely to succeed.

Often, they were odd. For many, high school was the most painful time, as the pressures for conformity beckoned.

Often, too, high school creative youth will band together in what they call nonconformity but will still dress the same as their other nonconformist friends, listening to the same music, reading the same books, and rebelling togther. I read somewhere, years ago, that the "enfants terribles" of 1970s movie directors, the Spielbergs, Lucases, Bogdonoviches, Coppolas, were not, in high school, the boys that the pretty blond cheerleaders chose for boyfriends, and they spent a lot of time yearning for these ice goddesses. It was only when their creative talents were realized, years later, that they got to cast their high school dreamgirls, as Bogdonovich cast Sybil Shepherd in *The Last Picture Show.* That is probably why many adult women also love the movie *The Way We Were,* because the odd rebel Streisand got the gorgeous blond hunk Redford; and perhaps it is why teenagers like *Pretty in Pink* and *Carrie.*

## For Teachers

The schools often see their major roles as socializing children so they fit into a mold and become acceptable to the society that the schools serve. This is considered to be as important as teaching the children to read and write and figure, for this is what the "real world" demands, say some educators. But as the research reported in this book shows, creative people are often at odds with the world and are prickly, rebellious, and nonconforming. Often their nonconforming is actually conforming, but conforming to a stereotype similar to how they perceive creative people to behave. Often creative students act out in class, are argumentative, and consciously underachieve; that is, they do well in classes they like but don't care about classes they don't like or see as relevant to their futures.

Rimm (1986) recommended that such creative students may need therapy. I disagree, because often their rebelliousness carries over to the therapist's office as well. The teenage creative writer whose responses to the Overexcitability Questionnaire were discussed in Chapter 4 said she sat silently and stubbornly when she was sent to a therapist. Another creative child videotaped for a case study by one of my students said that even though her mother made her go to therapy because of her nonconforming behavior, she didn't feel she had benefited because she felt smarter than the therapist. One of our creative adolescents in 1989 spent the whole Institute on psychotropic drugs and fell asleep in her morning classes. Her parents insisted that she take them because she had taken to wearing black clothes and black lipstick and they were worried about her so they sent her to a therapist who prescribed the drugs.

Perhaps when considering whether a creative child needs therapy, families and the schools should themselves be willing to undergo therapeutic questioning. The selection of the therapist is also quite important. Creative people generally understand creative people, recognize kindred spirits. Sending a creative child to a rigid therapist may not work.

### Approach Children with a Creative Style: Use Humor and Get Creativity Training

*For Parents and Teachers*

Besides enjoying and being frustrated by that child's "sense of humor," we as parents and teachers should monitor our own ways of dealing with creative children. Do we enjoy children? Do we laugh with children (or at them, if appropriate)? Do we have fun with children? In other words, is being with creative children the pleasure it can be?

Bryant and Zillman (1989) studied the use of humor in classrooms. Elementary school teachers use more humor than junior high teachers. Junior high teachers most frequently use funny comments, funny stories, and jokes, though male junior high teachers told jokes more often. Junior high, high school, and college teachers used hostile and tendentious humor such as ridicule and sarcasm more often than did elementary teachers. In fact, almost half the humor used by these teachers was sarcastic. Humor used in a hostile manner is not what is meant here, but humor used in gentler ways creates a happier, more relaxed classroom, and thus may help students to have positive attitudes towards learning. Bryant and Zillman said,

> A good, positive classroom environment is a setting and situation in which communication is free and open, children are stimulated and do not feel threatened, strong empathic bonds are established between teacher and students and among students, and feelings of happiness, goodwill, and the joy of learning prevail. (p. 61)

Ziv (1988) has shown that humor contributes to the development of creative thinking, and one can see why, for nonhostile humor creates the feeling of freedom and play that is necessary for creative thinking.

Get creativity training. A 1990-91 $100,000 statewide grant in Ohio in the development of creative thinking offered creativity training to elementary and middle-school teachers in two suburban districts. It was called Project Vanguard. As a result of this creativity training, which consisted of 30 hours for each teacher, participants were able to identify creative children, to utilize open-ended techniques of teaching, and were trained to value the creative thinking of the children they taught.

If school districts are serious about effectively teaching creative thinking, they must provide the necessary backup training. As detailed in Chapter 4, there are many commercial programs available and many trained people who can provide creativity training to school districts. School districts also should provide the rigorous instruction in the fields in which the creativity training can be applied.

## Frank Lloyd Wright

A final example of how these thirteen suggestions worked in the life of one of the most creative people of the century, Frank Lloyd Wright, will illustrate. In his stunning poetic *Autobiography* which he revised many times (1932; 1943; 1977), Wright detailed the experiences that made him a creative, productive adult. He referred to himself in third person, as "the boy" and "he," in describing his early years, and only began to refer to himself as "I" when he broke away from his home ties and left Madison, Wisconsin, for Chicago, at the age of eighteen.

Wright's mother was a schoolteacher from an immigrant Welsh Unitarian family that valued Education with a capital "E." She found her ideal educated mate in Frank's father, whom she met near their family valley in Wisconsin, where he worked for awhile as a circuit rider and music teacher. When they married, Frank's mother was in her late twenties, his father in his mid-forties. The father was a dilettante, "tirelessly educating himself, first at Amherst, then to practice medicine, soon found by him to be no genuine science. Then the law, but again — disillusion." The spectre of the ineffectual father seems apparent here. Finally taking up the call to be a Baptist preacher, he moved the family back to the Weymouth, Massachusetts, when Frank was three years old and his sister was one.

But the mother's loyalties swerved from the father to the son after Frank was born, and they were to continue that way. Anna's "extraordinary devotion to the child disconcerted the father," and the father began to recede into the background in her affections, for she "now loved something more, something created out of her own fervor of love and desire. A means to realize her vision." They lived in genteel poverty in Massachusetts. Frank's father took solace in music and would play into the night in the empty church on the organ. Frank, only seven at the time, would have to pump "with all his strength at the lever" and would be "crying bitterly as he did so." But Wright came to love music through these nocturnal experiences.

Meanwhile, his mother became very interested in the Froebel methods of education, similar to our present emphasis on manipulatives and concrete experiences for young children, and brought home gifts of blocks and paper in geometric shapes to the young boy. He was encouraged to play with them for hours. She had in mind that he was to build buildings, and besides helping him with these manipulative maple blocks, she hung his room with drawings of English cathedrals. The family moved back to Madison, Wisconsin, and one April, when Frank was eleven, his Uncle Frank came to take him to the family valley to work on the farm. Frank worked there every year from April to September, when he would go back to Madison to school.

At the farm he protested about the heavy labor, the milking of cows, the chopping of wood. He often ran away but was always brought back. One of his uncles pinched his flabby upper arm and told him that he must work so hard he would "add tired to tired — and add it again." Frank saw his physical and mental strength grow. He learned that "work is an adventure that makes strong men and finishes weak ones." He was a dreamy boy, a reader, a lover of music, imagining the time away, and his summers at the family farm, while strengthening him physically, also provided him solitary time, working to the rhythm of machinery, ranging in the woods listening for the tinkle of the bells of the cows he had been sent to find. He said that his uncle would see him go into a trance of dreamy thought and would shout, "Frank, come back! Come back, Frank!" Wright described it thus: "One eleven-year-old was turning to inner experience for what he heard, touched, or saw."

Back to school each September in Madison, Wright and a friend who was crippled and mercilessly teased by the other boys formed a comradeship of outsiders. The two boys were odd and didn't fit into the group of other boys. They read together in secret hideouts, basements, and attics, even reading the forbidden Nickel Library books. They developed crushes on the girlfriends of Frank's sister, and spent a lot of time tinkering and inventing things. Wright said, "Both Frank and Robie had real passion for invention, and were banged, pinched, stained or marred or were 'had' somewhere by perpetual invention going on." Designing and drawing always, they invented a water-velocipede, a catamaran, a cross-gun, bows and arrows, a bobsled, kites, a waterwheel, a scroll saw, a turning lathe. Their real life was lived outside of school. Wright said, "But — of the schooling itself? Not a thing he can remember! A blank! Except colorful experiences that had nothing academic about them."

The boys were enterprising also, and they went into partnership with another boy, forming a printing firm. They began publishing a newspaper in their mid-teens, and Wright again commented that the formal education occurring simultaneously with all these wonderful enterprises meant nothing: "But the schooling! Trying to find traces of it in that growing experience ends in finding none. What became of it? Why did it contribute so little to this consciousness-of-existence?" Wright said that even though his memories of school were so negative, school perhaps was not purely harmful, for one of the purposes of school is to civilize wild young people, and if the school can't do it, perhaps the art school can:

> You can't let boys run wild while they are growing. They
> have to be roped and tied to something so their parents
> can go about their business. Why not a snubbing post
> or — school, then? A youth must be slowed-up, held
> in hand. Caged — yes — mortified too. Broken to harness as colts are broken, or there would be nothing left
> but to make an "artist" of him. Send him to an Art
> Institute. (p. 56)

Wright's imaginational intensity was strong. Once he imagined that his mother was going to have a party for him. He began to discuss it with his friends, describing the food and the presents. They believed him and came at the appointed time in their Sunday best. His mother was surprised to see them, but when they said they had come for the party, she looked at Frank, understood, and made a party, even getting Frank's father to play for them on his violin. She went along with her beloved son, even though they were poor. Frank's intensity of imagination was so great, he didn't think he was lying to his friends; he believed his own fantasy. His real life was the life of his imagination.

During the summers, when he helped fix and improve the farm machinery, he used the rhythms of the farm to internally compose music: "All machinery makes some recurrent noise, some clack or beat above the hum that can be made into the rhythm of song movement — a rhythm that is the obvious poetry in the mathematics of this universe." His apprenticeship in pumping the organ for his distracted father paid off in his being able to relate the structure of music to the pounding of machinery.

"After one thousand two hundred and sixty todays and tomorrows like those yesterdays," he turned sixteen and prepared to enter the University of Wisconsin. The farm experiences left him with "a self-confidence in his own strength called courage" and with no fear but a fear of people. He was very shy with girls: "The sight of a girl would send him scampering like a scared young stag." Meanwhile, his father and mother were not getting along. His scholarly father was now teaching himself Sanskrit and escaping into his music, and their poverty was so overwhelming that his mother would wait to eat only what the family had left on their plates. Wright had become so muscular and strong that, at age sixteen, when his father tried to beat him, he held his father down on the floor until his father promised he would beat him no more.

Anna asked the father to leave when things got unbearable, and "Father disappeared. Never seen again by his wife and children." He took only his violin and his clothes. The marriage was quietly dissolved, and the family felt great disgrace and shame. Wright felt his mother had been dealt a great injustice, as divorced women were not usually found in society, especially divorced wives of ministers. She kept working in an engineer's office and kept pushing him, getting him a job with a civil engineer at the University of Wisconsin. Wright entered college then, to study civil engineering. Glad to be spared what was called architectural schooling at the time, he instead got a practical education, in civil engineering. He continued his voracious reading and dreaming, and he kissed a girl for the first time. At college, he was still an outsider. He never graduated, and he left Madison for Chicago, feeling a "sense of shame in accepting the mother's sacrifices for so little in return."

During college he experienced an event that was to haunt his vivid dreams for years afterwards. A new wing on the state capitol building collapsed because of the criminal negligence of the architect. Wright said the horrible carnage "never entirely left" his consciousness.

Thus went the childhood of one of the world's foremost architects. He was encouraged to be creative, to dream, to range freely. He had artistic parents interested in education. He was provided with music lessons, tools, and books, even though his parents were very ppor. His mother suggested architecture to him at an early age and then moved heaven and earth to influence him in that direction. He was engaged in many projects and had a few friends who were interested in the same things. His father was viewed by the son as ineffectual, and the mother was viewed as a major influence in his creativity. In his family mythology, the attainment of an education was emphasized, as well as an ethic of hard work. The family experienced hardship and took it in stride. Wright was not chided for being odd; rather, his family encouraged him. All of these seeds of his later accomplishment were planted in his early years.

## Summary

1. Provide a private place for creative work to be done.
2. Provide materials (e.g., musical instruments, sketchbooks).
3. Encourage and display the child's creative work. Avoid evaluating it overly.
4. Do your own creative work and let the child see you doing it.
5. Value the creative work of others. Attend museums, theater, and movies, and talk about books.
6. Pay attention to what your family mythology is teaching.
7. Avoid emphasizing sex-role stereotypes.
8. Provide private lessons and special classes.
9. If hardship comes into your life, use the hardship positively, to encourage the child to express him or herself through the arts.
10. Emphasize that talent is only a small part of creative production and that discipline and practice are important.
11. Allow the child to be "odd": avoid emphasizing socialization at the expense of creative expression.

12. Approach children with a creative style: use humor. Get creativity training.

13. The life of Frank Lloyd Wright is illustrative of many of the above suggestions.

# APPENDIX

# Creativity Theory

*There are no virgin births in the realm of ideas. Everything is connected to something else.*

— Robert T. Jones

## The Need for Theory

It was a meeting of the American Educational Research Association, and several researchers were presenting their papers about the education of the gifted. The Discussant was Dr. Robert Sternberg of Yale University. When he got up to give his reactions to the papers, he called for a theory. "What if we propounded a theory of murderosity?," he asked (Sternberg, 1990). Using this example, he showed how we would want to understand the construct of murderosity. The construct of intelligence and of intellectual giftedness also needs a theory. If the presenters had based their research on a theory, any theory, even a theory that was a rival to his theory, the papers would have been better. He pointed out that none of the presenters named their implied theory, the theory that giftedness equals high IQ, even though that implicit theory is in great dispute among researchers. He noted that none of the papers said anything about creative intelligence, nor about practical intelligence, but continued the myth that giftedness is high IQ.

Sternberg's comments are appropriate in considering how to address creativity. Theories seek to explain what and why, and the question of what creativity is has many answers. A theory is a framework explaining the relationships among factors that pertain to creativity. Depending on a theoretician's predilection, field of expertise, and sense of self, the answer differs. The impetus for theorizing about creativity may come from a person's thinking about his or her own creativity. Even so, there are several basic species of creativity theory; these are psychoanalytic theory, psychological theory, philosophic theory, and domain-specific theory.

The reason psychoanalysts theorize about creativity is to probe the psyche of the creative person, looking for the key incidents or events that lead creative persons to be as they are. One particular international group of psychoanalysts, therapists, and physicians belong to a group called "Creativity and Madness" which meets regularly to discuss the lives of creative people who had mental difficulties.

As stated in Chapter 1, psychological theorists also want to probe the psyche, but their interest is to find out what happens in the mind of the person creating (cognitive psychologists) or to make the perfect test for creativity in order to predict who will be creative (psychometrists), and to discover the traits of the creative person and the aspects of the creative process. Humanistic psychologists have a slightly different focus; they are not so much interested in a creative product as in enhancing the creative potential in every human being. Information processing theorists want to probe the brain in order to find out what dendrons flash with what speed so that the creative person's processing can be replicated, perhaps artificially, with computers.

Philosophers are among the most interesting creativity theorists. They want to assess the meaning of creativity, especially as it relates to certain philosophical problems. Those philosophers called existentialists seek to explore the meaning of freedom. Philosophers called aestheticians seek to explore the meaning of beauty.

The domain-specific theorists, or artist/scientist theorists, want to explain what it is that happens when they are "creative," and their accounts are generally fascinating to read. It is when they formulate a theory — that is, when they generalize for all artists, scientists, inventors, or mathematicians — that their accounts get a little questionable.

One basic book, *The Creativity Question* (1976), edited by a major psychoanalytic theorist, Alfred Rothenberg, and a major philosophic theorist, Carl Hausman, demonstrates the diversity of theories. Another interesting book that summarizes theories is the psychoanalyst Arieti's (1976) *Creativity: The Magic Synthesis*. The above-mentioned Sternberg summarized creativity theories in cognitive psychology in yet another book called *The Nature of Creativity* (1988), the title of which brought a strong reaction. Rothenberg, in *The Creativity Research Journal* in

1988, stated that through the title psychologists were falsely implying that they knew the "nature" of creativity, but that most of the book's theorists were just recycling their old ideas. His comment illustrates, again, the proprietary feelings that creativity incites.

The following list briefly summarizes the major theories and their proponents. Some of these ideas were implicitly stated and not fully developed; some were explicitly developed as full-blown theories of creativity. Some I have merely mentioned and have inadequately summarized their thoughts. This is not to minimize them, but to provide an overview of the deep morass one surveys when beginning to study creativity. A more complete introduction to creativity theory is the 1990 Ablex Press book, *Theories of Creativity* (1990), edited by Mark Runco. These thinkers have written, studied, summarized, and agonized over what creativity truly is. They have spent much of their professional lifetimes contemplating creativity, and their work is appreciated by us novices. Although you may have some objections as to which categories I placed people in — for example, I placed Hofstadter in the philosophical category, and Huxley into the domain-specific category — these categories provide broad outlines of theoretical summations. Think interdisciplinary, as we say in education.

## Philosophic Theorists

Kant (1778): Genius, or creativity, is found in the arts but not in science; there is a necessary interplay of the faculties of imagination and understanding in the production of art.

Bergson (1907): Creativity is the result of intuition when all precedents are absent.

Croce (1909): Creativity in art is the expression of intuitive pre-cognition.

Collingwood (1938): In creative people, imagination is the synthesizing activity that occurs before discursive or relational thought.

Maritain (1953): Human creativity can be traced to the power of the divine, through poetic insight and mystical illumination.

Langer (1957): Creativity is found where the abstract apparition of a form produces a symbolic emotional reaction in the perceiver.

Blanshard (1964): What the creator creates is an end that results from inner necessity. The subsconscious is present in invention.

Hausman (1964): Creativity is spontaneous, nonrational, and produces true novelty.

Hofstadter (1985): "The crux of creativity is the ability to manufacture variations on a theme."

## Psychologists

Galton (1869): Special talent or genius in diverse areas is inherited.

Thorndike (1911): Relevant experience is essential to creative problem solving.

Wallas (1926): The creative process takes place in four specific phases occurring in a fairly regular sequence including a phase of incubation where creative work occurs outside of consciousness.

Rossman (1931): There are seven steps to the creative process. These are similar to Wallas's.

Patrick, Catherine (1937-1938): Artists, poets and scientists do go through Wallas' four stages of preparation, incubation, illumination and verification.

Guilford (1950, 1967): "Divergent production," an intellectual factor, is present in the creative response; the divergent producer provides alternate solutions to open-ended problems.

Osborn (1953): There are seven stages in the creative process. These evolved to the Creative Problem-Solving Process.

Stein (1953): There are three stages in the creative process.

Rogers (1954): The creative individual has an openness to experience, an internal locus of evaluation and the ability to toy with elements and concepts.

Watson (1958): Creative problem solving comes because of transfer. Similar old problem solutions are generalized to the new solution.

Taylor (1959): Creativity exists at five different levels.

Gordon (1961): Previous theories of creativity were elitist and stressed inspiration and genius. Everyone can be creative. Making metaphors is the creative process.

Vygotsky (1962): Creative imagination is developmental, requiring the collaboration of concept formation.

Mednick (1962): Remote associations are combined to form creations by contiguity, serendipity, and mediation.

Roe (1963): The creative process is separate from the final product. It happens in most people and is not unique to only those who produce superior final products.

Dabrowski (1964) and Piechowski (1989): Creativity is talent in a specific field, exemplified by intense emotional, imaginational, intellectual, sensual, and/or psychomotor overexcitability, or intensity.

Wallach and Kogan (1965): Creativity can be differentiated from IQ or g-factor intelligence.

Torrance (1966, 1979): Certain aspects of creativity can be tested, especially divergent thinking.

Barron (1968, 1972): Creative people have the parodoxical presence of high degrees of ego strength along with psychopathologic qualities.

Maslow (1968): Creativity is in everyone, and many of the people who created tangible achievements were not self-actualized. He differentiated "special talent creativeness" from "self actualizing creativeness."

Bogen and Bogen (1969): Creativity results from the coordinated function of the repositional mind and the appositional mind. The connecting structure between right and left hemispheres is the seat of creativity.

Skinner (1971): Creativity is a result of natural selection over evolved time.

Gowan (1972): The creative individual develops as a result of certain childhood experiences.

Krippner and Murphy (1973): The capacities for extrasensory perception, telepathy, precognition, clairvoyance, and psychokinesis are very necessary for creativity.

Gruber (1974, 1988): Creativity is an evolving system: key phases of this system are insights, metaphors, the transformation of experience, and organization of purpose.

Getzels and Csikszentmihalyi (1976): Creativity comes about in problem-finding, and not in problem solving.

Renzulli (1978): Creativity is a necessary component of gifted behavior, along with above-average intelligence and task commitment.

MacKinnon (1978): Creative people have certain personality attributes that are different from those of noncreative people.

Willings (1980): Creative people have defensive, productive, adaptive, elaborative, or developmental personalities.

Perkins (1981/1988): Creativity is inevitable invention produced by people with certain personality attitudes using tactics of selection, planning, and abstracting.

Feldman (1982, 1988): Creativity is the developmental transformation of insight into novelty that makes a product that changes the field.

Amabile (1983): Creative people have certain personality traits such as intrinsic motivation, which can be temporarily affected by external interference.

Tannenbaum (1983): Creativity is necessary for giftedness and is integrated into all five aspects of what makes giftedness.

Brown (1986): Transpersonal psychology helps to understand creativity through exploring higher states of awareness.

Weisberg (1986): This anti-theorist systematically dismantled what he called the "Myths of creativity," stating that creativity is incremental, that is, grounded in the work of those who came before.

Csikszentmihalyi (1988): Creativity is the interaction of domain, person, field, and time.

Gardner (1988): Creativity is the interaction of a certain time in history on a certain mind in a certain domain.

Langley and Jones (1988): Creativity involves reasoning by analogy and qualitative mental models.

Schank (1988): The creative person can program him or herself to ask the right questions.

Simonton (1988): Creativity comes about through the chance-configuration theory, which postulates that social factors interact with personality factors to produce genius. Also, high productivity and great ego strength are involved.

Sternberg (1988/1991): Creative giftedness is dependent on insight and novel reactions to the insight.

Cohen (1990): Creativity is developmental, adaptive.

## Psychoanalytic Theorists

Lombroso (1895): Creative genius is related to insanity; he differentiated between ordinary insanity and the insanity associated with genius.

Freud (1908): Fantasy is essential in producing literary works. Such fantasy is primarily a manifestation of preconscious thoughts and feelings. The Unconscious also has a role in creation.

Jung (1923): Creativity is located in autonomous complexes which unearth the Collective Unconscious. These have a determining effect on consciousness in creation. The Collective Unconscious accounts for an audience's favorable response to a creation. The creative act can never be explained.

Lee (1940): Artistic creation is the result of symbolically compensating for disabilities.

Kris (1952): "Regression in the service of the ego" or ego-controlled regression is the specific means whereby preconscious and unconscious material appear in the creator's consciousness.

Kubie (1958): Preconscious processes produce creations.

Schachtel (1959): Allocentric perception, or openness to the world, is necessary for creativity to occur. This characterizes the most mature stage of human perceptual development.

Rank (1960): An artist type is distinct from the neurotic type. He overcomes his fear of death by an act of will directed toward immortality. Male creativity is developed by jealousy of female ability to bear children.

May (1975): Creativity takes courage, in making form from chaos.

Arieti (1976): Creativity is a primitive magic synthesis performed by gifted people.

Rothenberg (1979, 1990): Janusian thinking is involved in creation; this is the capacity to conceive and utilize two or more opposite or contradictory ideas, concepts, or images simultaneously.

Miller (1990): Creative production is a result of childhood trauma where warmth was present.

## Domain-Specific Theories

Coleridge (1817): An active and constructive imagination is necessary for poetic creativity.

Poe (1846): Logic and deliberately controlled techniques are important in the creative process.

Morgan (1933): Predictability is perhaps not necessary for scientific creation.

Cannon (1945): Creativity is an extraconscious process rather than unconscious, with no necessary determining effect upon consciousness. Hunches are important in certain phases of the scientific approach.

Huxley (1963): The use of psychedelic drugs can enhance creativity.

Koestler (1964): Bisociation — the combination of two consistent but habitually incompatible frames of reference — is meant to account for creations in all areas: culture, societies, nature, individuals.

Ehrenzweig (1967): The role of the unconscious in artistic creation follows a specific process called "unconscious dedifferentiation."

Findlay and Lumsden (1988): Creativity is evolutionary. Creative products and people have evolved through a mutational process.

# References

Abbs, P. (1989). *A is for aesthetic.* New York: Falmer Press.

Abell, A. (1946). *Talks with the great composers.* Garmisch-Parten-kirchen, Germany: G. E. Schroeder-Verlag.

Adler, S. (1970). In T. Cole & H. Chinoy (Eds.). (1970). *Actors on acting* (pp. 601-05). New York: Crown.

Albert, R. S. (1975). Toward a behavioral definition of genius. *American Psychologist, 30,* 140-51.

Albert, R. S. (Ed.) (1983). *Genius and eminence: The social psychology of creativity and exceptional achievement.* New York: Pergamon.

Alter, J. (1984a). A factor analysis of new and standardized instruments to measure the creative potential and high-energy action preference of performing arts students. A preliminary investigation. *Personality and Individual Differences, 5,* 693-99.

Alter, J. (1984b). Creativity profile of university and conservatory dance students. *Journal of Personality Assessment, 48,* 153-58.

Amabile, T. (1989). *Growing up creative: Nurturing a lifetime of creativity.* New York: Crown.

Amabile, T. (1983). *The social psychology of creativity.* New York: Springer-Verlag.

Argulewicz, E. N. (1985). Review of Scales for Rating the Behavioral Characteristics of Superior Students. In the Buros Institute of Mental Measurements. *The Ninth Mental Measurements Yearbook.* Vol. II. The University of Nebraska Press. 1311-12.

Arieti, S. (1976). *Creativity: The magic synthesis.* New York: Basic.

Arnheim, D. (1975). *Dance injuries: Their prevention and care.* St. Louis: C. V. Mosby.

Bagley, M. & Hess, K. (1983). *200 ways of using imagery in the classroom.* New York: Trillium.

Bakker, F. (1988). Personality differences between young dancers and nondancers. *Personality and Individual Differences, 9,* 121-31.

Bamberger, J. (1986). Cognitive issues in the development of musically gifted children. In R. Sternberg & J. Davidson (Eds.), *Conceptions of giftedness* (pp. 388-415). New York: Cambridge.

Bariaud, F. (1988). Age differences in children's humor. *Journal of Children in Contemporary Society, 20,* 15-45.

Barron, F. (1968). *Creativity and personal freedom.* New York: Van Nostrand.

Barron, F. (1972). *Artists in the making.* New York: Seminar Press.

Bateson, M. C. (1989). *Composing a life.* New York: Atlantic Monthly Press.

Belenky, M. F., Clinch, B. M., Goldberger, N. R., & Tarule, J. M. (1986). *Women's ways of knowing.* New York: Basic.

Bell, Q. (1972). *Virginia Woolf: A biography.* New York: Harcourt Brace Jovanovich.

Bergson, H. (1976). The possible and the real. In A. E. Rothenberg & C. Hausman (Eds.), *The creativity question* (pp. 292-95). Trans. M. Andison. Durham, NC: Duke University Press. (Original translation published 1946.)

Bernstein, D.K. (1986). The development of humor: Implications for assessment and intervention. *Topics in Language Disorders, 6,* 65-71.

Berryman, J. (1950). *Stephen Crane.* New York: William Sloane Associates.

Blanshard, B. (1976). The teleology of the creative act. In A. Rothenberg & C. Hausman (Eds.), *The creativity question* (pp. 97-103). Durham, NC: Duke University Press. (Original work published 1964).

Bloom, B. (Ed.). (1985). *The development of talent in young people.* New York: Ballantine.

Bloom, B. (1986). The hands and feet of genius. *Educational Leadership, 43,* 70-77.

Blumberg, S. A. & Panos, L. G. (1990). *Edward Teller: Giant of the golden age of physics.* New York: Macmillan.

Bogen, J. & Bogen, G. (1969). The other side of the brain III: The corpus callosum and creativity. *Bulletin of the Los Angeles neurological societies, 34.* Los Angeles: Los Angeles Society of Neurology and Psychiatry.

Bold, A. (Ed.). (1982). *Drink to me only: The prose (and cons) of drinking.* London: Robin Clark.

Bookspan, M. & Yodkey, R. (1981). *Andre Previn: A biography.* New York: Doubleday.

Borland, J. (1986). A note of the existence of certain divergent-production abilities. *Journal for the Education of the Gifted, 9,* 239-51.

Bowers, N. (1990). The contest racket. *Poets and Writers, 18,* 37-39.

Boyle, T. Corraghason (1990). *East is East.* New York: Penguin.

Braisted, J., Mellin, L., Gong, E., & Irwin, C. (1985). The adolescent ballet dancer: Nutritional practices and characteristics associated with anorexia nervosa. *Journal of Adolescent Health Care, 6,* 371-76.

Brandwein, P. (1955). *The gifted student as future scientist.* New York: Harcourt, Brace, & World.

Brennan, M. (1982). Relationship between creative ability in dance and selected creative attributes. *Perceptual and Motor Skills, 55,* 47-56.

Brennan, M. (1985). Dance creativity tests and the Structure-of-Intellect model. *Journal of Creative Behavior, 19,* 185-90.

Brody, L. (1989, Nov.). Characteristics of extremely mathematically talented females. Paper presented at National Association for Gifted Children Conference, Cincinnati, Ohio.

Brook, P. (1989). The act of possession. In T. Cole & H. Chinoy (Eds.). (1970). *Actors on acting* (pp. 223-29). New York: Crown.

Brooks-Gunn, J., Burrow, C., & Warren, M. (1988). Attitudes toward eating and body weight in different groups of female adolescent athletes. *International Journal of Eating Disorders, 7,* 749-57.

Brooks-Gunn, J., & Warren, M. (1985). The effects of delayed menarche in different contexts: Dance and nondance students. *Journal of Youth and Adolescence, 14,* 285-300.

Brooks-Gunn, J., Warren, M. & Hamilton, L. (1987). The relation of eating problems and amenorrhea in ballet dancers. *Medicine-and-Science-in-Sports-and-Exercise, 19* (1), 41-44.

Brown, F. (1968). Bereavement and lack of a parent in childhood. In E. Miller (Ed.), *Foundations of Child Psychiatry.* Oxford, England: Pergemon.

Brown, K. (1990). *You'd never know it from the way I talk.* Ashland, O: Ashland Poetry Press.

Brown, M. (1988, Aug.). Transpersonal psychology: Exploring the frontiers in human resource development. Paper presented at the Annual Meeting of the American Psychological Association, Atlanta, Georgia.

Bryant, J. & Zillman, D. (1989). Using humor to promote learning in the classroom. In McGhee, P. (Ed.). *Humor and children's development* (pp. 49-78). Binghamton, NY: Haworth Press.

Buchanan, D. & Bandy, C. (1984). Jungian typology of 37 prospective psychodramtists: Myers-Briggs Type Indicator analysis of applicants for psychodrama training. *Psychological Reports, 55,* 599-606.

Buckle, R. (1988). *George Balanchine, ballet master.* New York: Random House.

Bulfinch, T. (1855). *Bulfinch's mythology: The age of fable.* Boston: S. W. Tilton.

Buros Institute of Mental Measurements. (1985). *The Ninth Mental Measurements of Yearbook.* James V. Mitchell (Ed.). The University of Nebraska Press.

Callahan, C. (1991). The assessment of creativity. In N. Colangelo, & G. A. Davis (Eds.), *Handbook of gifted education* (pp. 219-35). Needham Hts., Mass: Allyn & Bacon.

Campbell, D. T. (1960). Blind variation and selective retention in creative thought as in other knowledge processes. *Psychological Review, 67,* 380-400.

Campbell, J. (1968). *The masks of god: Creative mythology.* New York: Viking.

Cannon, W. (1945). *The role of hunches. The way of an investigator.* New York: W. W. Norton.

Cattell, R. (1964). The personality and motivation of the researcher from measurements of contemporaries and from biography. In C. W. Taylor and F. Barron (Eds.) *Scientific Creativity,* New York: Wiley.

Cattell, R. & Cattell, M. C. (1969). *Handbook for the High School Personality Questionnaire (HSPQ).* Champaign, IL: Institute for Personality and Ability Testing.

Cattell, R. & Drevdahl, J. (1955). A comparison of the personality profile (16 PF.) of eminent researchers with that of eminent teachers and administrators, and of the general population. *British Journal of Psychology, 16,* 248-61.

Chafe, W. (1987). Humor as a disabling mechanism. *American Behavioral Scientist, 30,* 16-26.

Citino, D. (1990). *The house of memory.* Columbus, OH: Ohio State University Press.

Clark, R. (1971). *Einstein: The life and times.* New York: World Publishing.

Cohen, L. (1989). A continuum of adaptive creative behaviors. *Creativity Research Journal, 2,* 169-83.

Colangelo, N. (1991). The development of a scale to identify mechanical inventiveness. *Proceedings.* The Henry B. and Jocelyn Wallace National Research Symposium on Talent Development. Iowa City, IA: The University of Iowa.

Cole, T. and Chinoy, H. (Eds.). (1970). *Actors on acting.* New York: Crown.

Coleridge, S. T. (1817). *Biographia literaria, I.* London: Rest Fenner.

Coles, R. (1989). *The call of stories: Teaching and the moral imagination.* Boston: Houghton Mifflin.

Collingwood, R. (1976). Consciousness and attention in art. In A. Rothenberg & C. Hausman (Eds.), *The creativity question* (pp. 334-43). Durham, NC: Duke University Press. (Original work published 1938).

Cortazar, J. (1986). *Around the day in eighty worlds.* San Francisco: North Point.

Cowger, H. & Torrance, E. P. (1982). Further examination of the quality of changes in creative functioning resulting from meditation (Zazen) training. *Creative Child and Adult Quarterly, 7,* 211-17.

Crabbe, A. & Betts, G. (1990). *Creating more creative people II.* Greely, CO: Autonomous Learner Press.

Crews, H. (1987). From a childhood: The biography of a place. In D. McCullough (Ed.). *American childhoods* (pp. 327-44). Boston: Little, Brown.

Croce, A. (1990, Oct. 15). Angel. *The New Yorker,* pp. 124-27.

Croce, B. (1976). Intuition and expression in art. In A. Rothenberg & C. Hausman (Eds.), *The creativity question* (pp. 327-33). Durham, NC: Duke University Press. (Original work published 1909).

Cross, J. W. (1903). *George Eliot's life as related in her letters and journals.* New York and London: Abbey.

Csikszentmihalyi, M. (1988). In R. Sternberg (Ed.), *The nature of creativity* (pp. 325-39). New York: Cambridge.

Csikszentmihalyi, M. (1990). *Flow.* New York: Cambridge.

Dabrowski, K. (1965). *Personality shaping through positive disintegration.* Boston: Little Brown.

Dabrowski, K., & Piechowski, M. M. (1977). *Theory of levels of emotional development.* Oceanside, N.Y.: Dabor.

Damarin, F. (1985). Review of Creativity Packet. In [Buros Institute of Mental Measurements] *The Ninth Mental Measurements Yearbook,*

Vol. I, The University of Nebraska Press, 410-11.

Davis, G. A. (1981). *Creativity is forever.* Cross Plains, WI: Badger Press.

Davis, G. A. (1989). Testing for creative potential. *Contemporary Educational Psychology, 14,* 257-74.

Davis, G. A. & Rimm, S. G. (1980). *Group inventory for finding interests.* (II). Watertown, WI: Educational Assessment Service.

Davis, G. A. & Rimm, S. B. (1982). Group inventory for finding interests (GIFFI) I and II: Instruments for identifying creative potential in the junior and senior high school. *Journal of Creative Behavior, 16,* 50-57.

deBono, E. (1970). *Lateral thinking.* New York: Harper Colophon.

deBono, E. (1978). *CoRT thinking lesson series.* Blanford Forum, Dorset, UK: Direct Education Services.

de Mille, A. (1980). *America dances.* New York: Macmillan.

*A Directory of American Poets and Fiction Writers.* (1989-1990). New York: Poets & Writers, Inc.

Drevdahl, J. & Cattell, R. (1958). Personality and creativity in artists and writers. *Journal of Clinical Psychology, 14,* 107-11.

Eberle, B. (1982). *Visual thinking.* Buffalo: D.O.K.

Eccles, J. (1985). Model of students' mathematics enrollment decisions. *Educational Studies in Mathematics, 16,* 311-14.

Eccles, J. (1991). Gender differences in educational and occupational patterns among the gifted. Proceedings. The Henry B. and Jocelyn Wallace National Research Symposium on Talent Development. Iowa City, IA: The University of Iowa.

Edwards, B. (1979). *Drawing on the right side of the brain.* Los Angeles: Tarcher.

Ehrenzweig, A. (1976). Unconscious scanning and dedifferentiation in artistic perception. In A. Rothenberg & C. Hausman (Eds.), *The creativity question* (pp. 149-52). Durham, NC: Duke University Press. (Original work published 1967).

Einbond, B. (1979). *The coming indoors and other poems.* Tokyo: Charles E. Tuttle.

Ephron, N. (1983). A few words about breasts. In M. Richler (Ed.), *The best of modern humor* (pp. 467-75). New York: Knopf.

Fabrizi, M. S. & Pollio, H. B. (1987). Are funny teenagers creative? *Psychological Reports, 61,* 751-61.

Farrell, S. (1990). *Holding on to the air.* New York: Summit.

Feldhusen, J. & Clinkenbeard, P. (1986). Creativity instructional materials: A review of research. *Journal of Creative Behavior, 20,* 176-88.

Feldman, D. (1982). A developmental framework for research with gifted children. In D. Feldman (Ed.), *New directions for child development: Developmental approaches to giftedness and creativity, 17,* (pp. 31-46). San Francisco: Jossey-Bass.

Feldman, D. (1986). *Nature's gambit: Child prodigies and the development of human potential.* New York: Basic.

Feldman, D. (1988). Dreams, insights, and transformations. In R. Sternberg (Ed.), *The nature of creativity* (pp. 271-97). New York: Cambridge.

Feldman, D. (1990, November). Universal to unique: Developmental domains of giftedness. Paper presented at National Association for Gifted Children Conference, Little Rock, Arkansas.

Ferucci, P. (1990). *Inevitable grace.* Los Angeles: Tarcher.

Findlay, C. & Lumsden, C. (1988). *The creative mind.* London: Academic Press.

Foley, P. (1986). The dual role experience of artist mothers. Unpublished doctoral dissertation. Northwestern University, IL.

Fitzgibbon, C. (1965). *The life of Dylan Thomas.* Boston: Little, Brown.

Friend, T. (1990, December 9). Rolling Boyle. *New York Times Magazine,* pp. 50, 64-68.

Freud, S. (1976). Creative writers and daydreaming. In A. Rothenberg & C. Hausman (Eds.), *The creativity question* (pp. 48-52). Durham, NC: Duke University Press. (Original work published 1908.)

Fuller, B. (1981). *Critical path.* New York: St. Martin's.

Fuller, B. (1983). *Grunch of giants.* New York: St. Martin's.

Gablik, S. (1976). *Magritte.* New York: New York Graphic Society.

Galton, F. (1976). Genius as inherited. In A. Rothenberg & C. Hausman (Eds.), *The creativity question* (pp. 42-47). Durham, NC: Duke University Press. (Original work published 1869.)

Gardner, H. (1982). *Art, mind, and brain.* New York: Basic.

Gardner, H. (1983). *Frames of mind.* New York: Basic.

Gardner, H. (1985). *The mind's of new science: A history of the cognitive revolution.* New York: Basic.

Gardner, H. (1988). Creative lives and creative works: A synthetic scientific approach. In R. Sternberg (Ed.), *The nature of creativity* (pp. 298-321). New York: Cambridge University Press.

Gardner, H. (1989, December). Learning Chinese style. *Psychology Today,* pp. 54-56.

Gardner, J. (1978). *On moral fiction.* New York: Basic.

Garfield, P. (1974). *Creative dreaming*. New York: Ballantine.

Gawain, S. (1978). *Creative visualization*. New York: Bantam.

Getzels, J. (1987). Creativity, intelligence, and problem finding: Retrospect and prospect. In S. Isaksen (Ed.), *Frontiers of Creativity Research* (pp. 88-102). Buffalo, NY: Bearly Ltd.

Getzels, J. & Csikszentmihalyi, M. (1976). *The creative vision: A longitudinal study of problem finding in art*. New York: Wiley.

Getzels, J. & Jackson, P. (1962). *Creativity and intelligence: Explorations with gifted students*. New York: Wiley.

Ghiselin, B. (Ed.). (1952). *The Creative Process*. New York: Mentor.

Gilligan, C. (1990, April). Invited address. Paper presented at the meeting of the American Educational Research Association, Boston, Mass.

Gilligan, C., Lyons, N. P. & Hanmer, T. J. (Eds.). (1990). *Making connections: The relational worlds of adolescent girls at Emma Willard School*. Cambridge, Mass: Harvard University Press.

Glover, J. S., Ronning, R. R. & Reynolds, C. R. (1989). *Handbook of creativity*. New York: Plenum.

Goertzel, V. & Goertzel, M. G. (1962). *Cradles of eminence*. Boston: Little, Brown.

Goertzel, V., Goertzel, M. G. & Goertzel, T. (1978). *Three hundred eminent personalities: A psychosocial analysis of the famous*. San Francisco: Jossey-Bass.

Gondola, J. (1987). The effects of a single bout of aerobic dancing on selected tests of creativity. *Journal of Social Behavior and Personality, 2*, 275-78.

Gordon, W. (1961). *Synectics: The development of creative capacity*. New York: Harper & Row.

Gough, H. G. (1952). *Adjective Check List*. Palo Alto, CA: Consulting Psychologists Press.

Gough, H. G. (1979). A creative personality scale for the Adjective Check List. *Journal of Personality and Social Psychology, 37*, 1398-1405.

Gough, H. G. & Heilbrun, A. B. (1983). *The Adjective Check List Manual*. Palo Alto, CA: Consulting Psychologists Press.

Gourley, T. J. (1981). Adapting the varsity sports model for nonpsychomotor gifted students. *Gifted Child Quarterly, 25*, 164-66.

Gowan, J. (1972). *Development of the creative individual*. San Diego, CA: Robert R. Knapp.

Green, J. (1961). *Diary: 1928-1957*. New York: Carroll & Graf.

Greer, G. (1979). *The obstacle race: The fortunes of women painters and their work.* New York: Farrar Straus Giroux.

Gruber, H. (1982). *Darwin on man.* 2nd ed. Chicago: University of Chicago Press.

Gruber, H. (1982). On the hypothesized relation between giftedness and creativity. In D. Feldman (Ed.). *New directions for child development: Developmental approaches to giftedness and creativity* (pp. 7-29). San Francisco: Jossey-Bass.

Gruber, H. & Davis, S. (1988). Inching our way up Mount Olympus: the evolving-systems approach to creative thinking. In Sternberg, R. (Ed.), *The nature of creativity: Contemporary psychological perspectives* (pp. 243-70). New York: Cambridge University Press.

Gruen, J. (1988). *People who dance.* Princeton, NJ: Princeton Book Co.

Guilford, J. P. (1950). Creativity. *American psychologist, 5,* 444-54.

Guilford, J. P. (1967). *The nature of human intelligence.* New York: McGraw-Hill.

Guilford, J. P. (1970). Traits of creativity. In Vernon, P. E. (Ed.), *Creativity* (p. 167). London Harmondsworth: Penguin.

Guilford, J. P. (1988). Some changes in the Structure-Of-Intellect model. *Educational and Psychological Measurement, 48,* 1-6.

Gulbenkian Report (1978). *The arts in schools.* London: Calouste Gulbenkian Foundation.

Halperin, J. (1986). *The life of Jane Austen.* Baltimore: Johns Hopkins.

Halpin, G. and Halpin, G. (1973). The effect of motivation on creative thinking abilities. *Journal of Creative Behavior, 7,* 51-53.

Hamachek, D. (1990). *Psychology in teaching, learning, and growth.* 4th edition. Boston: Allyn & Bacon.

Hanson, L. & Hanson, E. (1954). *Noble savage: The life of Paul Gauguin.* New York: Random House.

Harmon, W. & Rheingold, H. (1984). *Higher creativity: Liberating the unconscious for breakthrough insights.* New York: Houghton Mifflin.

Hausman, C. (1976). Creativity and rationality. In A. Rothenberg & C. Hausman (Eds.), *The creativity question* (pp. 343-51). Durham, NC: Duke University Press. (Original work published 1964).

H'Doubler, M. (1968). *Dance: A creative art experience.* Madison, WI: The University of Wisconsin Press.

Heausler, N. & Thompson, B. (1988). Structure of the Torrance Tests of Creative Thinking. *Educational and Psychological Measurement, 48,* 463-68.

Helson, R. (1983). Creative mathematicians. In R. Albert (Ed.), *Genius and eminence: The social psychology of creativity and exceptional achievement* (p. 211-30). London: Pergamon Press.

Hennessey, B. A. & Amabile, T. M. (1988). Storytelling as a means of assessing creativity. *Journal of Creative Behavior, 22,* 235-47.

Hillesum, E. (1985). *An interrupted life: The diaries of Etty Hillesum, 1941-1943.* New York: Washington Square Press.

Hocevar, D. (1980). Intelligence, divergent thinking, and creativity. *Intelligence, 4,* 25-40.

Hofstadter, D. (1985). *Metamagical themas.* New York: Basic.

Hoge, R. D. (1988). Issues in the definition and measurement of the giftedness construct. *Educational Researcher, 12-16,* 22.

Hollander, L. (1987). Music, the creative process, and the path of enlightenment. *Roeper Review, 10,* (1) 28-32.

Horowitz, F. & Degan, M. (1985). *The gifted and talented: Developmental perspectives.* Washington, D.C.: American Psychological Association.

Hurwitz, A. (1983). *The gifted and talented in art: A guide to program planning.* Worcester, MA: Davis.

Huxley, A. (1963). *The doors of perception.* New York: Harper & Row.

Janowitz, T. (1986). *Slaves of New York.* New York: Washington Square Press.

Jarvie, I. (1981). The rationality of creativity. In D. Dutton & M. Krausz (Eds.). *The concept of creativity in science and art* (pp. 109-28). The Hague: Martinus Mijhoff.

John-Steiner, V. (1985). *Notebooks of the mind: Explorations of thinking.* New York: Harper & Row.

Jones, R. (Ed.). (1987). *Music by Philip Glass.* New York: Harper & Row.

Jung, C. G. (1976). On the relation of analytical psychology to poetic art. In A. Rothenberg & C. Hausman (Eds.), *The creativity question* (pp. 120-26). Durham, NC: Duke University Press. (Original work published 1923.)

Jung, C. G. (1965). *Memories, dreams, reflections.* New York: Vintage.

Kaltsounis, B. & Honeywell, L. (1980). Instruments useful in studying creative behavior and creative talent. Part IV. Noncommercially available instruments. *Journal of Creative Behavior, 5,* 117-26.

Kant, I. (1952). Genius gives the rules. In A. Rothenberg & C. Hausman (Eds.), *The creativity question* (pp. 37-41). Durham, NC: Duke University Press. (Original work published 1790.)

Karnes, F., Chauvin, J. & Trant, T. (1985). Comparison of personality profiles for intellectually gifted students and students outstanding in the fine and performing arts attending self-contained secondary schools. *Psychology in the Schools, 22,* 122-26.

Keating, D. P. (1983). The creative potential of mathematically gifted boys. In R. Albert (Ed.), *Genius and eminence: The social psychology of creativity and exceptional achievement* (pp. 128-37). London: Pergamon.

Kemp, A. E. (1981a). The personality structure of the musicians I: Identifying a profile of traits for the performer. *Psychology of Music, 9,* 3-14.

Kemp, A. E. (1981b). The personality structure of the musician II: Identifying a profile of traits for the composer. *Psychology of Music, 9,* 67-75.

Kemp, A. E. (1982a). The personality structure of the musician III: The significance of sex difference. *Psychology of Music, 10,* 48-58.

Kemp, A. E. (1982b). Personality traits of successful music teachers. *Psychology of Music, Special Issue,* 72-73.

Khatena, J. (1978). *The creatively gifted child.* New York: Vantage.

Khatena, J. & Torrance, E. P. (1973). *Norms-technical manual: Thinking creatively with sounds and words.* Lexington, MA: Personnel Press/Ginn.

Kington, M. (1990, October 28). How Calvin Trillin changed my life. *New York Times Book Review,* p. 10.

Kizer, C. (1990). A muse. In L. Lyfshin (Ed.), *Lips Unsealed* (pp. 26-32). Santa Barbara: Capra.

Klein, E. (1967). *A Comprehensive Etymological Dictionary of The English Language.* New York: Elsevier.

Knapp, R. H. (1962). Stylistic consistency among aesthetic preferences. *Journal of Projective Techniques & Personality Assessment, 16,* 61-65.

Koestler, A. (1964). *The act of creation.* New York: Macmillan.

Kogan, J. (1987). *Nothing but the best: The struggle for perfection at the Juilliard School.* New York: Random House.

Kozinn, A. (April 11, 1991). Shulamit Ran and the Pulitzer Prize. *New York Times,* p. B4.

Krippner, S. & Murphy, G. (1973). Humanistic psychology and parapsychology. *Journal of humanistic psychology, 13,* (4), 2-24.

Kris, E. (1976). On preconscious mental processes. In A. Rothenberg & C. Hausman (Eds.), *The creativity question* (pp. 135-42). Durham, NC: Duke University Press. (Original work published 1952.)

Krutetskii, V. (1976). The psychology of mathematical abilities in school-children. In J. Wirszup & J. Kirkpatrick (Eds.), J. Teller (Trans.). Chicago: University of Chicago Press. (Original work published 1968.)

Kubie, L. (1976). Creativity and neurosis. In A. Rothenberg & C. Hausman (Eds.), *The creativity question* (pp. 143-48). Durham, NC: Duke University Press. (Original work published 1958.)

Langer, S. K. (1953). *Feeling and form.* New York: Charles Scribner's Sons.

Langer, S. K. (1957). *Problems of art.* New York: Charles Scribner's Sons.

Langley, P. & Jones, R. (1988). A computational model of scientific insight. In R. Sternberg (Ed.), *The nature of creativity* (pp. 177-201). New York: Cambridge University Press.

Lee, H. (1940). A theory concerning free creation in the inventive arts. *Psychiatry, 3.* The William Alanson White Psychiatric Foundation, Inc.

Leonard, L. (1989). *Witness to the fire: Creativity and the evil of addiction.* Boston: Shambhala.

Lewis, C. S. (1955). *Surprised by joy: The shape of my early life.* New York: Harcourt, Brace, Jovanovich.

Lissitz, R. & Willhoft, J. (1985). A methodological study of the Torrance Tests of Creativity. *Journal of Educational Measurement, 22,* 1-11.

Loeb, K. (1975). Our women artist/teachers need our help: On changing language, finding cultural heritage, and building self image. *Art Education, 18, 10.,*

Lombroso, C. (1895). *The man of genius.* London: Charles Scribner's Sons.

Lowenkopf, E. & Vincent, L. (1982). The student ballet dancer and anorexia. *Hillside Journal of Clincial Psychiatry, 5,* 53-64.

Lozanov, G. (1978). *Suggestology and outlines of suggestopedia (psychic studies).* New York: Gordon & Breach.

MacKinnon, D. (1962). The nature and nuture of creative talent. *American Psychologist, 17,* 484-95.

MacKinnon, D. (1978). *In search of human effectiveness: Identifying and developing creativity.* Buffalo, NY: Bearly Limited.

McAleer, N. (1989, April). On creativity: The roots of inspiration. *Omni,* p. 42.

McConnell, J. V. (1982). *Understanding human behavior,* 6th Edition. New York: Harcourt.

McDonough, P. & McDonough, B. (1987). A survey of American colleges and universities on the conducting of formal courses in creativity. *Journal of Creative Behavior, 21,* 271-82.

McDonnell, D. & LeCapitaine, J. (1985). *The Effects of Group Creativity Training on Teachers' Empathy and Interactions with Students.* ERIC ED294858.

McGhee, P. (1988). The contribution of humor to children's social development. *Journal of Children in Contemporary Society, 20,* 119-34.

Madigan, C. & Elwood, A. (1984). *Brainstorms & thunderbolts: How creative genius works.* New York: Macmillan.

Malina, J. (1983). In K. Malpede (Ed.), *Women in theatre* (pp. 196-217). New York: Limelight.

Marshall, M. J. & Barritt, L. S. (1990). Choices made, worlds created: The rhetoric of AERJ. *American Educational Research Journal, 27* (4), 589-609.

Maritain, J. (1953). Creative intuition in art and poetry. Trustees of the National Gallery of Art, Washington, D.C. The A. W. Mellon Lectures in the Fine Arts. Bollingen series XXXV. Princeton, NJ: Princeton University Press.

Martindale, C. (1972). Father absence, psychopathology, and poetic eminence. *Psychological Reports, 31,* 843-84.

Maslow, A. (1968). *Creativity in self-actualizing people. Toward a psychology of being.* New York: Van Nostrand Reinhold Company.

Maslow, A. (1973). *The farther reaches of human nature.* London: Harmondsworth.

May, R. (1975). *The courage to create.* New York: Bantam.

Mednick, S. (1962). The associative basis of the creative process. *Psychological Review,* 220-32. Washington, D.C.: American Psychological Association.

Meeker, M. N. (1973). *Divergent production sourcebook.* Vida, OR: SOI Institute.

Meeker, M. N. & Meeker, R. (1975). *Structure of Intellect Learning Abilities Test — Examiner's Manual.* El Segundo, CA: SOI Institute.

Mellow, J. R. (1974). *Charmed circle: Gertrude Stein & company.* New York: Praeger.

Miklus, S. (1989, April). Forum. *Omni,* p. 16.

Miles, B. (1989). *Ginsberg.* New York: Simon and Schuster.

Miller, A. (1987). *Timebends.* New York: Harper & Row.

Miller, A. (1990). *The untouched key: Tracing childhood trauma in creativity and destructiveness.* New York: Doubleday.

Miller, A. (1981). *Drama of the gifted child.* New York: Doubleday.

Monson, K. (1983). *Alma Mahler: Musto genius.* Boston: Houghton Mifflin.

Mora, V. (1990, July). Historia del tango. Lecture presented at the University of Cordoba, Argentina.

Morgan, C. (1933). *The emergence of novelty.* London: Williams & Norgate.

Morse, D. & Khatena, J. (1989). The relationship of creativity and life accomplishments. *Journal of Creative Behavior, 23,* 23-30.

Myers, I. B. & McCaulley, M. H. (1985). *Manual: A guide to the development and use of the Myers-Briggs Type Indicator.* Palo Alto, CA: Consulting Psychologists Press.

Myers, S. A. (1983). The Wilson-Barber Inventory of Childhood Memories and Imaginings: Children's form and norms for 1337 children and adolescents. *Journal of Mental Imagery, 7* (3) 83-94.

Nachmanovitch, S. (1990). *Free play: Improvisation in life and art.* Los Angeles: Tarcher.

Navarre, J. Piirto (1978). A study of creativity in poets. Paper presented at National Association for Gifted Children Conference, Houston, Texas.

Navarre, J. Piirto (1979). Incubation as fostering the creative process. *Gifted Child Quarterly, 23,* 792-800.

Navarre, J. Piirto (1980). The blanket. Sing, Heavenly Muse!, 79-85.

Nietzsche, F. (1979). *Ecce homo.,* tr. R. J. Hollingdale. London: Harmondsworth.

Noller, R. B., Parnes, S. J. & Biondi, A. M. (1976). *Creative actionbook.* New York: Scribners.

Nowell, E. (1960). *Thomas Wolfe: A biography.* New York: Doubleday & Co.

Oates, J. C. (1988). *(Woman) writer: Occasions and opportunities.* New York: Dutton.

Olivier, L. (1967). In Burton H. (Ed.), *Great acting* (pp. 23-32). New York: Hill & Wang. Reprinted in T. Cole & H. Chinoy (Eds.). (1970). *Actors on acting* (pp. 410-17). New York: Crown.

Osborn, A. (1963). *Applied imagination.* New York: Scribners.

Ostrander, S. (1979). *Superlearning.* New York: Delacourte.

Owens, H. M. & Hogan, J. D. (1983). Development of humor in children:

Roles of incongruity, resolution and operational thinking. *Psychological Reports, 53,* 477-78.

*Oxford English Dictionary,* 2nd Ed. (1989). Oxford: Clarendon Press.

Parloff, M. B., Datta, L., Kleman, M. & Handlon, J. H. (1968). Personality characteristics which differentiate creative male adolescents and adults. *Journal of Personality, 36* (4), 528-52.

Parnes, S. (1967). *Creative behavior guidebook.* New York: Scribners.

Parnes, S. (1981). *The magic of your mind.* Buffalo, NY: Creative Education Foundation.

Parnes, S. (1987). The Creative Studies Project. In S. Isaksen (Ed.), *Frontiers of creativity research: Beyond the basics* (pp. 156-88). Buffalo: Bearly.

Passarro, V. (May 19, 1991). Dangerous Don DeLillo. *The New York Times Magazine,* 34-38, 76.

Patrick, C. (1937). Creative thought in artists. *Journal of Psychology, 4,* 35-40, 51-54, 66-67.

Pendarvis, E., Howley, C. & Howley, A. (1990). *The abilities of gifted children.* Boston: Allyn & Bacon.

Perkins, D. (1981). *The mind's best work.* Boston: Harvard University Press.

Perkins, D. (1988). The possibility of invention. In R. Sternberg (Ed.), *The nature of creativity* (pp. 362-86). New York: Cambridge.

Piechowski, M. M. (1978). Self-actualization as a developmental structure: A profile of Antoine de Saint-Exupery. *Genetic Psychology Monographs, 97,* 181-242.

Piechowski, M. M. (1991). Emotional development and emotional giftedness. In N. Colangelo & G. Davis (Eds.), *Handbook of gifted education* (pp. 285-307). Needham Hgts., Mass.: Allyn and Bacon.

Piechowski, M. M. & Tyska, C. A. (1982). Self-actualization profile of Eleanor Roosevelt, a presumed nontranscender. *Genetic Psychology Monographs, 105,* 95-153.

Piechowski, M. M. & Cunningham, K. (1985a). Patterns of overexcitability in a group of artists. *Journal of Creative Behavior, 19,* 3, 153-74.

Piechowski, M. M., Silverman, L. & Falk, F. (1985b). Comparison of intellectually and artistically gifted on five dimensions of mental functioning. *Perceptual and motor skills, 60,* 539-49.

Piirto, J. (1985). *The three-week trance diet.* Columbus, OH: Carpenter Press.

Piirto, J. (1987). The existence of writing prodigy. Paper presented at the National Association for Gifted Children Conference, New Orleans.

Piirto, J. (1989a). Does writing prodigy exist? *Creativity Research Journal, 2,* 134-35.

Piirto, J. (1989b, May/June). Linguistic prodigy: Does it exist? *Gifted Children Monthly,* 1-2.

Piirto, J. (1990). Profiles of creative adolescents. *Understanding Our Gifted, 2,* 1.

Piirto, J. (1990, March). Creative adolescents at a Governor's Institute. Paper presented at the Ohio Association for Gifted Children Conference, Columbus.

Piirto, J. (1991a). Encouraging creativity in adolescents. In J. Genshaft & M. Bireley (Eds.). *Gifted and talented adolescents* (pp. 104-22). New York: Teachers College Press.

Piirto, J. (1991b). Why are there so few (Creative women: visual artists, mathematicians, musicians). *Roeper Review, 13* (3), 142-47.

Piirto, J. (1991c). The existence of writing prodigy: Children with extraordinary writing talent. *Proceedings.* The Henry B. and Jocelyn Wallace National Research Symposium on Talent Development. Iowa City, Iowa: The University of Iowa.

Plato. *The republic.* In R. Ulrich (Ed.). (1954). *Three thousand years of educational wisdom: Selections from great documents* (pp. 31-62). Trans. P. Shorey. Cambridge: Harvard Univ. Press.

Plimpton, G. (Ed.). (1988). *Writers at work.* 8th series. New York: Penguin.

Plimpton, G. (Ed.). (1989). *Women writers at work.* New York: Pengiun.

Poe, E. (1846, April). The philosophy of composition. *Graham's magazine of literature and art, 28,* 4, 1963-64.

Predock-Linnell, J. (1987). Comparison of Barron-Welsh Art Scales of artists and nonartists and between dancers of two training styles. *Perceptual and Motor Skills, 65,* 729-30.

Project Vanguard: *A manual for the identification of creatively gifted students.* (1991). Ohio Department of Education.

Radford, J. (1990). *Child prodigies and exceptional early achievers.* New York: Macmillan: The Free Press.

*Random House Dictionary of the English Language.* 2nd Ed. (1988). New York: Random House.

Rank, O. (1960). *Art and artist.* New York: Knopf.

Razik, T. (1970). Psychometric measurement of creativity. In P. Vernon (Ed.), *Creativity* (pp. 147-56). Harmondsworth: Penguin.

Redgrave, M. (1946). The Stanislavsky myth. New Theatre. 3, 16-18. Reprinted in T. Cole & H. Chinoy (Eds.), (1970). *Actors on acting* (pp. 403-08). New York: Crown.

Reese, W. (1980). *Dictionary of philosophy and religion: Eastern and western thought.* New Jersey: Humanities Press.

Renzulli, J. (1978). What makes giftedness? Re-examining a definition. *Phi Delta Kappan, 60,* 180-84, 261.

Renzulli, J. & Harman, J. (1971). *Scales for Rating the Behavioral Characteristics of Superior Students.* Mansfield Center, CT: Creative Learning Press.

Renzulli, J. & Westberg, K. (1990, November). The 1990 revision of the *Scales for Rating the Behavioral Characteristics of Superior Students.* Paper presented at National Association for Gifted Children Conference, Little Rock, Arkansas.

Rico, G. (1983). *Writing the natural way: Using right brain techniques to release your expressive powers.* Los Angeles: Tarcher.

Rimm, S. B. (1986). *Underachievement syndrome: Causes and cures.* Watertown, WI: Apple Publishing Co.

Rimm, S. B. (1990, November). Identifying creativity: The characteristics approach. Paper presented at National Association for Gifted Children Conference, Little Rock, Arkansas.

Robinson, R. (1989). *Georgia O'Keeffe: A life.* New York: Harper & Row.

Roe, A. (1952). *The making of a scientist.* New York: Dodd, Mead.

Roe, A. (1963). Psychological approaches to creativity in the sciences. In Coler, M. & Hughes, H. (1963). *Essays on creativity in the sciences.* New York: New York University Press.

Roe, A. (1975). Painters and painting. In C. Taylor & J. Getzels (Eds.), *Perspectives in creativity* (pp. 157-72). Chicago: Aldine.

Roedell, W., Jackson, N. & Robinson, H. (1980). *Gifted young children.* New York: Teachers College Press.

Rogers, C. (1954). *Toward a theory of creativity. ETC: A review of general semantics,* 11, 250-58. New York: International Society of General Semantics.

Root-Bernstein, R. S. (1987). Tools of thought: Designing an integrated curriculum for lifelong learners. *Roeper Review, 10* (1), 17-21.

Rosen, C. L. (1985). Review of *Creativity Packet.* In [Buros Institute of

Mental Measurements] *The Ninth Mental Measurements Yearbook,* Vol. I, The University of Nebraska Press, 411-12.

Rosenthal, A., DeMers, S. T., Stilwell, W., Graybeal, S. & Zins, J. (1983). Comparison of interrater reliability on the Torrance Tests of Creative Thinking for gifted and nongifted students. *Psychology in the Schools, 20,* 35-40.

Rosner, S. & Abt, L. (Eds.). (1970). *The creative experience.* New York: Grossman.

Rossman, J. (1931). *The psychology of the inventor: A study of the patentee.* Washington, DC: The Inventors Publishing Company.

Rothenberg, A. (1979). *The emerging goddess: The creative process in art, science, and other fields.* Chicago: University of Chicago Press.

Rothenberg, A. (1990). *Creativity and madness.*

Rothenberg, A. & Hausman, C. (1976). *The creativity question.* Durham, NC: Duke University Press.

Rothenberg, A. & Hausman, C. (1988). A comment on *The nature of creativity. Creativity Research Journal, 1,* 123-24.

Rugg, H. (1963). *Imagination.* New York: Harper & Row.

Runco, M. (1986). Maximal performance on divergent thinking tests by gifted, talented, and nongifted children. *Psychology In The Schools, 23,* 308-15.

Runco, M. (1987). The generality of creative performance in gifted and nongifted children. *Gifted Child Quarterly, 31,* 121-25.

Runco, M. (1990). *Divergent production.* New York: Ablex.

Runco, M. & Albert, R. (1986). The threshold theory regarding creativity and intelligence: An empirical test with gifted and nongifted children. *The Creative Child And Adult Quarterly, 11,* 212-18.

Rust, J. O. (1985). Review the *Scales for Rating the Behavioral Characteristics of Superior Students.* In The Buros Institute of Mental Measurement. *The Ninth Mental Measurements Yearbook,* Vol. II. The University of Nebraska Press, 1312-13.

Samples, B. (1976). *The metaphoric mind.* Reading, Mass: Addison-Wesley.

Sarton, M. (1973). *Journal of a solitude.* New York: W. W. Norton.

Sartre, J. (1947). *Existentialism,* tr. Bernard Frechtman. New York: The Philosophical Library.

Schactel, E. (1959). *On the development of affect, perception, attention, and memory.* New York: Basic Books, Inc.

Schank, R. (1988). *The creative attitude.* New York: Macmillan.

Schickel, R. (1986). *Intimate strangers: The culture of celebrity.* New York: Fromm.

Schorer, M. (1961). *Sinclair Lewis.* New York: Random House.

Scribner, C. (1990, Dec. 9). 'I, who knew nothing, was in charge.' *New York Times Book Review,* pp. 1, 39.

Sears, P. S. (1979). The Terman studies of genius, 1922-1972. In A. H. Passow (Ed.), *The gifted and the talented: Their education and development* (pp. 75-96). The Seventy-eighth yearbook of the National Society For The Study Of Education. Chicago: University of Chicago Press.

Sears, R. (1977). Sources of life satisfaction of the Terman gifted men. *American Psychologist, 32,* 119-28.

Schneiderman, L. (1988). *The literary mind: Portraits in pain and creativity.* New York: Insight.

Sheets, M. (1966). *The phenomenology of dance.* Madison, WI: University of Wisconsin Press.

Shekerjian, D. (1990). *Uncommon genius.* New York: Viking.

Sherry, N. (1989). *The life of Graham Greene, I.* New York, Viking.

Shone, R. (1984). *Creative visualization.* New York: Thorstons.

Simonton, D. K. (1975). Age and literary creativity: A cross-cultural and transhistorical survey. *Journal of Cross-Cultural Psychology, 6,* 259-77.

Simonton, D. K. (1984). *Genius, creativity, and leadership.* Cambridge, Mass. Harvard University Press.

Simonton, D. K. (1986). Biographical typicality, eminence and achievement styles. *Journal of Creative Behavior, 20,* (1), 17-18.

Simonton, D. K. (1988). *Scientific genius: A psychology of science.* New York: Cambridge Unversity Press.

Simonton, D. K. (1991). The child parents the adult: On getting genius from giftedness. Invited Paper. The Henry B. and Jocelyn Wallace National Research Symposium on Talent Development. Iowa City, Iowa. May, 1991.

Simpson, E. (1982). *Poets in their youth.* New York: Random House.

Skinner, B. (1971). *Beyond freedom and dignity.* New York: Knopf.

Sloane, K. D., & Sosniak, L. A. (1985). The development of accomplished sculptors. In B. Bloom (Ed.), *Developing talent in young people* (pp. 90-138). New York: Ballantine.

Solomon, D. (March 31, 1991). Elizabeth Murray: Celebrating paint. *New York Times Magazine,* p. 20-25, 40, 46.

Sosniak, L. (1985). Learning to be a concert pianist. In B. Bloom (Ed.), *Developing talent in young people* (pp. 19-66). New York: Ballantine.

Spearman, C. (1927). *The abilities of man*. New York: Macmillan.

Spoto, Donald. (1985). *The Kindness of Strangers: The life of Tennessee Williams*. Boston: Little, Brown.

Stanislavsky, S. (1935/1964). *An actor prepares*. New York: Routledge.

Stanley, J. & Benbow, C. (1986). Youths who reason exceptionally well mathematically. In R. Sternberg & J. Davidson (Eds.), *Conceptions of giftedness* (pp. 361-87). New York: Cambridge University Press.

Stanton, D. (1991). An interview with John Irving. *Poets and Writers, 19* (3), 15-21.

Stein, M. (1953). Creativity and culture. *Journal of Psychology, 36*, 311-22.

Sternberg, R. (1991, May). Creative giftedness. Invited Address. The Henry B. and Jocelyn Wallace National Research Symposium on Talent Development. Iowa City, Iowa.

Sternberg, R. (Ed.). (1988a). *The nature of creativity*. New York: Cambridge.

Sternberg, R. (1988b). *The triarchic mind: A new theory of human intelligence*. New York: Viking.

Sternberg, R. (1985). *Beyond IQ: A triarchic theory of human intelligence*. New York: Cambridge University Press.

Sternberg, R. & Davidson, J. (Eds.). (1986). *Conceptions of giftedness*. New York: Cambridge.

Stone, I. (Ed.). (1937). *Dear Theo*. New York: Doubleday.

Storr, A. (1988). *Solitude: A return to the self*. New York: The Free Press.

Subotnik, R. & Steiner, C. L. (In press). Problem identification in academic research: A longitudinal case study from adolescence to young adulthood. In M. Runco (Ed.), *Problem finding, problem solving and creativity*. Norwood, NJ: Ablex.

Subotnik, R., Duschl, R., & Selmon, E. (In press). Retention and attrition of science talent: A longitudinal study of Westinghouse Science Talent Search winners. *International Journal of Science Education*.

Suzuki, S. (1983). *Nurtured by love: The classic approach to talent education*. Smithtown, NY: Exposition Press.

Tannenbaum, A. (1983). *Gifted children: Psychological and educational perspectives*. New York: Macmillan.

Tannenbaum, A. (1986). The enrichment matrix model. In J. Renzulli & S. Reis (Eds.), *Systems and models for the gifted and talented* (pp. 391-428), Watertown, Conn: Creative Learning Press.

Taylor, C. W. (1969). The highest talent potentials of man. *Gifted Child Quarterly, 13,* 9-30.

Taylor, D. B. (1990, October 17). Asian-American test scores: They deserve a closer look. *Education Week,* p.22.

Taylor, I. (1959). The nature of the creative process. In P. Smith (Ed.), *Creativity: An examination of the creative process* (pp. 51-82). New York: Hastings House.

Terry, W. (1971). *Dance in America.* New York: Harper & Row.

Thorndike, E. (1911). *Animal intelligence.* New York: Macmillan.

Torrance, E. P. (1966). *Torrance tests of creative thinking: Norms-technical manual.* Princeton, NJ: Personal Press.

Torrance, E. P. (1974). *Torrance tests of creative thinking: Norms and technical manual.* Lexington, MA: Personal Press/Ginn-Xerox.

Torrance, E. P. (1979). *The search for satori and creativity.* Buffalo, NY: Bearly Limited.

Torrance, E. P. (1987a). Teaching for creativity. In S. Isaken, (Ed.), *Frontiers of creativity research: Beyond the basics* (pp. 190-215). Buffalo, NY: Bearly Limited.

Torrance, E. P. (1987b). Recent trends in teaching children and adults to teach creatively. In Isaksen, S. (Ed.), *Frontiers of creativity research: Beyond the basics* (pp. 204-15). Buffalo, NY: Bearly Limited.

Torrance, E. P., Bruch, C., & Torrance, J. P. (1978). Interscholastic futuristic problem solving. *Journal of Creative Behavior, 10,* 117-25.

Torrance, E. P., & Goff, K. (1989). A quiet revolution. *Journal of Creative Behavior, 23,* 112-18.

Torrance, E. P., & Myers, R. E. (1970). *Creative learning and teaching.* New York: Dodd-Mead.

Torrance, E. P. & Safter, H. T. (1989). The long range predictive validity of the Just Suppose Test. *Journal of Creative Behavior, 23,* 219-23.

Treffinger, D. (1987). Research on creativity assessment. In S. Isaksen (Ed.), *Frontiers of creativity research: Beyond the basics* (pp. 103-19). Buffalo, NY: Bearly.

Updike, J. (1989). *Self-consciousness: Memoirs.* New York: Knopf.

Van Gogh, V. (1937). *Dear Theo.* I. Stone (Ed.). New York: Doubleday.

Vygotsky, L. (1962). *Thought and language.* Boston: MIT Press.

Wakefield, D. (1988). *Returning: A spiritual journey.* New York: Doubleday.

Wallach, M. & Kogan, N. (1965). *Modes of thinking in young children: A study of the creativity-intelligence distinction.* New York: Holt, Rinehart & Winston, Inc.

Wallas, G. (1926). *The art of thought.* New York: Harcourt Brace Jovanovich.

Watson, J. (1958). *Behaviorism.* Chicago: University of Chicago Press.

Weiner, J. (1990). *The next one hundred years: Shaping the fate of our living earth.* New York: Bantam.

Weisberg, R. (1986). *Creativity: Genius and other myths.* New York: W. H. Freeman.

Weisskopf-Joelson, E. & Eliseo, T. (1961). An experimental study of the effectiveness of brainstorming. *Journal of Applied Psychology, 45,* 45-49.

Welsh, G. S. (1975). *Creativity and intelligence: A personality approach.* Chapel Hill, NC: Institute for Research in Social Science.

Wertheimer, M. (1959). *Productive thinking.* New York: Harper & Row.

Williams, F. (1970). *Classroom ideas for encouraging thinking and feeling.* Buffalo, NY: DOK.

Willings, D. (1980). *The creatively gifted.* Cambridge: Woodhead-Faulkner.

Winchester, I. (1985). Creation and creativity in art and science. *Interchange, 16,* 76.

Wolff, T. (1989). *This boy's life: A memoir.* New York: Atlantic Monthly Press.

Woolf, V. (1954). *A writer's diary.* New York: Harcourt Brace Jovanovich.

Wright, F. L. (1932/1977). *An autobiography.* New York: Horizon Press.

Zakrajsek, D. B., Johnson, R. I. & Walker, D. B. (1984). Comparison of learning styles between physical education and dance majors. *Perceptual and Motor Skills, 58,* 583-88.

Zarnegar, Z., Hocevar, D. & Michael, W. (1988). Components of original thinking in gifted children. *Educational and Psychological Measurement, 48,* 5-16.

Ziv, A. (1976). Facilitating effects of humor on creativity. *Journal of Educational Psychology, 68,* 318-22.

Ziv, A. (1988). Using humor to develop creative thinking. *Journal of Children in Contemporary Society, 20,* 99-116.

Zuckerman, H. (1977). *The scientific elite.* New York: Free Press.

# Index

Meeker, Mary 87, 98, 99, 215
Meeker, Robert 87, 98
Mehta, Ved 162
Meier, Deborah 142
Mejia, Paul 262
Mellin, Laurel 264
Melville, Herman 7, 155
Mensa 25, 168
Mental Measurements Yearbook 70, 103
Mentors 207, 302
Merton, Thomas 36
Metaphorization 100
Method, The 247, 253, 255
Metropolitan Achievement Test 17
Michael, W. 76
Michelangelo 104, 148, 210
Miklus, Sam 99
Miles, Barry 147, 159-60, 164
Millay, Edna St. Vincent 148
Miller, Alice 140, 153, 206, 247, 272, 305, 306, 322
Miller, Arthur 155
Miller, Henry 300
Minnesota Multiphasic Psychological Inventory 132, 212
Miro, Joan 124
Monet, Claude 118
Monson, K. 239
Moore, Henry 139
Morgan, C. Lord 322
Morphological analysis 100
Morris, Mark 259, 260
Morrison, Toni 149
Morse, D. 79
Moscow Art Theater 247
Moses 24

Moses, Grandma 24
Mott, Michael 241
Multiple Talent Model 99
Murphy, Gardner 319
Murphy-Meisgeier 109
Murray, Elizabeth 130
Muse 36, 37, 47, 145
Music 219
Musical intelligence 22, 220
Muska, Nick 161
Myers, Isabel B. 108, 134, 154, 256
Myers, S. A. 109
Myers, R. E. 99
Myers-Briggs Type Indicator 108, 130, 154, 256
Nabokov, Vladimir 153
Nachmanivitch, Stephen 58, 237
Naivete 56, 124
National Endowment for the Arts 26
Navarre, Jane Piirto 272, 280
Nevai, Lucia 292
New Age Movement 31, 51
New Directions in Creativity 100
New York City Ballet 259, 260
Nietzsche, F. 153
Nijinsky, Vaslav 257
Nin, Anais 300
Noller, Ruth 96, 97
Noonan, Patrick 142
Novelty 8, 11, 13, 23, 33
Nowell, E. 187
Nureyev, Rudolph 257
Oates, Joyce Carol 5, 145, 146, 161
O'Brien, Tim 149
O'Connor, Flannery 153
O'Connor, Frank 147

Reed, John 299
Relaxation 52
Reliability 81-84, 103, 109
Remote Associates Test 76
Renoir, Auguste 118, 135
Renzulli, Joseph 10, 17, 66, 106, 320
Renzulli-Hartman *Scales* 103, 104
Rexroth, Kenneth 147
Reynolds, Cecil 11
Rheingold, Howard 55
Rich, Adrienne 161
Rico, Gabriele 46
Rimm, Sylvia 75, 106, 305, 306, 307
Robbins, Jerome 260
Robinson, Halbert 183
Robinson, R. 129
Roe, Anne 130, 131, 195, 204, 319
Roedell, Wendy 183
Roethke, Theodore 157, 158, 245
Rogers, Carl 51, 319
Rogers, Ginger 257
Rolling Stones 160
Ronning, Royce 11
Roosevelt, Eleanor 58
Root-Bernstein, Robert 148
Rorschach, Hermann 44, 131
Rosen, C. L. 103
Rosenthal, A. 83
Rosner, S. 238
Rossman, J. 319
Rothenberg, Albert 153, 317, 322
Rothko, Mark 163
Ruffin, David
Rugg, Harold 7
Rukeyser, Muriel 147
Runco, Mark 80, 81, 82, 91, 318
Runyon, Damon 168

Rushdie, Salman 151
Rust, J. O. 103
Safter, H. T. 78
Saint-Saens, Camille 148
Sampen, John 240
Samples, Bob 99
Sarton, May 50
Sartre, J. P. 31
Sayles, John 142, 150, 162
Scales for Rating the Behavioral Characteristics of Superior Students 103, 104
Schachtel, Ernest 322
Schank, Roger 321
Schema 59, 169, 222, 223
Schickel, Richard 246, 250
Schneiderman, Leo 153
Schoenberg, Arnold 239
Schorer, Mark 187
Schwartz, Delmore 157, 158, 159
Scientists 194
Scribner, Charles 161
Sculptors 137
Sears, P. S. 341
Sears, R. 341
Seashore Measures 222
Seberg, Jean 163
Selmon, E. 342
Sendak, Maurice 124
Severy, Bruce 160
Sexton, Anne 161
Shakespeare, William
Shearer, Moira 257
Sheets, Maxine 258
Shekerjian, Denise 24, 141, 149, 162, 246
Shelley, Mary 44
Shelley, Percy B. 43, 219
Shepard, Sam 254

# Epilogue

Is everyone creative? Does everyone have an urge to be creative? Can people be creative through hobbies if their professions don't allow creativity?

Yes, to all of the above. All of the research presented, all of the creative people quoted, all of the experts, converge on this fact: creativity is a basic human need — a need for expression, for release, for attaining a feeling of well-being. On the other hand, the quality of what is created is enhanced by discipline, by practice, by talent or proclivity. Some people feel a need to change a field, to explore beyond the boundaries, to see what will happen when they try this gewgaw or that mix of colors. Others are content to use their creative instinct as therapy, as rest, as peaceful pleasure.

This book has tried to show that the circumstances which arise in life — and how a person deals with those circumstances — determine whether one will become a creative adult pushing through the boundaries of her field. Creative children seem to have resiliency, to be able to make it through somehow, and to go on to change the world with their creativity.

# About the Author

**Jane Piirto** teaches in the School of Education and is the Director of Gifted Education at Ashland University, in Ashland, Ohio. A native of the Upper Peninsula of Michigan, she has attended Suomi College, Augsburg College, and has her undergraduate degree in English and theater from Northern Michigan University. She has an M.A. in English from Kent State University, an M.Ed. in counseling from South Dakota State University, a Ph.D. in educational administration from Bowling Green State University. She has been a high school teacher, a counselor, a college instructor of humanities, a coordinator for gifted program, principal of a school for gifted children, and an artist in the schools in Michigan, South Dakota, Ohio, and New York City. She has served as a consultant and speaker in the Near East, Southern Asia, South America, and throughout the United States. She is a published scholar, novelist, poet, and short story writer, and has received an Individual Artist Fellowship from the Ohio Arts Council, and a grant from the Fulbright-Hays Foundation. She has two grown children.